RADICALISM IN BRITISH LITERARY CULTURE,
1650–1830

In this volume of interdisciplinary essays, leading scholars examine the radical tradition in British literary culture from the English Revolution to the French Revolution. They chart continuities between the two periods and examine the recuperation of ideas and texts from the earlier period in the 1790s and beyond. Contributors utilise a variety of approaches and concepts: from gender studies, the cultural history of food and diet and the history of political discourse, to explorations of the theatre, philosophy and metaphysics. This volume argues that the radical agendas of the mid-seventeenth century, intended to change society fundamentally, did not disappear throughout the long eighteenth century only to be resuscitated at its close. Rather, through close textual analysis, these essays indicate a more continuous transmission. This book will be of interest to cultural historians as well as literary scholars.

TIMOTHY MORTON is Associate Professor of English at the University of Colorado at Boulder. He is the author of *Shelley and the Revolution in Taste* (Cambridge, 1995), and *The Poetics of Spice* (Cambridge, 2000).

NIGEL SMITH is Professor of English at Princeton University. He is the author of *Perfection Proclaimed* (1989) and *Literature and Revolution in England, 1640–1660* (1994).

RADICALISM IN BRITISH LITERARY CULTURE, 1650–1830

From Revolution to Revolution

EDITED BY TIMOTHY MORTON AND NIGEL SMITH

CAMBRIDGE
UNIVERSITY PRESS

PUBLISHED BY THE PRESS SYNDICATE OF THE UNIVERSITY OF CAMBRIDGE
The Pitt Building, Trumpington Street, Cambridge, United Kingdom

CAMBRIDGE UNIVERSITY PRESS
The Edinburgh Building, Cambridge CB2 2RU, UK
40 West 20th Street, New York, NY 10011–4211, USA
477 Williamstown Road, Port Melbourne, VIC 3207, Australia
Ruiz de Alarcón 13, 28014 Madrid, Spain
Dock House, The Waterfront, Cape Town 8001, South Africa

http://www.cambridge.org

First published 2002

Printed in the United Kingdom at the University Press, Cambridge

Typeface Baskerville Monotype 11/12.5 pt.   *System* LATEX 2ε   [TB]

A catalogue record for this book is available from the British Library

Library of Congress Cataloguing in Publication data
Radicalism in British literary culture, 1650–1830: from Revolution to Revolution / Timothy
Morton and Nigel Smith, editors.
p. cm.
Includes bibliographical references and index.
ISBN 0 521 64215 9
1. English literature – 18th century – History and criticism.   2. Radicalism in literature.
3. English literature – Early modern, 1500–1700 – History and criticism.   4. English
literature – 19th century – History and criticism.   5. Revolutionary literature, English – History
and criticism.   6. Politics and literature – Great Britain – History.   7. Radicalism – Great
Britain – History.   I. Morton, Timothy, 1968–   II. Smith, Nigel, 1958–
PR408.R36 R34   2002
820.9′358 – dc21   2001 035692

ISBN 0 521 64215 9 hardback

Contents

Illustrations

Notes on contributors

JUSTIN CHAMPION teaches the history of early modern ideas in the Department of History, Royal Holloway College, University of London. Since the early 1990s he has been working on the history of the early English Enlightenment. His most recent work is *John Toland: Nazarenus and Other Writings* (1999). He is currently working on a study of clandestine and public irreligion in England *c*. 1680–1720 to be called *Republican Learning: John Toland and the Crisis of Christian Culture* (Manchester University Press).

PAUL HAMILTON is Professor of English at Queen Mary and Westfield College, University of London. He has published books on Romanticism and historicism and is currently finishing one on metaromanticism.

DONALD JOHN is Professor of Religion and History and Lecturer in Romantic Studies at Pacific Union College, Oregon. His study of William Blake and eighteenth-century religious debate is forthcoming.

PETER J. KITSON is Chair of English at the University of Dundee. He is the editor of *Romantic Criticism, 1800–25* (1989); (with T. N. Corns) *Coleridge and the Armoury of the Human Mind: Essays on His Prose Writings* (1991); *Coleridge, Keats and Shelley: Contemporary Critical Essays* (1996); (with Tim Fulford) *Romanticism and Colonialism: Writing and Empire, 1780–1830* (1998); and (with Debbie Lee) *Slavery, Abolition and Emancipation: Writings in the British Romantic Period* (1999). He has published several essays on the relationship between the English and French Revolutions.

JON MEE is Margaret Candfield Fellow in English at University College, Oxford, and Lecturer in the Faculty of English, Oxford University. He is the author of *Dangerous Enthusiasm: William Blake and the Culture of Radicalism in the 1790s* (1992) and one of the editors of *An Oxford*

Companion to the Romantic Age (1999). He is currently working on a book exploring the disturbing presence of enthusiasm in literary, cultural and political discourse in the period to which the chapter in this volume is related.

JAMES C. MCKUSICK is Associate Professor and Chair of the Department of English at the University of Maryland, Baltimore County. He is the author of *Coleridge's Philosophy of Language* (1986), *Green Writing* (2000) and numerous essays on the English Romantic period.

TIMOTHY MORTON is Associate Professor of English at the University of Colorado at Boulder. He is the author of *Shelley and the Revolution in Taste: The Body and the Natural World* (1994, 1998); *The Poetics of Spice: Romantic Consumerism and the Exotic* (2000); *Radical Food: The Culture and Politics of Eating and Drinking, 1780–1830* (2000); and numerous articles on food, ecology and literature in the long eighteenth century, especially the Romantic period.

MICHAEL SCRIVENER has been teaching in the English Department at Wayne State University in Detroit for over twenty years. He has published a study of Percy Shelley (*Radical Shelley* (1982)) and an anthology of Romantic-era political poetry (*Poetry and Reform* (1992)).

JANE SHAW is Dean, and Fellow and Tutor in History, at Regent's Park College, Oxford University. She is co-editor of *Culture and the Nonconformist Tradition* (1999) and is currently writing a book on miracles in Enlightenment-period England.

NIGEL SMITH is Professor at Princeton University, which he joined in September 1999. Before then, he was Reader in English at the University of Oxford, a Fellow of Keble College and Chair of the English Faculty. He is the author of *Perfection Proclaimed: Language and Literature in English Radical Religion 1640–1660* (1989) and *Literature and Revolution in England, 1640–1660* (1994). He has edited the Ranter pamphlets, the Journal of George Fox, and the complete poems of Andrew Marvell (forthcoming), and is also the author of numerous articles on seventeenth-century literature.

CHARLOTTE SUSSMAN is Associate Professor of English at the University of Colorado, Boulder. She is the author of *Consuming Anxieties: Consumer Protest, Gender and British Slavery, 1713–1833* (2000). She has also published on Aphra Behn, Charlotte Smith and Samuel Richardson.

Acknowledgements

This book was written with the help of grants from the Graduate Committee on the Arts and Humanities at the University of Colorado at Boulder. These enabled Timothy Morton's research assistants, Daniel Peddie and Terry Robinson, to do invaluable copy-editing. The editors are grateful to the staff of the following libraries: the Bodleian Library, University of Oxford; the British Library; the Norlin Library, University of Colorado at Boulder.

The editors wish to thank Cambridge University Press for its help in publishing this collection. Josie Dixon saw the volume through its early days and Ray Ryan skilfully helped to finish the task. Our thanks are also extended to the contributors to this volume for their patience and diligence.

For their encouragement, advice and support, both intellectual and otherwise, the editors would like to thank: Iain McCalman, Jeffrey Cox, Kate Flint, Mark Philp, Kate Stephenson and those subscribers to the e-mail discussion list for the North American Society for Studies in Romanticism, especially Paula Feldman, Robert Griffin, Dave Haney, John Isbell, David Latane, Tom Lloyd, William McKelvy, Hugh Roberts, Nanora Sweet and Miriam L. Wallace. Timothy Morton also wishes to thank those who attended a Work in Progress seminar at the Center for the Humanities and the Arts at the University of Colorado, Boulder, at which the Introduction was discussed, and especially Jeffrey Cox, Stephen Epstein, John Murphy, John Stevenson and Charlotte Sussman.

Introduction

Timothy Morton and Nigel Smith

A CONNOISSEUR EXAMINING A COOPER; OR, 'A CHAOS OF THE ELEMENTS OF CHARLES THE FIRST'

Radicalism in British Literary Culture, 1650–1830 studies the transmission of radical texts, ideas and practices from the period of the English Revolution to that of the Romantic revolution. This is a new, developing field of enquiry, and we are aware that not everything in this field has been settled. In this Introduction we examine the nature of this emerging area. 'Radicalism' is explored in its diverse, plural meanings, and questions of historiography are considered. References to the individual contributions are made throughout, and at the end we examine each in turn, laying out the organisation of the whole volume.

'Radical' originally meant 'pertaining to the roots', from the Latin 'radix'. It was used in a broad set of fields of knowledge in the Middle Ages and Renaissance, from philosophy, mathematics and biology to astrology. The use of 'radical' to mean a thoroughgoing transformation of a system, a set of ideas or practices, from the 'root' upwards, dates from the late eighteenth century. *The Oxford English Dictionary* records the first usage of 'radical reformer' as 1802. One could in consequence take a nominalist view, and argue that 'radicalism' only exists in this period and afterwards. Everything else that came before was something else, and those who use the term for earlier events (e.g., the 'radical Reformation' in sixteenth-century Germany, the 'radicals' in the English Revolution, the 'radicals' in the Glorious Revolution) are guilty of anachronism.

But this would, we believe, be a disservice to historical reality. The class politics evoked in the word 'radical' – the overthrow or mitigation of the high by the low – surely did not arise spontaneously, but emerged historically. The period in English history between 1640 and 1832 was marked by some common conditions and characteristics, bestowing a consistency upon those who pursued a political or religious vision different

from that required by the state. In particular, we would point to an unchanged franchise, and, with the exception of the experiments of the
1650s, an unchanged representative. We might also add a persistent debate about the most appropriate form of Protestant worship. However
different theologies and ecclesiologies were accommodated within or
without the established national church, that sense of a continuity of
national religious experience remained. And thus, all those who sought
extreme change, or who chose to live in an alternative way, or publish
an alternative vision, were responding to a broad and continuous set of
circumstances, howsoever mitigated by their own position in history and
their own perceptions. If they found themselves interrogated or on trial in
a court of law for an offence, such as seditious activity, the law dealt with
them in roughly similar ways. Hence the significance of trial accounts,
either official or remembered by the accused or their followers, and their
transmission as texts in the period. John Thelwall, Thomas Holcroft,
Thomas Hardy and others were arrested and arraigned in 1794 under a
special charge of 'Constructive Treason'. They had found inspiration in
the English Revolutionary period, as demonstrated elsewhere and here
in particular in the work of Michael Scrivener and Peter Kitson.

The essays gathered here analyse a number of written and usually
printed texts that may be said to belong to a radical tradition as we have
just defined it. Towards the end of the period, there is an undoubted sense
that such a tradition existed, and that it was an animating principle for
the radicals of the 1790s. Republicanism, democracy, 'English liberties'
and a religious practice that did justice to the workings of the Holy
Spirit within individuals, are the chief components of this tradition as it
was understood in the late eighteenth century. This latter category was
largely understood as 'enthusiasm', the great bugbear of reactionaries
throughout the eighteenth century. Several of the chapters explore the
ways in which 'enthusiasm' survived and was perceived during the later
seventeenth and eighteenth centuries.

We also have to address a substantial problem in offering a volume that
spans two turbulent periods (1640–60 and *c.* 1780–1800), when radical
activity was at a height. The period in between, and certainly from
1689 to 1770, was not distinguished by widespread 'radical' activity.
During that time, stable government, successful campaigns in foreign
wars and imperial commerce, made Great Britain a world power. The
world pre-eminence that would arrive in the nineteenth century was
enabled in large part by the agricultural and industrial revolutions of

this previous period. Yet, in a discernible way, and sometimes with a substantial impact, the components of seventeenth-century radicalism were carried forwards in this most stable of periods in ways that are not always obvious. Some of these pathways are the subjects of the chapters that follow.

'Radicalism' is not the word that many seventeenth- and earlier eighteenth-century people would have used to describe their projects or their writings. The body of this Introduction is sensitive to the other words that these people used, and to the particular fields of vision to which they belonged, however different they were from the viewpoints of the radicals of the early nineteenth century. Some of the complex dimensions of this historical and lexical problem are evident in the two following examples.

James Gillray's picture seems simple enough (see Figure 1), but it embodies a series of verbal puns that reveal a tale of two kingships one hundred and fifty years apart.[1] It is a Gulliverian moment: as if the King of Laputa were examining the tiny Gulliver for the first time. The King looks curious and interested, but despite the light, he strains to see the detail in the portrait. Is this a reflection on his eyesight or his intelligence or his sanity? By contrast, Oliver Cromwell looks back at the King with piercing eyes, a stern, resolute visage and apparent anger. Oliver becomes the spectre of revolution from the past, a warning about events across the Channel in 1792 and a humiliating admonition to an impotent king. The monarch to whom Cromwell was compared was William III, not George III.[2] The candlestick-holder, fashioned as a classical column, suggests a pillar of liberty, from which the light of liberty, and hence of (French) Enlightenment, extends. It also resembles the columns of justice between which both Oliver Cromwell and William III stand in famous, generically identical, pictorial representations of their rule.

Samuel Cooper (1609–72), who painted the miniature depicted in Figure 1, was the most famous and successful painter of miniatures in England during the mid-seventeenth century. His art flourished during the Commonwealth, although he had gained some fame at court during the 1630s. Like the earlier phase of Lely's career, his portraits of famous Parliamentary and Commonwealth figures helped generate a distinctive style for the non-monarchical regime.[3] In doing so, Cooper transformed a major element in late Renaissance court sensibility: miniatures were widely exchanged as private tokens and diplomatic gifts. Cromwell and his family were painted by Cooper in the 1650s. If George III were

Pub. June 18.th 1792. by H.Humphrey N.º 18. Old Bond Street   J.G. del.et fec.

A CONNOISSEUR examining a COOPER.

*George 3.rd examining a miniature of Oliver Cromwell
by Cooper.*

*Gilray accompanied Louthabourg to France to assist him in making sketches
for his picture of the Siege of Valenciennes. When they returned, the King desired
to see their sketches, and was much pleased with those by Louthabourg, but
Gillray's being merely slight memoranda of the officers portraits, his Majesty
observed "I do not understand these caricatures". Gilray was very much dis
pleased at this observation, and shortly after made the above sketch, saying
"I wonder if the Royal Connoiseur will understand this!"*

Figure 1. James Gillray, *A Connoisseur Examining a Cooper* (1792).

a real connoisseur, he would have known that miniature painting was accompanied in the 1650s by the popularity of the commemorative medal, which often combined a miniature portrait struck on one side with an image on the other of anti-monarchical action during the Civil Wars.

George III is looking back on a moment when courtliness itself was transformed. He might expect the Cooper miniature to be a gift, but it is in fact the product of a violent transformation. To that extent it is paradoxically an iconoclastic image. Just so, all of the surviving artefacts of the 1640s and 1650s become potentially powerful agents in a revival of revolutionary energy in the 1790s, or a warning against those energies.[4] There is one further insight. Art collecting during the eighteenth century was no longer a specifically aristocratic activity. The collection of republican and Whig paintings and busts by the middle classes was one way in which that political tradition was sustained and transmitted.[5] Oliver Cromwell and George III have become equal figures, both meeting in the marketplace of bourgeois art-collecting. The sublime gaze of the revolutionary hero (or rebellious usurper) meets the idiot gaze of a king.

The energies represented in Gillray's picture are also present in the literature of the period. In 1818 Percy Bysshe Shelley started work on *Charles the First*, a drama depicting the crucial moments of the English Civil War. Attempting perhaps to mollify his more reactionary friend, Thomas Medwin, Shelley wrote to him on 20 July 1820 that he meant 'to write a play, in the spirit of human nature, without prejudice or passion'.[6] Shelley later claimed to his publisher Charles Ollier that 'it is not coloured by the party spirit of the author'.[7] This is quite untrue, given the evidence we have of the play, but perhaps Shelley was trying to adumbrate the grand aesthetic form needed to imagine a broader history. On 26 January 1822 he complained to John Gisborne that he was procrastinating on the project because he could not 'seize the conception of the subject as a *whole* yet'.[8] That Shelley was *trying* and yet struggling and ultimately failing to write such a drama indicates both the need for it and the difficulty of executing it.

Shelley had requested that a box of materials on the period be sent to him. The idea of covering the English Revolutionary period had been working on both him and Mary for four years. Mary Shelley's *Frankenstein* (1816) describes how Victor Frankenstein and Henry Clerval

visit Oxford (from which Percy had been expelled in 1811 for writing
an atheist pamphlet), a royalist stronghold 'after the whole nation had
forsaken [the king's] cause to join the standard of parliament and liberty'.
Oxford is a metonym for Victor's arrogant egotism, the entrepreneurial
science that leads him to spurn his own creation. Victor comments on
the Civil War, Charles I ('that unfortunate king' – *Frankenstein*'s judicously
disguised republicanism here asserts that it was unfortunate that he *was
ever* king), Hampden, Falkland and Goring. When visiting the tomb of
Hampden, Victor, contemplating 'the divine ideas of liberty and self-
sacrifice', dares for a moment to 'shake off [his] chains, and look around
[him] with a free and lofty spirit'.9 By 1818, Mary's republican father
William Godwin had suggested that she work on 'a great desideratum in
English history and biography, to be called "The Lives of the Commonwealth's Men"'. In reply Percy Shelley wrote: 'I am exceedingly delighted
with the plan you propose of a book illustrating the character of our
calumniated Republicans.'10 The box of materials for such a project,
however, was lost in a shipwreck in mid-1821. In a letter to John and
Maria Gisborne, Shelley exclaimed: 'My unfortunate Box! it contained
a chaos of the elements of Charles the first.'11

   This mishap is an allegory of the reputation and fortune of the transmission, survival and continuity of radical texts and ideas from the period
of the English Revolution to the British Romantic period. Shelley's fragmentary drama demonstrates the attempt by radical writers in the later
period to reassess and reappropriate the radicalism of their revolutionary
past. Its surviving parts reveal his focus on a radical view of the English
Revolution, offering an alternative perspective to one that pointed out
the military prowess of Oliver Cromwell. In fact, Shelley's play might
appropriately have been entitled *Sir Henry Vane*.12

   It is the presence of the disfigured Alexander Leighton that strikes the
strongest radical chord in the opening scene of the play. His face has
been branded and thus disfigured; in a sense his 'true face' has been torn
off. The real Leighton (1568–1649) was fined, defrocked, pilloried and
whipped (twice), had both ears and nostrils cut off, and his face branded
with 'S.S.' ('sower of sedition'), for publishing *Sion's Plea* (1628); he was
then imprisoned for life.13 Thomas Medwin's life of Shelley was keen
to stress the poet's dislike of the beheading of Charles I, but the presentation of Leighton complicates matters. At the very least, Medwin may
have been responsible for a conservative misrepresentation of Shelley's
views.14

Leighton portrays the violence done to him as a kind of writing that has removed his own identity:

> I *was* Leighton: what
> I *am* thou seest. And yet turn thine eyes,
> And with thy memory look upon thy friend's mind,
> Which is unchanged, and where is written deep
> The sentence of my judge.[15]

Through Shelley's characteristic rhetoric of 'silent eloquence', the presence of the disfigured person, Leighton, reclaims an identity beyond physical (dis)figuration.[16] Terror is unmasked: Archbishop Laud has dared to overwrite the law of God, inscribed on the very body of man. It is a typically strong Shelleyan image of ugliness and horror amidst aestheticised pomp. As Walter Benjamin observed, every 'cultural document' can be read as a 'record of barbarism'.[17] Shelley's *A Vindication of Natural Diet* (1813), his major statement of vegetarian ideas, also locates violence within civilisation, establishing a contrast between republicanism and the ideology of commercial capitalism. He writes, 'The odious and disgusting aristocracy of wealth is built upon the ruins of all that is good in chivalry or republicanism; and luxury is the forerunner of a barbarism scarce capable of cure.'[18] Capitalism may have ruined republicanism for Shelly, but radical voices could still be heard in the wreckage, even in 1818. In *Charles the First*, the presence of Leighton is radical: he *is* a document, a radical text and ghastly presence. His presence on stage testifies to the transmission of radicalism, and it appears to be retrieving a message of pacifism from that violent past.

We now consider the different kinds of radicalism: how may they be understood within the parameters of key historical determinants in the period? We discuss the significance of the party system, commerce, religion, popular politics and dominant philosophical fashions. We assess the long-term survival of heretical ideas in the eighteenth century, and the themes of social justice and crime. The section after next, 'Literature and history', explores the recent convergence of approaches between literary scholars and historians, which makes our volume possible. It discusses the republication and alteration of seventeenth-century literature associated with radicalism in the longer eighteenth century, indicating a number of genres that are crucial in this respect, such as the epic, the spiritual autobiography and the novel, in addition to forms of publication always associated with protest: the petition and the trial narrative. Most

ν

...tions deal with writings that were circulated and inter-
..rticular contexts. Accordingly, we elucidate the distinction
on the one hand studying the formal, rhetorical features of
..g, and on the other, attending to the discursive contexts in which
..e rhetorics function. We also outline different considerations of time
..nd chronology, since most of the contributions in the volume straddle
conventional period boundaries in literary and social history.

WHAT IS RADICALISM?

The source of creative tension for Gillray and revolutionary vision for
Shelley is a substantial difficulty for modern historians. J. G. A. Pocock
states the problem succinctly at the start of his essay 'Criticism of the
Whig Order in the Age between Revolutions': 'To begin our study in
1688 involves us in some problems of continuity [notably] . . . the problem of relating radical criticism . . . to the great explosion of plebeian
and sectarian speech and action which had marked the years of the Civil
War and Interregnum.'[19] It is indeed the age 'between' revolutions that
is precisely the problem. Was the eighteenth century a buffer or block
between moments of radical change? In which case, how did it block
those energies? Or was it a medium, however viscous and resistant, for
the transmission of these energies? By starting a conversation between
the radicalism of the 1650s and that of the Romantic age, *Radicalism in
British Literary Culture* is intended to open up ways in which to answer these
questions. The emerging answers indicate that the eighteenth century
may be understood as a medium of transmission.

Of course, there is no accounting for historical contingency. It is probably fair to say that most educated people in, say, 1740, wanted to forget
about the violence of the Civil War. They saw their country progressing
along a very different path. But then structural weakness in the body
politic was exposed, and it was followed by a successful revolt into independence by a distant colony, and the spread of popular discontent. The
late 1780s did begin to look a lot like the 1640s.[20]

There were also elements in eighteenth-century political life that may
constitute a bridge between the radicalism of the mid- and later seventeenth century, and that of the late eighteenth century. While few were
prepared to challenge mixed monarchy, the solidification of the Whig
oligarchy, with its dependence on what were seen to be corrupt practices of patronage and placement, produced an unlikely consonance of
radical Whig and Tory voices of criticism. Resistance to executive abuse

took the form of calls for more regular Parliaments, for the redistribution of seats from rotten boroughs to new, under-represented areas
of population. There were attempts, either by restriction of the voting
qualification, or other means, to return MPs who would resist corrupt
practices, and hence better look after the liberties of their constituents.
Standing armies, it was argued, should be replaced by citizen militias,
each of whose number would have a direct stake in the liberties their
arms would defend. The secret ballot was advocated by popular republicans in the 1650s, again by ex-Levellers in 1689 and again still by
opposition 'patriots' in the 1730s and 1740s. These small groups were
able to have a powerful voice, out of proportion with their actual numbers, by using the periodical press, which became progressively better
established in the provinces, as well as in London. The development of
political clubs, Whig and Tory, put further pressure on MPs – to 'instruct'
them, as the contemporary phrase had it.[21]

The dates for the publication of these views extend evenly from 1689
to the 1760s: 1701, 1721, 1732, 1747. So, if out and out radicalism was
not present, the concerns and practices that characterised the 1640s and
the 1790s certainly were.

Many of the more extreme suggestions in this body of writing remained apparently undiscussed, their implications unrealised. This is so,
for instance, of Locke's idea that the natural equality of all men should
be the basis for political representation – an idea that could be developed
into an argument for universal manhood suffrage. Yet if franchise reform
was not enjoined, the perception that all men had an equal right to freedom and to scrutinise the government was a prominent part of radical
Whig views. But there was no sustained and coordinated platform for
such reforms. Still, in addition to a vigorous press and a political culture
of associations, there were moments throughout the eighteenth century
when effective protests or campaigns were fought. There were often
bitterly contested general elections. The special nature of London produced effective resistance from the less wealthy middle-class merchants to
the court-connected magisterial elite. 'Street demonstrations, organised
petitions and addresses, judicial proceedings and tumultuous elections'
made London the centre of focus for a more open kind of politics.[22]
In many respects, these activities looked identical to those of the civic
Levellers of the 1640s, rewritten within the terms of the eighteenth-
century commercial metropolis. And London was but the most prominent example of the increasing involvement of the middling sort in
politics.

It is thus not surprising that a well-formulated popular republicanism, tied closely to the distribution of printed material, and accompanied by an advanced notion of the relationship between liberty and print, should flourish in the 1650s at the hands of journalists like Marchamont Nedham and John Streater, apparently disappear after 1660, reappear sporadically in the 1690s and then re-emerge in near-identical terms in the writings and activities of John Thelwall at the end of the following century. The relationship between literacy, liberty and bearing arms is most striking in this material. The presence of Machiavellian thought is never far below its surface, a vision of classically influenced civic culture glimpsed at different moments through the eighteenth century.[23]

While elements of seventeenth-century radical literature survived, and in some instances were republished, and can be shown to have had a readership, the terms in which that radicalism could be understood were being remade by social developments. The rise of commercial society is one important factor. Another related factor is the emergence of a literary culture, organised around serial publications as well as books and meetings (notably the coffee house) in which cultural values were discussed. A society divided by confession might have survived from the seventeenth century, although it was transformed by a literary and civic culture with common interests. Furthermore, within that culture, the new philosophy that had emerged in the later seventeenth century, and in particular the views on cognition of John Locke, were broadly disseminated. On the whole, the radical ideas of the seventeenth century were not present in these circles. People read Locke, Mandeville and Berkeley, rather than Lilburne and Walwyn. Accordingly, a multifarious dissemination of ideas about sense perception, taste and ethics occurred. By the later eighteenth century, this collective knowledge had become a complex body of thought that related language usage to class, status, notions of judgement and relative degrees of civilisation. Most of the prominent radicals of the 1790s had written on language usage.[24] The terms in which the trials for sedition in the 1790s were conducted were cultural and aesthetic as much as they were political and concerned with civil liberties.[25] Late eighteenth-century radicalism reinvented seventeenth-century radical issues inside eighteenth-century discussions of psychology, language, literature and ethics.

Furthermore, there emerged and flourished reflections upon what made a successful society, from systems of education and literary cultivation to political economy. Though the late seventeenth century was marked by the emergence of political economy, such formulations were

relatively primitive. Late eighteenth-century radicalism was in fact empowered with superior tools of analysis because the sciences of man had
arrived. Yet they may still have had a populist agenda. For example,
Abraham Rees's *Cyclopaedia* (1810–24), an attempt to mimic the French
Enlightenment, indicates that those studies that were eventually labelled
'anthropology' were spurred by an Enlightenment urge to avoid teleological histories of the victories and losses of monarchs and the fortunes
of the uppermost classes.[26]

These contexts make a history of intellectual radicalism in the period
difficult to construct. The continuities apparent within the boundaries
of intellectual history (if not political theory) have inspired distinguished
commentators. Pocock's 'Post-Puritan England and the Problem of
Enlightenment' contains a rich general discussion of the influence of
Interregnum hylozoism upon deist thought, although detailed reference
to the primary texts is absent: the account remains rather speculative.[27]
Justin Champion's work has sought to broaden this agenda, and to root
it in the debates concerning the Church of England between 1660 and
1730.[28] The more we travel into detailed considerations of arguments,
and to the continuing use of texts popular with earlier radicals, the more
a firm historical entity appears. And it is enhanced by the constellation
of the debate remaining within and around the established church, an
institution that had survived across a long period of time.

The impact of heterodoxy upon wide segments of eighteenth-century
culture has been demonstrated. This is a very fruitful way of understanding how orthodoxy was conceived, and how orthodoxy and heterodoxy
determined each other's identity and outlook.[29] While this is indeed an
aspect of the historical process with which we are concerned,[30] there is
the danger that we lose sight of the heterodox or oppositional as it is seen
to belong to, or be defined by, a particular context. Wit, for example,
plays a role in eighteenth-century religious controversy; but the chapters in this volume focus on specific texts and their contexts rather than
general cultural properties such as humour.

Yet there are ways, more remote than specific textual transmission, in
which the debates of one age recur distantly and differently in another.
As Mark Jenner has shown, the fascination with medical advance and
the application of cures was directly related to the theological controver-
sies of the mid-seventeenth century, and in some cases, this was directly
related to radical practices.[31] In a similar way, the occult and vegetarian
theories discussed in this volume continued the probing of the relationship between matter and spirit, soul and body, that concerned so many

mid-century radicals. There is ample evidence that radicalism, once it has a history conferred by the passing of time, can be measured by its impact in quite distinct areas of culture. Moreover, in investigating the radical genesis of a practitioner, we rapidly construct a picture of radicals accommodating their practice to an environment very different from the one in which they emerged. Such is the case with the vegetarianism, temperance and anti-colonialism of Thomas Tryon.[32]

Another broad theme in social history can be linked to radical agendas. Peter Linebaugh's *The London Hanged* (1991) uses the preoccupation with social justice of the mid-seventeenth-century radicals to launch a wide-ranging discussion of property crimes and their legal treatment in the eighteenth century. Those who suffered rough justice in the eighteenth century were the natural heirs of the Levellers. Legal disputes involving popular freedoms may be an important locus for future discoveries. Andy Wood's important account of the 'free miners' of Derbyshire shows how independent working miners in the mid-eighteenth century resisted the attempts of landowners to evict them through a recourse to 'ancient liberties'. The terms of their resistance look suspiciously like Leveller arguments in the 1640s.[33] It was even seen that oppression could take economic as well as political forms, and hence liberty was connected to sufficiently high wages, and perhaps even to the necessity for property redistribution.

No one isolated theme will satisfy an account of the journey of the ideas of the English Revolution. Here, we have to beware of some singular viewpoints. There is a wholly secular account of radical political ideas in the eighteenth century. It is, in effect, a Whig view of history that entirely discounts a religious view of the period, and it has adversely affected disciplines, such as literary criticism, borrowing from the works of historians.[34] The histories of religious dissent, the evangelical movement and rational dissent are beginning to receive the attention they deserve from modern historians. There is still much to be discovered, especially with regard to the relationship between dissent and national politics, and the cultural dimensions of the dissenting world.[35] *Radicalism in British Literary Culture* engages with a number of different moments of religious radicalism. Donald John, for instance, investigates the role of theodicy in Milton, Law and Blake; Timothy Morton explores the radical Behmenism of Thomas Tryon; Jane Shaw examines the role of women prophets; Charlotte Sussman considers the significance of women reading the Bible in the long eighteenth century; and Jon Mee examines the radical legacy of the Puritan doctrines of the sufficiency of the spirit's teaching.

What survived from mid-seventeenth-century radicalism was not only the politically controversial or the religiously heterodox but also the cultural traditions that resisted the meat-eating, alcohol-drinking ways of western Europe that were becoming increasingly fuelled by the quest for luxury and the rise of colonialism. Vegetarianism emerges from several different places, but in the English Revolution, it was part of radical Puritan theology. The survival of these ideas, texts and practices amounts to a vegetarian tradition that can be seen in the activities and works of Thomas Tryon. His widespread influence opens up a universe of occult theories, astrology and applied heresy, so much of the fashionable hinterland of radicalism during the 1650s. Swift was right to identify this material with enthusiasm in his satires, and to see it as part of a bizarre kind of circulation and unnatural consumption, in that it offended the customary order of things. Vegetarianism was also widespread in the middle classes. In the wider picture, radical meals and toasts formed, as James A. Epstein notes, 'a long-standing pattern of oppositional convivial activities' from the mid- and later seventeenth century.[36] *Radicalism in British Literary Culture* has conceived of radicalism as emerging in culture, defined in Raymond Williams's sense as a whole way of life, rather than merely in a history of republican ideas. In some ways, the 'oppositional' in any absolute sense is unnecessary, since the object of our attention begins to look like a phenomenon observed in a later period in English history, the 'radical domestic': 'Change does take place in England, but it is rarely the sort of sharp break that one might find in other societies... But change there is, and it is likely to take place on a domestic scale.'[37] In this context, enthusiasm became an aspect of what Jon Mee calls radical 'self fashioning', always contesting the boundaries of the polite public sphere: 'The notion of culture as a kind of polite conversation was ubiquitous in the late eighteenth century, but the nature of "politeness" and who was to be included in the conversation were questions continually at issue.'[38]

In conclusion, there were continuities of religion, of commerce and of radical political ideas through the long eighteenth century. Religion and capitalism were media for the transmission of English Revolutionary radicalism. But how may one describe these continuities?

LITERATURE AND HISTORY

The subject of radicalism encourages us to discard the simple search for formal literary and rhetorical techniques: otherwise our enquiry would be reduced to the worship of a kind of expressive avant-garde in each period. We are not simply searching for radical pamphlets and radical novels. Any approach must be concerned with 'discourse' rather than just 'rhetoric': a lived relation to cultures of fundamental social change. Radicalism implies certain ways of *inhabiting* historical moments, and this inhabiting would include the reading of history. In this collection, the contributors are to a great extent reading radicals reading other texts.

Transmission by means of reading and writing is precisely how the revolutionary discourse of Puritan inwardness is usually perceived, from Milton to the Romantics. We must address the question of the role of literary representation in a book in which literary texts are investigated extensively. From a historian's point of view, literary texts may appear to lack the significance of, say, works that offer sophisticated commentary on their own period, such as Hobbes's *Leviathan* or Burke's *Reflections*. It is, however, increasingly agreed by historians as well as by literary scholars that specifically literary texts did play political and cultural roles in their own times, and can be measured as so doing. This may be achieved either within those texts, through direct discussion, allusion and figurative language, or in the contexts in which they are received, transmitted and discussed. Recent work on the reading of books during the English Revolution yields startling evidence of the interaction of a knowledge of contingent events and books that compel one to think in new ways about those events, as well as events making one read books in a new way.[39] We are further comforted by the fact that boundaries between literary and other sorts of texts have been blurred throughout the literary criticism of at least the last twenty years. A literary scholar may be just as interested, these days, in Hobbes's use of figurative language as in Milton's.

The epic was revised in the seventeenth century to treat the emerging rhetoric of inwardness, which was part of the development of radical Puritan subjectivity: *Paradise Lost* is the most obvious example of such a revision. The way in which this rhetoric was transmitted to the poets of the Romantic period such as Wordsworth and Shelley is a very familiar story. It is not often remembered, however, that Wordsworth's famous conversation poem known as *Tintern Abbey* contains an allusion to Samuel Daniel's poem on the Civil War, or that Henry Vane makes his way into Thomas de Quincey's *Confessions of an English Opium-Eater*.[40] An 1809 stanza by Felicia Hemans reveals her youthful use of the anti-tyrannical trope of the sword of Harmodius, though Hemans's precise orientation towards republicanism is currently being contested. Lord Byron used the trope in in *Childe Harold* (1816), III (st. 20), where he counsels a post-Napoleonic Europe that 'all that most endears / Glory, is when the myrtle wreathes a sword / Such as Harmodius drew on Athens' tyrant lord'.[41] Many and varied poetic forms were capable of catching and re-presenting a seventeenth-century radical viewpoint.

The majority of research on the later period covered in our volume has tended to focus upon the continuity of republicanism of a certain sort. This argument has recently been made by Robert J. Griffin, who in his study of Wordsworth's Pope traces the persistence of a republicanism suited to the needs of the landed classes in the literature of the long eighteenth century, including the Romantic period. The influence of Pocock leads Griffin to state that this persistence is only a matter of degree: 'Swift, Pope, and Wordsworth are opposed to the same phenomenon [of commercial capitalism] but by Wordsworth's time the problem had become more acute. In Pocock's terms, all of these writers draw upon civic humanism as a weapon against the spread of commercial values.'[42] Pocock himself explains the potentially reactionary tendency of this formation: 'romantic radicalism, like other radicalisms before it, flowed from both a republican and a Tory source; this may help us understand the movement of Coleridge, Southey, and Wordsworth from republican youth to Tory old age'.[43] Moreover, attacks on commerce and consumerism were not the only forms of radicalism transmitted through the long eighteenth century; regarding that century as based on the rise of Whiggish aristocratic capitalism (and the classical republicanism that resisted it), may hinder a more broad and complex view of the kinds of radicalism that were transmitted.

Work is beginning to be done, for example by the late Joseph Nicholes, Terence Hoagwood, Kenneth Johnston and Greg Kucich, and in seventeenth-century studies by David Norbrook, on recovering this kind of textual transmission in Coleridge, Hazlitt, Shelley, Wordsworth and others. Norbrook, for example, demonstrates how Coleridge praised *Vox Pacifica* (1645), the sequel to *Campo-Musæ* (1643) by the popular, near-republican poet George Wither. The transmission is complex and disturbed: Norbrook observes that Coleridge's rephrasing of Wither's diction compromises the latter's view of democracy and Parliament. Norbrook's work stands in contrast to the recent re-Gothicising of the Romantic period by Geoffrey Hartman. The work of scholars such as Norbrook can only be done properly with a sensitivity to rhetoric, which includes not just tropology but argument and delivery – in its widest sense, historical context: the poem as speech act, as Norbrook theorises.[44]

Two further genres matter in this respect. First, the spiritual autobiography and various other kinds of experiential writing continued to be the means by which the traditions that had generated radicalism in the seventeenth century knew themselves. This was so even for relatively rational thinkers. The Methodists in particular liked to record their dreams (and Methodism has been known as a medium of radical transmission in the eighteenth century). And in a further sense of transfer, the texts of dissenting tradition sometimes found themselves in the libraries of their religious opposites. William Law, mystic, non-juror and translator of Jacob Boehme, possessed a library in which radical religious books from the Commonwealth were prominent.

Second, and in literary terms most important, is the nature of the novel. Its growth by the appropriation of other non-fictional genres points back to experiential writing. The novel depicted these genres at work. Thus, the conventional explanation of the cult of sensibility as a reaction to the absence of an empathetic description of humanity under the influence of rational thought, is incomplete.[45] Pamela's experiences are those of a pious woman: she bears the weight of domestic enthusiasm, while Moll Flanders is periodically tormented by the dreams that were so much at the heart of Puritan and Methodist literary experience. It is no surprise that the novel can so readily pick up on radical themes, articulating a series of debates in content and form on radical possibilities: witness the published works of Mary Wollstonecraft, Eliza Hays, Charlotte Smith, William Godwin and Robert Holcroft. The Romantic revolt depended on a stable and eclectic genre within which to discover itself, although the uses to which the language of sentiment was put were unpredictable.[46]

The more extreme proponents of Romantic radicalism took their endeavour forwards into experiments with expressible form, and this brought them full circle to the 'poetry' of the English Revolution's prophets. As Paul Hamilton puts it: 'In Romantic period writing, theories of imagination, irony and rhetorical reserve . . . are what energise writings calling out for their hidden rationale to be voiced. This occulted theory, in its turn, might, if properly expounded in all its Fichtean sensitivity to a Machiavellian heritage, have *recovered* not alienated [a] native, domestic, republican sublime.'[47]

In fact, British literary culture reconsidered its past during the long eighteenth century. An English literary canon, constructed on Whiggish lines, bolstered the claims of an emergent entrepreneurial class. The domestic antique was invented, comprising both textual and material objects. The past was contested. The ballad emerged in a constellation of radical thought and action. The debate between the antiquarians

Thomas Percy and Joseph Ritson over the role and authenticity of ballads was about who had the right to revise and appropriate the past: whose usable past was it? Henry Brougham made fun of radical petitions, figured as the recovery of texts: "'This, sir, is a specimen of the historical knowledge, – of the antiquarian research, – of the acquaintance with constitutional law of the wiseacres out of doors, who, after poring for days and nights, and brooding over their wild and mischeiveous schemes, rise up with their little nostrums and big blunders to amend the British Constitution!'"[48] Sarcastic as it is, this remark points out the textual nature of radical literature's transmission – its necessarily occult, underground textual nature. Aspects of radical literature in both the 1640s and 1790s have been described as kinds of 'bricolage'. A valuable future investigation might compare this kind of construction with what has been defined as the provisional, polyvalent literature of the Whigs (akin to their contractual and patronage politics; typified by the writings of Laurence Sterne), and the various registers of the 'natural' and uncorrupted Tory vision.

Whether formally defined rhetoric can be considered generally to participate in radical culture involves some complex issues. A lightning rod for such issues recently has been Mark Philp's recent essay on English republicanism in the 1790s.[49] Philp draws a significant distinction between rhetoric – that is to say a set of formal characteristics governing a piece of writing – and discourse – a set of social practices, beliefs, texts and assumptions, rhetoric in its lived relation to history. It is the *discursive* presence of elements considered radical that makes it possible to talk about transmission. We are not entirely happy with the thesis that English republicanism, for example, persisted as a rhetoric in the eighteenth century, if that implies that it died out as a result of Jacobinism and the reaction to it in Britain. If it can be shown that republicanism nevertheless persisted in some way in its exemplars, symbolism and so forth – in other words, in its rhetoric – then in accounting for this one should consider this rhetoric as part of wider discursive formations.[50] One of the problems with ideas such as 'discourse' and 'continuity' is the resistance of the contemporary literary historian to thinking of large groups and spans of time, inspired as literary history has been by anti-totalising post-structuralism. It is true that 'history' may too easily be seen as a head without a world, as *Zeit* or *Geist* or epoch. But to focus too closely on microscopic particulars without a sense of a larger pattern of chronological development, is to find oneself unable to analyse unorthodox but significant moments of cultural history.

Much extant work on eighteenth-century radicalism focuses upon political theory, but the boundaries of our discussion are not limited to a narrowly defined concept of the political. One might object to this position by declaring that the only kind of discourse that is significant is political discourse, and that historians of all stripes have to talk about historical reality, to limit themselves to some notion of the actual. To what extent, then, *is* there a discursive continuity of radicalism at all? Our rationale for disagreeing with this objection is that we are not dealing simply with political traditions of radicalism. For example, African-American culture in contemporary America is not confined to political institutions.[51] To tell the truth, its forms of radicalism have largely been excluded from such arenas. But that is precisely the point. The fact that the radical culture is still visible and vibrant in some way testifies to its strength, given the oppressive power of law and order.

There is another point to be made about the relationship between discourse and history, and it revolves around the question of diachrony. Transmission involves the passage of time. But what do we mean by this? The question is complicated by our objects of study themselves: radical discourse calls to the future, and is sometimes staged as a call *from* the future which activates radical conscience in the present and a subsequently authentic 'radical' inhabiting of one's culture. In other words, we are dealing with traditions that *create* their own 'time' and inhabit their own history. This is especially relevant to Paul Hamilton's analysis of Fichte's utopianism: 'In the absence of the requisite political community, at a time when Fichte could have no model for the German nationalism he tried to inspire, Machiavelli offers him a way of thinking a possible political agenda.'[52]

What we are *not* dealing with is time viewed as universal for all, an objective container of history consistent for all participants. An ideal study of radical cultures would view time in a Leibnizian or Heideggerian sense as a part of the world, not as an abstract and objective externality, as it is in Kant. An objective line implies a fixed present from which one may see an object called 'the past' and look to 'the future'. This is especially significant when it comes to theorising the nature of the textual transmission of radicalism. One may talk about radical traditions being 'anticipated' (in 'the past') or 'echoed' (in 'the future'): this is to evoke the objective line of time. To talk about 'anticipation' and 'echoing' is to fall into the Whiggish trap of a single, objective, linear temporal construct. This threatens to elide discourses marginal to the dominant Whig ones. The dice are already loaded against radicalism if we assume a solid line of time as the path of transmission from 1650 to 1830. A false

dichotomy between 'continuity' and 'recuperation' emerges as a result
of these loaded dice, giving rise to a further question: how could radical
culture have appeared if all we are talking about is the recuperation of
texts lost down a solid line of time? And as the continuity of the long
eighteenth century, from the Whig point of view, is really the triumph of
commercial capitalism and the birth of empire, then how can a radical
tradition possibly be said to continue in this narrative? This question
has recently been taken up by Peter Linebaugh and Marcus Rediker, in
their exploration of political strategies that resisted and challenged the
spread of global commerce in the eighteenth century. The narrative of
commercial power itself was challenged: the authors indicate a 'revolutionary Atlantic' that undermines the monological coherence of the
Whiggish narrative.[53]

The problem of transmission is bound up with the further problem
of how to conceive of liberty at any point in time. In the eighteenth
century, Rousseau's radicalism presupposed the spontaneous presence
of citizens to each other: a view promoted by republican theories of
representation. One of the features of Romantic-period radicalism is
the language of spontaneous presence: for example, the zetetic Richard
Carlile's dating of 1820 as the Year One in his journal the *Republican*, and
the republican cosmopolitanism that celebrated contemporary revolutions in South America.[54] Time is wound back, space is levelled. Zetetic
thought ('zetetic' is based on the Greek for 'seek') was inspired by the
Enlightenment. There is an anxiety about rhetoric in zetetic culture, an
elevation of what Epstein calls 'the gaze of pure reason'.[55] For all his
interest in reconfiguring the English Revolutionary past, Percy Shelley
was also strongly influenced by the Enlightenment, and for that reason
his radical poem *Queen Mab* was reviewed in *The Republican* and pirated
by Carlile.

What if radical actors and texts are taken unawares however, by
historical necessity? In the case of the radicals of the Romantic revolutionary period, the Gagging Acts necessitated forms of communication more tortuous than direct speech. The question goes deeper, as
all writing is based on the difference, deferment and dissemination
of meaning. Jacques Derrida sums up the problem as construed by
Rousseau:

speech always presents itself as the best expression of liberty. It is by itself
language at liberty and the liberty of language, the freedom of a speech which
need not borrow its signifiers from the exteriority of the world, and which
therefore seems incapable of being dispossessed. Do the most imprisoned an'
deprived beings not make use of that interior spontaneity which is speech?[56]

But as Jon Mee demonstrates at the start of his chapter on Richard 'Citizen' Lee, the conditions in which radical discourse emerged on trial – conditions which one would think guaranteed the full presence of spontaneous speech and its appeal to liberty – actually privileged the profusion of the written text, to radicalism's advantage.[57] Petitions to Parliament exemplify the textual nature of radical activity in the Romantic period. So does the way these petitions drew on readings of the British 'constitution' – whose non-textual status has frequently been contested as an organicist myth. This 'antiquarian research' (as Brougham called it) was a pervasive strategy. William Hone was roused to study constitutional law by reading the trial of Lilburne.[58] Evoking Hampden, Sidney and Russell was a radical liturgy, performed for instance by Thomas Jonathan Wooler, the editor of the *Black Dwarf*.[59] This is surely one reason why the history of radicalism must strive beyond the republican ideology of direct, face-to-face communication.

Finally, we must also reckon with the common view of history expounded in English literary studies in the last two decades. New Historicism has tended to have two effects, one quite obvious, the other less so. Obviously, it has reintroduced questions of history and politics into the study of non-contemporary periods. It has, however, also reduced history to a synchronic slice. Foucauldian readings of history tend to repeat, however unconsciously, Foucault's monolithic and static model of time as a sequence of epistemes. Ironically, *history* in New Historicist readings tends to assume the appearance of *poetry* in New Critical readings: self-contained, total, interrelated and self-reflexive in an almost paranoid way. *Radicalism in British Literary Culture* is a historical study, but not a New Historicist one. As our principal thesis is concerned with the idea of continuities of radical tradition, a nuanced sense of the flows of time and space must be entertained. In short, this study is necessarily diachronic. New Historicism has been suspicious of diachrony, preferring instead the brilliant explication of a spatialised chunk of time. We ɔ lay ourselves open to an unthinking charge of Whiggishness, if it is ᵼmed that any sense of continuity must be metaphysical. But is it ᵼss metaphysical to use for one's alternative view of time a set of ᵼical assumptions which make a fetish of the unique, extraordi- ᵼt, 'power on display' and the rest? The premise with which we ᵼbled these chapters is that there is no metaphysically absolute ᵼabsolute line of time is associated with the linearity of the ᵼrida calls 'a linear scheme of the unfolding of presence' in ᵼmogeneous, dominated by the form of the now and the ideal of continuous movement'.[60] But just as there is no single radical text, so there is no uniquely radical time, and in short no single radical *history*.

While this collection does strongly suggest that there is continuous radical textual transmission from 1650 to 1830, it is intended as the beginning of further scholarship. Our Introduction has sketched the current state of play on scholarship in this area, the theoretical underpinnings in literature and history that such scholarship should ideally consider and the different kinds of radicalism which appear as a result. Until a complete history, if that is ever possible, emerges, such an introduction will always be provisional, and will contain a degree of utopianism. But this is all the more reason for assembling the collection to motivate further discussion. We have collected a wide spectrum of chapters on radicalism, ranging from trial narratives (Jon Mee) to the history of philosophy (Paul Hamilton). This inclusiveness is appropriate to the phase of historical work on our theme, in which much ground needs to be broken.

The collection is divided into two sections. The first presents the passage of mid-seventeenth-century radicalism during the later seventeenth century and the eighteenth century. The second deals with the development of this tradition within Romantic-period radicalism. In demonstrating continuity between the mid-seventeenth century and the Romantic period, or by exploring an aspect of the period in between, the chapters explore how turbulent ideas, ideologies and textual traditions reshaped themselves. They also explain how major shifts of awareness, such as the rise of secular views, either adjust earlier modes of radical vision or refashion the conditions for the interpretation of those visions.

By comparing Britain and France, Justin Champion raises a series of fundamental questions regarding the conditions in which radical thought emerged, flourished or was hindered in the period. Arguing against a tradition that has refused to acknowledge an English Enlightenment, Champion shows how the irreligious ideas cultivated by the French *philosophes* (ideas that constituted in part the ideology of the French Revolution) can be traced to the actual dissemination of the writings and ideas of English deists and freethinkers in eighteenth-century France. But Champion presents no argument for English ascendancy in these matters. Especially where attacks on the authority of the Bible were concerned, English thinkers were often dependent upon earlier continental works. The circumstances of circulation of ideas and texts was often quite different between France and England, but, Champion argues, there was in both countries a common intellectual project in the period: a confrontation of the 'confessional state'.

Through a discussion of the survival of popular (as opposed to aristo-cratic) republicanism in late seventeenth- and early eighteenth-century civic culture, and in the particular instance of an anonymous play, *Timoleon, or the Revolution* (1697), Nigel Smith demonstrates that a col-lection of sentiments existed outside of contract and natural rights the-ory, and the other dominant terms of allegiance or resistance that were used after the Glorious Revolution. At a time when some of the actors of the English Revolution were still alive and active, neither popular republicanism nor radical Puritanism were silenced by the passage of time since the 1650s. But the forms of practice and expression they were able to take were determined by the shape of the 1689 political settle-ment, its associated implications for religious toleration and the impact of commercial society. Old agendas (the witness to violent persecution, or visions of Edenic perfection) could be buried inside recently introduced literary forms. Yet in the context of the bookmarket, and the lapse of the Licensing Act in 1695, radical expression was effectively commercialised. It was possible to consume the regicide in a form of ritual commemora-tion. These conditions encouraged the spread of an abundant literature of occult and mystical prophecy, and did not curtail the activities of such spiritual perfectionists, the forebears of whom were given far harsher treatment in the 1650s.

Extending these concerns, Donald John explores how a non-juror such as William Law, sometime chaplain in the household in which Edward Gibbon grew up, could use mystical texts that in the previ-ous century were largely the property of religious radicals.[61] In effect, John traces a process by which the theology of redemption was substan-tially altered, so that God was 'interiorised' in the believer. This had been the message of some of the mid-seventeenth-century radicals; in the eighteenth century, more searching forms of analysis and contem-plation discovered what a personalised God might be. One significant attraction of Boehme's writings was their location of evil and hell within the sphere of God. Jacob Boehme's writings were popular among mid-seventeenth-century radicals, as were some concepts associated with the German occult tradition, such as 'deification'. Much of William Law's library contents looks similar to the spiritualist reading matter of the mid-seventeenth-century radicals.[62] The eighteenth-century 'relearning' of

Boehme's perceptions was effectively a broadening of the reach of these ideas, as well as startling, profound theology: 'righteousness becomes more real; that is, it amounts to a constitutive change in the individual, in some cases stretching toward deification' (see pp. 89–100). These transformations can be projected backwards to the questions raised by Milton's theodicy in *Paradise Lost*. Much has been written of the impact of Milton on eighteenth-century literature, but it is usually assumed that Blake is the first inheritor of Milton's heterodox theology of the Son. John delineates a new context in which a far more widepread interest is apparent.

Timothy Morton explores the Behmenist legacy in another way, analysing the millenarian cultural thought of the vegetarian authority Thomas Tryon, emphasising his representation of plantations and colonies. In this instance, writing on vegetarian diet combines enthusiastic and Enlightenment agenda. Within the framework of the vegetarian vision, Morton also explores the persistence of utopian ideas about consumption and figuration through to the Romantic period, visiting a series of post-Behmenist, post-Tryonist thinkers: George Cheyne and Benjamin Franklin the foremost among them. A knowledge of the inner person, of being at one with oneself, is connected with ideas of political freedom, as Tryon's slave characters link the issue of diet with that of the problem of representation, both in the political sense and in the sense of being able (or not) to express extreme forms of brutalisation in words. That considerations of diet spread so widely across the literary spectrum means that we must, so Morton argues, reconsider the boundaries defining the 'radical' in the period. It was indeed the Behmenists, beginning with the apparently harmless Philadelphians, referred to in Nigel Smith's chapter, and in the figures discussed by Morton, who constituted the major resistance in the period to 'the wrathful appetites both of the body and of the market' (p. 85).

Jane Shaw investigates the changing role of the woman prophet in the later seventeenth and early eighteenth centuries. She reads their rôle as an index of the relationship between gender, radical opposition and the medical and theological theories determining the interpretation of, and response to, prophecy. In the case of Ann Moore of Tutbury, such radical opposition had persisted in women's allegiance to groups that transmitted seventeenth-century radicalism.

Beginning the second section, Michael Scrivener explores the comparable uses made of Reformation terminology, concepts of English popular liberty and classical republicanism in Leveller and Army tracts, and in populist writings of the 1790s. John Thelwall's republican writings are shown to be the true inheritors of the republican tradition, although in so doing they tend to appropriate the aristocratic republicanism of Algernon Sidney and Russell for a position in the 1790s that was populist, encompassing attacks on property and imperialism that are more characteristic of the Diggers. Thelwall knew about Lilburne if not other Leveller texts, but either did not or could not reproject Leveller ideas directly. Instead, he married 'elite' republicanism with more democratic ideas from the French Revolution. This is coupled with a use of English poetic tradition (especially Milton) that removed religion and the erotic from lyrical verse to present a verse of supposed authentic English liberty. The lack of detailed constitutional reflection in Thelwall's own verse produced an impression of belief in popular liberty that was neither Leveller, classical nor Puritan. Yet in fact it still projected all of these things as authentically British, and linked them to a conception of the literary that was oratorical rather than textual.

Considering the long eighteenth century, Charlotte Sussman identifies trends in the culture and politics of women's reading from the 1640s, which reached a decisive moment in the achievements of the Ladies' Anti-Slavery Societies of the early nineteenth century. In renewing the sentimental discourse of virtue, the Societies also refashioned the politicised notions of reading developed in the mid-seventeenth century. This in itself returns attention to the importance of reading in the making of prophecy in the seventeenth century, and in particular, the matter of women's private reading. Moreover, the significance of private reading is that the private sphere was not, as commonly supposed, symptomatic of female exclusion from political debate. Sussman gives us a startling picture. If Interregnum women prophets made public their private experiences through the politics of the gathered churches, the experience of the following period made the world of the female private sphere one that was eventually a site for reforming action.

Jon Mee writes on the Ranter influence in 1790s popular dissent and the contestation over its political meaning, through the example of Richard 'Citizen' Lee. Lee's violent republicanism, mixed alternately as Calvinism and universalism, and his poetry, are seen to produce a religion of the heart that was consistent with the experimental tradition of Puritan confession. Lee's works were marketed with reprints of seventeenth-century Antinomian tracts, and the works of unlearned 'mechanick' preachers, so that the two traditions were seen to coincide. Lee was a Ranting poet of the 1790s who seems to have intended his poetry to be used as a form of protest in the politics of the 1790s, especially during the imprisonment of radicals. Some of his works, such as *King Killing*, are in fact truncated but richly creative restatements of seventeenth-century tyrannicide tracts, such as Edward Sexby's *Killing no Murder*.

James McKusick examines Cobbett's self-help schemes for English peasants as a mode of political resistance to the capital-intensive agriculture of the Napoleonic wars. He elucidates Cobbett's historical understanding of the English Revolution, particularly the 'bloody and tyrannical' rule of Oliver Cromwell, as a direct result of the ongoing, sinister process of the Protestant Reformation. In a curious twist in the use of cultural artefacts, he also shows that John Clare's love of rural unity and calm was fed by an affinity with classic royalist literature. The Roundheads were the violaters of nature, Clare understood from a series of ballads, and his favourite book was his copy of *Eikon Basiliké*.

The collection closes with Peter Kitson's discussion of the representation of Cromwell and the English Republic in the early nineteenth century. Contrary to a received stereotype, Kitson shows that the survival of a positive appreciation of Cromwell's qualities and achievements was the basis of an Oliverian aesthetic among 1790s radicals, although the Terror and the rise of Bonaparte would lead to less favourable comparisons. The triumph of this movement was Godwin's history of the English Commonwealth (1824–8). This assembled a republican history at the point of the repeal of the Test and Corporations Acts, which had excluded dissenters from holding public offices. It was in Godwin's elision of religious Independency and the Protectorate with republicanism that a new understanding of the English Revolution emerged. However much it elevated Cromwell for serious historical consideration, and enabled Puritanism to be understood as a source of motivation for high political and moral ideals, it was one that marginalised Levellers and Presbyterians, in addition to dismissing royalists. Did Godwin notice that he was in fact falling into a royalist trap, and confirming Clarendon's own view?[63] The ghosts of the Commonwealth republicans would not have been amused.

It is the many voices of these ghosts, and their continuing power to suggest positive change as well as cultural fulfilment, that Paul Hamilton celebrates in his Afterword. If history includes self-consciousness, then history is in part the history of philosophy – in part, without wishing to say 'ultimately', for that would imply too firm a commitment to a brand of Hegelianism. Hamilton's essay, then, recapitulates the volume as it were in another key: the narrative of republicanism, not so easily separated from radicalism, in its transmission in philosophy. Hamilton draws on some of the chapters in this volume as he builds his case. This afterword is not intended as a totalisation of the previous essays, nor is it absolutely extrinsic to them. Instead, it is a coda which reasserts the case for the transmission of radicalisms thus:

Aesthetic, religious, civic and cultural discourses of all kinds do not diminish but amplify radical voices as part of an exercise of containment. The dominance the aesthetic comes to occupy in this exercise has recently been one influential way of describing Romanticism. But the radical voices themselves of course reject this repressive tolerance. In so doing, they recover that originary moment in which they reveal what gets politics going in the first place. They expose the arbitrariness of current constituencies, the accident of hereditary and traditional authority, the possibility that things might be completely different.[64]

Hamilton construes the long eighteenth century as the movement of wider and wider 'repressive tolerance' (an Adornian term) of radical discourses. As the net of tolerance widened, however, so the potential area in which radicalisms could exert their influence also widened.

The history of radical literary cultures between 1650 and 1830 is then a double movement, of 'containment' (Hamilton's word) and dispersal, a 'creative effervescence'.[65] Hamilton's discussion focuses on Fichte, who bridged the Enlightenment and the Romantic period, to illustrate the English turn to Machiavellian political theory. Machiavelli is important in the history of radicalism, argues Hamilton, because his view of politics as contingency was apposite to revolutionary moments. History-as-contingency, as decisive opportunity, is radicalism's orientation towards the future. Machiavelli appears in Hume's view of government, and Hamilton then traces this appearance through Gibbon, Burke and Cobbett. An 'oppositional public sphere' emerges in a contrary motion against the hegemonic public sphere of the long eighteenth century.

PART I

From revolution

CHAPTER 1

'May the last king be strangled in the bowels of the last priest': irreligion and the English Enlightenment, 1649–1789

Justin Champion

Writing on *The Rise and Dissolution of the Infidel Societies in the Metropolis* (1800), W.H. Reid excoriated the diffusion of continental irreligion amongst the 'lower orders' in London. Popular songs and reading clubs pilloried bishops and kings. 'May the last king be strangled in the bowels of the last priest' was a common toast in the public houses and hairdressers' of Shoreditch, Whitechapel and Spitalfields. Meetings in club rooms that were timed to coincide with church services, promoted discussion where 'every religious obligation, in civilised society, was resisted as priestcraft'. Through associations such as the London Corresponding Society, 'doctrines of infidelity' became 'extensively circulated among the lower orders'. This popularisation was heinous: books alone corroded order, but when the 'principle of infidelity [was] transferred from *Books* to *men*; from *dead* characters to *living* men' then the *status quo* was threatened. Much of Reid's diagnosis of the pathological quality of English irreligion was attributed to the importation of French ideas of dechristianisation after 1789. Alongside classics of English unbelief, like Paine's *Age of Reason*, the lower orders had become corrupted by a litany of continental writings by Mirabaud and d'Holbach, the 'paragon of French atheism'.[1] A central theme of Reid's text, echoed in many other contemporary works, is of English culture tainted by radical French impiety.[2]

It has been a scholarly commonplace to regard this 'French impiety' as significant in the history of European society. Celebrated as the moment when liberty of thought transcended tradition and religion, the Enlightenment saw the 'Kingdom of Reason' triumph over the superstition of custom and faith.[3] This process of religious disenchantment has been described as a radical moment. It has also been characterised as essentially French. One of the themes of historiography concerning the Enlightenment underscores the significance of anti-clerical and irreligious discourses in the eighteenth century. The argument proposed here is that this should also, by implication, commit historians to appreciating the English contribution to this radical rupture of *ancien régime* ideologies.

In recent years, historians have been reluctant to write about the Enlightenment as a radical movement. Accounts understanding it as a crucial turning point in the history of human society, whether Marxist, liberal or idealist, have been cast aside in favour of work that explores the idiosyncratic, the provincial, the oppressive and the clandestine dimensions of the period. Until recently the moment was described as the accession of philosophical rationality. Scientific progress, economic liberalism and modern literary discourses were all thought to have been born in the period. In contrast to these historiographies, which placed the processes of thought and cultural change in the larger map of human progress, we now have 'Enlightenments' that explore, among other themes, exoticism, sexual underworlds and secret societies.[4]

Exploring fragmented, liminal or counter-cultural 'Enlightenments' is a valuable and indeed important enterprise enabling, for instance, a deconstruction of the grander claims of traditional historiography. There may still be the intellectual space, however, to address the significance of some of the broader changes of the period. Perhaps the most powerful was the attack upon religion, which, it will be argued, was prefigured if not prompted by the crisis of Christian culture in England, one of the legacies of the revolutions in church and state in the 1640s.

That France was the font of irreligion in the eighteenth century is a scholarly commonplace. By contrast England has been construed as being blissfully free of such infidelity. As John Pocock has insisted, 'to try to articulate the phrase "the English Enlightenment" is to encounter inhibition; an ox sits upon the tongue'.[5] Although there have been recent attempts to 'shift the ox', or at least to render the notion of an English Enlightenment less of a mouthful, such accounts suggest that the Enlightenment in England was a conservative and clerical movement without destabilising propensities. It was a sensibility that throve within rather than without piety: a programme of religious reform rather than revolution.[6] In England after 1660, as a result of the profound social and intellectual inversions of the revolutionary decades, it is possible confidently to speak of a society that was divided by competing ideological prescriptions for true religion and government. As the research of many historians has stressed, this bipolarity was manifest not just in the realm of ideas, but embedded in the material practices of everyday life at all levels of the social hierarchy.[7]

The significance of this cultural polarity has received little attention in recent accounts of eighteenth-century life. The eighteenth-
century British are presented as a polite and respectable people. Linda
Colley has written about the social inclusiveness of British national identity in the period rather than the oppositional interests of social identity.
E.P. Thompson has described the period as one of 'class struggle without class'.[8] Much of this historiography has made the significant assumption that religion played little role as a destabilising factor in either
politics or society. Colley describes a broadly Protestant culture that
opposed the Catholic 'other', while Thompson writes of a plebeian culture that had all but escaped the 'hegemony of the Church'.[9] Although
Thompson insists that the elite governed in England through a process of 'cultural hegemony' the rôle of established religious authority
was only 'acknowledged in . . . perfunctory ways'. It seems paradoxical
to marginalise religion at the same time as placing the concept of cultural hegemony at the centre of an understanding of eighteenth-century
social relations.[10]

It is clear that the eighteenth-century Church of England loosened its
ritual authority over the people. The Toleration Act of 1689 set the legal
context for the practical fragmentation of unitary religious worship which
had become the experience of post-revolutionary England. But to claim
this, or that 'the early eighteenth century witnessed a great recession
in Puritanism', is not the same as arguing for a decline in the cultural
hegemony of religion. The institutional structure or membership of the
Church of England may have become 'erastian' and dominated by the
'cousins of the gentry'. The change from a 'magical' form of authority
to different cultural techniques of power did not imply a transcendence
of 'religion', so much as a mutation of the social and literary form by
which it was represented. The legal establishment of the restricted right
to worship in non-Anglican variants of Christianity did have profound
sociological effects in the number of individuals who attended Anglican
Churches. To suggest, however, that it overthrew the cultural authority of
religion (understood as an all-encompassing structure of social authority,
practice and belief) is dangerously reductive.[11]

Recent collections of essays addressing relationships between religion and society in eighteenth-century England indicate the continuing vibrancy of pastoral and theological institutions.[12] The efflorescence
of non-established and private forms of Christian worship, although
divergent in doctrine and dogma, were still forms of religious behaviour,
even if *ecclesiolae* rather than *ecclesia*. Toleration of Christian belief may

be regarded as an expansion rather than a decline in religion. What toleration did enfranchise was heterogeneity in public debates about the authority of true religion, rather than the rise of secular modernity. Although it is possible to agree with de Certeau's assertions that 'prophetic beginnings [made] room for a socio-political opposition', and that 'religious language turned into social discourse'[13] during the eighteenth century, this discursive transformation was enacted under the carapace of religious formality. As historians such as Clark and Hole have illustrated, orthodox Anglicanism seems to have been as effective a player in the battle for cultural hegemony in the 1790s as it had been in the 1690s: this is not to argue that it was the singular participant.[14] Yet to say that religion remained a vibrant, powerful cultural practice is not to insist that English radicalism was mute or peripheral. Indeed it was precisely because confessional imperatives remained so embedded in the infrastructure of social power that the anti-clerical and irreligious discourses of the Commonwealth tradition retained their relevance and power.

This theme has been strongly supported by Margaret Jacob. She proposes that the militant atheism of the High Enlightenment was spawned by a radical English Commonwealth tradition.[15] Her argument has distinguished precursors. Contrary to current orthodoxies, earlier historians inverted the commonplace narrative of French radicalism and English innocence. In France, Alexis de Tocqueville insisted upon the central rôle that irreligion played in challenging the 'sanctity' of the established political and religious order, while also suggesting that the intellectual origins of that impiety lay in English rather than French discourses. He commented boldly, 'There is no question that the nationwide discredit of all forms of religious belief which prevailed at the end of the century had a preponderant influence on the course of the French Revolution.'[16] The church was 'if not the most oppressive' then certainly the 'chief of all the powers in the land'.[17] There was, as de Tocqueville put it, a sort of 'give and take' between civil and ecclesiastical authority: 'the secular power insisted upon obedience to the ecclesiastical authorities and the Church saw to it that the King's authority was respected'. With the spread of the 'revolutionary movement', the consecrated alliance between church and state became fragile given that the 'power' was founded 'not on constraint but belief'.[18] In describing the ideological origins of this attack upon organised religion de Tocqueville was unequivocal: 'our anti-religious ideas had found exponents in England before our famous French philosophers were born'. Voltaire took his cue from English writers 'throughout the eighteenth century great skeptics made their voices heard in England, and brilliant writers and profound thinkers sponsored the views we now associate with Voltaire'.[19] De Tocqueville argued that the irreligious spirit of the age (the Enlightenment) prompted the Revolution of 1789. The modish impiety that wreaked such havoc on the continent was imported from English shores.

There is then an assumption in some quarters that the Enlightenment attack upon religion was in some manner significant in determining the shape of revolution in France. Exploring the precise connection between the diffusion of radical ideas and the coming of the Revolution has occupied (mainly French) historians since the early twentieth century. Daniel Mornet's classic studies between 1910 and 1938, based upon his researches into the diffusion of ideas through an examination of book ownership, argued that 'incredulity and indifference' derived from the arguments of many writings created a revolution in 'men's mind's', setting the context for 1789. If one intention was to play down the rôle of the 'great texts' in creating the impious culture of eighteenth-century France, Mornet's corollary was to emphasise the rôle of a widely diffused public opinion in creating the ideological circumstances for the breakdown of the *ancien régime*.[20] Mornet's early attempt at answering the question of what the French read in the eighteenth century spawned a massive body of quantitative research into book ownership, publishing houses and the circulation of clandestine literature, but not much at addressing the relationship between reading and revolution.

Two recent works by Baker and Chartier have endeavoured to re-pose the question of the 'ideological origins' of the Revolution.[21] Both Baker and Chartier set out to go beyond Mornet and explore the cultural implications of changes in reading and writing. In effect, they explore how new ideas or languages contributed to ruptures in the traditional discursive forms of social authority. There are, however, important distinctions between Baker and Chartier. For Baker, the Revolution was constituted in the realm of linguistic practice. The Enlightenment evolved critical discourses that tore French culture away from its absolutist foundations. Stressing the 'linguisticality' of political life, Baker's account of the ideological origins of 1789 is premised upon a confrontation between competing absolutist and anti-monarchical discourses. The traditional ideology of the *ancien régime* was undercut by *mauvais discours*: the men of letters, the *sociétés des pensées*, transformed the traditional 'symbolic representation' of absolutism into the 'socio-political action' of revolution in 1789; opinion was brought to power.[22]

If Baker locates the ideological origins of 1789 in the invention of restructured languages of opposition to *ancien régime* discourses of absolute monarchy, Chartier has adopted a less abstracted model of cultural change. Expanding on Habermas's work on the structural transformation of the public sphere, Chartier proposes a wider social context for the process of 'ideological erosion' focusing upon the idea of the 'public' use of reason. While Baker seems content to explore the changing configurations of political languages, Chartier insists upon their sociological dimensions. The new public sphere, embodied in new forms of intellectual sociability such as 'the salons, the cafés, the clubs and periodicals', defined alternative 'modes of representation' that became embodied in 'public opinion'. The 'tribunal of opinion' was ultimately constituted by the 'way of print'. More people read and owned a transformed literary product. Philosophic texts, pornography, satires, libels and salacious narratives circulated with increased frequency in both Paris and the provinces. Pirated and clandestine titles, 'books under the cloak', fashioned French culture from the mid century. Reading Voltaire or d'Holbach alongside the denuciatory *libelles* unpicked the charismatic authority of orthodox discourses.[23]

Although Chartier expresses some caution in 'linking philosophical books and revolutionary thought', by which he means connecting reading to belief, he contends that the period witnessed a transformation of reading practices. The new relationship between reader and book was the crux of the matter. This innovation was not just a matter of the content of philosophic texts, but, as Chartier writes, 'rather a new mode of reading that, even when the texts it took on were in total conformity with religious and political order, developed a critical attitude freed from the ties of dependence and obedience that underlay earlier representations'.[24] This 'disengagement from tradition' was manifest not just in linguistic practice (*qua* Baker) but in cultural and social practice. The processes of dechristianisation and secularisation were part of the early modern transition from a theocratic organisation of society to the political.[25] The decline of the social role of the parish and priest, the desacralisation of the monarchy and the diffusion of practical and theoretical incredulity, provided the components of a 'new political culture', that ultimately destroyed the established order in 1789.[26]

Recent scholarship then broadly reinforces the arguments of writers like Mornet, and before him de Tocqueville. The corrosion of the religious sensibilities of the *ancien régime* by high and low life *philosophes*, *gens des lettres* and hack journalists fractured the traditional structure of authority. As Chartier summarises, 'if the French of the late eighteenth century fashioned the Revolution, it is in turn because they had been fashioned by books'.[27] Although many of the these 'books' had English origins, with very few exceptions neither modern French nor English historiography has attended closely to the rôle anglophone irreligion may have played in the formation of this Enlightenment culture.[28] Earlier historians, however, in pursuing the influence of irreligion on the Revolution, located the provenance of this critical discourse in earlier eighteenth-century English sources.

Reading the series of literary studies written between 1900 and the 1930s, it is common to encounter arguments insisting upon the 'great intellectual liaison' between France and England in the first half of the eighteenth century.[29] Examinations of the networks of correspondence and literary journals that constituted the public forum of the *res publica litteratorum* stress the primacy of the English contribution. Central in the diffusion of radical ideas to the continent were Dutch journals, such as the *Nouvelles de la République des Lettres* and the *Bibliothèque Universelle*, which acted as conduits conveying 'substantial information on the English deistic movement . . . to French readers'. As one commentator put it, 'the English movement was thought to be the source of the French movement which followed'.[30] Robert Darnton regards Voltaire and d'Holbach as the two most popular writers of 'forbidden books' in the period. To take them as cases of English influence is instructive.[31] The early twentieth-century historiography treats these writers as publicists rather than innovators: Voltaire was the means by which 'the whole movement of English ideas was channelled into France'. D'Holbach's widely diffused materialist tracts contained translations of substantial portions of earlier eighteenth-century English writings.[32] As the research of Miguel Benitez on the circulation of clandestine literature in the eighteenth century has established, many of the more dangerous works were translations or adaptations of the English works of men like Hobbes, Blount and Toland.[33]

The historiographical suggestion that the roots of Enlightenment discourses of 'écrase l'infâme' are to be found in the soil of English anti-clericalism might be expected to provoke some shaking of scholarly heads. John Pocock has suggested that early modern England had a political culture in which radical ideas were 'invented but never put into practice'.[34] Because historians have generally explored the 'origins' rather than 'consequences' of 1649 there has been very little examining of the wider ideological significance of the Revolution.[35] It is

widely assumed that the radicalism of the 1640s and 1650s died with
the restoration of the king and bishops in 1660. Indeed, the idea of the
persistence of the traditional order has been painted in bold brushstrokes
by J.C.D. Clark. Far from being constitutionally distinct from the continent, for Clark, England with its 'confessional state' remained part of the
ancien régime throughout the eighteenth century. Since religious institutions, beliefs and practices remained robust and vibrant, Commonwealth
traditions were marginalised to the radical fringes.[36]

The logic of this argument rests upon a false opposition between a
religious configuration of social power and a secular or civil alternative.
The radical legacy of the 1640s and 1650s, mediated by the materialis-
tic and anti-clerical rearticulations of men such as Toland, Blount and
Gordon, was calculated as a contribution to the debate about the legitimate relationship between religious confessionalism and civic order.
Indeed, recent work on the 'politics of religion' after the Restoration
would argue that the confrontations between radical and traditional interests took place within rather than without the margins of 'religion':[37]
the struggle for 'power' was not a teleological plot whereby politics replaced theology, but a competition for the appropriation of authority
within the sphere of the 'religious'.[38] The irreligious discourses born in
ecclesiological debate in seventeenth-century England, and refined in
the crucible of revolutionary exchange in the 1640s and 1650s, were
not mere parochial ephemera but remained pertinent to the continuing
eighteenth-century contestation over the status of 'religion'. In this sense
the radical consequences of 1649 were intimately relevant to the cultural
origins of the French Revolution.[39]

The current historiographical inertia characterising eighteenth-
century England as a cynosure of theological stability is ripe for challenging. The cosmopolitanism of early modern culture has been obscured
in recent decades. To argue for a more permeable intellectual culture, is
not to jettison the idea of the cultural differences between early modern
states as a historical tool of explanation. To explore here just one tribu-
tary of the irreligion of the High Enlightenment, the intention is to point
out some of the continuities, as well as differences, between England and
France in the period.

Published first in 1719 and frequently reprinted after 1768, the *Traité
des Trois Imposteurs* has been long considered as the epitome of Enlightenment irreligion: a 'complete system of atheism'.[40] As the researches of
Wade, Spink and Allen illustrated, the manuscript had a massive clandestine circulation throughout the eighteenth century.[41] Recent studies by

Miguel Benitez, Silvia Berti and Françoise Charles-Daubert have traced
the location of the surviving manuscripts and compiled a bibliography
of the variant editions. That only two English versions seem to have survived of a total of some 300 copies still extant, reinforces the impression
that the *Traité* represents a peculiarly French phenomenon ('les tendances
les plus radicales de la critique antireligieuse de l'époque').[42] Eventually
republished by d'Holbach's printer Marc-Michel Rey in the late 1760s
and 1770s, the text indicted all organised religion as imposture. Compiled as a *bricolage* of early modern sources, Judaism, Christianity and
Islam were vilified as products of the 'absurd imaginations' of priests
and tyrants. Moses, Christ and Mohammed were the three religious impostors, who, masked as divine prophets, had duped the world: 'Toutes
les religions sont l'ouvrage de la politique.'[43] Theological institutions
and beliefs – priests, sacraments, heaven, hell, even God – were false systems, founded upon human ignorance and fear. These false ideologies
contrived not only spiritual deviance but civil tyranny.

   The *Traité* has been described as a 'preamble' to the systematic irreligion of d'Holbach's *System of Nature or Essay on Prejudices*. It exposed the
history of religion as a history of error: imposture was both irrational and
unjust. Kings and priests were condemned as conspirators against human reason and liberty. This polemic, while extreme, was not new. The
dissection of the *Traité* has shown its sources to be a collage of much earlier discourses: Hobbes, Spinoza, Vanini, Pomponazzi, Campanella and
Machiavelli all rubbed shoulders with classical standards such as Cicero,
Lucretius and Epicurus. Although there have been many candidates for
authorship ranging from Frederick II to various French *libertins érudits*, it
now seems most likely that the compiler was a minor Dutch diplomat,
Jan Vroesen, associate of the circle focused on Benjamin Furly's house in
Rotterdam, which included men such as John Toland, the third Earl of
Shaftesbury and John Locke.[44] The intellectual milieu which provoked
the *Traité* was Anglo-Dutch rather than French. The 'origins' of the most
radical 'oeuvre de combat' of the French Enlightenment seems to have
been in an author whose main inspiration was 'la letteratura deistica
inglese'.[45] More recent work has suggested that the pantheistical John
Toland may also have had a key rôle in the development of specific
elements of the clandestine text related to the construction of Moses
as a political legislator.[46] This research prompts some rethinking of the
relationship between English and French thought in the period. That
English writers could 'invent' such radical discourses between 1649 and
the 1700s, should prompt reconsideration of the cultural legacy of the

English Revolution and its relationship to the discursive origins of the French Revolution.

After 1649 English culture experienced (to use Baker's vocabulary) a rupture in the symbolic representation of monarchy and religion eroding the coherence of traditional authority. While writers on the French Revolution have described this conceptual fracture with absolutism as the 'origin' of the socio-political action of 1789, in the English context it is more typical to write of the 'Revolution' in 1649 as an accidental aberration. Recent research would however insist that the Revolution had profoundly irreligious consequences. Indeed, by exploring debates about the politics of religion between the execution of Charles I and the accession of the Hanoverian monarchy, it is possible to identify a series of republican and anti-clerical discourses that provided the conceptual cloth for Vroesen's *bricolage* in the *Traité*. Whatever the social, political or religious causes of the outbreak of revolution in 1642, there surely can be little controversy in insisting that the world was turned upside down in 1649. Although it cannot be said that there was any systematic and co-ordinated ideological programme that toppled both church and state, the result of practical disorder and heterodox practice was that the traditional economy of spiritual authority was disrupted. The Bible became a bagatelle, priests became popish rogues and princes mere dogs. Combined with the social disintegration of the established clerical and monarchical order were intellectual assaults on *ancien régime* ideology. While the writings of Hobbes, Spinoza and La Peyrère attacked the sanctity of the Bible as politically prescriptive, theorists such as Harrington promoted a civic republicanism that undercut the patriarchal ideology of later Stuart society.[47]

Although the English Revolution did not effect any profound social or economic transformation, there was then one important ideological legacy identified as the problematic of the 'politics of religion'. Between the Restoration in 1660 and the early eighteenth century, the central political debate revolved around the axis of religion rather than that of constitutionalism. The political and social power of the established church came under intense scrutiny. While high churchmen and royal apologists persevered in restating the sacrality of church and state, republican and anti-clerical writers such as Charles Blount, John Toland and Thomas Gordon designed polemics undercutting the 'halo of sanctity'. This antagonistic discourse, identified as a 'history of priestcraft', can be considered a first move in the history and sociology of religion.[48]

The crisis of authority engendered a series of texts, many of which were translated, paraphrased or plagiarised in later French books, treating religious belief, ceremony and ritual as a social and historical phenomenon. 'Religion' was conventional rather than transcendental, a product of human psychology and priestly manipulation. For example, Hobbes's *Ecclesiastical History from Moses to Luther* (1689 Latin edition, 1722 English translation) provided a simplified historical analysis of the decline of true theology and the rise of priestcraft. Primitive Christianity was originally a sociable religion that promoted natural morality rather than worldly gain. Using a corrupt apparatus of pagan philosophy and scholastic 'jargon', the priests turned religion into empire. False miracles, superstition, ghosts and goblins, the kingdom of fairies and darkness established clerical power over the fearful and ignorant laity. In language strikingly similar to the *Traité*, Hobbes insisted that the clergy had 'deified their dreams'. The sacerdotal order established dominion over the laity, which, hand in hand with corrupt monarchs, they forged into civil tyranny.

Other important texts, Robert Howard's *History of Religion* (1694), John Trenchard's *Natural History of Superstition* (1709) and Toland's *Christianity Not Mysterious* (1696), reinforced the anti-clerical polemic: mystery, cunning and priestcraft had corrupted natural religion. Although many of these attacks upon religion and the church were polemical *livres de circonstance*, they drew from a large body of scholarly research that investigated the history not only of Christianity, but also of heathenism, Judaism and Islam. Drawing from the critical writings of Herbert of Cherbury and John Spenser, populist pamphlets such as Blount's *Anima Mundi* (1680) and Toland's *Letters to Serena* (1704) exposed Christian beliefs in the soul and the afterlife as opinion and idolatry: the history of theology became the history of error. The underlying theme was the distinction between the virtuous injunctions of the law of nature and the conventional aspirations of positive institutions. Almost inevitably, natural religion became corrupted by the priests.

In tandem with reviling the priesthood for corrupting religion and establishing civil tyranny by imposing their false opinions as prejudices in the popular mind, the anti-clerical writers also exposed the techniques of priestly hegemony. Developing the radical Biblical criticism of the 1650s, the work of Toland and Thomas Burnet divested Scripture of its authenticity as the word of God by insisting upon its historicity. Scripture was 'a heap of copy confusedly taken'; the Canon was manipulated by priestly forgers. Toland scandalously attempted to negate the New Testament by supplanting it with his newly discovered 'Gospel of Barnabas'.[49] The word of God was wrested and wried by church self-interest: mistranslations, interpolations and mystification had obscured the true meaning of Scripture. Reformation of the 'Word' meant revolution in the church.[50]

The anti-clerical writers of the 1680s–1710s developed a conception of religion as sociological construct rather than divine truth. This formulation was not merely a scholarly point but a political discourse aimed at countering the church's social power. Some texts, such as Blount's edition of the *Life of Apollonius* (1680), another book translated for a French audience twice in the 1770s, and circulated in manuscript versions, were elegant, learned and even erudite deconstructions of Christian myth.[51] Others, such as Trenchard's and Gordon's journals *Cato's Letters* and the *Independent Whig*, were directed at a popular audience.[52] The central point of this English discourse, just as with the *Traité*, was that irreligion was part of a political agenda. Priestcraft corrupted both theology and society. As Trenchard pithily commented, Christianity was 'a deadly engine in the hands of a tyrant to rivet his subjects in chains'. The first step on the road to reform was to desacralise the church. The battle was not to overthrow religion but to purify it.

It is commonplace to suggest that the freethinking anti-clericalism of English works was tame compared with the outrageous elements in the *Traité* or d'Holbach's writings. On the contrary, in England the 'three impostors' thesis was mooted in print and in public from the 1650s. Richard Popkin's work on the Oldenburg circle reveals a current anxiety about the existence of a treatise presenting Moses, Christ and Mohammed as political legislators. Oldenburg was desperate for Adam Boreel to compose a rebuttal. As early as 1643 Thomas Browne had written against the author of 'the miscreant piece of the Three Impostors'. Henry Stubbe was familiar enough with the arguments to write a manuscript life of Mohammed displaying him as a much more successful politician that either Christ or Moses.[53] The bibliographer Richard Smith wrote an account of the 'rumour' of the treatise some time in the 1660s giving a detailed prospectus of both the types of argument such a work might propose as well as a useful list of sources for further reading.

Evidence that the 'three impostors thesis' had become part of popular currency could be derived from the trial in London of John Baptista Damascene, 'an impious and profane and irreligious person' in June 1672. Although acquitted later, Damascene was accused of proclaiming that 'Jesus Christ, Moyses and Mahomet were three great rogues'.[54]

Blount's much ignored *Life of Apollonius* (1680), a book that was burnt by order of the Bishop of London, used many of the sources contained in the *Traité* to parody the life of Christ with the example of the pagan magician Apollonius. The irreligious footnotes to the classical text contained a trialogue between a Jew, a Christian and a Moslem debating the relative merits of their religions. Blount made similar allusions to the theory of triple imposture in letters to Rochester published in the 1690s. Perhaps the closest parallel to the *Traité* is Toland's *Nazarenus* (1718), another English text widely disseminated and discussed on the continent (in print and scribal form) and ultimately translated by D'Holbach in 1777. Using a very suspect and highly heterodox gnostic gospel, which he had disinterred in Holland, Toland proposed that Judaism, Christianity and Islam were all part of the same 'religious' phenomenon concerned to promote moral virtue rather than sacrament and ritual. The subtext of *Nazarenus*, explored more explicitly in Latin works such as *Origines Judicae* (1709), was that the so-called religious prophets (Moses, Christ and Mohammed) were really political legislators adapting their religious institutions to national and historical circumstances.

English Commonwealthmen such as Toland adapted the clerical idea of religion to the needs of the state: they aimed to create a civil religion modelled upon classical examples. The indictment of priestcraft was not because it was 'religion', but because it was corrupt religion. Reform of religion was the stepping stone to reform of society. Pre-empting the civic religion of Rousseau, the inauguration of the Cult of Reason and worship of the Supreme Being in 1792–3, republicans suggested that Commonwealth religion was to be 'a minister of God on Earth, to the end that the World may be governed with Righteousness'.[55] Studies such as Walter Moyle's discursus on Numa Pompilius applauded the Roman's politic use of religion and credal minimalism. Harrington's *Oceana* (1656, reprinted in 1700), popular in eighteenth-century French political theory, promoted a 'public leading' in religion to establish national virtue. The republican model was predicated upon a stoic vision of the personal and political battle between reason and the passions. Priestcraft corrupted the soul and the state with ignorance and tyrannous private interest; virtue blessed the soul with reason and the state with public interest. For the republicans the false sacrality of priestcraft was to be transferred to the civic religion. This religion was to teach reason, virtue and public interest to the populace. Priestcraft reformed to civic religion was a central theme of the attack upon the Church of

England between 1660 and 1714 by writers such as Toland, Gordon and the third Earl of Shaftesbury. Precisely these writings were translated for French readers in the 1760s and 1770s.[56]

Although the period from 1650 to 1800 has consistently been described as an era of secularisation, it is now apparent that relationships between religion and reason were not as clear as Victorian logic might have it.[57] Discursive contestations between church and state rather than between monarchies and representative institutions determined the nature of conflict in both England and France. After the 1660s the public debate about relationships between the Church of England and civil power produced a profoundly radical critique of clerical authority. This collection of writings became an intellectual resource for later European anti-clericalism.[58] This is not to argue that the radical anti-clerical discourse of the English Commonwealthsmen 'caused', 'inspired' or 'provoked' the crisis of 1789. Because common themes of public debate focused on the correct institutionalisation of religion, French writers such as Voltaire and d'Holbach could appropriate and rearticulate the language and arguments of earlier English authors.

The radical texts of English anti-clericalism found new, and perhaps more elite, audiences in the clandestine circles of eighteenth-century France.[59] In contrast to the remarks of Reid that opened this chapter, complaining about the corrosive influence of French impiety on English readers, it was possible for Edmund Burke to comment that no one read the works of Toland, Tindal and Blount in the 1790s. Although English Commonwealth anti-clericalism, between 1660 and 1720, engaged in a robust, and public, attempt to grapple public power from the established church, by the 1730s and 1740s the power of this discourse was neutered by the institutional dominance of the Whig political establishment. This radical public discourse was also powerfully rebutted by clericalist response. The battles for the capture of the 'confessional state' in England saw freethinker and priest competing in the same public forum of print for the power to inform 'public reason'.[60] If one were searching for reasons for the distinction between the 'performance' of radical discourses in England and France in the eighteenth century, one clear element can be seen in the powerful and learned response of the clerical elite. English freethinking attacks upon priestcraft did not go unchallenged: impiety was rebutted by vigorous polemic. As Brian Young has recently asserted, the language of 'enlightenment' in England was successfully captured by profoundly clerical figures. Articulating an anti-dogmatic 'reasonable' defence of Christian orthodoxy, 'Enlightened ecclesiastics' such as William Law, Daniel Waterland and William Warburton, preserved the cultural and intellectual status of religious institutions.[61]

Acknowledging the persisting cultural authority of a churchmanship that successfully plotted a steady course between Enlightenment and counter-Enlightenment discourses should not, however, imply a consequent deflation of the 'radicalism' of equally persisting anti-clerical and Commonwealth ideologies. The continuing success of religious apologetics also meant the enduring political relevance of irreligious ideologies. An older intellectualist account of Enlightenment argued that rationalist conceptions of human nature and society necessarily vanquished traditional religious and theological values during the course of the eighteenth century. In contrast to this now moribund account an alternative view might insist that throughout the eighteenth century religious and heterodox ideas were in continual contestation: although orthodox Christianity claimed a dominant or hegemonic status, this was persistently, and sometimes successfully, challenged by a variety of different affinities or interests who deployed a language of religious reform to defend their positions.

By rehearsing the arguments of the current historiography of political culture in eighteenth-century France, the intention has been to suggest that the emphasis upon the politically corrosive dynamic of anti-clerical irreligious ideas also has significant application to the English context. If we accept the arguments of Chartier and Baker, which suggest that the production, circulation and reception of anti-monarchical and anti-clerical ideas were intimately connected with the rupture of 1789, then there are clear implications for the historiographical understanding of such discourses in England in the eighteenth century. It is possible, then, to argue that there was a critical discourse that had a radical reaction in the *ancien régime* societies of both England and France. By exploring the intellectual genesis of such radically anti-traditional ideas and locating them in English Commonwealth traditions, it is possible to underscore their portability and permeability. There is a twofold implication here. First, that there was a textually continuous relationship between an early radical (English) Enlightenment and a later high (French) Enlightenment. Secondly, these ideas were not only portable and adaptable, but also the product of a specific politico-religious moment. Between 1660 and 1730 there was a contestation in intellectual culture between clerical and anti-clerical interests: neither simply 'religious' nor 'secular', this

was certainly internecine. While it is possible to assert, *pace* Clark and
Young, that this 'radical' moment was compromised, and, even perhaps,
marginalised from the central stage of public debate after the 1730s in
England, its significance is undeniable: both for providing a resource
for later (French) writers and polemicists, and for establishing a radical
agenda for the contours and parameters of eighteenth-century European
debate about religion.

CHAPTER 2

Radicalism and replication

Nigel Smith

2nd Cit. Then we'll all govern by turns.
Juca. Ay, but who'll govern first?
Omnes. I, I, I.

Timoleon (1697)

In futurity
I, prophetic, see
That the earth from sleep
(Grave the sentence deep)

Shall arise and seek
From her maker meek,
And the desert wild
Become a garden mild.
William Blake, 'The Little Girl Lost',
from *Songs of Innocence* (1789)

I dreamed I saw a tree full of angels, up on Primrose Hill
And I flew with them over the Great Wen till I had seen my fill
Of such poverty and misery, sure to tear my soul apart
I've got a socialism of the heart, I've got a socialism of the heart.
Billy Bragg, 'Upfield', from *william bloke* (WEA *Elektra*, 1996)

INTRODUCTION: FROM GLORY DAYS TO GLORIOUS REVOLUTION

The publications of 1640–60 are rightly looked upon as a heyday of inventive writing and publishing in politics and religion. In special circumstances that enabled the uncontrolled production of pamphlets and books, radical Puritan theology and, eventually, Leveller and republican politics, were established. It was such an intense two decades that it is no surprise that several scholars have been able to focus on almost nothing else for their entire careers.

But with the Restoration all that invention ceased. After the intense flurry of voices that followed the recall of the Rump Parliament in 1659, including a revived Leveller platform, all went quiet with the return of the monarch. What did not go quiet was the voice of hard Protestant dissent. Hence the very considerable outpouring of dissenting literature during the Restoration.[1] But, since the conditions by which Nonconformity now operated were governed by the restrictions of the Act of Uniformity of 1662 and subsequent legislation, it was issues of toleration rather than disputes over church ordinances that dominated the agenda. While exchanges between Anglicans and dissenters resulted in a distinguished controversial literature, the mental qualities of dissenting experience are evident in numerous works that were visionary rather than theoretical.[2] In the opinion of the most distinguished commentator of Restoration Nonconformist literature, political defeat led to literary triumph.[3] For instance, the voice of dissent against the Restoration came with a series of prophetic tracts distributed by some of the radical publishers of the 1650s, in particular the Calverts.[4] Thus, the *Mirabilis Annus* pamphlets of 1661–2 found evidence in natural phenomena, such as comets, to prove that the restored monarchy was displeasing to God, and would be punished.[5] These publications may be set alongside the disgusted or disappointed expression of more magisterial Puritans and republicans, like Ludlow and Milton, whose response to April 1660 was quickly distilled into literary tradition. The Restoration was, for all supporters of the Commonwealth, a huge psychic blow, as the Puritan writings of 1660–3 reveal, and as particular individual witnesses – such as George Fox and his early 1660s depression – suggest.[6] The visionary quality of the *Mirabilis Annus* tracts is indeed remarkable, a fitting example of the peculiar attentiveness induced in the Puritans by their fall from political grace:

A Strange Cloud, sending forth great flashes of Fire, seen
in the Air; and on the top of it the form of a Man's Head,
of a very large proportion

Upon the 30th of July, 1662, three credible persons going from London to Newington-Green, about eight of the clock at night, saw a great Cloud before them, which hung very low in the Air: It sent forth very many and great flashes of Fire, which were very terrible to behold. At length there appeared on the top of the Cloud, the form of a Man's Head, of a very large proportion: his hair was of a perfect black colour; they saw Fire ascend out of the Cloud, against the Head, as it had come out of a Musket. One of the Spectators being a Woman, was so extreamly affrighted, that she would not go further in that way wherein they were, but prevailed with the rest to turn into another path which led to Sir *George Whitmoor's* house, and so are able to give no further account; but they do all constantly affirm the truth of what hath been here related.[7]

It is no surprise then that a broad Protestant consensus, defined largely by its hostile treatment in the law, consolidated itself as a wrongly abused religious community – the very heart of the godly nation. Those who supported Monmouth's rebellion thought that they were supporting a true king because he had not reneged on Protestantism. The popular literature of Keach and others in this period, some of which sold well, and was read very widely indeed, together with the instances of the execution of rebels, all speak a popular Protestant martyrology.[8]

In one sense, however, the literature of Restoration dissent did change. The publishing practices of royalists when they were under scrutiny in the 1650s were now used by dissenters and republicans in the 1660s and 1670s. The coffee house had arrived in England in the later 1650s, but it now provided a suitable context for an opposition. Likewise, royalism had survived and made itself known partly through the use of ballads in the 1640s. The form was now employed to pillory Clarendon's regime in the late 1660s, and the censors came looking for the culprits.[9]

A kind of middle way, between abuse and complaint, occurred in the pamphlets of Ralph Wallis of Gloucester. The influence of Marprelate is evident, but Wallis is too rude and too blunt to be identified firmly even with that tradition. Wallis's *Room for the Cobler of Gloucester* (1668) fuses the dialogue of the Marprelate tradition as it had been mutated during the Civil War at the hands of writers like Richard Overton, with the popular verse traditions of the ballad. The journalist Marchamont Nedham famously advocated the use of laughter and jesting wit in order to retain a wide readership for his newsbooks in the 1650s.[10] In Wallis, laughter becomes a form of harsh abuse that plays on national stereotypes:

Wife, being wiling to have a little more discourse with you, I think it not amiss, if we and our Children sing a *Tantrum*.
Wife. What do you mean by a *Tantrum*, Husband?
Husb. Wife, I borrow that Word of a Welchman, who made this request to his wife; *Market, thee go me to Quire Einsome, and hear my Poy Ropin sing two three Tantru* from whence in *Herefordshire* they call *Anthems Tantrums*.

To the tune of *Room for Cuckolds*: It will be thought a strange tune, but it will be a suitable tune to us, as the tune of *Tory Rory Betty*, which they plaid upon their Organs at *Oxford*: A sweet *Tantrum*![11]

The following abusive 'song' makes it easy to see why the 'Bawdy House Riots' of 1668 were caused by angry dissenters:[12]

> Room for Prelates, and for their company,
> 　　Room for Prelates, and for their Spawn;
> Room for Dumb Dogs, and all Croaking Frogs,
> 　　And Vermin hid under the Lawn ...
> That with the Herd run at right as a Gun,
> 　　Like Pigs possest with a Legion.[13]

Having set the context for subsequent judgements, the reader is assaulted with a thirty-five-page-plus array of episcopal abuses, many of them stories derived from provincial sources. The replication of Catholic prayers, rendered as invocations of the pagan god of wine Bacchus, is matched by scatological stories:

At a place called *Lurgashal* in *Wiltshire*, (as I have been informed from very good hands) the People having sung a Psalm, expected the Priest would begin his Sermon; but staying somewhat long, a Gentleman, one Mr *Poussain*, sent to him to begin his Sermon; but the Messenger found him in the Pew, where he had beshit himself, and was wiping his breech (as was conceived) with his Sermon-notes; and in that condition would have got up into the Pulpit to have preached, but the people would not let him.[14]

For Wallis, a Leveller-style genealogy prevails in the Church of England: bishops are derived from the Norman yoke, and every man is free and equal by nature. He pointedly associates his tract with Samuel How's *Sufficiency of the Spirit's Teaching* (1640), the dynamic anti-clerical justification of preaching by the unordained and the uneducated, which would be published again in the 1790s.[15]

THE GLORIOUS REVOLUTION AND THE RADICALS

The settlement that followed the Glorious Revolution provided a different kind of political culture, and as time passed, so it gathered to be ~~~akeable foundation for an increasingly powerful nation state. As ~~~: 'What did end ... after 1688, was the experience of ~~~alism had been sustained.'[16] Indeed, one of ~~~t was the way in which the element that had survived from mid-century radicalism was effectively built into the political system, because Whig politicians had relations with dissenting interests at the level of local, corporation politics. At the very end of his life, and almost as a living symbol of the change that had taken place in 1688–9, the former Leveller John Wildman found himself holding public office as Postmaster-General.

The history of the ideas and individuals who constituted the founders of Whig ideology is very famous indeed: the first Earl of Shaftesbury, Algernon Sidney and John Locke; Andrew Marvell too. Between them, they invented the ideological foundations of the new state, although only one of them lived to see it. Through heroic suffering (notably and in an absolute way, Sidney), they found much popular support and a clear context in which to be celebrated as wronged champions of liberty. This reputation survived continuously down to the nineteenth century and into our own day. However, in spite of their defence of liberties, and the right of Englishmen to resist tyrants, they belonged to a political elite. With very few exceptions, they had nothing to do with the people who made up the body of mid-century radical and Restoration dissenting support, even though they had been involved in the popular politics of the Restoration.[17] Their principles might have been enshrined in the 1689 settlement, which contained a broad degree of toleration, but this had almost nothing to do with the worlds of consciousness in which these people lived. There are a few published exceptions to this rule, where a popular appeal for a republican government was made to Parliament.[18]

The contested issue of allegiance to the new regime, and the lingering military threat of a major Catholic power, France, made the Settlement seem tenuous at first. But as time progressed, its durability became apparent. Radicalism became part of a national culture that was divided but nonetheless inclusive. Radicalism was both a memory and a practice, subject to tendencies of repetition and replication, as the political actors of the day themselves sought to find authenticity.

Indeed, much energy hitherto committed to religious and political protest found an outlet in cultural and aesthetic pursuits. The institutions of literary culture – journalism, a tradition of literary criticism, public debate concerning standards of taste and judgement – might have had their foundations in the seventeenth century, even in the English Revolution, but their first sustained flourishing was in the fifty years after 1689. John Dennis's influential essays on the nature of poetry were rooted in a literary canon that was undeniably republican. The relationship between politics and literature changed after 1689 with the concerted patronage by the Whigs of literary productions.[19]

Timoleon: Or, The Revolution (1697) is an anonymous[20] play published early during the campaign against proposals for the maintenance of a standing army, meant clearly to appeal to William III, who is figured in the eponymous hero. It is largely concerned with the virtuous qualities of Timoleon, who left a private life in the mother city of Corinth to defeat the tyrant Dionysius in the colony of Sicily.[21] The immediate context for the play was the assassination plot against William III of early 1696: the play contains an unsuccessful attempt against Timoleon's life. It is concerned with courtly corruption, a theme that echoed constantly in the period. The two villains of the play, Pharax and Alphonso, are venal time-servers, who have survived from the government of the banished tyrant. They represent Robert Spencer, Earl of Sunderland, and Thomas Osborne, formerly Earl of Danby, now Duke of Leeds; they are sensationally linked with the assassination plot, and are torn to pieces by the people.[22] It is, then, a play of party loyalty: Whig anger appears to focus upon the survival of pernicious Tories in government.

But at the end of the play, the citizens suddenly begin to discuss a form of government in which the people participate:

> *1st Cit.* They say our Prince will govern no longer, and we must now chuse a new one.
>
> *2nd Cit.* Nay, hold therefore, good neighbours; if our old Prince will not govern us, why should we be govern'd by any others? Therefore, I say, if he will leave us, let us see whether or no we cannot govern ourselves.
>
> *Juca.* Heark ye, Friend, I find thou art but a Mountebank of the Body-Politick; dost thou not know what belongs to Government.
>
> *2nd Cit.* Yes, Friend, I think I do: For, look you here, in Government there be two sorts of People, there be those that govern, and then there be those that are governed; now the governed, being allways more in number than the governing, 'tis fit they should have their share as well as the other: Therefore, I say, we will all be Governors.[23]

The authors in the state have finally found their voice, albeit one that voices democracy through the mouth of a clown. Timoleon was a hero of the mid-century radicals, especially Lilburne.[24] Here he is in the play, figuring William III, decreeing liberty, equality and prosperity, as he founds a popular republic:

> *Tim.* Hear ye *Sicilians*, you whose free-born Minds
> Disdain the Yoke of Slavery to bear,
> Heav'n has restor'd you what Heav'n gives
> To all, till proud imperious Man invades
> His Fellows Right, couzening or robbing him
> Of what the Gods freely do bestow;
> Henceforth both *Noble* and *Plebians* too,
> Shall each a just share of Government partake,
> The Rich no longer shall the Poor oppress,
> Whil'st Justice flows with uninterrupted stream;
> But let not Pride or Avarice destroy
> The Freedom you have sought, and now enjoy.[25]

The play cuts a fine line between ridicule and respect for a popular republic, a state in which all participate in government. Timoleon/William
is figured as *rex absconditas*: having defeated a tyranny, he wants to give
power away so that a free state is born. On the other hand, it is not clear
that all of the citizen participants are yet ready for political responsibility. They enter as an uncontrollable beast: '*the Mob, hallowing*'.[26] Other
plebeian characters believe that government should be left to those fit to
govern: violent anarchy always threatens to destroy calm debate.[27]

And yet the play ends with Timoleon evoking a future in which the
freedom of citizens is guaranteed by the limiting of executive power,
and by the establishment of a militarily strong state, 'that no lawless
Might / May rob or spoil them of their Native-right'.[28] As in the writings
of John Toland (Milton's editor and biographer) and the Calves-Head
Club at about this time, the English monarchy, established by the 1689
settlement, is recast as a popular republic in terms that would have been
pleasing to many of the radicals of the 1640s and the 1650s. 'Let not one
Man grow greater than the rest'[29] dekings the king, recasting him as a
citizen in office.[30] The author was clearly familiar with Milton's *Paradise
Regained* (1671), since he echoes the anti-monarchical sentiments at the
end of Book II:

> 'Tis easier to complain of Power,
> Than, when possess'd, to lay it down;
> With far less Pain a Crown of Thorns you'll wear,
> Than from your Brow the conqu'ring Lawrel tear.[31]

The play is sufficiently confident to suggest a future in which a popular
republic will produce security enough for men to live virtuous private
lives: so many domestic utopias in harmony with the laws of nature.

From where does this voice come? Is the play a Machiavellian fantasy in which a follower of Henry Neville articulates a rôle for the populace? The attack on flattery and the corruptions of preferment in the dedicatory epistle, together with a direct reference to Machiavelli's *Discorsi*, and his praise of that other selfless hero of the ancient world, Cincinnatus, might suggest so.[32] Is the play Toland's fantasy? Controlling the people with powerful oratory, so that the physical energy of mobs, such as apprentices, could be harnessed for the sake of a strong republic, was certainly one of his concerns.[33] Yet the play's republicanism does not voice the frustration with William III felt by radical Whigs, nor fears the emergence of a new kind of tyranny, a reborn Cromwellian Protectorate. The play's vision is altogether distinct from the known positions with which we might associate it, although it might have fitted the aristocratic republican perspectives of the Whig grandees when they tried to assert a constitutional reform much later in 1722.[34]

In the absence of any further information concerning the author of *Timoleon* and his intentions, some sociological questions might unravel the play and its context. What were the 'people' doing in the decade after the Glorious Revolution, the urban population of London, who might earlier have been Leveller supporters? Were they the 'happy slaves' who, according to a recent account, willingly surrendered their rights in exchange for the security offered by the post-1689 regime?[35] Are these the people portrayed by the author of *Timoleon*?

Popular politics after 1689 very much took the shape of interest groups trying to influence by petitions debates in Parliament.[36] By a reverse flow of influence, popular interests began to be infected exclusively with major political concerns: Defoe's populist writings on the Protestant succession are exemplary here. Hence, as the Whigs gradually ascended to the position that enabled them to hold on to power for most of the first half of the eighteenth century, they no longer remained the obvious representatives for the people. The age of party has surprises for the relationships we might suppose exist with popular politics. A Tory or Jacobite appeal to social justice (such as Swift on Irish matters) might satisfy many who in other circumstances would have been the natural supporters of the radicals.[37]

Yet the literary history of this period has been concerned largely with the emergence of the professional author and a defined literary market. This view acknowledges the existence of party, and the rôle of literature in the life of political parties, but its concern with the economic misses the resonances that the Glorious Revolution left for those at the margins

of representation.[38] This is true both in respect of the survival of former
political identities and agendas and in respect of the transformations
that party politics was producing in the body politic. The one exception
to this has been the exposure of the flurry of republican activity during
the last three years of the seventeenth century, notably in the realm of
publication, in the aftermath of the Treaty of Ryswick and during the
Standing Army controversy.[39]

Certainly, the democratisation of the London Corporation government in the 1690s was akin to moves that had taken place earlier in
the 1640s. Those involved in city government after the 1690s had often been involved in the Monmouth Rebellion in the previous decade.
They believed in the 1690s that they were restoring to London its ancient liberties after the infringements of James II's reign. Surely, then,
they are the citizens of *Timoleon*? They were nearly all merchants, even
though this group too retreated from its relatively libertarian position
as mercantile success within the ruling oligarchy led to a subtle limiting
of the franchise, particularly after 1694. By the end of Anne's reign the
London Tories had not only absorbed their opponents' former populist
following but had also appropriated their populist rhetoric. And in the
years following the Treaty of Ryswick, not only did the 'country' Whigs
split from the governmental 'Junto', but they divided into the 'Roman'
Whigs, who believed in a broad application of ancient prudence to current governance, and the out-and-out republicanism of the Calves-Head
faction.[40] Yet both collaborated between 1697 and 1699. Where were
the people situated for these groups?

Political identity is even more slippery: some of the high Augustan authors, Swift foremost among them, were chiming with the agendas of later
libertarians or socialists, such as the Fabians.[41] Even the Jacobites offered
an alternative model of politics, religion and society that at some points
appealed even to republicans.[42] Ultimately, the exclusion of the Tories
from power after the Hanoverian succession resulted in an association
of Tories with a number of popular grievances and franchise issues until
the 1760s. To many contemporaries, the Tories looked like republicans
and democrats.[43]

THE TROOPER'S HOME

But there was not enough in the world of party politics to satisfy the urban,
Puritan mind, and especially those active during the Commonwealth.
The prophetic imagination, formed in mid century, and sometimes

transmitted into the next generation, was expressed in another arena. We have to look in unusual corners to find it. One excellent example is the last work of the sometime New Model officer, admirer of Oliver Cromwell, and follower of Major-General Lambert, Richard Franck.[44] His piscatorial works, including his attack on Walton, which, remarkably, is linked with his defence of the New Model Army, and his love of occult theory, have been the subject of occasional critical attention, but his very last work has gone unnoticed. *The Admirable and Indefatigable Adventures of the Nine Pious Pilgrims*, 'written in AMERICA, in a time of Solitude and divine Contemplation' (1707),[45] looks like a pious allegory, strongly influenced by Bunyan's *The Pilgrim's Progress* (1678). But amidst the rather bland and obvious religious discourse, comes a kind of experiential writing that is the self-expression of the surviving radical. The prefatory epistle dissociates true religion from 'politick' religion,[46] but the allegory has place-names derived from Italian cities and kingdoms: 'From Venecina Italiana, A City in the Kingdom of *Exorbitancy*; where *Proserpina* was Princess'.[47] The real world is in fact never far away, and like Franck's other allegories, the public world is plainly visible in his hermetic and occult account of biblical history: Adam is a 'universal monarch'.[48]

One of a series of visionary adventures involves a female speaker being attacked by Apollyon.[49] It is based on one of Bunyan's most well-known episodes, but it is also very much Franck's version of confrontation with torture for religious belief. Allegory is supplemented by a physical and mental anatomy of torture:

O Heretick! (said he) you have con'd your Responses, drawn out by the Figure of a *Geneva* Metaphor; let the Furies torment thee for an impertinent Sorceress, I'll rummage thy Skelleton Carcass to find out this Relique.[50]

So bending his Charm till it almost broke, his furious Hell-hounds let fly upon me . . . So with Pincers some of them began to pull my Flesh, and some with Tongs, as if my Skin was too hot for their Fingers to touch, and some brought Rakes, some others Forks and Shovels; and a Gridiron was brought, supposing me St *Lawrence*.[51]

However illusory it may be, the loss of security suffered by the self points to the precariousness of a military life; the reader recalls earlier passages concerned with soldiers being harshly treated as mutineers.

The narrative mode is apparently pilgrimage, but it expresses the sense of isolation or loneliness as a political subject, as well as before God. This

was the 'naked space' of many a pike-trailer: a consciousness of being reduced to a sense of frail basic birthrights when a person is removed from
his or her habitual social context.[52] Such narratives are related to but distinct from the rogue or vagabond narrative of the late sixteenth century.
Existence is a pilgrimage: the greatest threat to the pilgrim is to be convinced that he or she lives in a fictitious world. To sustain a belief in the reality of what appears to the eyes constitutes a victory. While the narrative
is constructed as a spiritual autobiography, felicity and piety are figured in
a female speaker. She is called Charity, but unlike Bunyan's Christiana is
far more autonomous, and apparently part of a virtuous sisterhood. The
'adventures' involve escapes from living hells, figured through images
of the modern city of Rome.[53] There are references to Michaelangelo's
pictures of hell,[54] and an escape from the alluring and cloying clutches
in hell of Proserpina,[55] the wife of Pluto, king of the underworld.

Proserpina was taken to the underworld while gathering flowers in the
fields of Enna.[56] For Franck, such innocent environments are the living
Edens still available to us:

In like manner the Ocean super-abounded with Fish, which by reason of their
unctuosity become profitable to the Merchant; whiles some others not so unc-
tuous are by renewed acts, fitted and accomodated for bodily Health; besides
Shell-fish innumerable that are not so edible, which in another Case become
useful and ornamental. So that what to say of the Treasures in the Ocean, since
so vastly enrich'd by the Bounty of Heaven, my Pen wants Rhetorick to put an
Estimate upon them.[57]

True recreation involves a prudent use of nature: catching and cook-
ing a trout.[58] These moments fit with the pastoral idylls that punctuate
Timoleon, an Edenic state of nature that is looked to as the end of successful political organisation. Franck resided in London during the 1690s,
but his vision in his writing is based on provincial life, exile and itineracy,
suggesting separation from the political centre.

No one familiar with the English literary canon will miss the obvious
point that Franck's book is somewhere between Bunyan and Defoe. It
is in ideological terms radicalised Defoe, and in psychoanalytical terms,
politically unrepressed Bunyan. The pilgrimage motif in fact restates a
version of the godly, Levelling self originating in the pamphlets of the
1650s. In his way, Franck was continuing the literature of Restoration dissenting resistance after 1699, against the trend of quietism. To this extent,
he was making allegory a dangerous form, despite Roger L'Estrange's

(Charles II's press censor) hope that allegory would make the dissenters disappear into their own literary ghetto.[59] But at the start of the Augustan peace, allegory may be said to have taken on new powers.

Franck's self-representation was close to hostile depictions of him, for in the eyes of his enemies he was worse than a rogue: a penniless Don Quixote. In 1673, after Franck's release from prison, Richard Head, the Irish hack and bookseller then resident in London, published *The Floating Island: Or, A New Discovery, Relating The Strange Adventure on a Late Voyage, from Lambethana to Villafranca*. Head was something of a rogue himself: his popular and influential *English Rogue* (1666) was supposedly autobiographical in part. The chief character in *The Floating Island* is Captain Robert Owe-Much, a reference to Franck's state of want, and the publisher is described as 'Franck Careless'. Enough of subjects, if not of authors, has been given away, and we can credibly accept the substitution of 'Richard' with 'Robert' as another faint disguise. Head impersonates Franck's own awkward style: his love of the occult and of clumsy allegories. Usually, however, Franck writes out of genuine interest, whereas Head makes his impersonation of Franck sound as though he is describing London as if its places were part of a sea voyage made for the sake of mere profit.

Head's narrative constructs Franck as a mock-heroic subject in a way that entirely erases his New Model Army identity. And the fact that Head published his book long before Franck published his first work must have enhanced this false image. Such erasures were common in political practice as well as in literature in the period. Many of the radicals active after 1660 lend themselves extremely well to depiction in picaresque terms. Perhaps the best example is Thomas Blood, once a JP in Cromwellian Ireland, then an actor in several anti-government plots in Ireland, Scotland and England during the 1660s. His unsuccessful attempt to steal the Crown Jewels on 9 May 1671 is usually seen as an act of revenge against the crown for property taken from him at the Restoration. Accordingly he is seen as a mere 'adventurer', as if ideology did not matter to him. But is this really the case? Is it not rather the case that he was in fact a serious conspirator, whose ability to make friends with strangers not only saved him from the pursuit of government agents, but was also an expression of his own definition of being a 'good and just person'? And in any case, the pursuit of lost property, which was originally paid in return for services rendered, seems entirely justified. Blood was sufficiently committed to throw in his lot with the Scottish covenanting force, which was defeated at Pentland Hills on 27 November 1666. The conventional description of him as an adventurer is, to say the least, un-satisfying. Blood found a personal way to make an accommodation with Charles II; after 1689, Franck found his own fishing utopia in his head.

Not surprisingly, these fictions are embodied in the utopian literature of the period. Gregory Claeys's description of Defoe's *Robinson Crusoe* (1719) and its great impact is equally applicable to Franck's book: 'Here the ideal of a well-ordered society is lived out mostly in solitude, partly taking the form of a fantasy of power (Crusoe becomes governor of his island), and rumination on the development of conscience and the idea of returning to a state of nature.'[60] Much of this writing points back to the critique of luxury, excess and slavery to be found in the temperance writings of Thomas Tryon, and helps to explain their continuing popularity in the eighteenth century.[61]

One group that sought Edenic states of being through the collective interpretation of fantasies was the Philadelphian Society, at the centre of which was the prophet Jane Lead. The other joint founder of the Society was John Pordage. Lead may have been in an antinomian congregation during the Civil War and Interregnum, and Pordage was at the centre of the 'antinomian revolt' of 1649–51, in which the Ranters and the Diggers played a major role. He lost his living at Bradfield in Berkshire in 1655 because of a Protectoral investigation. The Philadelphians were followers of Jacob Boehme, Pordage being the first substantial English Behmenist thinker.[62] After his death, the Society focused upon the circulation of Jane Lead's visionary dreams, by which followers were assured of their salvation. To be 'reborn' in one of Lead's dreams (expressed through a imagistic repertoire of childbirth) was to be redeemed. She had seemingly replaced Christ in the role of providing grace.

The Philadelphians were regarded as a fairly harmless body. Some of the prominent members were Anglican clergymen, and it was only when some of these were felt to be threatening their role in the estab-lished church that they were challenged. Otherwise, the Philadelphian Society flourished modestly in the late seventeenth and early eighteenth centuries, generating a substantial following in Holland and Northern Germany. It was in fact a key element in the origins of continental Enlightenment mystical religion. In effect, the Philadelphians replayed the mystical sectarianism of the Interregnum within the quiet world of (largely urban) middle-class respectability.

Lead's visions, as we shall see, are in fact interiorised versions of the account of purity envisioned by the vegetarian Tryon. They are no less detached from 1690s and 1700s civic life than are the contemplations of Richard Franck. Public space – the Philadelphian meeting – has been made for that part of a rehearsal of prophecy that emerged from a largely domestic setting. The prophecies themselves are undoubtedly Paracelsan, Hermetic and alchemical material, and we learn that Lead's words are indeed the 'pure language of nature' that had been lost at the Fall (elsewhere the original language is also discussed). To refine the human body in these terms requires the discovery of the 'All-healing Pool, where the corrupt and Putrifactious Matter, in the Body Elementary may through the continual rising Spring of this Water of Life, receive Clarifying and Healing – Ezek. 47:9: this River of Life must never cease to run through the Corporeal Forms'.[63] So this is spiritual sanitation, fused with an optimism in the powers of medical science: 'there will also be outward Medicines discovered that have not yet been, that will have a wonderful Efficacy for the preserving and fortifying Nature, and recovering the lost Paradisal Body'.[64]

Crises of birth become the way of describing imperfect or uncompleted enlightenment. A vision in which 'Almighty Strength' becomes stuck in the 'place of breaking forth' (the birth canal) intimates the failure of people to understand this reality. In these circumstances, and, since the Philadelphians appear to have practised chastity, imagery of birthing, reproduction and the erotic is relocated to a space in which it serves to describe perpetual creations rather than earthly and hence mortal ones. A kind of alchemy underwrites this. We all have inside us a 'Mould and Paradisal Matter' that will be quickened by 'that pure azure stream or breath'. Blue, azure is associated with the alchemical catalyst that brings into life the elixir (or a sapphire tree). Accordingly, Lead has a vision of a man 'in a clear blue Firmament, enclosed as in an oral frame, Rainbow-like'.[65] This is a sexed man, it would seem, visible from the loin upwards, but with missing legs and feet, although elsewhere, Lead claimed that angelic beings had no sexual characteristics. In effect, a feminised religion is founded, although it is no surprise that even those Anglicans divines who were attracted by Lead's message did not exploit the possibilities of these insights. To suggest that women have men in them, and men have women in them is to reinvent sexuality, but no one has been locked up in Newgate Prison as a consequence.

An extensive literature grew up in the Philadelphian Society, by which its history was known and by which the knowledge of salvation was imparted. Since the salvation narrative was generated by the prophetic activities of the chief prophet, these texts began to function as novels in the limited public sphere of the Philadelphian Society. In publishing their visionary literature, they also had a considerable impact upon the late seventeenth- and early eighteenth-century book market.[66]

There is no doubt that one strand of utopian literature provided an opportunity to think through republican possibilities of good government, and to parody, from a republican perspective, the orthodox justification from Scripture of the monarchical nature of society. Such is the case with Henry Neville's *The Isle of Pines* (1668), which, by the late seventeenth century, was already accruing the extra sections of text and extraneous commentary that would turn it into an exploration of natural law.[67] The significance of utopian writing amongst dissenting radicals of the later eighteenth century was such that they engendered debate as to their usefulness for the cause – precisely the kind of problem with regard to the relationship between theory and practice that had preoccupied Commonwealth supporters in the late 1640s and 1650s.[68] We should see the Digger Gerrard Winstanley's writings from the 1650s and the Quaker John Bellers's from the 1690s as the begetters of a tradition that included Defoe.[69] Bellers's proposals for wealth, enhancing the profits of the rich and keeping the poor in a living, begin in Quaker injunctions to neighbourly love, and in recommendation of the excellence of the 'inward light'.[70] His proposed colleges of industry and communal hospitals were offered as a means of improving the stock of trading companies, the South Sea Company in particular, although his vision of plenty derived from the Golden Age imagery of Edmund Waller's sacred poetry.[71] As late as 1724, Bellers was recirculating George Fox's own warnings from the 1650s for magistrates to look after the poor of London.[72] But nearly thirty years before this, Bellers revealed that he misunderstood history, since 'Levelling' for him is a dirty word. He understood that it meant making the rich work alongside the poor, which is indeed a long way from the proposals in the Agreements of the People, although not remote from Digger ideas.[73]

A broader degree of religious toleration might make possible the unhindered generation of many 'utopias', or experiments in living, from Lead's heaven of the androgynous imagination to Mary Astell's Protestant nunneries. *The Sophick Constitution* (1700) is one of a number of utopias of this period that projects a fantasy of the facets of godly life that had *not* been achieved in the previous century. There is a complete liberty of conscience for Christians, and a mixture of compelled attendance

and compulsory communication that maintains attendance at the worship of both national church and various sects, while also ensuring that
church and sects keep in touch with each other. *The Sophick Constitution*
is dedicated to the Adepts, a society of alchemical magi devoted to the
doing of good and preserving of knowledge in the expectation of the
future arrival of 'God our Saviour'.[74] They do not go out of their way
to become involved in politics, but it is expected that they will be treated
with as much honour as a prince. Within their urban college, they live in
a total democracy. Since the Adepts specialise in producing gold, it is assumed that they will realise literally the prophecy of the New Jerusalem
in Revelation 21:2; 11; 18–21, where the streets will abound in gold and
precious stones. For their part, the 'Governours' should make it their
duty to ensure the welfare of all, which would mean making available
appropriate labour for those who had lost an income from property.

CONCLUSION: COMMERCE AND REVOLUTION

The Glorious Revolution and the Settlement of 1689 provided a resolution to the crises of the previous half-century. They caused a rethinking
of political and religious identities. For this reason radicalism took on
a reflective rather than a confrontational and protesting character. And
this was enhanced by a society that finally came to terms with the reality
of using public media as informational and reflective tools, as opposed to
instruments of subversion or control. Both the theatre and the newsbook
were important in this respect.

These conditions were prefigured during the Restoration in the drama.
Before 1660 drama represented rebellion, but no actors had taken part
in such activities.[75] But after the Restoration actors appeared on the
stage who had taken part in the Civil Wars. One such was John Lacy,
whose portrait in several roles stares out at the viewer, startlingly masking
a kind of forbidden knowledge.[76] Dryden's Tamburlaine-like hero from
The Conquest of Granada (1672) returned in the 1690s as a figure around
whom the possibility for action in the name of freedom has to be debated.
This evidence lends some support to the general thesis that the long
eighteenth century was a theatrical society.[77]

Likewise, the newsbooks in the 1690s no longer took sides in any
absolutely partisan sense. By the 1680s, Restoration newsbooks were
returning to some of the battlegrounds of the Civil War and Interregnum
years. This is especially to be noted with regard to the persecution of
dissenters, and the resistance to it.[78] But after 1689, the urbane *Athenian*

Mercury could publish articles in the 1690s on vegetarianism, which before was more rather than less of a political issue. Its editor, John Dunton, was happy to discard writings he regarded as part of an outdated religious warfare, not least of all because they did not sell well. He preferred an ideal of dissent that was neo-aristocratic and civilised rather than engaged.[79]

Many of those who supported the Glorious Revolution were also supporters of a mercantile, capitalised society. In this respect, the rise of a commercial society, with a place within it for aesthetic reflection, led to a commodification of 'radical' content. Henceforth, it was no longer a matter merely of allegiance. Radicalism had become an art object and could be consumed. Hence Toland's interest in the 'taste' of artisans.[80] True radicals of the mid century and the Restoration (those that survived that long) were both stranded after 1689 and commodified within the terms of utopian or (mock-) romance discourse and practice.

When widespread radical activity rose again in the 1780s, it was by means of the marketability of discursive events. In a recent analysis of the debating societies of the 1780s (and 1780 in particular), Donna T. Andrew celebrates the emergence of the debating societies in this era, societies that charged a modest admission fee, and debated on a great variety of subjects, but which permitted women both to attend and to speak, and which had, albeit within genteel parameters, broken down the barriers between high and low culture and personnel, between the public world of politics and the private sphere of domestic life.[81] Late eighteenth-century radicalism was actually produced by part of the commercial profile, accommodating within itself practices of debating that had once been found in conventicles and then pubs. Quakers were allowed to speak to these meetings, effectively a bringing back of dissent into a very eighteenth-century public sphere. The debates about the significance of the French Revolution were formed through and took place within a language of aesthetics.[82]

In the 1690s, when this world of commercialised and aestheticised politics was emerging, did the Calves-Head Club reach out to include those who in the 1650s would have counted as Levellers? Would the elderly Richard Franck, who was living at the time in the Barbican, have felt happy in this company? It is an interesting point of departure for further historical enquiry. Richard Ashcraft's attempt to see Locke as an inheritor of Leveller ideas is compromised by its inability to identify such connections.[83] *Timoleon* puts this question entirely in the balance. In its theatrical fiction, the Calves-Head Club position is represented as the question of whether true republicanism can be launched in the populace. Yet in its publication it is certainly an attempt to articulate undiluted republican ideology: it might even have been too much for a 'Roman Whig'.

The Calves-Head Club represented and celebrated the memory of revolution. It replayed the regicide in a ritual form. This was fundamentally different from earlier rituals since a very recent political event was being celebrated, as opposed to an event in the remote past, or a legend. And the ritual was performed not in public, but in a reserved space of civility, possibly even the coffee house, as well as a dinner. The rehearsal of the possibility of resistance in the context of a tolerant polity was an especially startling turnaround given the violence of persecution, and the serious plotting, in the decade preceding the Glorious Revolution.[84]

Repetition by ritual within commercial society was one possibility for a radical vision after 1689. Another possibility was a critical assessment of the energies that had generated revolution. In his famous writings, the third Earl of Shaftesbury was effectively debating the possibilities of the energies of enthusiasm. His objections to the dangerous powers of enthusiasm is well known, a fear that the Philadelphians proved was ill-founded. But we should see the *Characteristicks* as an attempt to learn from the mistakes of earlier times in order to generate a model of civil society that would endure and be faithful to human nature. In his way, Shaftesbury aestheticised revolution, but in a meaningful context.

Timoleon is as it is precisely because the directions in which its energies might go were unclear. It had a complex memory of revolution, and some hints of where to go, but no context in which to do so. This is no index of failure at a time when so many of the ideals to which republicanism and Puritanism had dedicated themselves were realised or imaginable. So much imaginative and utopian literature confirms this sense. *Timoleon* was a hope for William III and a memory for the future. That future would always depend upon the shape that public enthusiasm took, or was allowed to take.

In Julian Barnes's novel *England, England* (1998), historical development is replaced by the performance of great moments and myths in English history on the Isle of Wight, and sold as a holiday experience to Europeans and Americans. Real England, renamed Albion, is abandoned to poverty and a kind of local anarchism. On his way out to the Isle, the King of England is accompanied by a flying escort of two Spitfires and a Hurricane, the holiday flying display team, who recreate the Battle of Britain for the tourists. When an enterprising journalist interrupts the royal flight in a light aircraft, the squadron leader in one of the Spitfires decides to give the journalist a scare by firing off some blank rounds from his machine guns. But the ammunition is live, and the Piper Cherokee falls flaming from the sky. There is always that possibility. The contemporary 'post-modern' notion that 'history' is replaced by a series of more trivial 'games' within a timeless master narrative of late capitalist consumerism is analogous to the sense of escape from a violent century that many in the decade or so after the Glorious Revolution sought. Yet there were always sufficient hints that replication would slip back into a thoroughly Machiavellian *occasione*. And all the time, replication guaranteed a rapid expansion of the inward dimensions by which those central seventeenth-century questions, redemption and Paradisal perfection, could be imagined.

CHAPTER 3

The plantation of wrath

Timothy Morton

INTRODUCTION

By the Romantic period, a long tradition of vegetarian radicalism had peaked in the works of a wide range of writers. There are links between vegetable diet in the radical seventeenth century and vegetarianism in the Romantic period.[1] This chapter explores continuities of vegetarianism as a form of radicalism. First it investigates two radical writers, Thomas Tryon and Robert Wedderburn. Then, to place these in context, it discusses two writers less inclined to radicalism but operating within a similar rhetorical framework: the more conservative figures John Evelyn and Benjamin Franklin.

One of the underlying continuities is the way in which the natural world became a complex signifier of liberty. Despite conventional views of georgic replacing pastoral in the seventeenth century, often seen as a symptom of encroaching bourgeois mentality, the landscape could be celebrated in itself in Sir John Denham's *Cooper's Hill* and Marvell's 'Upon Appleton House'. It is commonly assumed of the later eighteenth century that georgic is really disguised pastoral, and that what is really being presented is an aristocratic poetics of slumming (*otium*). Scholarly blinkers prevent seeing the continuity of representing nature in itself as a radical enterprise. Pastoral poetics *might* culminate in the triumphalist and anti-ecological writing exemplified by Pope's 'Windsor Forest'. But Pope's landscape and forgetting should be contrasted with other strains of seventeenth-century writing: radical Puritanism's internalised landscapes, Marvell's figures of levelling the land, the Diggers' ecological communism, Roger Crab's vegetarian prose, or Walton's and Richard Franck's fishing narratives. In Franck's *Northern Memoirs*, as Nigel Smith writes, 'Food provides a departure point for the consideration of the uses of nature. What are the boundaries of man's legitimate use of nature, and where can he be said to do violence to it?'[2]

Vegetarianism and radicalism had a complicated relationship. Robert Pigot (1736–94) was the brother of Charles (d. 1794), whose *Political Dictionary* (1795) was the publication for which Daniel Isaac Eaton was prosecuted. Pigot was a vegetarian, influenced like General John 'Walking' Stewart by James Graham (1745–94). He emigrated to Paris, became a Jacobin and wrote on vegetarianism and politics. His ancestors, however, were royalists, and later Jacobites. Pigot was born at Chetwynd Park in Shropshire. Charles I, travelling from Oxford to Naseby in 1645, stayed three nights with Pigot's great-grandfather, Walter. Walter's wife, Anne, was the daughter of Sir John Dryden, and the poet Dryden's cousin. Walter's grandson Robert, the father of the vegetarian Robert, was an MP to whom the Pretender presented a portrait while at Rome in 1720: he was not only royalist but also Jacobite. He lived in Geneva and Dijon and in 1701 condemned the use of bread preferring potatoes, lentils, maize, barley and rice. Like Joseph Ritson, Robert Pigot the younger objected to the American, but supported the French, Revolution.[3]

Relationships between vegetarians separated in time were formed through reading and writing. Attacks on radicalism in the seventeenth century spawned new forms that assumed the shape of the image attacked.[4] This is legible in the transmission of vegetarian texts from the Civil War to the Romantic period. The Jacobin Joseph 'Citizen' Ritson (1752–1803) became a vegetarian ironically by reading remark P in Mandeville's ambiguous excoriation of the culture of luxury, *The Fable of the Bees* (1714).[5] Ritson went on to use Thomas Tryon (1634–1704) in his vegetarian prose; Percy Shelley, coming into contact with vegetarianism via Ritson and John Frank Newton, could not have helped but be aware of Tryon's presence. As members of a growing culture, gradually expanding from the province of mystical thinkers, hermits and radicals into the more modern realms of those concerned with diet and health, vegetarians shared each other's work frequently. The exacting antiquarianism of Ritson is only a strong example of a general trend. Percy Shelley marked a long quotation from Tryon in his copy of Ritson's *Animal Food*.[6]

Vegetarianism rewrote Civil War radicalism. The Diggers' holistic view of nature, while not necessarily giving rise to vegetarian practices, was in the right spirit. During and after the Interregnum, some retreated physically and imaginatively from what they construed as the potential violence of revolutionary politics, relocating themselves in the countryside or writing about the importance of the natural world. As Smith states, 'only the landscape provided an environment of sufficient liberty, in which civilisation (which, paradoxically, was the [Civil] war) could be assessed with relative detachment'.[7] The Tory Thomas Tryon was one of those whose vegetarian work engages with issues of violence, not least in his writing on slavery.

Vegetarian recipe books continued in popularity. *Adam's Luxury and Eve's Cookery* was published anomymously in 1744, and at the turn of the century, George Nicholson published *On Food* (1803), containing 'Sallads by Tryon' and salad dressings by John Evelyn.[8] It was published with Benjamin Franklin's account of his coming to be a vegetarian through reading Tryon. *Vegetable Cookery* was published in 1821 by the wife of Joseph Brotherton, who was a member of the church for three hundred vegetarian Swedenborgians founded in Salford in 1809 by William Cowherd (Brotherton also wrote a teetotal tract in 1821).[9] The growth in vegetarianism's popularity was due largely to two interrelated factors. These were, first, what Smith observes to be the fusion of Enlightenment and enthusiastic discourses in vegetarian rhetoric: for Tryon, 'the energies provided by the immediacy of the indwelling Spirit are reimagined as a programmatic overcoming of the terrors of worldliness'.[10] Secondly, there developed an economic view of the body and its role in society. The body was disciplined according to secularised notions of temperance deriving from radical Puritanism. It became an economy: a restricted system of energy flow. This emergent view is the subject of this chapter.

BOEHME: SPIRITUAL ECONOMICS

That revolution was mystical was commonly held in the millenarian circles of the Romantic period. How did this view arise? I bracket the question of mysticism's nature, and approach those mystical writers whose works inspired Romantic millenarians in a different manner. What seems mystical in the writings of Boehme, for example, becomes quite ordinary in the late eighteenth century: it is the language of economics.

An economic approach to reality, in which constant flows are chanelled and regulated, derived in Tryon from his reading of Jacob Boehme, to whom he transferred allegiance from his original Anabaptism. Hegel described Boehme's language as *Natursprache*, the spontaneous rhetoric of nature itself.[11] For Boehme, God is utterly transcendental: what is left for us to conceive of is the *Ungrund* or 'Abyss'.[12] This is similar to the Buddhist idea of emptiness (because Buddhism is non-theistic);

and it is also very similar to Cabbalistic thought.[13] This abyss is 'active and fertile possessed by a motivating energy and Desire (Trieb)' 'for self-knowledge and moves both the knower and the known'. For Schleiermacher, the Romantic-period hermeneuticist, Boehme's writings 'are in fact "esoteric psychology" or, the psychology of the depths'.[14] This internality made Boehme popular in the radical thought and prophecy of the English Revolutionary period, suggesting strongly that God and man are the same and that humans can aspire to Godhead.[15] Thomas De Quincey gave Samuel Taylor Coleridge Law's edition of Boehme's works; Coleridge annotated them copiously.[16] One biographer assumes that Boehme's reputation waned during the eighteenth century, but there is in fact a continuity of reception in vegetarian writing going through Law and George Cheyne (1671–1743, vegetarian doctor to the literati in Samuel Richardson's circle), and arriving at Percy Shelley via Joseph Ritson.[17]

Lucifer's tragedy could be our own because heaven and hell are within us; this is exactly how Percy Shelley writes about Satan in his vegetarian prose.[18] An economic regulation of energies is required. As in the Cabbala, the wrath of God is tempered by mercy and love, as if they were the left and right hands of God. For Boehme, 'good and evil are not simply inextricably bound up together in all things. They are the mutually conditioning, opposing powers, without which the world could not have arisen and could not go on recreating and revitalizing itself in time.'[19] Wrath untempered breaks away from God and is turned into '"the radically evil, into Gehenna and the dark work of Satan"'.[20] The human body was originally pure and uncorrupted until the eating of the fruit in Eden. Boehme makes much of this mishap, explaining it in alchemical terms: 'If *Adam* had continued in innocency, then he should in all fruits have eaten paradisiacal fruit, and his food should have been heavenly, and his drink should have been out of the mother of the heavenly water of his source [or fountain] of the eternal life.'[21] Imagination becomes the key to a Christianity viewed historically as a sequence of Creation, Fall and Rebirth. This is literalised by a digestive metaphor: faith is '"an eating of God's being"' (the prefiguring of Schelling is unmistakable).[22] The divine mystery is seen as a tincture, an alchemical view of Fall and Redemption which necessitates the activity of medical and culinary elements.[23] In *Signatura rerum* Boehme explains disease: 'every disease in the body is nothing else but a corruption or poysoning of the Oyl, where-from the Lifes-light burneth or shineth; for when the Light of the Life shineth or burneth clear in the

Oyl, it doth expel and drive away all poysonful influences and operations, as the day expelleth the night'.[24] We always have the potential
for 'wrathful Hunger' which must be changed into love.[25] Likewise, in
Tryon's book on dreams, *Pythagoras His Mystic Philosophy Revived* (1691),
a temperate diet of vegetables and water enables the body to become
'penetrable' by good influences and dreams to become lucid, free of
wrathful humours.[26]

The economic view propagated by Behmenism was later articulated
by the iatromechanical doctor George Cheyne. If the world is a prison
in which the merely mechanical body of Hobbesian '*Ropes, Pullies, Levers,
Tubes, Glands, Strainers*, and the like' is punished in order to '*polish*' it,
then this process, winning back the soul for God, is an '*Œconomy of
Redemption*'.[27] Animal flesh contains more of the Behmenist materials
of wrath, salts and sulphurs that make it harder to digest.[28] Eating
such food is done in a larger, truly economic, in fact proto-ecological,
context:

> it is not impossible, that a whole Race, and all the inhabitant Mass of such cor-
> rupted and putrified Bodies [of flesh-consumers], and deprav'd and degenerated
> *Spirits*, may have had such an insensible and gradual Influence on a whole *Globe*,
> its *Atmosphere* and different Regions, as quite to alter its *original* Nature; as we
> see Heaps of putrifying *Fish*, *Insects*, and the carcases of Men, by the *Fermentation*
> and *Volatilization* of the animal Salts, (from intense Heat) produce an universal
> *Plague* and *Pestilence*, as was that of *Athens*, and many others.[29]

The whole world has become the plantation of wrath, where flesh be-
haves like alcohol, fermented to an intoxicating liquor. This notion is
evidently not entirely secular: arguments that the eighteenth century was
an age of secularisation, of Locke supplanting Habakkuk, as Marx puts
it, are too generalising. In fact, the mysticism of a seventeenth-century
vision of the body has been adapted to a scientific view of the effects of
flesh and drink.

If wrath is planted in the heart, then goodness can be transplanted in its
place. This is the key to the Behmenist language of the Romantic-period
vegetarian and millenarian prophet Richard Brothers (1757–1824), in
his employment of a tree metaphor in *Prophetical Passages*: 'Men cry *Mordio*
[*Murder; confusion to their enemies;*] and yet there is no strange enemy, but
it is only the *Turba* [*wrath*] only, which hath grown up in the midst of
Babel in her wickedness and unrighteousness.'[30] Babel is England, and
later, London specifically. England is being assailed not from without but
from within, as in Tryon's model: the problem is not a foreign enemy

but her own wickedness.[31] Through Christ's voice the whole lineage of prophecy shall be

> transplanted into one kingdom; viz. into the first tree of *Adam*, which is no longer called *Adam*, but Christ in *Adam* . . . This high Tree doth disclose, and clearly open itself what it hath been in time, and what it shall be eternally, and in its disclosure Moses puts away his veil, and Christ his parables in his doctrine; and then the *prophetical mouth* of this *Tree of Wonders*, doth express in Divine Power, all the voices of the powers of the tree, whereby Babel taketh her end . . . and this no man can hinder.
>
> For that which is in the spirit of the letters shall be again found; and the spirits of the Letters . . . in the formed word of the creation . . . when the branches shall know that they are (or stand) in the tree; they will never say, that they are peculiar and singular trees; but they will rejoice in their STEM; and they will see that they are altogether boughs and branches of one TREE; and that they do all receive power and life from one only STEM.[32]

According to Iain McCalman, 'Men and women like Brothers and Southcott evoked memories of the radical prophets of the seventeenth century.'[33] Brothers was born in Newfoundland, and served in the navy. In 1787 he came to London and lived as a vegetarian. In 1793 he described himself as a 'nephew of the Almighty', and in 1794 began to preach his interpretations of prophecy. On 19 November 1795 he was to be revealed as prince of the Hebrews and ruler of the world, and in 1798 the building of Jerusalem was to begin. He was arrested in March 1795 for treason, though a Gillray cartoon of 5 March identified him with the Whig party. Brothers was caught up in the wider culture and politics of the age: his visionary politics is in the lineage of Boehme. His view of redeemed, millenarian monarchy emphasises a sense of economy:

> The form is planned by God himself; and as he has ordained the government shall be in a king; he has also ordained that he shall live with all the splendour suitable to the rank; but never to dishonour it by a departure from modesty and justice temperance and economy; – that the rich may praise him as an example to imitate, – the poor as an example of wisdom, – and every stranger as an example of admiration[.] His residence will be a noble palace, on the north side of the great central square that incloses the park, or Garden of Eden, for the public to walk in.[34]

What is being walked around here? It is a form of exteriorised interiority, an outward manifestation of the spirit's radical inwardness. The interiorised epics of the English Revolutionary period gave rise to the utopian interiority of Romanticism. This is especially evident in the Romantics' use of Milton. The inner cleanliness of the spirit was what mattered

to vegetarians such as Tryon and Shelley. But the inverse of this could
also be held: the inside could be rendered exterior, as in Blake's view of
Jerusalem, or Brothers's. Blake's psychological poetics actually performs
the reverse of Wordsworth's psychic landscapes: 'A Poison Tree', for example, from *Songs of Experience* (1794), creates a view of what would now
be called passive aggression: a psychic state – anger – is exteriorised.
Blake's inversion of interiority is Behmenist and thus Tryonesque. The
poison tree is a perfect image of exteriorised wrath, and in the Romantic
period was taken as a metaphor for the spread of commercial capitalism,
for example in Shelley.[35] It has often been argued that the interiority of
Romanticism is counter-radical: the radical theatre of the age, for example, is collapsed into the mental theatre of the six 'major' male poets.[36]
In the utopian diet and architecture of Shelley, Ritson and Brothers,
we see that the inside could be manifested in the outside: the outside
could resemble the dreamlike ideality of the utopian inside. A tendency
to make things dreamlike was one of capitalism's radical potentials, as
Marx noted in the *Communist Manifesto*: all that is solid melts into air. The
English Revolution and the Romantic period shared the radical continuity of commerce, its ability to sweep hardened exteriors away and
replace them with new visions. So in opposing commerce, the Romantic vegetarians were drawing upon it. What were they opposing? The
kind of dystopian externalisation which they saw in the culture of the
plantation.

THE PLANTATION OF WRATH

In 1684, Tryon published *Friendly Advice to the Gentlemen-Planters of the East
and West Indies*. Tryon's vegetarianism linked the rights of animals to
human rights, most radically in this work of anti-slavery. The rhetoric
in favour of the slaves in *Friendly Advice* suggests nothing so much as the
sentimental discourse of anti-slavery.

   Montaigne had articulated relationships between vegetarianism and a
critical view of Christian culture in its dealings with other cultures. What
is new in Tryon is the harnessing of an emergent economic language of
self-discipline and temperance to suggest that the remedy for European
corruption lies in the body. It was this kind of language, with its emphasis
on regulating impulses, which appealed to Benjamin Franklin when he
became a Tryonist vegetarian in his teens. Vegetarianism was a critical
edge of the growing ideological support for commercial capitalism.

Much of *Friendly Advice* is devoted to 'The Negro's Complaint of their Hard Servitude, and the Cruelties Practised upon them by Divers of their Masters Professing Christianity in the West-Indian Plantations'.[37] This follows 'A Brief Treatise of the Principal Fruits and Herbs that Grow in Barbadoes, Jamaica, and other Plantations in the West-Indies', and 'Some brief Directions for the Preservation of Health, and Life in hot Climates'. The reader's sympathies are solicited through natural-historical, and then medical, rhetoric. Tryon's interest in diet was, like Pythagoras, in *diaitia*, a culture or (as Raymond Williams would say) a whole way of life. The reader gradually focuses on the planter's body, then wonders what has been excluded from the planter's *diaitia*: care for the bodies of the slaves. The language of politics and sympathy is thus embedded in the languages of science and medicine. Tryon's rhetoric is strikingly modern.

Tryon puts his words into the mouth of a slave. It may be unfashionably Whiggish to say so, but in doing this he opens a space for the ventriloquism of the culture of sympathy a century later:

> *Complaints* and *Lamentations* are the natural Language of the *Miserable*. 'Tis some kind of *Easement* to Hearts swell'd with *Grief*, and almost broken with the Rigors of *Oppression*, to *tell the sade Stories* of their *Woes*, and when they have lost all other *Liberty*, to *bemoan* themselves with *Freedom*: More especially, since Nature does not so readily furnish *us* with *Tears*, (the usual Expressions of Sorrow) we hope we may be allow'd to make our *Groans* articulate, and declare in words how intollerably we suffer by the deeds of unreasonable men.[38]

A politicised culture of sympathy developed within the wider culture of sensibility: here emotional reactions to the world were rendered as distinctively physical, in the form of groans and tears. These physical manifestations were valued as more directly communicative than speech or writing. As in Mary Shelley's *Frankenstein*, words of sympathy and liberty are placed in the mouth of the oppressed. A notion of language is broached, transcending articulate speech or writing; elsewhere I have called this 'silent eloquence',[39] a phrase used in John Field's critical pamphlet on Tryon. Harping on the trite debate about whether vegetarians should wear animal products, Field wonders 'whether the Beasts will not send up their Complaints against him in a silent Eloquence to Heaven' like the blood of Abel.[40]

Tryon's slave monologue establishes relationships between internality and an idea of political freedom. There is an inwardness about how an object such as a pair of shoes, a commodity such as a slave, or a suffering animal, could seem to cry out in pain. This inwardness is derived from Tryon's radical Puritanism, signalling a continuity between ideologies of the English Revolution and the Miltonic rhetoric of the Romantic poets.[41] Percy Shelley frequently used the rhetoric of 'silent eloquence', both in explicitly vegetarian writing and in supporting the working class and the rights of slaves. Thomas Taylor (1758–1835), the translator of the Neoplatonist vegetarian writing of Porphyry and a friend of William Blake and Mary Wollstonecraft, parodied the link between human rights and animal rights in *A Vindication of the Rights of Brutes* (1792); to be brute is to be silent.

To evoke silent eloquence is to question the validity of sign systems. It is a kind of radical empiricism: the evidence alone should be enough to demonstrate a case. 'The facts speak for themselves.' Language cannot merely be pasted on to reality but must emerge from it. The slave in *Friendly Advice* speaks in a crisis of representation. What language should he use? His countrymen are too far away, his stories unbelievable in their extremity: 'Such *superlative Inhumanity* amongst *Nominal Christians* will surpass all Belief, and the Extremity of our *Calamities* making them seem *Romantick*, debarrs us even of *Pity* and *Commiseration*, those general Slaves of helpless Misery: Shall we then fling our selves at our Masters feet, and with universal Cries importune them to Compassion and Charity?'[42] This disjuncture between the fictionality of the stories (their '*Romantick*' quality) and their truth value is precisely the emerging gap in radical Puritan discourse between the authenticity of the body and the artificiality of the languages used to represent it. It is tempting to see the 'universal Cries' as a proto-Rousseauist solution, just as the notion of liberty expanded to a universal limit.

What ultimately hardens the dilemma into a crisis, is commerce – the structural continuum underlying the period 1650–1830. There is a gap between the oppressive economics of commercial capitalism and the ideological constructs – civilising Christian missions, the promotion of softening, refining taste and so forth – used to support it: 'Alas! those Vertues are Plants that scarce grow in these Islands; nothing thrives here so fast as *poysonous Tobacco* and *furious Pride*, *sweet Sugar* and most *bitter ill Nature*: a false conceit of *Interest* blinded their Eyes and stopped their Ears ...'[43] Commerce is not being supported by true Christianity. Playing on the meaning of 'virtue' (just moral action or a plant's vital juice), Tryon internalises the commodities which grow outwardly in the West Indies. The love of money is named the root of all evil. God, invoked in Behmenist fashion as a universal principle of creativity who 'didst pour forth the Ocean-Sea, who formedst the glorious Sun', has been deserted. Man has

turned away the eye of his Mind from thy Counsels, and hath precipitated his Imagination into the Centre of Wrath and Fierceness, thereby defaming his Noble Birth . . . he is now become a *Tyrant*, a *Plague*, a *professed Enemy, Hunter, Betrayer, Destroyer* and *Devourer* of all the Inhabitants of *Earth, Air* and *Water*, and to those of his own kind no less fierce and cruel . . . they fight and tear each other like *Tygers*, and he is the bravest Fellow that can invent the most mischievous Weapons and Engines of Destruction.[44]

Commercial capitalism has unleashed a wrathful energy that directly seizes and mutilates the bodies both of its victims and its perpetrators: 'the *devilish Wrath* has such power over [our masters] that they will not forbear their Oppressions, though to their own *Detriment*, as well as our *Destruction*'.[45] This corporeal explanation indicates how far contemporary society has fallen from a natural state, a Golden Age of spontaneous production and peace.

Tryon's argument for better treatment of the slaves is ultimately an economic one. Some degree of rest is required to get the most out of the workers' bodies:

The end of all Natures Motions is Rest [emphasised in Gothic script], nor can she perform any of her Operations without Refreshment; *Ground* always plow'd yields little encrease, but must lie fallow now and then, if you expect a Crop: A *Bow* always bent will hardly send an *Arrow* to the *Mark*, but our inconsiderate Masters regard neither the voice of *Nature* nor *Reason*, but with Cruelty compel us to Labour beyond our strength . . . in so much that often-times we are forc'd to work so long at the *Wind-Mills*, until we become so *Weary, Dull, Faint, Heavy* and *Sleepy*, that we are as it were deprived of our natural Senses, or like men in a maze, that we fall into danger, and oft times our Hands and Arms are crusht to pieces, and sometimes most part of our Bodies.[46]

Exploitation is unreasonable precisely insofar as it *prevents* the efficient operation of the plantation.

The rhetoric of crushing and mangling at the end of this passage is reminiscent of the vegetarian rhetoric of *macellogia* – the description of the butchery of the animal body. This is continued in: 'Beat and Whip us, and hang us up by the hands, Feet, and the like, and so *Bastinado* us till our Bodies become like a piece of raw Flesh, and we are just ready to give up the Ghost.'[47] To mangle is to treat somebody as an object. If a body has 'become like a piece of raw Flesh', then it is no longer a body but just a metonymic part. Moreover, the body has become *unlike*

itself, enough to warrant the metaphorical 'like', reduced as it is to a
corpse, mere stuff. The slave compares slavery with being a tool or raw
materials, such as earth. As fallow ground implies sowing seeds, so the
slave is conscious of himself as an economic unit: there is a faint echo of
the parable of the talents. Later the slave berates 'the vast Consumption
or Destruction that is made of us' in America and the Caribbean, naming
slavery as a state of commodification.[48] As it continued in the Romantic
period, anti-slavery rhetoric played between treating the slaves as subjects
endowed with voices and as objects deprived of them. The slave could
cry out as an oppressed subject, or be portrayed as cruelly objectified.
Here both poles are in play. This sense of subjects-as-objects, and vice
versa, is part of the topsy-turvy language of the fetish: slaves are treated
like objects, while the sugar they farm is treated like a subject. As we will
see, Tryon brilliantly exploits this language, with its ambivalence about
subject–object relationships.

The concept of the fetish was devised to explain what the Portuguese
encountered on the west coast of Africa in their journey around the
Cape to reach the Spice Islands, the goal of early commercial capitalism. It is precisely this concept that the slave uses in Tryon's ensuing
dialogue, 'A Discourse in Way of Dialogue, between an Ethiopean or
Negro-Slave and a Christian, that was His Master in America'.[49] Tryon
turns Christian universalism on its head, just as Marx was to turn Enlightenment economics on its head, by invoking the idea of the commodity
fetish. A supposedly universal concept, in this case of an all-powerful
deity, is held against those who devised it:

I was the Son of a *Phitisheer*, that is, a kind of *Priest* in our Country and Way; he
was also a *Sophy*, and had studied the Nature of things, and was well skill'd in
Physick and natural *Magick*, I have heard him often discourse of a *great* and *mighty*
Beeing, (greater far, and *brighter* too than either Moon or Sun) which framed both
Land and *Sea*, and all the glittering Glories of the *Skie*; and he was wont to say,
Men were the Children of the great King, *who if they were good, would take them up . . . into*
spangled Regions, *where they should do no Work, nor endure any Pain, nor* Fight *one with*
another.[50]

Far from being enmeshed in a false idolatry of the object, the '*Phitisheer*'
articulates the highest ideals of the subject. Radical rhetoric's ability to
flip-flop between subject and object like this inevitably continued in the
rhetoric of Romantic-period vegetarianism and anti-slavery. As the slave
says to his master, 'that which you call *Trade* or *Traffick . . .* is little better
than an Art of *Circumventing* one another'.[51] There is a complex pun on

the language of commerce, involving words such as adventure, venture
and vents (of trade).

Eating, then, becomes an issue for radicalism as it involves the fundamental metaphysical distinctions that pattern political life: inside and
outside, subject and object, cooked and raw. Raw materials, if over-used,
become wrathful. The slave complains, 'So also we are forced to stand
and work at the Coppers, in the hot sulpherous Fumes, till Nature being
overcome with weariness and want of proper Rest we fall into the fierce
boyling Syrups.'[52] It is a question of balancing the vital fluids of the
body. Sweat endangers the loss of 'the sweet Oyl and Radical Balsom of
Nature'.[53] Biblical and Behmenist language resonate. Slaves and what
they farm co-create harmful wrath.

The plantation of wrath becomes the central anti-slavery trope. The
very dialectic of fluids (both bodily and and outside the body) enrages
the masters:

O you brave and swaggering Christians! who exercise this strange and severe Master-
ship over us, who sport your selves in all manner of superfluity and wantonness,
and grow fat with our Blood and Sweat, gormandizing with the fruits procured
by our *Slavery* and sore *Labour*; set by your *Rum-Pots*, your *Punch-Bowls*, your
Brandy-Bottles, and the rest of your *Intoxicating Enchantments* for a while, and stand
still a little, and suffer the cool of the day to overshadow you, and the long
obstructed Fountain of Reason in your Hearts to send forth its streams.[54]

Alcohol, for vegetarians from Tryon to Percy Shelley, was a serious problem pertaining to the issue of the plantation of wrath. It inflamed the animal spirits and provoked, quite literally, a mad rage whose murderousness
was related to the murderous wrath that compelled the killing of animals.
Vegetarianism was not only against meat, but also against alcohol.

ROBERT WEDDERBURN: THE CONTINUITY OF ANTI-SLAVERY

Unlike Olaudah Equiano, a respectable member of the London Corresponding Society, Robert Wedderburn was a free mulatto child in
Kingston, Jamaica, in charge of slave obeah (shamanic ritual), and a
smuggler's agent.[55] He lived in London in St Giles, in what were called
the 'rookeries' (a name for black communities) where other 'blackbirds'
lived.[56] There is no evidence that Wedderburn was familiar with other
black autobiographers such as Equiano, Ignatius Sancho and Ottobah
Cugoano.[57] But he was aware of a continuous tradition of anti-slavery
since the English Revolution. McCalman notes how in *The Axe Laid to the*

Root (1817), Wedderburn invokes 'the days of "Cromwell the Great, who humbled Kings at his feet and brought one to the scaffold"'.[58] The title of Wedderburn's text suggests Paine and Spencean agrarian radicalism. In its figuration of the Tree of the Knowledge of Good and Evil, it also alludes to the radical Puritanism of the seventeenth century.

In the fourth number of *The Axe Laid to the Root* Wedderburn draws strongly upon the continuity of radicalism. He articulates it in ways familiar to race activists today, asserting the incompletion of the project of universal rights: 'Yes, the English, in the days of Cromwell, while they were asserting the rights of man at home, were destroying your ancestors then fighting for their liberty; but the Calamantees, as the late Pitt declared, in the House of Commons, led to victory, other tribes less valiant.'[59] This is to marry the language of the English Revolution with the Enlightenment discourse of rights and the black activism and anti-slavery movements of Wedderburn's time. In placing 'the rights of man' back in time, 'in the days of Cromwell', Wedderburn is both creating and sustaining a radical tradition.

Wedderburn showed how the Romantic-period poetics of sensibility were caught up in radical discourse. His quotation from 'The Slaves, an Elegy' makes use of what I have elsewhere called the 'blood sugar' topos, associated with the soft reformism of humanitarian anti-slavery. Here, however, the metaphor of blood turning into sugar is radically recontextualised:

> The drops of blood, the horrible manure
> That fills with luscious juice the teeming can [*sic*]
> And must our fellow-creature thus endure,
> For traffic vile, th' indignity of pain?
>
> Yes, their keen sorrows are the sweets we blend
> With the green bev'ridge of our morning meal,
> The while we love, mock mercy we pretend,
> Or for fictitious ills pretend to feel.
>
> Yes, 'tis their anguish mantles in the bowl,
> Their sighs excite the Briton's drunken joy;
> Those ign'rant suff'rers know not of a soul,
> That we enlighten'd may its hopes destroy.[60]

Smith has shown how Tryon indicated 'the sweet violence of sugar' in a radical enthusiasm that could dovetail into (not contradict) the radicalism of the Enlightenment.[61] The politics of the radical Unitarians provides a parallel example of this dovetailing. Samuel Taylor Coleridge had a

Pantisocratic interest in animals as brothers, and Richard Holmes has noted the popularity of Susequehanna-like schemes with Quakers and Unitarians.[62]

Wedderburn was aware of the continuity of anti-slavery. McCalman adds: 'like Winstanley, Wedderburn wanted prisons abolished'; like the Fifth Monarchists he believed in the exclusion of lawyers and the established clergy from his ideal society.[63] Indeed, in *Cast-Iron Parsons* (1820), Wedderburn suggests that we replace parsons with automata. On being sentenced for blasphemy, Wedderburn addressed the King's bench:

The early Quakers were a stern and stubborn set of men, determined both to risk and to suffer persecution in the attainment of their object; and by this means they ultimately secured, and do still enjoy, greater religious liberties than any other sect without the pale of the state religion. Why then may not the numerous *Latitudinarians* of the present day hope, by zeal, industry, courage, and perseverance, to gain that toleration which is granted to others . . . [64]

Wedderburn, a member of what McCalman has described as the 'radical underworld', was establishing continuity between the English Revolution and Romantic-period radicalism.

The first number of *The Axe Laid to the Root* invokes the language of non-violence: 'Oh, ye oppressed, use no violence to your oppressors, convince the world you are rational beings, follow not the example of St Domingo, let not your jubilee, which will take place, be stained with the blood of your oppressors, leave revengeful practices for European kings and ministers.'[65] Wrath is on the side of the oppressors. Regarding the slave revolution on the Caribbean island of Santo Domingo, this is an approach quite different from the less empathetic and more triumphant rhetoric of the sidelined Robert Southey.[66] Wedderburn continues in a strongly Spencean manner: 'the earth was given to the children of men, making no difference for colour or character, just or unjust; and . . . any person calling a piece of land his own private property, [is] a criminal'.[67] He addresses the planters, as Tryon did: 'Their weapons are their billhooks; their store of provision is every were [*sic*] in abundance; you know they can live upon sugar canes, and a vast variety of herbs and fruits, – yea, even upon the buds of trees.'[68] Ploughshares may be radicalised back into swords, in the name of a struggle against a more sustained violence, that of the commodification of the natural world – including the republican view of land as private property.

There is a long history of reactions to the commercial culture of luxury. Tryon's *The Way to Make all People Rich* (1685) criticised luxurious excess by evoking civic humanism. When luxury abounds, the nation is ripe for riots and tumult, these becoming 'apt Fewel for *Sedition* and the flames of a *Civil War*'.[69] Aphra Behn's encomium at the start of Tryon's book establishes a figurative connection between luxurious diet and the vagaries of commerce:

> Unprun'd the Roses and the Jes'mine grew,
> Nature each day drest all the World a-new,
> And Sweets without mans aid each moment grew;
> Till wild Debauchery did the mind invade,
> And Vice and Luxury become a Trade. (lines 17–21)

The exterior world (the garden) and the interior world (appetite) are coterminous. As Tryon has it: 'all kinds of Violence, whether towards our own kind or inferior Creatures, arises from the *awakened Wrath* in *Nature* . . . the same does by *Simile* excite the fierce Wrathful principle in the man that kills and eats them, and renders him prompt and ready for any Acts of Cruelty, or Oppression'.[70] The greatest luxury at the feasts of Heliogabalus and Caligula is 'The *Blood of the Poor*'.[71]

VEGETARIANISM AND THE PEACEFUL REPUBLIC: JOHN EVELYN

In 'Romantic Sobriety', Orrin Wang points out that writers in the Romantic period were interested in notions of sobriety arising out of civic humanism and French revolutionary republicanism.[72] Are there any relationships between this configuration and the culinary and dietary writing of the seventeenth century? The natural world came to be figured in the continuous transmission of radicalism. In investigating this transmission, we must gauge the extent to which the figuration of the natural world could become an autonomous genre: radical pastoral. There is no better way to see this than to examine the work of John Evelyn. Evelyn was no Wedderburn. But that is precisely the point: radical pastoral could be detached from its specific historical and political determining contexts.

The theme of vegetarianism as peaceful diet was articulated in *Acte-taria*, a playful but significant work on salads published in 1699 by John Evelyn (1620–1706), a founder of the Royal Society who had joined the king's army during the Civil War and retreated into his garden until the Restoration. The dedication to John Lord Somers, High-Chancellor and President of the Royal Society, contains constant digs at Apicius, the Roman chef whose work was being reappropriated in the emergent culture of luxury. Vegetarianism opposed not only cruelty to animals and alcohol abuse, but also the indulgences of commercial capitalism, tending to favour a Golden Age view of spontaneous and wholesome production. As Evelyn puts it: 'I am so far from designing to promote those *Supplicia Luxuriæ*, (as *Seneca* calls them) by what I have here written; that were it in my Power, I would recall the World, if not altogether to their Pristine *Diet*, yet to a much more *wholsome* and *temperate* than is now in Fashion.'[73] The use of 'Pristine' is significant in its evocation of a prelapsarian purity. For Evelyn, meat and 'exotic Sauces' 'debauch' the stomach.[74] The only thing that could disturb Evelyn's temperate vision is the culture of luxury. Citing Isaiah, and speaking of a future Utopia, he remarks: 'But after all . . . there's a *Snake* in the Grass; Luxury, and Excess in our most innocent Fruitions.'[75]

Evelyn reinvestigates the theme of radical pastoral, citing Pythagoras' theory of reincarnation to berate a flesh diet: '*Grillus*, who according to the Doctrine of *Transmigration* (as *Plutarch* tells us) had, in his turn, been a *Beast*; discourses how much better he fed, and lived, than when he was turn'd to *Man* again, as knowing then, what Plants were best and most proper for him: Whilst Men, *Sarcophagists* (Flesh-Eaters) in all this time were yet to seek.'[76] Evelyn celebrates vegetarianism for its prolongation of life, employing Tryon, who had published *The Way to Health and Long Life* in 1683: 'But to return again to *Health* and *Long Life*, and the Wholesomness of the Herby-Diet, *John Beverovicius*, a Learn'd Physician . . . treating of the extream Age, which those of *America* usually arrive to, asserts in behalf of Crude and Natural Herbs.'[77] The idea of America here as a Utopia in which the natural potential of humans could be played out is present in the experimentalism of Benjamin Franklin's Tryonist vegetarianism in the following century.

Evelyn's celebration of the Golden Age is also a reaction against (explicitly militarised) violence. Vegetarianism had been part of a re-action against the violence of civil war, as it would later:

> The *Golden Age*, with this Provision blest,
> Such a *Grand Sallet* made, and was a Feast.
> The *Demi-Gods* with Bodies large and sound,
> Commended then the Product of the Ground.
> Fraud then, nor Force were known, nor filthy Lust,
> Which Over-heating and Intemp'rance nurst:
> Be their vile Names in Execration held,
> Who with foul Glutt'ny first the World defil'd:
> Parent of Vice, and all Diseases since,
> With ghastly Death, sprung up alone from thence.

Ah, from such reeking, bloody Tables fly,
Which Death for our Destruction does supply.
In *Health*, if *Sallet-Herbs* you can't endure;
Sick, you'll desire them; or for *Food*, or *Cure*.[78]

The idea of the body's 'Over-heating' generating such conflicting emotions as wrath and lust was thus not restricted to Behmenism. Evelyn declares that European blood-eating comes from their mixture with Goths, Vandals and other 'spawn' of the Scythians, implying something monstrous, inhuman.[79] By contrast, the natural world participates in a Eucharistic metaphor in which humans eat themselves, a startling elaboration of a proto-ecological language of interconnectedness: 'Nor is it an inconsiderable Speculation, That since *all Flesh is Grass* (not in a *Figurative*, but *Natural* and *Real* Sense) *Man* himself, who lives on *Flesh*, and I think upon no Earthly Animal whatsoever, but such as feed on Grass, is nourish'd with them still; so becoming an *Incarnate Herb*, and Innocent *Cannibal*, may truly be said to devour himself.'[80] The '*Snake* in the Grass' is the body's internal attachment to the culture of commercial capitalist luxury. The elements of an ecological discourse had been established, before so-called 'Romantic ecology'.

Evelyn's thoughts on diet also have implications for the human community. Vegetarianism becomes the currency of a peaceful republic: 'In a Word, so universal was the *Sallet*, that the Un-bloody Shambles (as *Pliny* calls them) yielded the *Roman* State a more considerable Custom . . . than almost any thing besides brought to Market.'[81] This fits with Evelyn's vision of great swathes of green space mitigating oppression and violence.[82] True nobility is the georgic view: there was a time when 'the *Pease-Field* spread a Table for the Conquerors of the World . . . The greatest Princes took the *Spade* and the *Plough-Staff* in the same Hand as they held the Sceptre.'[83] The georgic model and the vision of the peaceful republic contain potent economic notions of self-sufficiency. Evelyn quotes Cowley's reworking of luxury as peaceful Epicureanism, echoing Virgil:

Happy the Man, who from Ambition freed,
A little Garden, little Field does feed.
The Field gives frugal Nature what's required;
The Garden what's luxuriously desir'd;
The specious Evils of an anxious Life,
He leaves to Fools to be their endless Strife.[84]

The non-violence of Tryon and Evelyn contradicts the view stated by John Field in *The Absurdity & Falsness of Thomas Trion's Doctrine Manifested*

(1685): 'For tho Christ forbad doing Violence to any Man, can T.T. prove he forbid to kill Fish, Fowl, or Beasts? or did account his Disciples and Apostles Murderers; and tell them that they should *perish with the Sword*, because they with their Nets caught the Fish, and also ate them?'[85] Field's real object is Tryon's critique of Christianity. Through the long eighteenth century, a rearguard action was fought against critical notions of humankind's place in the natural world by those who would assert a radical difference between matter and spirit. This implicated vegetarians, for whom material, alimentary affairs had a direct bearing on spiritual ones. There were different sorts of vegetarians, however. William Law corresponded with Cheyne, whose vegetarian influence can still be felt in the Shelleys. Law recommended some mystical writings which led to Cheyne's acquaintance with Boehme, thus alienating the vegetarian Wesley. Tryon and Law were both concerned to establish a clear boundary between the spiritual realm and the gross physical body. As Cheyne puts it in *An Essay on Regimen* (1740), citing 1 Corinthians, 15:44: 'There is a natural Body, and there is a spiritual Body.'[86] In his pamphlet on Mandeville (1726), Law makes telling use of a herbal metaphor, berating those for whom 'the Death of Man implies no more than the Fall of Leaves'. Opposing deism, and criticising what he sees as Mandeville's equation of moral concepts with the natural world, Law declares that Mandeville has 'made the Difference between Good and Evil as fanciful as the Difference between a *Tulip* and an *Auricula*'.[87]

CONCLUSION: THE ETHICAL ECONOMICS OF DIET

Cheyne is at his most Behmenist when he declares: 'this now *Adamical* and gross Tabernacle of ours, must necessarily contain under it, the Principles, *Elements*, Springs and *linear Root* of that *ethereal* or *Paradisaical* Body it was created in, and of that perhaps *glorious* Body it will be restor'd to at last in the final Recovery'.[88] Cheyne's use of 'final Recovery' nicely balances the spiritual and the medical. All intelligent creatures are '*Effluxes, Emanations*, and analogous *Infinitesimals* of the *Deity*', as in Boehme, and thus borrow the spirit which they return to God at death: a physical and spiritual economy.[89] This economic sense of diet was reused by Joseph Ritson, an ardent supporter of the French Revolution whose work was a major influence on Shelley's vegetarianism.[90] Ritson was familiar with Tryon and cited him at length in *An Essay on Abstinence from Animal Food* (1802).[91] But perhaps the most significant indicator of just how far the economic view of the ethics and politics of the body had come in is Ritson's use of Adam Smith: '"It may . . . be doubted whether butchers-meat is any where a necessary of life."'[92] Despite his overt ideological commitment to a critique of Smith, Shelley likewise relied on a Smithian economic perspective. Those cultures which *were* seen to rely on flesh were criticised throughout the century, in Gibbon, Rousseau, Ritson and Shelley. The Tartars, Calmucks and others were seen as vicious, warlike and wrathful. European polish could only suffer from a comparison with such rapacity; thus Ritson lambasted the slave trade.[93] The plantations had become a symptom of European corruption. Poetry that tended towards anti-slavery, such as Cowper's *The Task* and Shelley's *Queen Mab*, contained figurative links with vegetarian poetry.

Benjamin Franklin also considered the implications of digestion, writing to George Whatley in 1785 'that he believed that God had created the universe "with great Frugality, as well as Wisdom" and had provided for "the natural Reduction of compound Substances into their original Elements, capable of being employ'd in new Compositions" with "nothing annihilated . . ."'[94] Both Tryon and Franklin were preoccupied with economic discourses of self-improvement: the way to make everybody rich (Tryon) or 'The Way to Make Money Plenty in Every Man's Pocket' (Franklin). Franklin wrote on the slave trade and luxury. In his autobiography (1793) he describes his seventeenth-century ancestors: his father 'never discussed whether [the foods on the table] were well or ill dressed, of a good or bad flavour, high-seasoned or otherwise, preferable or inferior, to this or that dish of a similar kind. Thus accustomed, from my infancy, to the utmost inattention as to these objects, I have always been perfectly regardless of what kind of food was before me.'[95] There is a Puritanical distaste for representational iconography in this passage. Evidently, Franklin's vegetarianism was not aesthetic.

Franklin continues by describing his introduction to vegetarianism:

When about sixteen years of age, a work of Tryon fell into my hands, in which he recommends vegetable diet. I determined to observe it. My brother, being a batchelor, did not keep house, but boarded with his apprentices in a neighbouring family. My refusing to eat animal food was found inconvenient, and I was often scolded for my singularity. I attended to the mood in which Tryon prepared some of his dishes, particularly how to boil potatoes and rice, and make hasty puddings. I then said to my brother, that if he would allow me per week half what he paid for my board, I would undertake to maintain myself. The offer was instantly embraced and I soon found that of what he gave me I was able to save half. This was a new fund for the purchase of books; and other advantages resulted to me from the plan. When my brother and his workmen left the printing-house to go to dinner, I remained behind; and dispatching my frugal meal, which frequently consisted of a biscuit only, or a slice of bread and a bunch of raisins, or a bun from the pastrycook's with a glass of water, I had the rest of the time, till their return, for study; and my progress therein was proportioned to that clearness of ideas, and quickness of conception, which are the fruit of temperance in eating and drinking.[96]

Franklin describes himself 'dispatching my frugal meal' – an example of the language of temperance. He establishes himself as an atypical bachelor: he cooks for himself. This self-sufficiency disrupts the household – a form of individualism that is also explicitly economic: Franklin is able to save money for (radical) books. Vegetarianism, then, is part of a softening, almost feminising regime which civilises and makes the consumer independent. This squares with those languages that promoted commercial activity as a softening pursuit, which clashed with older ideologies of civic humanism and their emphasis on masculine virtue. What is radical is the *non*-republican quality of this discourse.

Sacvan Bercovitch has recently shown how Franklin's individualism transmutes the radical forces in American society. If for Emerson there is no history, only biography, which is really autobiography, then this was possible because of the internality with which Franklin converted the libertarian and subversive qualities of independence and naturalised individualism in civic and cultural values.[97] Thus there emerged a Romantic style of autiobiography, in which the 'protean imagination' becomes the benchmark, supplanting Augustianian grace; Bercovitch cites Carlyle's example of Cromwell. The result in English culture is that 'the titanic individual often finds himself in conflict with the norms of free-enterprise individualism – witness the dandy, the Romantic medievalist, and especially the secular Antinomian'. This is different from American culture, where there is 'an arrogance of the culture, not of the self. Or rather . . . an arrogance of the self conceived as an emblem of the culture.' Franklin contributed to this by linking 'the conversion handbook (replete with maxims and precepts) and the success story'.[98] Spirituality has been transmuted into an economic mode. It has recently been shown that Franklin was less immersed in capitalist ideology than Weber's famous citation of 'time is money' maintains.[99] However, this revision does not entirely contradict the view of Franklin as an avatar of capitalist individuation. And it is evident that his interest in diet was related to his interest in economics, and that he learnt this from Tryon.

A recent analysis of Franklin's vegetarian rhetoric demonstrates its economic flavour. Sailing from Boston, Franklin encountered a crisis of conscience:

During a calm which stopped us above Block-Island, the crew employed themselves in fishing for cod, of which they caught a great number. I had hitherto adhered to my resolution of not eating any thing that had possessed life; and I considered on this occasion, agreeably to the maxims of my master Tryon, the capture of every fish as a sort of murder, committed without provocation, since these animals had neither done, nor were capable of doing, the smallest injury to any one that should justify the measure. This mode of reasoning I conceived to be unanswerable. Meanwhile I had formerly been extremely fond of fish; and when one of these cod was taken out of the frying-pan, I thought its flavour delicious. I hesitated some time between principle and inclination, till at last recollecting, that when the cod had been opened some small fish were found in its belly, I said to myself, if you eat one another, I see no reason why we may not eat you. I accordingly dined on the cod with no small degree of pleasure, and have since continued to eat like the rest of mankind, returning only occasionally to my vegetable plan. How convenient does it prove to be a *rational animal*, that knows how to find or invent a plausible pretext for whatever it has an inclination to do![100]

For David Levin, Franklin opens with 'pair of complex, balanced sentences'. The rationale for vegetarianism is presented in a clause 'that emphasizes both rhetorical parallels and a persuasive, commonsensical justice based on reciprocal, proportional premises'. This is followed by the shortest sentence, preparing for the switch. Levin finds that 'The young vegetarian balances, here, between the two abstractions that contend in eighteenth-century views of psychology' of principle and inclination.[101] The language of balance, reciprocation and proportion which Levin uses is aptly economic, evoking Franklin's judicious, humorous middle style.

Leigh Hunt's review of his friend Shelley's *The Revolt of Islam* places vegetarianism in the context of self-regulation:

[Shelley was living] As much like Plato, – or rather still more like a Pythagorean. This was the round of his daily life: – He was up early; breakfasted sparingly; wrote this *Revolt of Islam* all the morning; went out in his boat or into the woods with some Greek author or the *Bible* in his hands; came home to a dinner of vegetables (for he took neither meat nor wine); visited (if necessary) *the sick and the fatherless*, whom others gave Bibles to and no help; wrote or studied again, or read to his wife and friends the whole evening; took a crust of bread or a glass of whey for his supper; and went early to bed. This is literally the whole of the life he led, or that we believe he now leads in Italy.[102]

This is a life of benevolent, temperate *otium*, surely a revision of Coleridge's Pantisocratic mixture of poetry and labour. Here (in *The Examiner*, 10 October 1819) is the riposte to John Taylor Coleridge's attack on the poem in the *Quarterly Review*, 21 (April 1819), in which the vegetarianism is made to seem explicitly *radical*: 'A good deal of mummery follows, of national fêtes, reasonable rites, altars of federation, &c. borrowed from that store-house of cast-off mummeries and abominations, the French revolution.'[103] Leigh Hunt is putting Shelley in the same context as those artisans whose diet Francis Place described: Place thought that by the 1820s an artisan 'could only expect social respect if he also *behaved* respectably and acquired sober, self-improving (though non-deferential) values'.[104] (Indeed, evidence from the radical journalism of Richard Carlile suggests that Shelley's vegetarianism was popular amongst the artisanal w orking class.)[105] It was no longer just a case of 'Economic independence and possession of a skilled status'.[106] In the long history of radicalism, forms of temperance had been developed which resisted the wrathful appetites both of the body and of the capitalist market. But vegetarian language could also be employed radically, in realising the image of a nonviolent community of all races and species.

CHAPTER 4

They became what they beheld: theodicy and regeneration in Milton, Law and Blake

Donald John

From the last quarter of the seventeenth century to the Romantic period, a heightened sensitivity prevailed in English theology regarding the relation between a Christian's conception of God's character and the specifications of salvation. To a large extent, theology and soteriology had always been so linked. But throughout the period from Milton to Blake, the proliferation of differing arguments in theodicy – the investigation of God's existence and purpose – drastically redefined Christian redemption. Increasingly equated with constitutive restoration in society as well as in the individual, redemption redounded on discussions about the nature of God. Both the Deity, and the nature and effects of the reconciliation process, in many circles became less arbitrary and alien to the religious subject. God could not be a 'god far off', nor could contemporary conceptions of salvation.[1] The extreme Puritan theologies of the English Revolution are famous for the different ways in which they personalised the divine. This chapter explores one of those traditions as it was successively shaped by three influential figures in the long eighteenth century.

Theodicean discussions aimed to justify the ways of God in a larger sense than explaining metaphysical, natural and moral evil in an all-good and all-powerful Creator's universe: authors worked fundamentally to recast the Deity's image or personality.[2] Arguing along the lines of Matthew 7:11, 'If ye then, being evil, know how to give good gifts unto your children, how much more shall your Father which is in heaven give good things to them that ask him?',[3] they portrayed God's character as the most benevolent human qualities writ large.[4] At the very least, God could be no less humane than the best of human beings. Redemption, moreover, was conceived as having more to do with regeneration, restoration, self-fashioning, soul-making, or the building up of identity, than with the accession by faith of an imputed, alien, or to use John Calvin's phrase, 'fictitious righteousness'. God 'becomes as we are, that we may be as he is'.[5]

Programmes of salvation were connected with theodicean concerns because of strong convictions that throughout the spiritual pilgrimage the religious subject would become ever more like the God he or she worshipped. The assumed plasticity of whatever was salvageable in humankind suggested that the believer was shaped by what he or she perceived to be the character of Deity. In 1686 John Scott, describing the purpose of a Christian life, wrote that 'God will have us praise him . . . because our praising him naturally excites us to imitate him, and to transcribe into our own natures those adorable perfections, which we do so admire and extoll in his . . . thereby we may glorifie our selves.'[6]

Toward the end of the period, writing from an entirely different religious tradition, David Bogue argued:

The importance of having right views of religion appears from the very nature of the thing. All goodness of disposition, all excellence of temper and conduct, arises from the influence of truth upon the soul. We see, in the vegetable world, that every seed produces a plant or tree of the same kind with itself, whether it be wholesome or poisonous. It is so in the moral world too: every doctrine, whether good or bad, has a tendency to produce its resemblance in the soul . . . compare the influence of religious maxims to the impression of the seal upon the wax: whatever the form of the seal is, it makes a corresponding impression.[7]

What follows is that the most successful theodicean efforts would offer the largest promise of constitutional change in the individual, and furthermore in society (and the creation). Culture would have to be reconfigured to accommodate such constitutionally altered individuals, and vice versa. That this did not occur on a widespread basis is well known. However, the number of people, as well as the variety of their ideological or theological orientations, who developed or subscribed to such constitutively affective theodicies are grossly underestimated and should not be considered an 'underground' which surfaced from time to time.[8]

The diagram below represents the theological implications which arise from a given writer's concept of creation:

| (a) ex nihilo | (b) ex deo | (c) emanation |
| Augustine | Milton | Boehme/Law |

Because of the ontological gap between the Creator and the creature, a soteriology tied to such concepts as imputed righteousness, penal-substitution, or satisfaction atonement would more likely be developed toward the (a) end of the spectrum: there, more arbitrary notions of salvation would prevail. But as one moves closer to point (c), the ontological gap is narrowed. An ontological bond is realised and righteousness becomes more real; that is, it amounts to a constitutive change in the individual, in some cases stretching toward deification.

The same is true of theodicy. At (a) the wrath of a Deity, whose justice has been offended, is depicted as being assuaged through a forensic metaphor. But, as one moves towards (c), a seemingly negative element in the Creator, creation, or creature is actually a positive element out of balance. In his inscription to the *Epitome of 'James Hervey's Meditations Among the Tombs'*, Blake writes, 'God out of Christ is a Consuming Fire.'[9] In Law's Behmenist scheme wrathfulness being held in tension or equipoise with love is thus not manifest in God; wrath as a negative force exists only in creatures who have wilfully skewed the constellation of the elements that constitute the image of God in them.[10]

THEODICY: 'METHINKS I GROW LIKE WHAT I
CONTEMPLATE'[11]

William King's *De Origine Mali* (1702; English, 1731) and G. W. Leibniz's *Essais de Théodicée sur la bonté de Dieu, la liberté de l'homme et l'origine du mal* (1710) addressed the classic theodicean dilemma attributed to Epicurus:

> God . . . either wishes to take away evils, and is unable; or He is able, and is unwilling; or neither willing nor able, or He is both willing and able. If He is willing and is unable, He is feeble, which is not in accordance with the character of God; if He is able and unwilling, He is envious, which is equally at variance with God; if He is neither willing nor able, He is both envious and feeble, and therefore not God; if He is both willing and able, which alone is suitable for God, from what source then these evils? or why does He not remove them?[12]

Of the theodicies of King and Leibniz, A. D. Nuttall rightly observes that 'the reasoning . . . has been severely *a priori*. The object of the exercise has been to reconcile the phenomena with what is known, at a higher level, of the nature of God'. Nuttall concludes that [these writers] 'cannot resist the temptation to reason backwards, *a posteriori*, from the given excellence of the world to the goodness of God'. This hope of 'imparting some *ethical colour, some warmth*, to an increasingly transparent deity', in their systems, failed.'[13] This effort, having failed, did not lead to the production of new theodicies *per se*; rather, it took place in the context of discussing aspects of Christian doctrines whose content had great potential either to impugn or to justify the character and ways of God. Such doctrines included eternal rewards and punishments, original sin, atonement and the divine inspiration of Scripture, especially that of the Old Testament.

We begin *in medias res* with the non-juror William Law (1686–1761) and a précis of an imagined monologue God delivers to prelapsarian Adam:

The world around thee . . . bears the marks of those creatures, which first made evil to be known in the creation . . . they began to . . . fancy that there was some infinity of power hidden in themselves, which they supposed was kept under, and suppressed . . . Fired and intoxicated . . . there was no end of their eternal sinking into new depths of slavery, under their *own self-tormenting natures.* As a wheel going down a mountain, that has no bottom . . . so are they whirled down by [their] wrong turned wills . . . into the bottomless depths of their own dark, fiery, working powers. *In no hell, but what their own natural strength had awakened; bound in no chains, but their own unbending, hardened spirits* . . . In that moment . . . their glassy sea in which they had dwelt, was . . . broken all into pieces, and became a black lake, a horrible chaos . . . of the confused, divided, fighting properties of nature. My creating Fiat stopped the workings of these rebellious spirits, by dividing the ruins of their wasted kingdom, into an earth, a sun, stars, and separated elements. Had not this revolt of angels brought forth that disordered *chaos,* no such materiality as this outward world is made of had ever been known . . . in eternity . . .

In heaven, all births and growths . . . are . . . so many manifestations of . . . the divine nature. But in this *new modelled chaos,* where the disorders that were raised by Lucifer are not wholly removed, [so] here every kind and degree of life, like the world from which it springs, is a mixture of good and evil in its birth . . .

. . . Therefore, my son, be content with thy angelical nature [and] to eat angel's food, and rule over this mixed . . . World . . . Thou canst not have [the animals' or devils'] sensibility, unless thou hast their nature . . . if the bestial life is raised up in thee, the same instant the heavenly birth of thy nature must die in thee.[14]

Law's Behmenist version of the Fall varies only slightly in his other works: the key elements remain the same. Instead of maintaining, like God, a tension between contrary elements – dark/light, wrath/love, astringency/sweetness – Satan fixes on the negative elements, breaks up the balance of these contraries held in tension and becomes what he beholds. The world comes into existence as a limit, albeit a chaotic one, to his fall. Adam is created androgynous and tripartite: his inner being is divine and is enclosed by a soul and material body. A material body enables Adam to make contact and bring healing to the material world. Only like can communicate with like. His task is to transmit a redeeming influx, which his divinity is capable of receiving and his humanity capable of imparting to the fallen creation. But Adam becomes enamoured with the material world, the divine influx reverses itself and his divinity is more or less destroyed.

As Adam becomes what he beholds, his Heavenly consort, Sophia (who is a reflection of the perfections of the divine Trinity), is replaced by Eve, who divides from the once androgynous Adam.[15] Law's key texts are Acts 17:24–8 and Genesis 3:15. The former assures us that an ontological bond between humankind and God has never been broken; the latter, that the defaced divinity in humankind received – simultaneous with the Fall – the inspoken Christ in the likeness of a seed which would bruise the serpent's head; that is, the power to reverse the influx as deriving from the material rather than the spiritual realm.

Law comments:

We are apt to think that our Imaginations and Desires may be played with, that they rise and fall away as nothing, because they do not always bring forth outward and visible effects. But indeed they are the greatest reality we have, and are the true reformers and raisers of *all that is real and solid in us*. All outward power that we exercise in the things around us, is but a shadow in comparison of that inward power, that resides in our Will, Imagination, and Desires; these communicate with eternity, and kindle a life which always reaches either heaven or hell. This strength of the inward man makes all that is an angel, and all that is a devil in us. Now our Desire is . . . always alive, always working and creating in us . . . It perpetually generates either life or death in us.[16]

A person who does not live with the conviction that every day he becomes, by his will's first love, either more devilish or more divine, is said by Law to be snared by the 'dream of life', losing all that eternity for which he was brought into being.[17] That such dreaming creates a Hell rather than a Heaven is owing to the nature of Adam's fall. Adam's eating of the Tree of Knowledge (knowledge of the material world) precipitated a fall into the senses, as it was rooted in the vegetated creation. Adam's sin did not consist in '*a single act of disobedience*', which brought a curse upon his posterity; nor was God's command '*arbitrary*' or 'a mere trial of man's obedience'.[18]

The following two basic theodicean elements thus appear in Law. First, a denial of *creatio ex nihilo* and an affirmation of emanation:

It is the same impossibility for a thing to be created out of nothing, as it is to be created by nothing . . . *Thinking* and *willing* are eternal, they never began to be. Nothing can think, or will *now*, in which there was not will and thought for *all eternity* . . . the soul, which is a *thinking, willing* being is come forth, or created out of that which hath *willed* and *thought* in God from all eternity. The *created* soul is a creature of *time*, and had its beginning on the *sixth* day of creation; but the *essences* of the soul, which were then formed into a creature and into a state of distinction from God, had been in God from all eternity, or could not have been *breathed* forth from God into the form of a living creature . . . The *essences* of our souls can never cease to be, because they never began to be.[19]

Second, that the nature and source of evil lies in self-skewed elements of the divine essence. Of the origin of evil, Jacob Boehme writes:

But there is yet a difference [to be observed], that evil neither is, nor is called God; this understood in the first principle [which Boehme calls the *Ungrund*], where it is the earnest fountain of the wrathfulness, according to which, God calleth himself angry, wrathful, and zealous God. For the original of life, and of all mobility, consisteth in the wrathfulness; yet if the [tartness] be kindled with the light of God, it is then no more tartness, but severe wrathfulness is changed into great joy.[20]

This first principle of wrath is not God until it mingles with, or is held in simultaneous tension with, light or love. Man contains God-like elements. But if one's will seizes on one or more of these elements to the point where contraries – which should be held in balance – become unbalanced, the divine equipoise is lost.[21]

Turning from Law to William Blake one could well question an enterprise that compares writers, amongst whose most famous lines are, on the one hand, 'Represent to your imagination that your bed is your grave; that all things are ready for your interment . . . and that it will be owing to God's great mercy if you ever see the light of the sun again or have another day to add to your works of piety', and on the other, 'Sooner murder an infant in its cradle than nurse unacted desires.' How, one wonders, would Blake have annotated a passage in which Law suggests that 'Moses was the legislator *par excellence*, the father of emanation-metaphysics, and the first Universalist'? Would Blake's marginalia read 'uneasy', 'all gold', or 'this man was hired to depress art'?[22] The fact remains that both were theodicean writers possessed by a lifelong vision of the building up of a personal identity by exercising an *innate* element which is ontologically derived from and bonded to Ultimate Reality.

One day, while meditating on the creation of the universe, Emanuel Swedenborg (1688–1772) was raptured into a society of celestial beings who were mulling over the same subject. The celestials expressed their dilemma to the Baron:

We could never come to any certain conclusion . . . our thoughts were perplexed with the idea of a chaos, as of a large egg (occupying one fourth part of the universe), from which the universe and all its parts were brought forth ... there was also another idea riveted fast to our minds, that all things were created by God out of nothing; and yet now we perceive that out of nothing nothing can be produced.[23]

Fortunately, Swedenborg knew the true story. God, who is Christ, resides in the centre of the *spiritual* sun. His essential love and wisdom radiates outward. Love corresponds to will, and wisdom to understanding, and the situation (state) of spiritual beings depends on how much of the influx of divine love and wisdom each imbibes. Hell is the state of mind of those who worship the natural world as God, even as Heaven is the state of mind of those who worship God *in* Christ.

Intuitively Blake – not as methodically or overtly as Law – rejects *creatio ex nihilo* (and *ex deo* in the Miltonic sense) in favour of (again intuitively) an emanation system, in which the natural world comes into being as a limit to fallenness. 'Many suppose that before [Adam] <the creation> All was Solitude & Chaos This is the most pernicious Idea that can enter the mind ... & limits All existence to creation ... to the Time & Space fixed by the corporeal vegetative eye ...'[24] His protestations notwithstanding,[25] the material world is no mere illusion; it is a salvific outbirth of 'the Eternal Creation flowing from the Divine Humanity',[26] a place in which 'The Ruins of Time build Mansions in Eternity.'[27]

Perhaps the salient difference is that in Blake we find Gnostic theodicean elements along with Behmenist or Swedenborgian ones. There is a demiurge figure, because for Blake, the creation's and creature's vegetated state is sustained by reasoning, imagining and acting in concert with the God of the Old Testament.[28] Blake asserts that 'in [Albion's] Chaotic State of sleep Satan & Adam & the whole World was Created by the Elohim'.[29] Men and women misperceive the Creator as well as the creation: 'Thinking as I do that the Creator of this World is a very Cruel Being & being a Worshipper of Christ I cannot help saying the Son O how unlike the Father <First God Almighty comes with a Thump on the Head Then Jesus Christ comes with a balm to heal it>.'[30] And as with Boehme, Law and Swedenborg, Blake's theodicy is enhanced by making the individual responsible for creating and maintaining 'mind-forg'd manacles': for becoming like that which they perceive to be most real and enduring.[31]

Blake wrote, 'I must Create a System, or be enslav'd by another Man's', and further in *Jerusalem* he asserts, 'Man must & will have Some Religion; if he has not the Religion of Jesus, he will have the Religion of Satan.'[32]

In his earliest illuminated works Blake offers a prospectus: 'Therefore God becomes as we are, that we may be as he is.'[33] God is ontologically bonded to His creatures: 'I am not a God afar off, I am a brother and friend; / Within your bosoms I reside, and you reside in me.' In an attempt to save Albion from further disintegration, Los (Blake's zoa of imagination, of prophetic vision) rages, 'Why stand we here trembling around / Calling on God for help; and not ourselves in whom God dwells . . . ?'[34]

Blake availed himself of 'rationalist' critiques of doctrines that represented an inhumane God. His imagery of sacrificial atonement sears like a paper cut. There are, for instance, such illuminations as the disembowelling of Albion (*Jerusalem*, Plate 25), or lines such as 'for Sacrifice to Tirzah . . . She ties the knot of nervous fibres, into a white brain! / She ties the knot of bloody veins, into a red hot heart.'[35] Blake more straightforwardly exposes the inhumane and irrational elements he finds in Christian doctrines: 'Saying, Doth Jehovah Forgive a debt only on condition that it shall / Be payed? . . . That Debt is not Forgiven / Such is the Forgiveness of the Gods, the Moral Virtues of the / Heathen, whose tender Mercies are Cruelty. But Jehovah's Salvation Is . . . without Price.'[36]

Much has been written about Blake's idea of John Milton, but we seem to have only two terse comments on Milton by William Law. In 1740 Law responded to Dr Joseph Trapp's 'The Folly, Sin and Danger of Being Righteous Over-Much', a piece in which Trapp (Oxford's first Professor of Poetry, 1708) had attacked enthusiasts in general and Law and the Methodists in particular. Trapp responded to Law, focusing on the latter's sustained and stringent critique of the clergy. Milton briefly surfaces in Law's animadversions to Dr Trapp's reply:

I own, when I was about *Eighteen*, I . . . should have been glad to have translated the *Sublime Milton*, if I had found myself able; but this *Ardour* soon went off, and I think it as good a proof of the *Sublime*, to desire the death of all that is diabolical and *Serpentine* in my own nature, as to be *charmed* with those *Speeches* which the *Devils* make in *Milton*.[37]

A similar comment appears in Law's last work: 'Instead of the depth, the truth and spirit of the humble publican, seeking to regain Paradise, only by a broken heart, crying, "God, be merciful to me a sinner," the high-bred classic will live in daily transports at the enormous Sublime of a Milton, flying thither on the unfeathered wings of high sounding words.'[38]

'Die he or justice must; unless . . .' The stated project of *Paradise Lost*[39] has generated a mass of literature on the poet's theodicy: much of this output focuses on traditional theodicean themes such as *felix culpa* and free will.[40] It seems difficult to find criticism of *Paradise Lost* that is not in some sense theodicean. It just may be that the reader-response criticism of Stanley Fish or the 'self-authoring' of Marshall Grossman represents as satisfying a response to William Empson – who was thinking of theodicy in our larger sense – as does Dennis Danielson's defence of Arminian free will.[41] That acknowledged, are there elements in Milton that will take us beyond the theodicies of Augustine, Bishop King and Leibniz and reveal a more organic universe in which neither the Creator nor the process of salvation is alien or arbitrary?

One may fairly object to what seems like placing a highly specified theological stencil over a great epic poem: nevertheless the theology of *Paradise Lost* disturbed – for aesthetic as well as theodicean reasons – great poets. In just over one hundred lines of dialogue Milton uses the words and phrases of a Deity and a programme of salvation that are 'afar off': 'to appease betimes / The incensed Deity . . . brings obedience due . . . breaks his fealty . . . To expiate the treason . . . Die he or justice must; unless for him / Some other pay . . . The rigid satisfaction . . . on me let thy anger fall . . . His crime makes guilty all his sons . . . merit imputed shall absolve' (III: 186–291). If Christ were essentially equal with the Father, we could read their dialogue in Book III as a Behmenist tension between wrath and love held in equipoise. But they are not ontologically equal and we have something more akin to a briefing session rather than a dialogic insight into the nature of God-head itself. So, I must set aside Irene Samuel's (and many others') warnings about reading the dialogue between the Father and Son as dogma rather than drama.[42]

From the point of view of the other two authors being discussed in this chapter, if – to put it colloquially – the Father really talked like that, then *pace* Stanley Fish, Satan did not fall as a result of willing not to see things as they really were; quite the contrary, he fell because he 'became what he beheld'.

In looking for signs of an immanent God and an organic universe, what immediately comes to mind is the seed metaphor so closely tied, at this point in history, to an internal lodestar-like divine principle. But aside from referring to Israel as God's chosen people (I:8), the seed of Genesis 3:15 comes to fruition with the defeat of Satan through the effects of Christ's Incarnation. And Milton's surprisingly Swedenborgian or Behmenist, 'Not by destroying Satan, but his works / In thee and thy seed' is quickly qualified by penal-substitution atonement, debts repaid, imputed righteousness and satisfaction (XII:379, 387–419).

In arguing for a Behmenist Milton, Margaret L. Bailey unintentionally throws into relief the theodicean problems in the poetic imagery just noted: in Boehme God cannot become fully God without Christ; in Milton Christ could not be even God-like without God.[43] Boehme personifies the divine element in humanity as the divine virgin, Sophia; in Milton there is no divine element in humanity in Law's Behmenist sense. At best there is the capacity to receive grace and moral strength by the Holy Spirit.[44] Hell and Heaven are states in Boehme; in Milton, while Hell can be a state (I:253–5; IV:75), it, as well as Heaven and Eden, are 'portrayed' as places for creatures with certain states of loyalty to God.[45] To what extent does Milton's *Paradise Lost* address theodicy in the larger sense?

That Milton had ready access to most of the raw materials for developing a theodicy in the larger sense but did not use them, is no surprise. Though he was standing on point (b) of the spectrum, he had his back turned to theodicies derived from point (c). This is for at least two reasons related to his Arian Christ. Milton's conception of the generation of the Son from the substance of the Father required a strong rejection of *creatio ex nihilo*.[46] Milton's *ex deo* position is a polemical reaction, designed to safeguard the ontology of Christ rather than, as with Boehme or Law, to explain the deiform nature of the universe, and therefore, in itself, does not go very far towards forming a thoroughgoing *ex deo* soteriology such as we find, for example, in Law. But even if this first point does not hold, Milton's God was 'a God out of Christ [and] a consuming fire', because Milton's revelation of God centres on the entire Bible rather than on the incarnate Arian Christ.[47] At the very outset readers are advised that Milton will draw the raw materials for his theology inclusively from the Old and New Testament Scriptures.[48]

REGENERATION OR, 'BECOMING PALATABLE TO GOD'

In this concluding section we are following the suggestion that during the period with which this book concerns itself, salvation is increasingly seen as involving constitutive transmutation in the religious subject.

Daniel Watkins argues that John Keats's 'vale of Soul-making' letter 'points towards a view of identity as the happy influence of painful circumstantial pressures in forming a *spiritually meaningful essence*: identity becomes synonymous with salvation*, and thus it is, finally, but a modified version of the Christian idealism to which Keats objects'.[49] From the last half of the seventeenth century, thinking about Christian salvation as a process of building up an identity of some kind was displacing such conceptions of salvation as being, for example, a change in one's legal status before God, or experiencing vicariously *at-one-ment* with Ultimate Being.[50] And still more radical was the tendency to consider the religious subject as containing within himself or herself the capability for building up an identity, call it a divine seed, poetic genius, imagination, or deified will and reason.

What, then, is the nature of Christian regeneration in Milton? Milton, like Law and Blake, will not allow for an arbitrary or divinely imposed 'glorification'. This is precisely the problem with predestination: 'God's restoration of fallen man [would be] a matter of justice not grace.'[51] As in *Paradise Lost*, untried reason which 'had served necessity, / Not [God]', cannot lead to regeneration (III:110–11). It is important for Milton that 'when God determined to restore mankind, he also decided unquestionably . . . to restore some part at least of man's lost freedom of will'.[52] The regenerated will is the primary constitutive change Milton seeks in the person of faith. There is a phrase in *Christian Doctrine* which may be more telling of Milton's concept of regeneration than are his later explicit arguments: 'For, as we shall show later, some traces of the divine image remain in man, and when they combine in an individual he becomes more suitable, and as it were, more properly disposed for the kingdom of God than another.'[53] To be sure the passage has to do with right reason and obedience firmly tried, yet it has what we have termed constitutive overtones, as in becoming willingly, if not ontologically, 'palatable to God'.[54] But, by comparison to Law and Blake, Milton's 'soul-making' is possibly hampered by his thnetopsychism and his eschatology as regards the final end of this world.[55] To the extent that the soul dies with the body, and 'sleeps', final glorification will tend to be arbitrary, graciously imposed from without. Some misreading on Blake's part notwithstanding, it was the impossibility of soul-making after death that led to Blake's most violent outbursts against Swedenborg.[56] And non-imposed 'soul-making was the engine that drove Law's Universalism'.[57]

Law died a few days after writing the last words of his most radical critique of the *ancien régime*, in which he anticipates Blake's phrase, 'religion hid in war', by laying the carnage of colonialism and warfare on the doorstep of the church. We might as well be reading here that rather less orthodox follower of Boehme, Thomas Tryon (see above, pp. 57–8, 64–6, 68, 70–83). Against the notion of just war Law writes 'that no one can subsist in safety from its neighbouring Christian kingdoms, but by weapons of war, are not all Christian kingdoms equally in an *unchristian* state, as two neighbouring *bloody Knaves?*'[58]

But immediately before this critique of warmongering, Law condemns a religion of *prudent* morality.[59] A forensic soteriology, made up of such doctrines as satisfaction or penal-substitution atonement and imputed righteousness, would be indicted for exactly the same reason. Both a theology which equated salvation with the building up of prudential moral virtue, and one which rested in legal metaphors, are developed by making analogies from the vegetated, unregenerate world. They both violate the argument of Blake's *There is No Natural Religion*: explicating Scripture by making rational analogies to the natural, fallen world will not move one above or out of a natural fallen state: 'If it were not for the Poetic or Prophetic character. the Philosophical & Experimental would soon be the ratio of all things & stand still, unable to do other than repeat the same dull round over again Therefore God becomes as we are, that he may be as he is.'[60]

There is generally thought to be an early, rigorist Law, best known for his *Treatise on Christian Perfection* and *A Serious Call to a Devout and Holy Life*; and a later, and radically different, post 1735–6 Behmenist-informed Law; but the notion of such a sea change cannot be exactly right. Law always held that justifying righteousness was more constitutive than imputed. When he was an undergraduate, Law discovered Malebranche by himself, on no one's recommendation, claiming him as his mentor.[61] Early on, Law had immersed himself in the major mystical writers, and to a significant extent in hermeticism. Law was an 'affective' mystic: a supernatural ontological reality could be infused into, or communicated to, man at the spiritual (eternal) point of his being.[62] And in this regard prayer is for Law what imagination is for Blake. They are constitutive, means for building up being, creating identity. Law describes prayer as the means of altering the 'states' through which individuals pass and of awakening that which is divine and eternal within them.[63] Prayer for him – as imagination for Blake – awakens one from what we have termed the 'dream of life'.

A somewhat unsavoury-sounding Swedenborgian term, 'vastation', highlights the similarity between Blake's and Law's view of regeneration. Vastation, not unlike Blake's 'last judgement', is the process whereby our first love completely fills out our identity or character. Like the movement of an earthworm, which extends its forward extremity and then draws the rest of its body towards it, the dominant value or first love

of the mind, the soul, or the identity – call it what you will – projects
itself forward into experience (Keats's 'vale of soul-making' or Blake's
'world of regeneration'), and, with each exertion, further fashions itself.[64]
This is a lifelong moment-by-moment process; but a process which, for
Swedenborg, races to its final end after death. Now in terms of regeneration in Blake and Law, something akin to 'vastation' takes place. In
a proto-existentialist manner, one's imagination and will compact and
confirm the objects of one's first loves and cherished beliefs; self-making
is underway.

When Lavater asks, '*What is a man's interest? what constitutes his God, the
ultimate of his wishes, his end of existence?*' and answers 'that to which
he makes every other thing a mere appendix; – the vortex, the centre, the
comparative point from which he sets out, on which he fixes, to which
he irresistibly returns . . . *The object of your love is your God*', Blake writes,
'Pure gold . . . This should be written in gold letters on our temples.'[65]

The imagination is both the means and the end product of regeneration in Blake. The fallen imagination reveals the process by which a
prelapsarian imagination is regenerated. Blake explores in great depth
the downside of identity-making in the haunting phrase, 'he/they became what they beheld', which perhaps draws on Romans 1 : 18ff,
which depicts those who exchange a vision of the true God for images
drawn from the vegetated creation and actually become like what they
behold.

Negative becoming and beholding, in Blake, is related either to theodicy or to regeneration. In terms of theodicy it is a fall into a world overseen
by a God 'afar off'. In terms of regeneration it is tied to forensic atonement imagery. The phrase, 'they became what they beheld', derives from
the Fall narrative in *The Book of Urizen*, but we first encounter it in Night IV
of *The Four Zoas*. A Behmenist limit has been put to Urizen's precipita-
tion into Eternal Death, but as Los surveyed 'enslaved humanity', he
'became what he beheld'.[66] *Milton* plate 3 recapitulates the Urizenic fall
into the senses, and once again Los 'became what he beheld', and as
a result a 'Female pale' separates from him.[67] *Jerusalem* emphasises the
dividing and division that leads to and becomes a staple feature of the
fallen world. Having divided Luvah into three bodies, the Daughters
of Albion, 'became what they beheld'.[68] Gwendolen, having divided
Rahab and Tirzah into twelve portions, 'became what [she] beheld',
and those looking on, Los included, 'became what they beheld'.[69] The
further divisions and fleeings apart of Blake's mythological characters
lead in the space of only seven lines of poetry to a staccato repetition

of the phrase.[70] And then Blake gives us a cosmic view of the unfallen Eternals observing all this 'beholding and becoming': 'Those in Great Eternity who contemplate on Death, / Said this. What seems to Be: Is: To those Whom / It seems to Be, & is productive of the most dreadful / Consequences to those to whom it seems to Be.'[71]

Forensic sacrificial imagery is both the cause and result of negative beholding and becoming, of explicating the Bible or drawing theological conclusions from a vegetated state of perception. In a conflated scene of knives, blood, Jesus, Luvah and other sacrificial imagery, Albion's sons, 'Terrified at the sight of the Victim: at his distorted sinews!... become like what they behold.'[72] The very next *Jerusalem* plate ends with these lines: 'As the Senses of Men shrink together under the Knife of flint, / In the hands of Albions Daughters, among the Druid Temples'.[73]

But, here for Blake, as for Law, we have a preference for Boehme over Swedenborg. Though the latter's Heaven is not a place but a state, it has to it a fixedness, a finality which we do not find in Law's Boehme. Beholding what we become is an ongoing process. Fallenness can recur if those in Eternity fix their wills and imaginations on the fallen world, as did Law's Behmenist Adam. This is why Blake's Eternals, following Los's fall and Enitharmon's separation from him, cry out in *Urizen*, 'Spread a Tent, with strong curtains around them / Let cords & stakes bind the Void / That Eternals may no more behold them.'[74] Identity building is real and ongoing, and concerns the Creator as well as the creation and the creature.

Blake advised his readers to 'Distinguish ... States from Individuals in those States. States change: but Individual Identities never change nor cease: / You cannot go to Eternal Death in that which can never Die':

'Judge then of thy Own Self: thy Eternal Lineaments explore / What is Eternal & what Changeable? & what Annihilable!... Whatever can be created can be Annihilated...

'For God himself enters Death's Door always with those that enter / And lays down in the Grave with them, in Visions of Eternity'.[75]

This sounds very like Swedenborg: 'Now whatever can be conjoined with the Divine Principle, cannot die to Eternity, for the Divine Being is with it, and conjoins it to himself.'[76]

Keats's 'soul-making' replaces the notion that, 'we are redeemed by a certain arbitrary interposition of God and taken to heaven'.[77] Keats is here juxtaposing the building up of a 'spiritually meaningful essence', with certain arbitrary aspects of evangelical theology. It has not been the purpose of this chapter to deny the existence of a strong thread of evangelical belief throughout the period. Nor have I intended to suggest that a theology which works itself out in forensic metaphors is inimical to the English Romantic movement. The goal has been to follow a multi-faceted movement of English Christianity which, in one way or another throughout the long eighteenth century, emphasised the constitutive nature of salvation by radically envisioning a God who 'becomes as we are, that we may be as he is', a conception very much related to the theological and aesthetic concerns of English Romantic artists. Far from being an underground movement, these revolutionising views of theodicy and regeneration had undeniably significant implications for radicalism in the fabric of social order and literary culture. Those seeking to understand the earthly ferment of the 1790s and 1830s would, in short, do well to reconsider the heavenly ideas of Law, Blake and a re-formed Milton.

CHAPTER 5

Fasting women: the significance of gender and bodies in radical religion and politics, 1650–1813

Jane Shaw

The history of fasting women from the mid-seventeenth century to the early nineteenth century has usually been seen as significant by historians and medical scientists because it is emblematic of a broader cultural and intellectual shift in this period: that is, from a world view which explained the unusual in religious terms to one which relied upon scientific and medical explanations for all such phenomena. Employing such a secularisation thesis, historians have suggested that as belief in supernatural explanations declined and trust in scientific analyses increased, women's fasting bodies were transformed from miraculous to medical wonders.[1]

The cases of Ann Moore of Tutbury and Anna Trapnel would seem, at first glance, to support this thesis. Trapnel, a Baptist who became involved with the Fifth Monarchists, in the 1640s and 1650s, prophesied and had religious visions and dreams while she fasted. Testing her survival without food was only one of the issues in the political and religious atmosphere in which she was engaged. Moore claimed that from 1806 she had lost all desire to eat and was surviving without food or even liquids. In 1808, a scientific investigation – by local worthy gentlemen – was undertaken and her claims of survival without food were substantiated. For the next five years, she attracted a great deal of attention, but in 1813 she was exposed as a hoax by a committee of medical men, magistrates and ministers of the Church of England. However, to explain the apparent differences in the stories of these two women by means of the secularisation thesis empties these stories of their political significance, thereby potentially robbing the women of their agency: Trapnel was a significant figure in the radical politics of the 1640s and 1650s, and Moore was visited by the Reverend Thomas Foley who was associated with the popular and heterodox religious group gathered around the prophet Joanna Southcott. Following Foley's visit to Moore, Southcott herself made prophesies concerning Moore. Further, the simple secularisation thesis ignores the complexity

and variety of interpretations of the many cases of fasting women in the
period between the two revolutions.

This chapter will explore the political, religious and cultural meanings
assigned to fasting women from the mid-seventeenth century to the early
nineteenth century, with particular emphasis on Trapnel and Moore,
the women who mark the beginning and end of the period. Cases in
the intervening years, particularly that of Martha Taylor, a woman who
survived without food for about a year in the late 1660s, and whose case
in many ways represents a turning point with regard to the relationship
between religious and scientific understandings of fasting, will also be
discussed. Why were fasting women such fascinating and potent symbols?
How did the women themselves understand their fasting? What was the
relationship between what they said in words and what they said through
their bodies? And given that the vast majority of such cases of fasting in
this period involved women, how was their gender significant?

FASTING AND RELIGIOUS AUTHORITY

Fasting is a central practice in many religions, and historians and anthro-
pologists have pointed to the ways in which 'Food habits are a language
through which a society expresses itself... Food practices have established and confirmed contact and contracts of care and responsibility
not only between humans but . . . even between humans and their gods.'[2]
Fasting evolved as an important religious practice in early Christianity,
especially in ascetical regimes which aimed to train the soul by regulating the body. This emphasis on fasting remained within many strands
of Christianity, taking on a variety of meanings that were beyond asceticism. While fasting was, as a religious practice, perhaps more clearly
associated with Catholic Christianity, nevertheless Protestants adapted
the practice for their own uses and attributed their own meanings to it.
For example, in England, this adaptation of fasting occurred especially
amongst the radical religious groups of the Civil War. George Fox and
other prominent Friends such as James Nayler and Thomas Ellwood
fasted for days and even weeks at a time, and in their diaries described
their survival after such fasts as miracles. Such fasting – and survival –
was interpreted by the Quakers as a sign of the special truth of their
religious and political claims, amongst the proliferation of such claims
by radical groups in the Civil War period.[3]

It was in this context, then, that women prophets in the radical groups
of the 1650s claimed spiritual and political authority through bodily

suffering, including fasting.[4] Trapnel came to public prominence in January 1654 when she went to Whitehall and for twelve days prophesied and poured forth her religious visions nearby the room where the Independent and Fifth Monarchist Vavasor Powell was being questioned by the Council of State. *The Cry of a Stone* is Trapnel's account of this time, and the opening pages make clear the strong connection between Trapnel's fasting and her prophetic practices:

> The first five days neither eating nor drinking anything more or less, and the rest of the time once in twenty-four hours, sometimes eat a very little toast in small Bear, sometimes only chewed it, and took down the Moysture only, sometimes drank of the small Bear and sometimes only washt her mouth therewith, and cast it out, lying in bed with her eyes shut, her hands fixed, seldom seen to move, she delivered in that time, many and various things; speaking every day, sometimes two, three, four, and five hours together . . . she uttered all in Prayer and Spiritual Songs for most part.

Trapnel had been prophesying from the late 1640s and continued into the 1650s – about the political situation, and primarily against Oliver Cromwell – after she had experienced her 'call', a religious experience in which the Lord had told her 'I will make thee an instrument of much more; for particular souls shall not only have benefit of thee, but the universality of Saints shall have discoveries of God through thee.' Fasting for Trapnel was always intimately connected with this personal authority received from God, so that her prophecies would come especially when she had been fasting for several days. Some of her companions obviously questioned this, for Trapnel reported that:

> I was judged by divers friends to be under a temptation . . . for not eating; I took that scripture, neglect the body, and went to the Lord and enquired whether I had been so, or had any self-end in it to be singular beyond what was meet; it was answered me, no, for thou shalt every way be supplyed in body and spirit, and I found a continual fulness in my stomack, and the taste of divers sweet-meats and delicious food therein which satisfied me.

Thus she tested the practice of fasting by Scripture and by asking God directly. Fasting was also a sign of purity; in February 1653, she reported, 'I durst not eat nor drink for four days together, because it was said to me, If thou doest, thou worshippest the Devil.'[5]

Sarah Wight, a Baptist who worshipped at Henry Jessey's church, and whom Trapnel visited, was another prophet who made fasting central to her practice of prophecy, understanding it as a sign of purity: she declared that she needed nothing but Christ to survive. 'Now I have my desire; I desired nothing but a crucifed Christ and I have him; a crucified Christ, a naked Christ; I have him and nothing else.' This meant that she was 'so full of the Creator that I can take in none of the creature'. So, she reported, 'I do eat, but it's meat to eat that the world knows not of. His words were found, and I did eat them.'[6] Thus Wight even refused the bread and wine of the Lord's Supper because she was already full of Christ. By contrast, Trapnel did rely on the Lord's Supper for sustenance; the day before she set out from London on her (ill-fated) 'prophesying tour' of Cornwall in 1654, she went to the All Hallows congregation of which she was a member:

And I that day saw great shinings and tasted much of my Saviour that day, who was presenting his loveliness in the ministery, and his sweetness in the supper of breaking bread, which filled my heart with joy unspeakable and glorious in the believing . . . And having thus spent the night in sweet communion with God I was prepared for my journey: I wanted not sleep nor food-preparation, having had the cordial revivement liquors from my Lord Jesus which strengthened me for my travelling to Cornwall.[7]

Both Trapnel and Wight used what was close at hand to exercise religious authority: namely, their bodies and food. Their fasting bodies were in turn read as 'signs' by the many people who visited them, and by other commentators and observers. As Nigel Smith has remarked, in this period fasting 'was constructed within the terms of saving souls, and the religious politics of the Interregnum'.[8] In Trapnel's case fasting was intimately entwined with her power to prophesy, and involved explicitly political prophecies against Cromwell. Sarah Wight's seventy-five days of fasting – and related illnesses – were rather an essential part of her wrestle with the forces of evil, so that her fasting body became an authoritative sign of the triumph of good, of the healthy state of her soul and of the ultimate triumph of the independent church of which she was a member. This in turn gave Wight the authority not only to pour out her various scripturally based prophecies, but also to offer spiritual advice to the many people who visited her, such as Dinah the Black, probably the 'Moor not born in England', a young woman to whom Wight offered counsel about her suicidal tendencies and pain at being and looking different.

Fasting women in the Restoration period and beyond rarely claimed religious authority through their fasting. This is one of the major shifts of this period. However, their fasting and surviving bodies continued to be read as religious and political signs. Martha Taylor (whose own religious affiliation is not clear) of Over-Hadon near Bakewell in Derbyshire, who survived without food for at least twelve months in 1668–9, illustrates this point.[9] News of Taylor's survival spread rather quickly, both by word of mouth and through the publication of several pamphlets. Amongst the many people who came to visit her was Thomas Robins, 'a well-wisher to the gospel of Jesus Christ', and, apparently, a Derbyshire ballad-maker, who wrote of the miracle of Martha Taylor in two cheap pamphlets. In the second of these, he described Taylor as a public, interpretable sign of a mysterious work of God. He suggested that God 'hath made his chosen vessel of this Damsel, for to work this marvelous work upon as a comfortable sign to a sinful and hypocritical nation'.[10] Her miraculous survival without food was also providential, a wake-up call to a sinful nation; her miraculous body symbolised what God might do for all who repented of their sins. In his interpretation, Robins was part of a culture of reading signs and prodigies in terms of the nation's religious and political fate, a culture which had flourished in the Civil War and Interregnum but also continued after the Restoration, amongst ministers of both the established church and the dissenting congregations. The anonymous author (who simply signed himself as H. A.) of another pamphlet about Taylor also saw her as a sign for others:

I look upon the Preservation without the use of Creatures to be the manifestation of Infinite Power, for the benefit and advantage of them that fear God, to let them see how God can preserve life by and of himself, and for the hardening of the obstinate and impenitent; for my own awakening and bringing into a way of holiness.[11]

H. A. saw God's providence at work in the prophet, writing of 'so great a wonder of Providence; the total fast of Martha Taylor'[12] and related that to Taylor's piety and suffering. In this, H.A. made a number of connections, often established in the Christian tradition, but particularly in the lives of the prominent female mystics of the Middle Ages, between female piety, suffering and food.[13] He transcribed a number of Taylor's 'ordinary sayings' in his work, in which Taylor expressed her own understanding of her fasting and piety: 'If I was able to feed upon all the good creatures of God, where as now I cannot, yet they could none of them satisifie or solace my poor, weak and hungry Soul; It is the enjoyment of him, who is the Bread of Life, the Life of my Life, that is my satisfaction, to whom be the glory.'[14] Here there are strong echoes of Wight's refusal of food (for she had Christ and was fed by him), but Taylor does not seem to have insisted on any claims of religious authority. She was the *object* of religious interpretation, curiosity and scientific investigation.

THE INVESTIGATION AND TESTING OF FASTING WOMEN

Fasting women were always the objects of attention. While at Whitehall Trapnel 'uttered all in Prayer and Spiritual Songs for most part, in the ears of very many persons of all sorts and degrees, who hearing the Report, came where she lay'. Among those who came to visit her were members of the Barebones Parliament, Independent Ministers, military men and Lady Darcy and Lady Vermuden.[15] Wight had a similar array of visitors: men involved in the politics of the day; Independent Ministers; people of a radical religious sensibility or who otherwise had an interest in unusual religious women, including the same Lady Vermuden who visited Trapnel, as well as medical doctors (a point to which I shall return, for of course ministers of the churches often performed medical tasks) and the various people who came to seek her spiritual wisdom. The authors of the various pamphlets on Taylor reported on the crowds who came to visit her, including the Earl of Devonshire and other local Derbyshire gentry, who could hear her hiccuping a hundred yards from the house and crowded into the downstairs sitting room of her humble house.

In all these three cases, the 'truth' of the fasting woman was tested, though in different ways and sometimes to different ends. The testing of Wight was not a testing by earthly power so much as by spiritual ones. Here spiritual and physical recovery happened concurrently. While Anna Trapnel was treated with considerable respect in London, on her tour of Cornwall, she met considerable hostility, for 'the clergie gave information in many places of the country, what an impostor, and a dangerous deceiver was come into Cornwall'. Ministers came to speak to her, though she regarded their words as mere 'clergie-puff,' and they were followed by justices and constables who came up the stairs crying witch, and pulled her eyelids up and pinched her nose. She went into a trance to avoid them, but she greatly feared the 'witch tryer-woman of that town' who had a 'great pin which she used to thrust into witches, to try them'. Nevertheless, she survived the accusations of witchcraft and continued her prophesying.[16]

In the cases of Wight and Trapnel, it was not so much their fasting as their spiritual authority which was tested. By contrast, in Taylor's case, her survival without food was the central issue. Her fast was in itself her central claim to fame, and a variety of interpretations were attached to this claim. Robins thought her a miracle. H. A. thought her a sign of the providential care of God. Others thought her a hoax; as H. A. reported, 'Divers sort of Persons there were who employed themselves to vilifie her, and cry her up for a cheat, about the Country.'[17] One John Reynolds, a physician, thought her survival could be explained in purely medical terms and, appealing to Thomas Willis's theory of fermentation, wrote a pamphlet saying so.[18] The Earl of Devonshire and local gentry therefore initiated an investigation of her claims, for they had 'a great desire to be more fully satisfied in the truth'. They selected twenty maids to watch and wait with her for seven days and seven nights; these maids then 'certified for very truth' that she had received no food in that time.[19] H. A. emphasised his own close observation of Taylor and conversation with other witnesses:

I writ the ensuing sheets upon the irresistible Importunity of some Friends, who know that I had seen and conversed with her several times; and with her Visiters, Gentlemen, Divines, Physicians, some of both the watch set upon her, and with some of her most sober knowing Neighbours on purpose to get the Truth concerning her; but upon further Trial, I became convinced of the reality of what I have been given an account of.[20]

The credibility of the witnesses was important, so that 'Gentlemen, Divines, Physicians,' as H. A. put it, all came to be deemed more reliable than a mere local neighbour of lowly social status. This was all part of the developing scientific method, in which increasing numbers of credible – that is, those of correct social status – witnesses were required for an experiment to be believed, especially by those who were not present.[21] Witnesses were always important (everyone was aware of the need for reliable witnesses, for the procedures of common law were generally known) but in the case of Wight, Henry Jessey presented those witnesses as reliable according to the criteria of the religious sensibilities of the readers he anticipated. In a postscript to the Reader, Jessey described the key witnesses as the father, Mr Thomas Wight, a preacher in Tewkesbury; the mother, Mrs Mary Wight who 'above seven years ago was also deep in terror and distraction of the Spirit . . . til the Lords good time of refreshing came'; and the maid who tended her, Hannah Guy, whose father went to Ireland 'to avoid the ceremonies here urged'. He claimed that 'the testimony of these two, the Mother and this Maid, of her drinking so little, and not eating at all, for so long (from 27 March till 11 June), both these being of approved faithfulness may be sufficient'. He then listed those who 'have been with this Handmaiden' in her days of fasting and illness, witnesses who were credible because 'of esteeme amongst many that fear the Lord in London'. His reason for naming so many, he said, was 'that some more incredulous, might the sooner beleeve, and reap benefit, and not reject the mysteries of God, against themselves, to their hurt (Luke 7.30)'.[22]

Scientific or medical investigation of the fasting woman became more central, and Taylor's case illustrates this,[23] especially when contrasted with the place of medical experts in Wight's case. Wight had been examined by various doctors during her long fast, but their diagnosis had covered both the physical and spiritual dimensions of her fast and illness. As Barbara Ritter Dailey has pointed out, these doctors (Thomas Coxe, Benjamin Worsley, Nathan Paget and one Dr Debote – probably either Gerald or Arnold Boate) had connections to the radical religious and political circles with which Wight herself was associated so while some of them may have demonstrated their scepticism in their questions to her, they could not dismiss the religious significance she attached to her illness, and the prophetic utterings she made in her weakened physical state.[24]

While medical and scientific interpretations of these fasting women were given increasing authority, the fasting woman's piety neverthess remained significant, so that – at least for some commentators – Taylor's piety was an important consideration, just as the piety of Wight and Trapnel had been significant some fifteen to twenty years earlier, and in a very different political and religious era. For as long as anyone attached religious significance to a fasting woman, her piety was an important test of her credibility. Fasting might be both a significant part of her cultivation of piety, and in turn her piety might prove the truth of her fasting. In *The Cry of a Stone*, Trapnel related the details of her conversion, her regular attendance at the All Hallows congregation to which she was attached and her many deeply personal conversations with God. This moment in her conversion narrative serves as a typical example of her religious practices: she 'remained silent, waiting with prayer and fasting, with many tears before the Lord' though she felt very low with 'much contention and crookedness working in my Spirit' and she asked God what was the matter and He said, 'I let thee see that thou art in thyself to keep thee humble, I am about to show thee great things and visions which thou hast been ignorant of.'[25] In other stories of fasting women which circulated, piety played a central part. For example, Rebecca Smith, a fifty-one-year-old servant of one Thomas White in Minster Lovell, near Oxford, survived without food for ten weeks, and then again for another year. When Robert Plot recorded the story in his *Natural History of Oxfordshire* in 1677, Smith was sixty years old and still very much alive. It was her great Anglican piety which led her to fast.

The varying interpretations of Taylor's fasting body led to different arguments about her faith. Reynolds, writing against those who saw Taylor's fast and survival as miraculous, maintained that she had no particular piety and that she herself made no claim that she was a miraculous maid. 'There's no cause from any antecedent sanctity to ascribe this miraculous production to miraculous causes.' Furthermore, he said in favour of his case, there were her own 'non-pretensions to any Revelations'.[26] By complete contrast, H. A. observed Taylor to be 'constant . . . either in Confessing Sin, Begging Mercy, or Praising God. She seemed to be made up of prayer when most afflicted.' His description of her prayers suggests that her weak, pious utterances led to quasi-mystical experiences:

Her voice, when at the weakest, would be spending itself upon her God, by fervent, pious Ejaculations, to hold up an heart-chearing Intercourse between Heaven and her hungering soul . . . She seemed by a sensible struggling, melting frame of Spirit, to go as it were out of her Self into an Upper Region; so that when a Rousing Prayer hath been ended, she would be puzzled to reduce her self, and compose the humane frame.

After a description of her prayer life, he went on to list her 'ordinary sayings', responses she gave to certain questions about the role of Christ in her life 'taken from her own mouth by the Hand of a Friend'. The place of suffering is central in these; in particular the suffering she experienced because of those who were sceptical about her survival without food. For example: 'The Reproaches of the World, which are many, and Crowd in upon me, do not, cannot rob me of my joy which I have in Christ Jesus, my Lord, my portion, my righteousness, my Life, my All.' For H. A., then, Taylor showed 'That spiritual comforts may be enjoyed, and Serious Holiness exercised, under great and continuous Bodily Afflictions.'[27] If we are to take the 'ordinary sayings' as Taylor's own words (rather than formulaic responses to H. A.'s questions, serving his agenda), then H. A.'s account both gives Taylor some agency and places her in the tradition of women for whom suffering, fasting and faith were deeply related, a tradition to which the mid-seventeenth-century female prophets, including Trapnel and Wight, very much belonged. Both Wight and Trapnel saw their suffering, through their fasting, as a symbol of their piety. Trapnel wrote, 'I bless the Lord, my sufferings are for righteousness sake, and I go not about to vindicate myself, but Truth.'[28] Wight's fasting body was a symbol of her suffering, her spiritual struggle.[29]

ANN MOORE OF TUTBURY

In the years following Taylor's case, various cases of fasting women were recorded, attracting a range of commentaries and interpretations. They were discussed in medical commentaries, such as that by Richard Morton, James II's physician, who attributed two cases of fasting to nervous causes and saw fasting as a symptom of consumption,[30] and they appeared in collections of wonder tales, such as Nathaniel Wanley's *The Wonders of the Little World* (1678) and William Turner's *A Compleat History of the Most Remarkable Providences* (1697), where they were seen as noteworthy prodigies, wonders of nature or religion. Thus fasting bodies continued to have a variety of meanings, according to context and interpreter, and conflicting meanings could co-exist. This was true in the case of Ann Moore of Tutbury at the beginning of the nineteenth century, though because she was ultimately revealed as a hoax, her case is seen as exemplifying 'how scientific and medical rationalism transformed the nature of abstinence cases'.[31]

A superficial narrative of Moore's story can easily be seen to exemplify the triumph of science. Certainly, the weight of scientific investigation and witnessing, as it had developed since the time of Taylor, was brought to bear on Moore's emaciated body. As Brumberg puts it in her history of fasting girls, 'By the eighteenth century, abstinence was a medical problem to be resolved by a set of predictable empirical validation techniques: around-the-clock watches, calculations of food intake, observation and measurement of excrement, and weighing of the body.'[32] In 1806, Moore apparently lost interest in food, and in 1807, her fasting first became publicly known. Her last food was, she said, a few blackcurrants on 17 July 1807, and her intake of liquids was gradually reduced in August so that eventually she drank no liquids. The first major investigation into her case was taken up by local doctors, Robert Taylor and John Allen, in September 1808. A watch was kept for sixteen days by a series of local people of the appropriate social status and thus credibility, 117 in all, whose names were published along with progress reports on Moore. At the end of that time, Moore's claim was declared valid. People were invited to come to Tutbury to see Moore for themselves, and large numbers of people did visit her over the next four years. She became something of a celebrity, known even in America, and received financial gifts from some of her visitors. During this time, Moore's fast was interpreted in a range of ways and a multitude of pamphlets about her were published, one suggesting she lived on air, another suggesting that she had a disease of the oesophagus, still others believing that a supernatural power kept her alive. But in 1813, a second watch was organised, partly in response to a sceptical discussion of the case written by a physician, Alexander Henderson. A committee was formed, consisting only of Church of England clergymen, medical doctors and magistrates (at Moore's request). After seven days it was announced to the public that Moore had lived without food for seven days. At the ninth day, at least two of the doctors present were concerned that she might not live, the watch was abandoned for a few hours, and Moore's imposture was detected when it was discovered that her daughter had been giving her liquids. The fact that Moore had survived only on liquids – remarkable in itself – was ignored, and she was declared an impostor. Legh Richmond, a prominent evangelical Church of England clergyman, who was the rector of Turvey in Bedfordshire, wrote the 'official' account of the detection of this imposture.

The various medical men and magistrates involved in the case ensured throughout that a 'number of persons highly respected in rank, talent and scientific attachments' were the investigators of the case, and witnesses in the very investigation.[33] Nevertheless, questions about Moore's character and piety were important to a range of commentators in order to prove her credibility. The author of a small cheap pamphlet about Moore's wonderful existence without food, published in 1810, wrote of her conversion to faith under the preaching of the Calvinists, and her simultaneous fasting for economic reasons: 'sooner than see her children starve, she frequently lived without food for several days together: yet she would read her Bible . . . and believed he [God] would support her, and that she felt no pain from hunger'.[34] Fasting and survival were thus seen (at least by this author) as an answer to Moore's prayer in hard economic circumstances when her husband had deserted her, and thus supported his claim that her survival had resulted from supernatural powers. This author was in part responding to attacks on Moore's character that claimed she had rather loose sexual morals. Richmond, writing the official report, used these rumours about her character to cast a sceptical interpretation of her piety, and thus her credibility.

Her former character had been very indifferent. Separated at an early period from her husband, she had lived in various places of service, in the last of which she became the mother of two illegitimate children . . . Many circumstances had excited a high degree of local prejudice against her. It is true, that during the two years preceding the first watch she began to make a religious profession, seemed to be sensible of the sinfulness of her past state, and to be sincerely anxious to obtain that forgiveness and peace of mind, which a right application of Christian principles can alone afford to a guilty conscience. A few benevolent individuals did entertain a belief of her sincerity, and hoped that extreme poverty with other afflictions of body and mind had been made instrumental, through divine mercy, to an important change in her disposition and conduct. These few friends, all of them in respectable stations of life, credited her profession on the score of abstinence, because they trusted in the hopeful appearances of a moral and religious amendment.[35]

While Moore relied on the reports of her repentance and piety to achieve credibility in the eyes of her visitors and investigators, she did not claim religious authority through or because of her fasting and survival. Another woman did this for her: the radical prophet Joanna Southcott. A Devonshire domestic servant by origin, Southcott was a visionary who in 1792 declared that she had been sent to announce the second coming of Christ. Her prophecies were made at the height of the revolutionary fervour of the 1790s and continued into the early nineteenth century, lasting until her death in 1814. She moved to London in 1802 and at her height she attracted thousands of followers. She became known in part because of the publication of her prophecies – she published some sixty-five pamphlets between 1792 and 1814 – but also because she attracted some influential supporters, including a number of Anglican clergymen. One such was the Reverend Thomas Foley, a rather flamboyant figure of considerable social status who was Rector of Old Swinford in Worcestershire. He heard about Southcott in 1801, corresponded with her, and after visiting her in London in 1802, became a follower. Foley had already been a supporter of the radical prophet Richard Brothers, whom the government had decreed a dangerous political figure in the revolutionary 1790s. J. F. C. Harrison describes Foley thus: 'It is clear that Foley had what we can by now recognise as a millenial mentality. He was always prepared to investigate a report of some unusual happening, to give credence to supernatural claims however suspect their source, and to interpret trifling events as divinely inspired.'[36] Foley visited Moore in 1809 and wrote the following account for Southcott:

Ann Moore was sitting up in her bed, and had pillows before her, which she rests upon. She appears about fifty years old, and looks well in the face, though she cannot stir the lower parts of her frame, they being dried up, and totally dead; her arms as far as her elbows, are not at all shrunk, but appear like those of a person who is thin and healthy. She seemed to be perfectly resigned to her very deplorable situation. She told me, she had lived two years and five months without food, and she had lost her appetite by degrees, before she laid aside all sustenance. Liquids, in very small quantities, she took some time after she had left off solid food: but from October 1808, she had never even wetted her mouth; and yet she had sufficient moisture in it for all the purposes of talking, and of comfort to herself – indeed, she is a living miracle.[37]

The various accounts of Moore had been interpreted by some of Southcott's followers before Foley's visit and without Southcott's direction, for she wrote that 'the believers drew various judgments from it; some thought it was the fulfilment of the vision shown to me in 1792, which is published in the third page of the warning to the world, for they thought the description of Moore was much like it; others drew their judgments, that it was not any fulfilment'.[38] In 1792, Southcott had had a dream of a woman coming out of a castle: 'The wind blew back her cloak, and I saw she was a skeleton, nothing but bones; as I saw her legs the same.'[39] The skeleton was interpreted by Southcott as a sign of God's judgement, which would bring 'The sword – the Plague, or some fatal disease like the Plague, to carry them off – and the Famine'. Southcott thus believed that nothing but such 'judgments would awaken the nation to believe in the visitation of the Lord, and be looking for the coming of Christ'.[40] Some of Southcott's followers therefore interpreted Moore as the skeleton of that 1792 vision, a presage of the judgement of the nation. However, in her direct prophecy about Moore, made after Foley's visit, Southcott declared that Moore was 'no fulfilment of the [1792] vision' but a 'sure and certain sign that the fulfilment of that vision will be seen and felt by Mankind'. In particular, Moore was:

a sure sign of the famine that will be three years, according to the words I have spoken to thee. And let them discern in what manner she hath lived these years – first, without meat, – and then without drink, – for all seemed dried up to her; and so that Nation will find, where I have pronounced the famine to appear.

Thus God spoke through Southcott : 'they will see from this woman what I have power to do'. While Moore was the shadow, 'the substance must follow before any fulfilment can be accomplished'. Thus Southcott continued: Then they may draw a clear judgment from the shadow that hath appeared in the woman, if they discern at what time that woman appeared; and what shadows of all things that I shewed thee before in dreams and visions, that hath already appeared before the ten years are up, that I mentioned to thee in 1801. And this they may discern from the wars and tumults that hath appeared abroad, and the distress at home.[41]

In fact, Southcott was remarkably accurate in her prophecies. She foretold the war with France, the bad harvests of 1794, 1795 and 1797, the effects of weather on the crops in 1799 and 1800. She predicted the death of the Bishop of Exeter and the Naval Mutiny of 1797. In Devon she had been known as a local wise woman and accurate prophet: farmers relied on her prophecies about the harvest.

By being drawn into Southcott's prophecies, Moore became a part of a radical political and religious movement that flourished in the 1790s and early nineteenth century and which had earlier origins, as the chapters in this volume illustrate. Many of Southcott's adherents had not only followed the 1790s prophet Richard Brothers but also traced their roots back to the dissenting radicalism of the seventeenth century.[42] However, Moore did not place herself in this tradition. While Wight, Trapnel and even Taylor to some extent, used their fasting to claim and express their religious authority (and for Wight and Trapnel religious authority was entwined with political authority), Moore used religion simply to demonstrate her piety in order to cultivate credibility. In this, as much as in the scientific detection of her imposture, Moore exemplifies the gendering of the modern scientific and medical paradigm. That is, she did not, for the most part, interpret herself. Female fasting bodies had always been signs, as this chapter has shown, but the seventeenth-century women gave their own meanings to the signs which were their bodies. Moore's female fasting body was interpreted by various (usually male) authoritative others, be they scientific, religious or otherwise. Historians, such as Brumberg, have focused their attention on the scientific and medical aspects of Moore's case, and have worked within the secularisation thesis, to show the shift in meanings of fasting women, from the miraculous to the anorexic. And yet Southcott's prophecies about Moore both reinforce and subvert that modern scientific paradigm. The paradigm is reinforced in that Southcott gave meaning to Moore, rather than seeking Moore's self-understanding. But the paradigm is subverted by the fact that Southcott was a *woman* interpreting Moore; moreover, she was a radical prophet who represented a popular religious movement, with radical political connections, a movement whose very existence throws into question the usual assumptions made about the increasing secularisation of English life in the eighteenth and nineteenth centuries. Furthermore, even when new medical explanations were becoming predominant in explanations of the survival of fasting women, the prophet of such a movement found religious and political meaning in a fasting woman. In the end, however, both Moore and Southcott were discredited by medical authorities. In 1813, when Moore was declared a fraud, Southcott simply declared that the Holy Spirit had revised his interpretation and declared Moore an impostor.[43] A year and half later, Southcott was herself declared an impostor. In 1814, she declared that she, a sixty-four-year-old virgin, would give birth to Shiloh, the man-child of Revelation 12:5 who would rule all the nations with a rod of iron. By November, she had still not given birth and she was becoming physically weak. On 27 December 1814, she died. Doctors performed a dissection and found she was not pregnant. Many declared her an impostor while the faithful continued to believe the birth of Shiloh to have been spiritual. Their hopes were revived in 1866 when Mabel Barltrop was born; she claimed to be the 'soul child' of Joanna Southcott, and the bride of Christ. She died in 1934, but the Panacea Society continues to this day, supporting both her and Joanna Southcott's claims.

PART II

To revolution

CHAPTER 6

John Thelwall and the Revolution of 1649

Michael Scrivener

The French Revolution controversy, according to a contemporary observer,

> revived, as it were, the royal and republican parties that had divided this nation in the last century, and that had lain dormant since the Revolution in 1688. They now returned to the charge with a rage and animosity equal to that which characterized our ancestors during the civil wars in the reign of King Charles the First; and it remained a long time in suspense, whether this renewed contest would not be attended with the same calamities; so eager were the partizans of the respective tenets contained in those performances, to assert them with unbounded vehemence.[1]

With some political vehemence, John Thelwall was a partisan of parliamentary reform and a critic of the aristocracy, its institutions and ideas. He did more than just unconsciously echo an earlier radicalism from the previous century; he consciously appropriated seventeenth-century radicalism in a variety of ways, both literary and political. Specifically, the republic of 1649 represents for Thelwall both an achievement by which to criticise subsequent political developments (the Cromwell dictatorship, the Restoration, the Glorious Revolution of 1688–9), and a historically specific failure that nevertheless suggested an ideal that could be realised in later revolutions. Whether writing about Milton or later republicans like Moyle, Thelwall uses 1649 as an organising point of reference for his thinking about republicanism, the public sphere, enlightenment and revolution.

A republican when most parliamentary reformers were not, Thelwall expressed his ardour for seventeenth-century radicalism by naming his two sons after John Hampden and Algernon Sidney, dramatically inscribing on his own progeny his enthusiasm for the earlier republicans.[2] He used the historical precedent of an English republic and the intellectual tradition of English republicanism to counter Francophobic suggestions that radicalism was foreign to English political culture. To illustrate

Thelwall's appropriation of 1649 – the most radical point of the Puritan Revolution following the regicide but before Cromwell's dictatorship – I will examine primarily his popularisation of Walter Moyle's republican tract but also several other texts. First I explore the volume of poems he wrote during his seven-month imprisonment in the Tower of London and then in Newgate awaiting his trial for treason. Next I will describe his strategic and rhetorical use of the Norman yoke myth, an aspect of seventeenth-century republicanism. Thirdly, one of his *Tribune* lectures compares and contrasts 1649 with the French Revolution in order to clarify the prospects for revolutionary change in 1795. Finally, he made his most extensive investigations of 1649 and its legacy during his lecture series of 1796–7 on classical history, designed to satisfy the letter but defy the spirit of the Two Acts prohibiting lectures on contemporary politics; his lectures relied in part on the treatise on Roman republicanism by Walter Moyle, a Commonwealthman and follower of James Harrington. Moyle (1672–1721) was no democrat, according to Caroline Robbins, for classical republicanism emphasised the aristocracy.[3] Thelwall wrote of these True Whigs that they 'stole the name from the *Scotch Sans Culottes*' and 'stood about 150 years ago so boldly and conspicuously forward in vindication of the rights of man'.[4] However, the lectures and the popular edition of Moyle that he published made radical use of Moyle to serve Jacobin rather than aristocratic ideology.

Thelwall turned to 1649 and English republicanism for a number of reasons. Milton and other examples of republican virtue (Russell, Sidney) provided Thelwall with ethical models that gave meaning to his imprisonment in 1794 and provided continuity with an English past. In contrast with the rights-based and more rationalistic arguments of fellow republicans such as Thomas Paine and William Godwin, Thelwall gained access to a constitutionalist rhetoric of ancient liberties that had been popularised in 1649. He was able to make the Puritan Revolution illustrate his ideas on revolution and enlightenment, steering his argument to the right of Thomas Spence's insurrectionist ideas and to the left of William Godwin's philosophical anarchism. The Puritan republic is also the unnamed ghost that haunts Moyle's essay on the Roman republic. Thelwall's lectures on classical history after the Two Acts complexly allegorise past and contemporary politics.

There were obstacles to Thelwall's easy assimilation of seventeenth-century radicalism. First, the Commonwealthman tradition was more elitist than Thelwall's own democratic politics, so that he had to factor out the aristocratic bias.[5] Secondly, seventeenth-century radicalism

was permeated with religious controversy, Biblical imagery and theological enquiry. Thelwall was so secular that he rarely made literary use
of Biblical material.[6] Thirdly, the very word 'Leveller' was anathema.
Thelwall made some spare references to the Levellers, but he called
Lilburne 'a virtuous and gallant patriot' who sustained the liberty of trial
by jury; in fact, Thelwall's own position is close to that of the Levellers.
According to a recent scholar, F. K. Donnelly: 'The problem faced by
radicals in the period from the 1790s through to the 1830s was that they
could not avoid the charge of Levellerism. The term had an entirely negative connotation and was extremely damaging if brought into political
discourse. Therefore, Leveller literature and precedents were not employed to any great extent, despite relatively easy access to them.'[7] To
enhance the appearance of objectivity, Thelwall cites socially conservative historians such as David Hume and Gilbert Burnet for details about
the Civil War, but he rarely quotes directly from Leveller tracts.[8] Nevertheless, despite these difficulties, seventeenth-century republicanism for
Thelwall was much more of a positive resource than a liability because it
connected secular Jacobin ideology with an *English* revolutionary republic and tradition, something that was especially useful during his lecture
tour of East Anglia, a dissenting stronghold.

PRISON POEMS

Thelwall appropriates seventeenth-century radicalism in *Poems Written
in Close Confinement in the Tower and Newgate, Under a Charge of High Treason*
(1795) at a formal level through Milton and at an ideological level through
republican stoicism. The first twelve poems are political sonnets in the
Miltonic tradition. The *form* of the sonnets is not Miltonic, but the tone
and political themes are Miltonic.[9] The motto for the entire volume is
from Milton. Thelwall deliberately omits some words from *Comus*, lines
662–5: 'Fool, do not boast: / Thou can'st not touch the freedom of
my mind, / [With all thy charms] – Altho' this corporal rind / Thou
hast immanacled [while heaven sees good].' He erases the eroticised
confrontation between Comus and the Lady, and secularises the extract
by omitting the Christian context of the Lady's spiritual resistance to
Comus's sensual temptation.

Although not directly quoted, Milton's *Samson Agonistes* and *Paradise
Lost* exert powerful modelling influences; both poems contain nu-
merous references to prison, exile and confinement. Although
Thelwall cites several times the republican martyrs, Sidney and

Russell, the republican poet is the dominant presence in the prison poems which defend against the weakness of merely personal loyalties and allay a guilt over separating from his family by justifying republican virtue.

The Miltonic and classical republican models pit patriotic virtue against family feelings. Milton's Delilah and Eve represent temptations to error that Samson and Adam cannot resist. In a 1796 essay Thelwall uses Samson for a metaphor signifying 'the manly spirit of Britain' that is threatened by the charms of Delilah.[10] Moreover, in republican culture, nothing illustrated virtue more starkly than Brutus' willingness to kill his own sons who had become traitors; Thelwall cites this topos in his second ode. The much maligned example of virtue from the second chapter of the second book of William Godwin's *Political Justice* – if only one person could be saved from a fire, one should save the more socially beneficial person like Bishop Fénelon rather than one's own family member – is another example of republican stoicism.[11] As a victim of tyranny, Thelwall figures himself as a woman, Comus's Lady, but as a virtuous republican he adopts the role of warrior. In the second part of the first ode, the 'enamour'd Youth' should resist meeting 'the Virgin's answering vows' and 'Love's endearments' until 'Patriot Virtue' has inspired heroic action against despotism.[12]

The master theme of the volume is emulation. For Thelwall's own republican emulation he has Hampden, Sidney, Russell, Brutus and Milton. In 1794, awaiting trial and possibly execution, Thelwall made literary sense of his experience by thinking through forms and examples of seventeenth-century republicans, but those models were more rigidly gendered as masculine and stoic than Thelwall ordinarily represented himself. Nevertheless, those models permitted him access to a politically inflected inwardness that was both English and traditional, repelling charges that Thelwall's radicalism was French and wilfully modern, unrelated to native British political traditions.

NORMAN YOKE MYTH

In addition to Milton's republicanism, Thelwall often utilised the myth of the Norman yoke and Saxon democracy to position his radicalism as natively British rather than imitatively French. Both in and after the 1790s he claimed Saxon democratic precedents much as seventeenth-century radicals had done, although he also argued for democracy on the grounds of rights and 'nature' rather than precedent. According to Christopher

Hill, the Levellers 'appealed to Anglo-Saxon against seventeenth-century practice' but eventually claimed 'natural rights'.[13] For Thelwall it was neither practice nor rights alone that undergirded democracy, but always both, as was typical in 1790s radicalism, although arguments based exclusively on rights were not in the radical mainstream. The Saxon precedent was very important for the seventeenth-century revolutionaries. 'Men looked to the Bible for solutions to moral and economic problems, to the Anglo-Saxons for solutions to their political problems.'[14] Sir Edward Coke, opposition leader in the House of Commons, 'believed that the common law had survived from the time of the ancient Britons, and that the Roman, Anglo-Saxon, and Norman conquests had left it virtually unchanged'.[15] According to R. B. Seaberg, whose view is somewhat different from Hill's, the Levellers saw continuity in history. The Norman invasion was not a fatal breach in tradition, as William changed the administration, but not the substance of the law.[16] Thelwall was not unique among radicals in appropriating a constitutionalist idiom in a manner similar to the Levellers because, as James Epstein calls to our attention, such an idiom was the only political language where power could be contested effectively from the 1790s through the Chartist period.[17] Political argument by precedent was not the exclusive preserve of traditionalists such as Burke.[18]

Thelwall's appropriation of the Norman yoke myth and Saxon democracy recurs pervasively throughout his political prose and poetry, early and late. Even his lyrical drama, *The Fairy of the Lake*, and his epic, *The Hope of Albion*, are informed by a radical republican antiquarianism.[19] Arthur in the former and Edwin in the latter are pre-Norman heroes who best symbolise Thelwall's ideological commitments. Milton's *History of Britain*, book 3, was one of the sources for the Arthurian material in *The Fairy of the Lake*, and book 4 was a source for *The Hope of Albion*. It is also intriguing that Milton had sketched plans for a tragedy on Vortigern, the monarch who figures prominently in Thelwall's own *The Fairy of the Lake*.[20]

In a planned speech at his treason trial that he published later as a separate pamphlet, Thelwall cites the 'Common Law' as legal precedent for the protection of political commentary and extols common law as: 'that still surviving fragment of the free and glorious Constitution of our Saxon ancestors'.[21] This is typical of his political prose. In another 1790s essay, Thelwall states that under the ancient Saxon constitution, kings were chosen; the hereditary line was established only in 1688.[22] One finds similar statements in writings of the 1790s and later. Indeed, in the essays written in *The Champion* (1818–21) and speeches he delivered in radical Westminster there are even more references to Saxon democracy. However much Thelwall used a rights-based rationalist discourse after Locke and Godwin, he refused to separate himself entirely from the constitutionalist idiom employed earlier by the Levellers.

THE FRENCH REVOLUTION AND THE PUBLIC SPHERE

Another extensive engagement with seventeenth-century radicalism appears in one of Thelwall's lectures (3 June 1795) later published in *The Tribune*.[23] He compares the English Revolution of 1649 with the French Revolution of 1792. Thelwall's defence of the French republic is largely at the expense of the earlier English Revolution. The Puritan republic and the Cromwell protectorate failed and the French republic succeeded, according to Thelwall, because of their different degrees of enlightenment. In 1649 England was not 'an enlightened nation'; rather, the Revolution was led by 'a few intelligent minds, who stimulated the people to act upon principles which they did not comprehend'.[24] Cromwell, the 'hypocritical fanatic' and 'ambitious usurper', could displace the republic because the Revolution was animated by the 'inward light' and 'the active spirit of fanaticism', rather than by the French Revolution's 'optics of reason'.[25]

Thelwall believes there is no possibility of a military dictatorship or reactionary restoration in France because the Revolution rests on such a secure foundation. He idealises the Revolution in France, ignoring the signs of Bonapartism and popular counter-revolution, while at the same time slighting the Revolution in his own country in order to defend his own political project.[26] As a secular democrat, Thelwall, wary of the religious 'enthusiasm' of the most radical forces in the Puritan Revolution, adopted the French model, according to which the middle 'orders' disseminated information to the classes below them to create a 'broad basis of public and almost universal opinion' in favour of revolution.[27] A true revolution, the French Revolution 'altered' the 'souls', 'habits' and 'modes of thinking' within the society, producing a 'universal moral revolution'.[28] Thelwall emphasises that the founding of a republic need not lead to the problems experienced during the Puritan Revolution. He concedes the weaknesses of the 1649 republic in order to save the *idea* of a democratic republic for 1795.

If a republic depends upon popular education for its security, then popular education depends upon the health of the public sphere. Thelwall defends public rationality rather than some version of 'inner light' enthusiasm. Here and elsewhere he shows an extremely optimistic opinion of the public sphere – so optimistic that reading, lecturing, debates and indeed public discourse of all kinds lead inevitably to truthful consequences. The unstable meanings of public discourse break down not into nonsense or chaos but truth. One of his favourite examples is Burke's diatribes against the French Revolution and democracy in general: 'if you wish to be a thorough democrat, read every aristocratic book that is published: Begin with *Burke's* Reflections, for I declare to you, that it was not *Tom Paine* but *Edmund Burke* that made me so zealous a reformer'.[29]

Another favourite example of his is also personal. As a young man he was an ardent royalist until his participation in the debating club turned him into a democrat.[30] In a speech at the Coachmakers' Hall he defended public discussion and free debate, at a time when the government intervened frequently to limit both.

I never knew an instance of men of any principle frequently discussing any topic, without mutually correcting some opposite errors, and drawing each other towards some common standard of opinion; different perhaps, in some degree from that which either had in the first instance conceived, and apparently more consistent with the truth. It is . . . in the silence and solitude of the closet, that long rooted prejudices are *finally renounced*, and *erroneous* opinions changed: but the materials of truth are collected in conversation and debate.[31]

In a later lecture he suggests a collaborative rationality with public discourse providing more than just the 'materials' for private reflection. Social reason within the public sphere is called an '*associated intellect*'.[32] A similar idea appears in *The Rights of Nature*, where he praises factories and workshops as 'favourable to the diffusion of knowledge, and ultimately promotive of human liberty'.[33] Thelwall's preference of 1649 to 1688, then, is ultimately based on the former's more extensive public rationality.

Even in Thelwall's later career, when he was politically more moderate, he spoke more highly of working-class culture than of middle-class *commercial* culture. The culture of the 'middling class' was the 'least *intellectually* informed'.[34] When Thelwall resumed his political activism in 1818 through the weekly newspaper *The Champion*, he discussed seventeenth-century radicalism in several ways. First, in several letters addressed to Lord Russell, he urged a political reformation of the Whigs in the spirit of Russell and Sidney, the republican martyrs. Like the Levellers,

he insisted upon the Saxon origin of the English Constitution and ascribed anti-democratic values and institutions to the Normans.[35] After
Peterloo, Thelwall criticised the Spenceans who had assumed leadership
in the reform movement, and he urged in lead articles in *The Champion*
that Whig aristocrats take a more active role in the reform movement.[36]
It is hard to tell whether he ever thought Russell, Bedford and Fitzwilliam
would champion universal suffrage and speak at open-air meetings
of labourers and artisans.[37] More likely, Thelwall was establishing
public accountability for future disorder and violence. If the Whigs
failed to promote vigorously meaningful reform – universal suffrage –
then they had no right to complain later when 'Maratists' became
powerful.

Thelwall's dispute with the Spenceans in 1818–22 is similar to
Godwin's dispute with Thelwall in 1795–6.[38] In 1795 Godwin wrote
specifically against the London Corresponding Society in general and
Thelwall in particular. Claiming that public meetings were dangerous, he
added: 'The collecting of immense multitudes of men into one assembly,
particularly when there have been no persons of eminence, distinction,
and importance in the country, that have mixed with them, and been
ready to temper their efforts, is always sufficiently alarming.'[39] (Thelwall
himself was outflanked on his left even in the 1790s by those who, like
Thomas Spence, were sympathetic to food riots and other forms of popular political intervention; Thelwall spoke and wrote consistently against
the food riots, although he did not call for their punishment and blamed
social and political injustice for causing the food shortages and high
prices.)[40] After Peterloo Thelwall makes a similar point in his leading
articles addressed to prominent Whigs, but there are differences: he defends public meetings and goads the Whigs for their 'supine' politics.
Thelwall defended the public sphere, even at the risk of the violence and
disorder he thought likely to follow if the enlightened leaders among the
privileged did not play a leading role.

The discussion of seventeenth-century radicalism in Godwin's *Political
Justice* provided a model against which Thelwall could react to refine his
own ideas. It is from Godwin that Thelwall derives the following: that
the 1688 Revolution was not bloodless because it led to two wars and
two rebellions;[41] and that the American and French Revolutions were
largely unanimous in comparison to the English Revolution that divided
the nation into 'two equal parts', as the process of popular enlightenment was complete in the former cases but incomplete in the latter.[42]
However, Godwin idealised the reforms of 1640 in a way that Thelwall

did not, mirroring rather precisely Thelwall's willingness and Godwin's unwillingness to risk revolutionary tumult.[43]

POPULARISING WALTER MOYLE'S *DEMOCRACY VINDICATED*

The popular enlightenment that made Godwin so anxious provides the foundation for Thelwall's edition of Walter Moyle's tract on classical republicanism. He published Moyle's *An Essay Upon the Constitution of the Roman Government*, provocatively retitling it *Democracy Vindicated*, supplying translations of the Latin, omitting the classical source material, and appending explanatory notes that also function as political commentary. Thelwall locates Moyle in the republican tradition of 'Machiavel, Sydney, Harrington and Bacon', the tradition of what Pocock calls civic humanism.[44] Although Pocock has delineated the lines of intellectual influence running from Machiavelli to the American creators of the Constitution, he has not focused much on the radically democratic appropriation of civic humanism by writers like Thelwall and Thomas Spence.[45]

Spence found a validating tradition for his agrarian socialism in three different sources: customary popular culture, civic humanism (especially that of Harrington) and radical dissent.[46] Thelwall's tradition is somewhat different. He also uses civic humanism, including the Harrington variety, but emphasises a particular strain of seventeenth-century republicanism identified with Milton and Sidney. He appropriates a nationalistic 'Saxon' tradition of democracy and a French Revolutionary version of classical republicanism. Thelwall evokes recurrently what we might call the missed or betrayed or incomplete revolution of the seventeenth century. Here we can see the stark differences from Burke, for whom the Restoration was a defining constitutional moment, corrected by 1688, when the 'flower of the Aristocracy' called in a Protestant monarch. The Restoration for Thelwall was catastrophic, 'the unfortunate restoration of the House of *Stuart*';[47] 1688 was only a partial correction of 1660 and it was also a betrayal of republican ideals. Cromwell was better than the Stuarts, and 1688 was better than 1660, but Thelwall's preference is unquestionably for 1649.

Thelwall borrowed from Moyle for his lectures on Roman history.[48] A copy of *Democracy Vindicated* in the British Library is annotated by Thelwall, suggesting he employed that particular text for his lectures or lecture notes.[49] Moyle himself uses the Roman republic to symbolise England. Like the other Commonwealthmen, Moyle saw Cromwell as a

usurper who had suppressed a republic. Moyle, because of possible prosecution, expressed his republicanism indirectly and in disguised ways. As
a Member of Parliament from Cornwall (1695–8) and as a London political writer, Moyle argued against crown and court power – a standing
army, for example – using an ultimately republican argument without
challenging monarchy itself. Similarly, Thelwall, prohibited from lecturing on contemporary politics by the Two Acts (1795), developed a
series of lectures on *classical* history. These lectures were barely disguised
commentaries on contemporary politics but they were within the letter
of the law. (The government-sanctioned disruptions of his lectures in
Lynn, Wisbech, Yarmouth and Derby by loyalist crowds, soldiers and
sailors in 1796–7 were proofs that Thelwall's lectures were of much more
than antiquarian interest; the government did not jail Thelwall but effectively silenced his political lecturing.) In the political context of 1796,
Moyle was a perfect choice for Thelwall. His use of Moyle was significant
not just because it aligned his efforts with an earlier republicanism but
also because it permitted political commentary. The double distancing –
Rome, Moyle – allowed a critique of the explosive issues of property and
violence.[50] Thelwall popularised the work of an aristocratic republican
author, but in the spirit of 1649, not 1688. Thelwall's bold commitment
to expanding the public sphere is in the spirit of the most radical forces
of 1649. Popularising texts was an important British Jacobin tactic in the
1790s to give artisans and others access to ideas and writing that had
been structured outside their social experience.

Among the actors of 1649 Thelwall finds most congenial with his
politics are the 'Independents'. According to Thelwall there were three
religious groups on the side of Parliament: the Presbyterians, Fanatics,
and Independents. 'Of all religious sects the Independents are the firmest
friends of political liberty', he remarks in a political lecture of 1794. While
the 'fanatics' endorsed 'Cromwell's usurpation', 'the only true republicans were the Independents and the Deists'.[51] By deists Thelwall means
probably the Commonwealthmen, many of whom rejected formal worship within a congregation. In David Hume's terminology the Fanatics
are the millenarians and antinomians, but Hume also merges Independents and Fanatics. The Levellers suppressed by Cromwell were mostly
Independents, and it is most likely Thelwall is referring to them. In contrast with Godwin, Thelwall defends indirectly his own activism and
popular politics by siding with the Levellers.

At a time when the British Jacobins were being repressed as the Levellers had been by Cromwell, Thelwall's preface to *Democracy Vindicated*

highlights the expansion of the public sphere. Using the metaphors of money and the priesthood, Thelwall argues that the 'ore' of intellectual culture has been insufficiently mined and refined; these 'treasures of literature' require publicity, as they have been until now 'shut up from vulgar use' and have had a limited 'circulation'. Who has been restricting the currency of literary culture? The 'priests of literature' have 'too frequently disposed to resist' the 'distribution of their sacred treasures'. Moreover, 'learning, like revelation, has been too generally employed to teach the few how to oppress the many, rather than to enable the many to throw off the oppression of the few'. Publishing this 'small and cheap edition' is part of the effort to throw 'open to the inspection of the multitude' the cultural treasures of literature. Unlike Godwin, ' a celebrated philosopher' who thinks that 'truth is only to be published in quartos, and discussed in the private conversations of the literati', Thelwall is committed to popularising the Enlightenment.[52] Thelwall himself could have written Moyle's defence of a republic, however unstable: 'And who is there that would not prefer a factious liberty before such a settled tyranny?'[53]

By wrenching Moyle's text out of its original context and placing it in a very different one, Thelwall creates a new text that addresses the French Revolution and the British democratic movement. Challenging the Two Acts but keeping within the parameters of legality, Thelwall in *Democracy Vindicated* uses parallel reference points: republican Rome, republican England of 1649, Moyle's own post-1689 England, Thelwall's own revolutionary Europe. Thelwall's footnotes at the bottom half of the page function both as a text unto itself and as a running commentary guiding the reading. An examination of some of the notes will reveal how skilfully the notes rewrite Moyle's text.

Thelwall's notes on Moyle's discussion of suffrage in the Roman Republic are not historical but directly political, for Thelwall insists that the people's interests can be promoted only by means of universal suffrage. Any concession to a propertied suffrage will result in the privileged representing their own interests, not the interests of everyone. Even if the recently passed Two Acts are abolished, Thelwall claims that without universal suffrage the abolition will be trivial.[54]

Moyle, holding close to one of Harrington's most characteristic ideas that property determines power relations, repeats on numerous occasions that 'land is the true centre of power, and that the balance of dominion changes with the balance of property'.[55] Moyle explicitly disputes the view of Polybius, for whom political change is due to moral determinants, which in turn alter according to the patterns of historical cycles. In one of Thelwall's most interesting notes, he disputes the views of both Polybius and Moyle. The French Revolution will give birth to a new 'sect of political theorists' who will effect 'the diffusion of political knowledge' as the source of power. 'The progress of intellect, the balance of property, and the insolence of oppression have their respective influences in the production of great revolutions. It must be confessed that when the balance of property inclines to the popular side, revolutions are less sanguinary and turbulent, than when knowledge and population have to struggle against property and power.'[56]

Thelwall reflects on the relative determinants, material and cultural, of political change. He envisions a society revolutionised by a rule of democratic reason but by un-Godwinian, popular means. According to the anti-Jacobins, the philosophers who created the Revolution were responsible for its violence. According to Thelwall, that political narrative is partially true, but 'property' and 'the insolence of power' are even more responsible for the degree of violence. In his notes on Moyle's discussion of the agrarian laws, Thelwall demystifies concentrations of property as a morally unjustifiable form of violence. The agrarian laws attempted to restore property rights that were originally egalitarian and that had been undermined by the patricians. The *people* originally gave land to the king and magistrates, so that legitimate property, according to Thelwall, rested on popular rights.[57] Several times Thelwall defends the agrarian laws as not 'levelling and plunder' but a defence of equality, the people's right to land and the illegitimacy of monopoly.[58] Thelwall's rhetoric suggests that the Roman agrarian laws apply to 1790s Europe in this regard: land is described, quite irrespective of national origins, as the 'common unappropriated gift of nature'.[59] Evoking explicitly British political conflict, he writes that the Roman agrarian laws tried to counter the patricians and their 'seizing and enclosing the common lands'.[60] In these notes on the agrarian laws that insist property was subject to criteria of justice and public rationality, Thelwall takes a position on property against possessive individualism that is closer to that of Winstanley and the Diggers than to that of the Levellers.

Moyle thought highly of Roman colonisation policies, echoing in this instance Cromwell's zealous imperialism (especially in Ireland), but Thelwall uses Moyle's praise as an opportunity to criticise British imperialism. He distinguishes between the least venal colonies (the Greek, products of surplus population) and the more venal (the Roman, which Thelwall finds less defensible than does Moyle), declaring the British colonies to be the most venal. Moyle's classical imperialism was the spread of republican institutions to new lands by a surplus population created by a thriving republic; Thelwall's modern imperialism extracts from a victim country wealth that is sent back to the mother country, which is then corrupted by it. The 'modern invention' of 'commercial colonization' Thelwall defines as: 'murdering one half of the people, and reducing the other half to bondage, that the victor may monopolize the plunder of the country'.[61] A genuine internationalist, Thelwall criticises Moyle's enthusiastic patriotism as too 'narrow'. 'The true actualizing principle of virtue is the love of the human race.'[62] Where the Puritan Revolution and republicanism failed to achieve the highest objectives of liberty, as here with imperialism, Thelwall corrects the error with a critique inspired by republican ideals.

CONCLUSION

The republic of 1649 functions in Thelwall's writing as an imperfect actualisation of liberty. Comparing the Puritan Revolution and the French Revolution in the 1795 lecture, Thelwall pays scant explicit attention to the public sphere of 1649.[63] Although he notes that '*Charles I* shut up the coffee-houses' in attempting to 'padlock the mind', he writes little about the tremendous expansion of the public sphere during the Puritan Revolution.[64] By 1795 the most egalitarian phase of the French Revolution had passed, making Thelwall anxious and defensive about revolutionary prospects; because France was more 'enlightened', Thelwall wants to think it will not succumb to a dictatorship like Cromwell's. During 1796, however, after the Two Acts and further decline in revolutionary equality in France, Thelwall turns to 1649 through Moyle and classical republicanism, employing the tactic of popularisation and allegorical, indirect political commentary. As a lecturer he upholds the public sphere with his own bodily presence threatened by loyalist violence in the East Anglia area that was strongly for Parliament in 1649. For this struggle neither republican stoicism nor the Norman yoke myth was as useful as the example of revolutionary defiance by the Levellers and Diggers.

Thelwall's appropriation of the classical republican tradition was not an attempt to appear more moderate than he actually was. Indeed, in *Sober Reflections on the Seditious and Inflammatory Letter of the Rt. Hon. Edmund Burke to a Noble Lord* (1796), Thelwall has high praise for Danton and severe criticism of the Brissot faction;[65] he even has some moderate praise for

Robespierre,[66] who in another lecture is praised at the expense of Pitt.[67] Because the most radical aspects of 1649 had been vilified for so long, Thelwall could deploy them only indirectly, not in a straightforward manner.

Classical republicanism assumed a propertied franchise, and the conflicts within the Puritan Revolution that finally were resolved by Cromwell's protectorate were fought over political representation. Accordingly, Thelwall argues that an unrestricted public sphere linked with universal suffrage, annual parliaments and rotation of officers will produce the institutional structures of non-repressive representation. Although direct democracy is possible only in a small society, a representative democracy is no less democratic: 'the whole body of the people may convey their will to the heart and centre of the government, and by means of representatives and properly appointed officers, conduct the business of the country according to the general voice of the people'.[68] Thelwall remedies what he saw as the weaknesses of 1649 with more democratic political structures and a stronger public sphere to promote popular enlightenment. Moreover, one finds in his comments on the agrarian laws a position on property that is reminiscent of the Diggers, whose egalitarianism was more thorough than the Levellers'. The republic of 1649, however imperfect, was an achievement upon which to build a durable actualisation of liberty and equality in Britain and elsewhere; it was not, as it was for the dominant political culture, a sign of 'disorder' that proved the inevitable evils of democracy and the necessity of authoritarian rule.

CHAPTER 7

Women's private reading and political action, 1649–1838

Charlotte Sussman

In 1654, the Fifth Monarchist Anna Trapnel fell into a trance while attending Vavasor Powell's sedition trial. Refusing almost all food and drink for over a week, she criticised Oliver Cromwell's government and commented on England's general condition. The writers who transcribed and framed her prophesies, however, indicate that despite her disruptive activities, Trapnel respects at least one form of authority. Unlike some Quakers and Ranters, she holds the Bible 'in very high regard' and remains 'exceedingly confirmed in her persuasions of, and love of, the truth, holiness, authority and precious usefulness of the Scriptures'.[1]

In a rare moment acknowledging the strangeness of her behavior, Trapnel herself invokes her experience of reading Scripture to legitimate her words. She says of her condition:

They will say the spirit of madness or distraction is upon her, and that it is immodesty; but thou knowest Lord that it is thy Spirit; for thou hast cast thy servant where she would not, and hast taken her contrary to all her thoughts . . . let them know that it is too, by the language of it, by the Rule through which it comes: How is the written word carried forth in it! thy Spirit takes the Scripture all along, and sets the soul a swimming therein.[2]

Trapnel describes a revelation that is also an experience of 'the written word'. This unconventional account of the effects of reading nonetheless provides an intriguing delineation of them. Reading, here an immersion in Scripture, results in congruence between Trapnel's own language and sacred language; her spoken words merely 'carry forth' the 'written word'. Her own agency is almost submerged – 'swimming' in the sacred text, she is 'taken contrary to all her thoughts'.[3] At the same time, however, the mental space of the reader expands into a vast and varied landscape, lending a dynamism to this encounter between reading subject and printed artefact. Reading thus becomes both active and passive, both a private experience and a publicly visible set of effects (in Trapnel's case, the acts of fasting and prophesying, as Jane Shaw discusses). Ventriloquising the possible criticism of observers, Trapnel further specifies this as the experience of a female reader. Her behaviour can be interpreted as departing from feminine modesty, but she pre-emptively refutes such accusations by insisting on her own passivity; her reliance on the Scriptural language provided by reading works to legitimate her right to criticise the existing government.[4] For a female reader, then, proper articulation of the simultaneously passive and active, public and private experience of reading bears directly on both her gendered identity and her right to political agency.

This chapter traces a history of the way certain modes of reading affected the representation and practice of women's political agency during the long eighteenth century, an agency understood as the capacity to comment upon and intervene in the socio-political changes of the period. Dealing with the intersection of print culture and politics, the chapter also considers the impact developing concepts of 'public' and 'private' spheres might have had on women's reading. Many historians have commented on the way women's engagement with print culture began to be relegated to the private sphere, as female reading became associated with the consumption of novels and other fictions; here, I am interested in exploring the degree to which the privacy of women's reading precluded their engagement with politics. Through this examination of female engagement with the political, the chapter also tackles the disposition of the female body as definitions of 'the private' changed during this time. That is, it treats reading as having a culturally significant physical or performative element, and assumes that regulating the female body affected women's political agency. Since it covers such a lengthy span of time, the chapter makes a number of historical generalisations that beg to be substantiated (or disproved) by more in-depth studies of particular readers and reading communities; it is worth looking at the big picture, however, to get a sense of the changing definitions of terms such as 'private' and 'political' over the long term.[5]

In mid-seventeenth-century England the social structure that has been called the public sphere began to emerge. Matters previously considered the exclusive domain of governmental or royal authority were entered into public debate, along with questions previously thought to be of private economic interest only. Such issues became available for discussion among an expanding, though still circumscribed, number of rational interlocutors. Although many discussions took place face to face, the growth of the public sphere was largely facilitated by the development and spread of print technology and printed materials. Much of this technology had existed since the late sixteenth century, along with vernacular translations of the Bible, but the breakdown of government censorship during the Civil Wars allowed many more people access to print culture. Participants in the public sphere were, almost by definition, readers – of newspapers, pamphlets and other materials. Around the same time, the area of social relations we now think of as the 'private' or 'domestic' sphere began to be more sharply defined. A shelter from the vagaries of business, politics and labour, such privacy was supposed to foster individual moral and emotional life, along with greater leisure time, particularly for middle-class women. This domain was also inhabited by readers – devotees of the new genres of 'secret histories', novels and the poetry of domestic life.[6]

These distinctions are broad enough to invite contradiction by individual experience, but they still raise these questions: how does the activity of reading straddle the public–private divide? And what are the ramifications of its simultaneously public and private nature? To some degree the answer depends upon what material is read and where it is read. In historical retrospect, we characterise reading a newspaper in a coffee house as a public act, and reading a narrative like Eliza Haywood's 'Fantomina' at home as a private one. Yet there are several ways in which the most exposed act of reading might still be considered private. One, which perhaps we now take for granted, has to do with the reading body's disposition, which during this period usually gave few physical signs of the intellectual process going on within. After the Middle Ages, such silent reading had replaced 'a tradition of one and a half millennia' in which 'the sounding pages [were] echoed by the resonance of the moving lips and tongue'.[7] Furthermore, reading, even about public matters in public places, also might be considered private when the text triggered personal interpretations, a problem that particularly bedeviled the triumphant counter-revolutionary forces of the later seventeenth and early eighteenth centuries. John Dryden, for example, saw the Interregnum as a time when 'the book' was 'put in every vulgar hand, / Which each presumed he best could understand'; he, like many others, worried that no form of social or governmental discipline could prevail over that silent space inside the reader's mind.[8]

Gradually, this sense of the privacy of the public reader was joined to a standard of physical decorum. This is particularly clear in the case of the coffee house, one of the main sites of public reading during the period. As Peter Stallybrass and Allon White point out: 'The coffee-house . . . combined democratic aspirations with a space of discourse less contaminated by the unruly demands of the body for pleasure and release than that of the tavern . . . Intoxication, rhythmic and unpredictable movements, sexual reference and symbolism, singing and chanting, bodily pleasures and 'fooling around', all these were prohibited in the coffee-house.'[9] For the silent reader in these spaces, the text does not translate 'directly into bodily movements and [pattern] nerve impulses'.[10] Rather, as Dorinda Outram has remarked about the ideal member of the public sphere during the French Revolution: 'he possess[ed] a body which was also a non-body, which, rather than projecting itself, retained itself', privileging 'the language of objectivity and rationality, rather than . . . energy or displays of integration between body and personality'.[11] It was precisely the lack of this kind of discipline that characterised the Interregnum as a less developed, chaotic form of publicity for Dryden, who decried the way 'the tender page with horny fists was galled, / and he was gifted most that loudest bawled'. For Dryden and similar thinkers, proper public discussion developed only when private interpretations stopped manifesting themselves on the body, when physical, as well as political, unruliness was curbed.

At the same time, the readerly experiences that seemed the most private and personal had their public elements. As Ian Watt long ago remarked about novel reading, 'it is paradoxical that the most powerful vicarious identification of readers with the feelings of fictional characters should have been produced by exploiting the qualities of print, the most impersonal, objective and public of the media of communication'.[12] The novel reader feels uniquely and powerfully connected to texts that were equally available to any number of other readers. In this way, the private reading of fiction resembles Benedict Anderson's account of newspaper reading: '[it] is performed in silent privacy, in the lair of the skull. Yet each communicant is well aware that the ceremony he performs is being replicated simultaneously by thousands (or millions) of others of whose existence he is confident, yet of whose identity he has not the slightest notion.'[13] This paradoxical joining of a sense of public knowledge and shared understanding with the right to individual, private interpretation characterises the experience of reading, and of print culture more generally, during the long eighteenth century.

The case of female reading, like Trapnel's, was, of course, more complicated, and many of its difficulties pre-date the Interregnum. A tradition stretching back at least to Dante's Paolo and Francesca saw women as more susceptible to the dangers of reading than men. Those dangers included the tendency to allow texts to mark themselves on the body, and for that body to become unruly, immodest or overly public. As early as 1543, Parliament restricted access to the Bible according to class and gender. Women from the nobility and gentry were allowed to read the Bible privately (that is, alone or silently) while women from the merchant and lower classes were forbidden even this; only men of the nobility and gentry could read Scripture aloud to their families and households.[14] This law implies that an idea of female decorum connecting improper reading to improper female speech was already in place by the mid-sixteenth century. But it also reminds us that during this period the household – a social entity incorporating the family within it – was not considered the private sphere; the idea that domestic space was private space developed only gradually.[15]

During the next century, ideas about the susceptibility of female readers proliferated. In 1645, for example, Samuel Torshell urged women, in *The Womans Glorie*: 'Away with your Tragedies and Comedies and Masques and Pastorals, & whatsoever other names they have, that soften the spirit, and take away your savour of heavenly matters . . . We are so easily fashioned into what we read much, and with delight, as our bodies take the qualities of such meat as we ordinarily feed upon.'[16] The female mind here becomes as malleable as the body – as liable to be shaped by outside forces. This idea persisted through the seventeenth and eighteenth centuries and well into the nineteenth.[17] The *Ladies' Magazine* of 1812, for example, warns that 'Books, merely entertaining, produce the same effect upon the mental faculties, which a luxurious diet does upon the corporeal frame: they render it incapable of relishing those pure instructive writings, which possess all the intrinsic qualities of wholesome, unseasoned food.'[18] The close connections between nourishing the mind and nourishing the body suggest, through a kind of analogy, that the badly fed mind would lead the body into improper actions. Many suspected that reading about transgressive sexual behaviour would lead young women to try it out for themselves. The second half of the eighteenth century, in particular, produced a number of representations of female readers whose 'powerful, vicarious identifications with texts' perverted their public behaviour, including Charlotte Lennox's Arabella (a 'female quixote'), Sheridan's Lydia Languish and Jane Austen's Catherine Morland. This ongoing cultural concern for the wayward body of the female reader links the fiction lovers of the eighteenth century with the female prophets of the seventeenth, at least in the rhetoric of their censors.

Where, then, did female reading fall along the public–private divide? The anxiety generated by women's potential to be overly performative readers implies that women were not thought capable of the decorum demanded of readers in the public sphere. This, certainly, is one of the factors that gendered the public sphere male by the late eighteenth century, if not earlier. Yet there are at least two ways of understanding the privacy of female reading, keeping in mind John Brewer's advice to regard 'the line between the public and private as a matter of spatial and political perspective and as a matter for persistent adjustment and dispute'.[19] For writers of Trapnel's time, privacy seems to mean interiority, a mental space for reading imagined as a site for the individual actions of the spirit. Although dissenting women did much of their reading in groups, their representations of the experience tend to focus on the articulation of interior states.[20] For later writers, however, female reading, both sacred and secular, involves the seclusion of the female body in the private space of the home. Indeed, for these women, the private 'lair of the skull' is potentially as treacherous for women as public debate; the ideal mode of reading is aloud among domestic groups.[21] Between the mid-seventeenth and the early nineteenth centuries, a significant shift in the understanding of privacy took place, with important implications for representations of women's political agency.

Most of the controversy surrounding women's reading focused on the ill effects of secular texts; yet from the Reformation on, female reading of sacred texts also raised questions about women's virtue, agency and their place in public debate. Citing the case of Anne Askew, Diane Willen observes that although even aristocratic and gentry women were rarely taught to write, reading the Bible often led to public activism.[22] Indeed, during the conflicts of the mid-seventeenth century, women's religious reading was often more closely connected to political issues than were the secular texts that generated so much censure. The ability to read the English Bible without clerical intervention underpinned many protests of social, legal and academic institutions during the Interregnum. Mary Pope, for instance, wrote in 1647: 'it may be that some will say, that . . . my writings are non-sense[.] But to such I answer, if they would study the scripture as I do, they shall find them very good sense.'[23] Often, however, this kind of political agency was gained through a paradoxical renunciation of will. When female prophets like Trapnel made their private study of Scripture public, they sometimes exploited the cultural perception of the malleability of the female body and mind. The prophet Sarah Wight, for example, believed that 'a Christian's true happiness lies in being emptied of all self, self refined, as well as gross self; and being filled with a full God'.[24] Using the already conventional analogy between text and food to bolster her authority, Anna Trapnel tells her readers (in verse this time) that God urges them to 'look into the written word / and there drink you of me, / for I am flagons of Wine, and / You shall partake of me'.[25] One can see how Trapnel constructed a stance of religio-political authority out of a feminised readerly passivity.

This submersion of the reader in the text was not simply an interior process, but often resulted in physical demonstrations of belief. Trapnel herself lay immobile and fasting in public sight for many days. The relegation of female reading to a private domestic sphere is not firmly in place, partly because both the privacy of the household and the decorum of the public body are still under construction. The idea that a rational interlocutor should publicly embody rational restraint was only sporadically enforced during the Interregnum. Yet, though Trapnel escaped immediate legal or extra-legal punishment for her actions, many Quaker women were chastised for their attempts to publicise their own interpretations of God's word.[26] Of the 360 Quakers punished for disrupting ministers between 1654 and 1659, 34 per cent were women.[27] As Rosemary Kegl points out, many of these women were treated as if they had violated the corporeal codes of gendered behaviour. The preachers Dorothy Waugh and Anne Robinson, for example, were led along the thoroughfare of Carlisle with iron bridles.[28] The fact that bridles were traditionally used on scolds suggests that these women were being punished both for the impropriety of their reprimand to the community, and the publicity and immodesty of their female bodies. Women's desire to bring personal religious beliefs to bear on public activities was interdicted by a sense of the impropriety of public speech.

Many of the indecorous connotations of such behaviour arose from the connections which some early Quakers forged between the reading body and the scriptural text. These resulted in the practice of acting out 'signs' in public. Elizabeth Adams, for example, 'stood in front of the houses of Parliament for two days with a vessel on her head; she then overturned it, as many things were turned, and aturning, sat down on it, and finally smashed it'.[29] As Nigel Smith points out, in early

Quaker protest 'body and language were inextricably linked as the sites
in which the workings of the inner light were known'.[30] By and large,
however, men participated in this behaviour more often than women.[31]
Its most notorious practitioner was a man: James Nayler. Nayler was
a prominent Friend from Wakefield, with a number of devoted female
followers.[32] On 24 October 1656, in what seemed the apogee of the
physical performance of scriptural truth, Nayler rode into Bristol on a
horse, re-enacting Jesus's entry into Jerusalem. He was surrounded by
his followers, including three women and three men, who sang 'holy,
holy, holy, Lord God of Israel', and scattered garments before him.
George Fox and the rest of the Quaker leadership repudiated Nayler:
he was tried before Parliament, publicly whipped, branded with a B
for blasphemy and had a hole bored through his tongue. Yet, as Leo
Damrosch has argued, Nayler's performance was a plausible interpretation of certain Quaker doctrines about the relation of Scripture to
the living reader, motivated by the belief that typology 'operates, as it
were, forward, rather than backward: the point is not so much that our
experience recapitulates events of the Bible as that reading the Bible
helps explain what the Spirit is enacting here and now'.[33] Nayler's en-
trance into Bristol was an experiment in connecting private reading to
public performance. And it seemed to mark a limit case of indecorous
interpretation.

Both contemporary and later historians associated Nayler's fall into
performance with the influence of 'extravagant', 'fanatical' and 'unbalanced' women – 'simple-minded literalists' who believed that Nayler
was Christ.[34] Some of his followers did indeed make a habit of disrup-
tively conjoining interpretation and performance; Martha Simmonds,
for example, used Bible reading to subvert what were becoming the conventional forms of Quaker worship. Even after Nayler's trial, Simmonds
caused chaos at one meeting by reading a chapter of Ezekiel over the
protests of Richard Hubberthorne: 'the lord has sent that chapter to be
read unto us', she declared. Phyllis Mack argues that the Nayler episode
was used to prove 'what many had suspected all along: the unsuitability of
the female for positions of public authority . . . the leaders' extreme reactions to Simmonds . . . show how quickly their own adoration of women
as vessels of God could reverse itself into virtual terror of women's diabolical energy'.[35] The controversy it provoked led to the establishment
of separate women's meetings, and the re-channelling of female energies
into 'the safer (and more feminine) waters of poor relief and oversight
of their own sex'.[36] Even before the Restoration, then, the legitimacy of

women's public performances of private interpretations of the Bible was growing more restricted.

There has been a tendency to see the period immediately following the Restoration, when laws were enforced denying the right of dissenting congregations publicly to meet for worship, as the moment when the relegation of female reading to the private sphere decisively led to women's exclusion from political debate.[37] In fact, struggles over women's public religio-political actions continued into the early eighteenth century. Many women protested the loss of public religious expression, either by continuing to act out signs, or by keeping public meetings going after their male co-religionists had been jailed. In 1671, the Quaker Margaret Whithart made an eloquent defence of publicity: 'We do not meet here in wilfulness or stubbornness, God is our witness, but we cannot run into corners to meet as some do, but must bear our testimony publicly in this thing, whatever we suffer.'[38] Such episodes illustrate, as Paula McDowell has recently argued, that women's interventions were crucial in the struggles over proper behaviour in the public sphere.[39] But such activities represented a residual form of publicity and were actively suppressed. Thus for many dissenting men and women, religious practice became, by necessity, a private affair, more than ever dependent on the written word. Although Quaker women like Katherine Evans and Sarah Chevers continued to travel and write, and Margaret Fell Fox argued for women's right to speak in church, the Clarendon Code forced many dissenting women underground, into clandestine communities of readers. Those sects that did survive were enabled by the particular kinds of privacy associated with print culture. As N. H. Keeble has shown, Nonconformists used printed sermons, letters and other texts not only to maintain their own communities, but also to argue against the laws that had forced them into seclusion; they used print 'to refute the government's presentation of them as seditious rebels and Episcopalian caricatures of them as hypocritical dissemblers'.[40]

Women took an active part in these new strategies for political intervention. The Quaker Rebecca Travers, protesting the Clarendon Code in 1663, invites her political adversaries to debate:

Hear a little, though you be mighty, and be entreated to weigh with seriousness, what one fearing the Lord says unto you, who are executing the Act made against such as meet to worship contrary to the Liturgy of the Church of England, which we have heard to be according to the Scriptures, for and in the Scriptures we have been trained up many of us from our childhood, and exercised therein.[41]

Like earlier women writers, Travers stakes her authority on her personal
knowledge of the Scriptures. In contrast to a prophet like Trapnel, however, she does not transmute that knowledge into extravagant physical
display, although she demands the right to public worship. Rather, she
calls for a contest of textual interpretation – a battle that can be carried
out in print, without personal, oral confrontation. Ann Docwra, another
Quaker, also seems to rely on the reader's ability to reflect in private
when she writes 'An Epistle of Love and Good Advice' in 1683. She
concludes her defence of Nonconformity: 'I shall leave you to search
the Scripture to see if these things be not true; for this is written in true
love to all, but most especially to awaken those that are asleep in their
mistaken Judgement and led away by the dreaming conceits of Imagination.' A veteran of Restoration religious controversy, Docwra 'came
to believe that the new public forum of print was in fact the safest place
to do battle with one's enemies'.[42] In this passage, she withdraws even
farther from the tumult of public debate, asking the reader to engage in
private, intellectual reflection.

Even after the Clarendon Code was overturned, the sense remained
that religious reading was a private, introspective matter, for Anglican
as well as dissenting women. During the early eighteenth century the
inward-looking, semi-mystical poetry of the dissenter Elizabeth Rowe
(1674–1737) became a much-admired model of female religiosity. Rowe's
poetry typically represents spiritual experience in terms of a kind of
ecstatic, pastoral solitude. In her poem 'To Mr Watts, on his Poems
Sacred to Devotion' (1709) she describes her reading in this way:

> Seraphic heights I seem to gain,
>   And sacred transports feel;
> While, WATTS, to thy celestial strain
>   Surpriz'd I listen still.
>
> The gliding streams their course forbear,
>   When I thy lays repeat;
> The bending forest lends an ear,
>   The birds their notes forget.[43]

We can see the value accrued by such private, even isolated, religious expression in 'On the Death of Mrs [Elizabeth] Rowe' (1737), written by a
slightly later exemplar of proper piety, the Bluestocking Elizabeth Carter:

> Long did romance o'er female wits prevail,
> Th' intriguing novel and the wanton tale.
> What different subjects on thy pages shine!

How chaste the style, how generous the design!
Thy better purpose was, with lenient art,
To charm the fancy and amend the heart;
From trifling follies to withdraw the mind,
To relish pleasures of a nobler kind.
No lawless freedoms e'er profane thy lays,
To virtue sacred and thy maker's praise.[44]

Carter here praises the way both the style and content of Rowe's religious writing embody the values of the private sphere; Rowe's verse encourages virtue, chastity and withdrawal from 'lawless freedoms'. Although Carter's poem seems more concerned with women's predilection for sexual transgression than political action, it nonetheless warns against the wrong kind of publicity. Female writers like Rowe properly enter the public sphere of print through the codes of domestic virtue.

The privacy of women's religious practice grew in importance throughout the eighteenth century. In his study of the late eighteenth-century reader Anna Larpent, John Brewer notes that however devout and energetic a reader of religious texts she was, she tended to keep her thoughts about those texts to herself, rarely recording them even in her diary; 'it was not a subject for polite conversation, like so much other material, but an act of personal devotion'.[45] In this practice, Larpent followed the social conventions of the day. Women were advised to avoid controversy in their religious reading. In her popular conduct book, *Letters on the Improvement of the Mind* (1776), Hester Chapone tells the young female reader:

Though religion is the most important of all your pursuits, there are not many *books* on the subject, which I would recommend to you at present. – Controversy is wholly improper at your age, and it is also too soon for you to enquire into the evidence of the truth of revelation, or to study the difficult parts of scripture – when that shall come before you, there are many excellent books from which you may receive great assistance.[46]

This passage reveals a clear contrast between what an eighteenth-century bourgeois conservative like Chapone expected from women's religious reading, and the hopes of seventeenth-century radicals like Trapnel or Travers. Young women should avoid not only controversy, but also difficult interpretation. Even mature women, this passage implies, need assistance in deciphering the truth of Scripture. Yet we should also note the legacy writers like Chapone inherited from seventeenth-century upheavals: the assumption that women's private reading of the English Bible is an acceptable occupation. By the late eighteenth century, this idea was shared by a broad spectrum of religious believers. In 1772, for example, Elizabeth Carter gave this advice to a troubled female correspondent about the statements of religious sceptics: '[T]hey are certainly entitled to no further regard than as they agree with the declarations of Scripture; and how far they do so, a diligent, religious and modest enquirer will easily be able to determine, so as not to be led into any fatal error.'[47] John Wesley, too, directed the female seeker of religious truth to the Bible. In a 'Female Course of Study' (1790), he advises women that 'everything one can know of God is to be found in the Bible', and it would be wise to spend 'at least two hours every day, in reading and meditating upon it'.[48]

Simultaneously, the conception of privacy seems to have altered somewhat by this period; privacy for Chapone means something taking place inside the home, rather than inside the reader's head. This shift coincided with increased cultural attention to the boundaries between the public and private spheres. And it is perhaps for this reason that during the mid-eighteenth century, representations of the folly of women turning private reading into public action began to proliferate, in regard to both sacred and secular texts. Chapone, for example, warns women away from sentimental novels:

both the writing and sentiments of novels and romances are such as are only proper to vitiate your stile [*sic*], and to mislead your heart and understanding. – the expectation of extraordinary adventures – which seldom ever happen to the sober and prudent part of mankind – and the admiration of extravagant passion and absurd conduct, are some of the usual fruits of this kind of reading.[49]

Clearly, what worries Chapone here is not simply the 'admiration' of indecorous emotions and behaviour, but 'the expectation' of 'extraordinary adventures'. The behaviour involved in such adventures would certainly be less than sober and prudent. She fears that private, emotionally engaging reading will lead to public absurdity.

Such corporeal emotionality could be sanctioned, however, if it were kept private. For example, when Samuel Richardson's respected correspondent Lady Bradshaigh reports her reading of *Clarissa* to him, she seems almost to revel in the physical effects of her reading. 'When alone in Agonies would I lay down the book, take it up again, walk about the Room, let fall a Flood of Tears, wipe my Eyes, read again, perhaps not three Lines, throw away the book crying out Excuse me good Mr Richardson, I cannot go on.'[50] Tears, actions and speech all seem legitimate responses to reading, but only when 'alone'. Although Lady Bradshaigh's emotionality seems self-indulgent, even histrionic,

Richardson, at least, regarded it as virtuous and Christian. Indeed, it differs only in degree from the response Chapone herself demands from female readers of the Bible. Describing the experience of reading of Jesus' death, she says:

what can I say, that can add anything to the sensations you must then feel? – No power of language can make the scene more touching, than it appears in the plain and simple narrations of the evangelists. – The heart that is unmoved by it, can be scarcely human: – but, my dear, the emotions of tenderness and compunction, which almost everyone feels in reading this account, will be of no avail, unless applied to the true end; – unless applied to the true and warm affection towards your blessed Lord – with a firm resolution to obey his commands [.][51]

Chapone expects women's reading of Scripture to be as powerful as do early Quaker writers. Yet the direction and quality of that emotionality has changed. The reaction is universalised – it is what 'everyone', all 'humans', feel. And it is channelled, ideally, into individual obedience, rather than public protest, into personal morality, rather than political intervention.

A similar concern with the connection between female reading and public action appears around the same time in the Methodist movement. During the 1760s and 1770s, responding to negative public reaction, John Wesley became more concerned with curtailing the activities of women preachers, many of whom had been very active in the early years of the movement. He enforced a distinction between prayer and preaching defined as the interpretation of Scriptural passages. In a letter of 1769, Wesley explains how a female follower should behave:

I advise you, as I did Grace Walton formerly, (1) Pray in private or public as much as you can. (2) Even in public prayer you may properly enough intermix *short exhortations* with prayer; but keep as far from what is called preaching as you can: therefore, never take a text; never speak in a continued discourse without some break, about four or five minutes. Tell the people, 'We shall have another *prayer-meeting* at such a time and place.'[52]

Although he still allows that some kinds of publicity may be appropriate, Wesley adjudicates the forms that female reading of Scripture can take. Methodist women were allowed to lead small groups of other women in prayer, reading and personal testimony in 'bands' and 'classes', but they were not allowed publicly to interpret what they had read. In 1802, ten years after Wesley's death, the Methodist Connexion formally excluded any women who continued to preach in this fashion. As Christine Krueger comments, this put female readers in a difficult position.

Allowed to quote, but not to interpret, these women, like the prophets of the seventeenth century, 'had to emphasize their spiritual gift at the expense of their own talents, characterizing themselves as passive mediums rather than self-conscious polemicists'.[53]

Such attempts to constrain women's religious reading seem to squeeze out the possibility of political action. Women's political activities were certainly circumscribed during the period – they were not able to vote, sign petitions, or even own property after marriage. But I would argue that it is a mistake to conflate their privacy with a denial of political agency. Although the rhetoric of separate spheres proliferated, the same period saw a burgeoning of women's philanthropical activities. If the late eighteenth and early nineteenth centuries evidenced an increasing sensitivity to female immodesty, the period also witnessed a pronounced rise in the level of organised female intervention into cultural affairs. In retrospect, these activities often look quite 'public'. Lawrence Klein declares: 'even when theory was against them, women in the eighteenth century had public dimensions to their lives. Moreover, engaging in those public practices involved a consciousness that they were behaving publicly and that their behavior implied its own sanction.'[54] The rhetoric of separate spheres was a double-edged sword – used by some to caution women against public behaviour, and by others to legitimate it.

We can see the way women used 'private' religious and moral beliefs to influence 'public' affairs in one example from the early nineteenth century. Among other ventures, religious women's longtime involvement in the anti-slavery movement led them to form their own philanthropical associations to focus on this issue; 'in 1825, three women's anti-slavery societies were formed, at Birmingham, Sheffield and at Calne in Wiltshire: by the end of the decade there were forty others'.[55] Such associations were composed primarily of middle-class religious women and 'evolved out of their already accepted roles in religious philanthropy and the religious societies aimed at the expansion of evangelical Christianity'.[56] These activities usually took place in the domestic sphere; 'in most [philanthropic groups], women worked only with women. If they addressed mixed-sex meetings, they did not speak in public but at "drawing room" or "parlour" meetings of invited guests.'[57]

Even these activities sometimes seemed too openly political for their male colleagues. Wilberforce once told Thomas Babington Macaulay that 'all private exertions for such an object become their character, but for ladies to meet, to publish, to go from house to house stirring up petitions – these appear to me proceedings unsuited to the female character as delineated in Scripture. I fear its tendency would be to mix them in all the multiform warfare of political life.'[58] Interestingly, Wilberforce does not question women's ability to inform themselves, meet in each others' houses, or influence those close to them. Their right to participate in public questions such as slavery as private readers seems incontrovertible. What bothers him is women's physical participation in politics – going door-to-door, attending meetings, even publishing seems too public, too exposed. Thus, he emphasises two crucial limitations for women's involvement in the public sphere during this period: that they are welcome as readers, but not as political polemicists; and that the proper positioning of their bodies is vital to any legitimate intervention.

Yet were the lines between suitable public and private behaviour for women really as clearly drawn as Wilberforce asserts here? Wilberforce's 'broadcasting of the language of separate spheres', might be read, according to Amanda Vickery, as a 'conservative response to the opportunities, ambitions and experiences of late Georgian and Victorian women'.[59] The ability of female abolitionists to defeat 'the opposition with its own weapons' emerges in the following exchange from an abolitionist pamphlet entitled 'A Dialogue between a Well-Wisher and a Friend to the Slaves in the British Colonies, by a Lady'.[60]

B: But I really think women ought not to interfere in this business, on account of its being a political question: for women have nothing to do with such subjects; they are quite out of their province, and I think it is not consistent with propriety and hardly with feminine modesty, that they should put themselves forward on this occasion.
A: I own I have never been able to affix any clear meaning to the expression you have just used, and which I have often heard before, that this is a political question. It appears to me to be peculiarly a religious and moral question.[61]

In order for anti-slavery feelings to conform with 'propriety' and 'feminine modesty', they had to be coded as religious or moral – that is, during this period, part of private life. Private concerns are construed here in terms that allow them to bear upon political questions, those formerly thought to be confined to parliamentary debate. Women thus laid claim to an agency in the world outside the home that had more to do with the cultural force of private domestic practices than with public, and thus overly physical, action.

If women's rôle in the political arena was to influence the men around them, one of the primary methods of influence they used was the dissemination of texts and the modelling of reading practices. In 1828, the

Dublin Ladies' Anti-Slavery Society noted in its 'Rules and Resolutions' that 'the primary objects of the Ladies of the society be, to procure and to circulate universally, throughout Ireland, copies of all such documents, as show the great evils of slavery'.[62] The dissemination of information 'through the medium' of these items informed the public of these women's ethical and political views about slavery, without involving them in public speaking or petition signing. The language of this passage, representative of most such appeals, highlights the rôle of women as transmitters of neutral information, rather than as creators or shapers of a pointed political message; the group 'introduces information', and 'awakens attention', rather than emphasising their own abilities as writers or rhetoricians. Thus these women negotiate late eighteenth-century ideas about gender and class that asserted that middle-class white women should be consumers rather than producers – exemplifying rather than sculpting emotion. They also reinforce those beliefs by emphasising the natural quality of female compassion, which only needs to be awakened, rather than fostered or produced.

For these reasons, reading, rather than writing, figures as the primary political activity of ladies' anti-slavery societies. It assumed such importance among these groups, that, in 1837, the Sheffield Association for the Universal Abolition of Slavery could declare, in its *Appeal to the Christian Women of Sheffield* that:

We place reading before praying, not because we regard it as more important, but because, in order to pray aright, we must understand what we are praying for; it is only then we can pray with the *understanding* and with the *spirit* also. We lay great stress upon reading – torturing to the feelings, as the dreadful evils produced by slavery must often prove; – for when you read these accounts you cannot help making them known to others; and the great thing wanted is, that the real nature of the system should become *known*; – it would then seem impossible that its continuance should be longer endured.[63]

This statement makes a number of interesting connections between reading and political action. It assumes that once readers gain knowledge of the 'real nature' of slavery through anti-slavery texts, they will no longer be able to 'endure' its existence, and presumably will be compelled to further agitation against it – or at least to prayer. Furthermore, it claims that such knowledge cannot remain personal – 'when you read these accounts you cannot help making them known to others'. Textual dissemination is characterised as the key to the growth of abolitionist consensus in Britain. The writers also make assumptions about the activity of reading itself. Reading produces an 'understanding' of slavery despite the fact that the details of 'the dreadful evils produced by slavery' often prove 'torturing to the feelings'. For them, the sympathetic pain produced by textual representations of suffering is indissociable from, even necessary to, an understanding of slavery.

Although it places reading before praying, the passage nonetheless emphasises the relationship between the two activities. Prayer, and the spiritual response to political injustice, take place in private, inside the home. The female body is engaged, not as a means of bringing conviction into public view, as seventeenth-century religious radicals might have done, but as a sentimental register of affect, of the pain of feeling. In its emphasis on 'understanding', however, the passage combines the rational, educational attitude towards reading and religion we saw in Chapone, with a sense of the political agency enabled by religiously informed reading more reminiscent of the seventeenth-century radicals. The sentimental body, secluded in the private space of the home, nevertheless makes an impact on the wider world.

Looking back from this vantage point, we can trace some continuities in the political consequences of women's private reading, along with some changes. It is not surprising to find that an interdiction against indecorous public behaviour that critiqued political or social structures, whether through prophesying, enacting signs, or canvassing for signatures, remains consistent throughout this two-hundred-year period, perhaps sporadically interrupted during the Interregnum. The effects of women's reading, then, were always supposed to be in some way confined to the private. Yet the definition of that privacy changed decisively during this time. Privacy expanded outward from the space of the mind to include the household, the domestic space Habermas calls the 'intimate sphere'. Under the older definition, public behaviour meant any kind of physicality stemming from reading, even reading aloud to the household. Under the later set of ideas, however, a greater degree of private physicality was condoned, while movement outside the domestic space became more restricted. These changes affected the way women were able to imagine their own political agency. During the conflicts of the seventeenth century, women legitimated their own political action through reference to a private, individualised experience of the text. Religio-political action took the form of manifesting one's interpretations in public – through prophesying, preaching, or more oblique gestures. By the late eighteenth and early nineteenth centuries, however, private spaces could accommodate the collective actions of groups of women like ladies' anti-slavery societies, who presented their experience of reading as universal; religio-political intervention thus took the form of modelling the private affect of prayer – tears, and other emotional responses – for public consumption.[64] This cultural shift reveals that in order to understand women's political agency during the age of print, we need to consider the history not only of the public, but also of the private sphere. We cannot assume that the private nature of women's religious practice precluded their ability to intervene in political affairs.

CHAPTER 8

The strange career of Richard 'Citizen' Lee: poetry, popular radicalism and enthusiasm in the 1790s

Jon Mee

A transcription from the Treasury Solicitor's papers of an interrogation which took place on 31 October 1795 illustrates the confusion of the authorities trying to understand popular radicalism in the 1790s:

> Q. Are these all the productions of Mr Lee's pen?
> A. Not all, But those that have his Name to them are.
> Q. You I suppose are Mr Lee's servant.
> A. No my name is Lee.
> Q. O, then you are Mr Lee himself?
> A. Yes sir.
> Q. You must be very industrious to produce such a quantity of matter.
> A. There are several persons employed.[1]

Insofar as it suggests that the government scarcely knew what it was facing, this exchange is a paradigmatic response to the phenomenon of a popular radical movement after 1792. Such a movement was novel, and its identity often mystified the political elite. Modern historians tend to identify the phenomenon most strongly with the aftermath of the publication of Thomas Paine's *Rights of Man* (1791–2). Paine's influence can scarcely be underestimated, but it can be distorting if it is used to separate popular radicalism from older traditions of popular protest and, especially, if the deism expressed in Paine's *Age of Reason* (1794–5) is assumed completely to have displaced Christian ideas of liberty. Even a historian as attuned to the political valorisation of religious language in popular culture as E. P. Thompson sometimes works with a normative idea of the typical member of the London Corresponding Society (LCS) – the most influential popular radical organisation in the 1790s – as a Painite deist.[2] This chapter attempts to account for a different kind of radicalism by following the strange career of Richard 'Citizen' Lee, the man whose identity was so difficult for his government interrogators to understand in 1795.

'Citizen' Lee has also remained a mystery for modern historiography, although he is often mentioned by historians. E. P. Thompson briefly described him as 'one of the few English Jacobins who referred to the guillotine in terms of warm approval'. Such passing comments aside, however, modern historians seem as much in the dark as the Treasury Solicitor. Thompson seems unaware that Lee appears in E. F. Hatfield's worthy tome *The Poets of the Church* (1884). Far from recognising Lee as a Jacobin, Hatfield remarkably commends the 'devout spirit' of his poetry. The existence of these parallel archives makes Lee an interesting case for any discussion of the complexities of popular radical literature in the period. This chapter brings the two sides of Lee's career into fuller contact and accounts for the role of his religion in his politics.[3] Although it is now often regarded as a forum for freethinking mechanics, Lee's religious 'enthusiasm' was not uncommon in the LCS, but there was a serious conflict between religion and irreligion which cannot be reduced to one between progressives and traditionalists or between radicals and reformers. Few LCS tracts were as violently republican as those Lee issued. Indeed the leadership of the LCS attempted to present the movement as a reforming rather than a revolutionary organisation precisely by distancing itself from the enthusiasm of such men. No less than the Enlightenment cry of universal reason, however, the appeal to the power of a grace freely given to the believer by Christ could be and was used to vindicate popular participation in political affairs.

Expressions of religious 'warmth' were not unusual in a period of evangelical revival. Free grace – the Calvinist doctrine of justification by faith alone – had continued its powerful resonance among the poor during the eighteenth century. John Walsh has stressed the role of the message that grace was available to all who repented and believed, in his account of the success of the Methodist movement among the lower classes, and also observes that more traditional Calvinists were often shocked by a confidence in salvation which could verge on antinomianism in the strength of its feeling of liberation from the restraints of the Moral Law.[4] The evangelistic gains of the message of free grace were always haunted by the spectre of undisciplined enthusiasm. Richard Lee was one of those who flouted the constraints of evangelical piety, but he began writing under the patronage of respectable revivalism, first appearing in the *Evangelical Magazine* between late 1793 and early 1794. The *Evangelical Magazine* had been founded in 1793 by a group of

dissenting and Anglican preachers of Calvinist orientation. It was produced in a style 'level to every one's capacity, and suited to every one's
time and circumstances', designed to protect 'true believers, exposed to
the wiles of erroneous teachers who endeavour to perplex their minds,
and subvert their faith'.[5] At its very inception, then, the *Evangelical
Magazine* was concerned to channel popular religious feeling into courses
properly secured against enthusiasm.

A series of Lee's religious poems appeared in the first two volumes
under the pseudonym 'Ebenezer'. These were collected together as
Flowers from Sharon and published at the beginning of 1794 in a volume proudly announcing Richard Lee as their author. Lee prefaces the
collection with the kind of apology for its defects typical of the self-taught
'peasant' or 'uneducated' poets of the eighteenth century:[6]

It is not from a vain Supposition of their Poetical Merit, that the ensuing Sheets
are offered to the Public; but from a Conviction of the Divine Truths they
contain: Truths, which I own, fallen and depraved Reason will always stumble
at; and which the unregenerate Heart will never cordially receive; they are too
humbling for proud Nature to be in love with; – too dazzling for carnal Eyes
to behold. But they are Truths which the CHRISTIAN embraces, and holds fast as
his chief treasure. From a real Experience of their divine Power in his Heart, he
derives his only Support and Comfort in this wretched Vale of Tears.

The pious rhetoric of this 'Advertisement' and its stress on the unmedi-
ated experience of grace recall many popular revivalist spiritual auto-
biographies. In James Wheeler's posthumous *The Rose of Sharon: A Poem*
(1790) an anonymous apologist for the poet makes a great deal of the author's 'being with respect to human learning an illiterate (though doubt-
less sincere) Christian'. The apologia goes on to suggest that the poem
'may very probably receive the censures of the critic. Yet the serious
Christian Reader will . . . discern so much of real experimental religion
as may afford him both pleasure and profit.'[7] In Lee's case, the *Evangelical
Magazine* extended its patronage to a review praising the genuinely
'experimental' feeling of the poetry, although it simultaneously registered
a concern over the poet's presumption that his incorrectness would be
overlooked in favour of the authenticity of his religious feelings:

This is perhaps more than a writer is entitled to expect, when he claims the
public attention; especially as defects in grammar, accent, rhyme, and metre,
might have been removed by the previous correction of some judicious friend.
However, these poems, published, apparently, 'with all their imperfections on
their head,' afford the stronger evidence of being genuine; and many of them are
superior, even in correctness, to what is naturally looked for in the production of

so young a person, who has received little assistance from education, and whose occupation we understand to be that of a laborious mechanic.[8]

Such prefaces and reviews were ways of circumscribing the possibilities available in print for the 'laborious mechanic' such as Wheeler and Lee. Self-taught poets could be valued for their 'genuine' effusions of the heart, but this was not quite the same thing as valuing them as 'poets' or 'writers' in their own right. That would have meant encouraging them to abandon what polite commentators perceived as their proper position within the social hierarchy, a fear repeatedly sounded in critical assessments of so-called 'uneducated' poets in the period.[9]

Lee seems to have believed, on the contrary, that inspiration, rather than correctness, could found a public career, and he was to extend the implications of this idea into a democratic politics. That politics does not appear in *Flowers from Sharon*, but what does breathe through the poetry is a fierce confidence in the saving power of the personal experience of divine grace. This confidence sustains the aggressive undertone of the 'Advertisement' and is the cornerstone of many of the poems which follow it. 'Eternal Love', the first poem in the collection, asserts the unity of the believer with the divine ('ONE with the FATHER, with the SPIRIT ONE'), and looks to a day when the shout 'GRACE! FREE GRACE!' shall 're-echo thro' the Skies!' Lee's collection is pervaded by the faith in the sufficiency of his own spiritual illumination which the more respectable dissenters James Bennett and David Bogue (a trustee of the *Evangelical Magazine*) regarded as the besetting sin of those uneducated men who had never read Calvin, 'the popular poison, a bastard zeal for the doctrine of salvation by grace'. Such zeal was feared by polite commentators such as Bennett and Bogue: they saw in it a tendency towards an antinomian disregard for respectable morality and social deference. Ironically, the *Evangelical Magazine* itself was criticised for giving rein to such excesses of popular religious feeling.[10] In 1800, William Hamilton Reid – who had been a member of the LCS in the 1790s before he turned his coat to work as a government hack – condemned 'the Evangelical and other Magazines, still in circulation' for retailing 'under the head of Religious, or Missionary Intelligence' accounts of popular enthusiasm which he felt undermined the power of religion to act as a bulwark against republicanism and atheism. A few years later, the liberal intellectual Leigh Hunt condemned the *Evangelical Magazine* again for whipping up precisely this kind of intense religiosity. Hunt thought that the magazine, whatever its good intentions, encouraged popular enthusiasm by opening its pages to the religious feelings of the uneducated. Chief among these suspect feelings he identified the Calvinist's conviction of salvation by grace. He believed it could lead the unlearned to an undue sense of their own abilities:

People of exuberant fancies and uncultivated minds cannot think too highly of themselves, when they hear the refuse of society claiming familiarity with all the persons in the Trinity and talking of going to heaven as they would of the one-shilling gallery: they are led on therefore from familiarity to confidence, and from confidence to a sense of equality, and thus become gods themselves.

Lee conforms closely to Hunt's image of popular Calvinism and his career confirms Hunt's worst fears about the *Evangelical Magazine*.[11]

The exact details of Lee's religious affiliations in 1793–4 are unknown, but one of the poems collected in *Flowers from Sharon* mentions a lecture 'at the Adelphi Chapel, by the Rev. Grove'. Thomas Grove (1747?–1817) had been expelled from Oxford in 1768 for 'Methodism'. He was in London in 1793–4 between pastorates and was one of several ministers preaching at the Adelphi, which had no settled minister at the time. John Feltham's *Picture of London* (1802) mentions Grove rather disapprovingly as one of a group of Calvinistic Methodists 'celebrated for their zeal in addressing large auditories'.[12] The list of booksellers on the title page of Lee's collection further helps to elucidate Lee's religious context. They include J. S. Jordan and Garnet Terry, who had collaborated in the previous year by republishing an 'old Ranter' tract from the seventeenth century, Samuel (Cobbler) How's *The Sufficiency of the Spirit's Teaching*, a pamphlet which W. H. Reid eventually cited as the source of Tom Paine's idea that 'every man's mind is his own church'. Jordan was, of course, the original publisher of Paine's *Rights of Man*. How's tract, much like Lee's preface, stresses the sufficiency of the faith of the poor believer over the knowledge of 'the wise, rich, noble, and learned'. It also demonstrates the self-conscious familiarity of religious seekers of the 1790s with their predecessors from the 1640s and 1650s. Indeed, Terry had collaborated with the hyper-Calvinist preacher William Huntington to reprint John Saltmarsh's antinomian tract *Free Grace* – originally published in 1645 – in 1792. Many polite commentators, encouraged in their response by Burke's *Reflections*, which compared the Rational Dissenter Richard Price to Cromwell's chaplain Hugh Peter, believed that this kind of publication signified the fanaticism of the Civil War re-emerging in the 1790s. Their fears were not entirely groundless. Sometimes a faith in the sufficiency of the spirit's teaching did pull the believer into radical politics. Huntington, for instance, was to split with Terry, who had been his publisher from the 1780s, when he discovered the latter distributing Painite propaganda to the congregation. 'Citizen' Lee was to follow a similar course from religious enthusiasm to radical politics.[13]

What needs to be emphasised is that such developments did not necessarily entail abandoning religion for politics; a secularising narrative of enlightenment cannot simply be assumed to define popular politics in the period. Freethinking for Lee remained bound up with religious experience. Free grace underwrote Lee's understanding of political liberty, no less than for his Civil War forebears. At this point, however, it is necessary to explain how Lee became involved in radical politics. One version comes in a letter from 1797 written by the spy James Powell to his paymaster, Richard Ford, at the Treasury Solicitor's office. Powell claims that Lee had become known in radical circles for his exertions on behalf of Thomas Hardy, John Thelwall, John Horne Tooke and others arrested for treason in May 1794. After his acquittal in November, Thelwall, according to Powell, established 'what was called a *conversatione* every Monday evening at his home to which the principal men of the party were invited'. Powell seems to have become acquainted with Lee, whom he describes as 'principal clerk at Perchards of Chatham Square', at these meetings, or one of the other similar debating groups, and subsequently began to encounter him continually at Daniel Isaac Eaton's shop.[14] Powell's chronology of Lee's association with the radical movement cannot be entirely accurate, because his poetry begins appearing in Thomas Spence's *Pig's Meat*, a cheap radical journal, before May 1794. What does seem accurate is Powell's claim that it was his exertions on behalf of the prisoners in the Tower which brought him to prominence. Lee made himself particularly popular as a poet within the movement with the publication of the sentimental verses *On the Death of Mrs Hardy* (1794). Hardy's wife died on 27 August 1794, while her husband was still awaiting trial. Lee's poem was published by the LCS printers Burks and Smith, who sold it for 1d or 7s per 100, with the profits going to the wives and families of persons imprisoned under the suspension of Habeas Corpus. Hardy himself later reproduced the poem in his autobiography, although his gratitude to the 'patriot bard', as he calls Lee, shows no particular sign of any intimate acquaintance with the poet. The following year (by which time Hardy had been released and was not playing much part in radical politics) was Lee's *annus mirabilis*, in which he was transformed from an anonymous 'friend to the distressed patriots', as he signed his poem to Mrs Hardy, into 'Citizen' Lee, the purveyor of the most flagrantly seditious literature in London.[15]

Lee made himself a poetic celebrity in radical circles, and then followed the example of others drawn into the popular radical movement by setting himself up as a bookseller-publisher. The circulation of literature, in its broadest sense, was fundamental to the aims of the LCS, and during 1795 tracts and handbills fell like ripe fruit from the Tree of Liberty (the name Lee gave to his shop). For all its fertility, however, Lee had to uproot the Tree of Liberty more than once in this period. A handbill in the Library Company of Philadelphia, dated 21 March 1795, suggests that he was under considerable pressure from 'the hostile Attacks of Church and King Rioters'.[16] Nevertheless, even during these tempestuous times, Lee still found opportunities to write and publish poetry, now combining his politics explicitly with his religious views in the verse collected as *Songs from the Rock*. Lee's name is not given on the title page, but it does tell us that the volume is by the author of *Flowers from Sharon*. It is not clear why the collection does not boast its author's name. Perhaps Lee had poetic ambitions for an audience, probably among dissenters and Methodists, beyond the radical movement in which he was becoming a celebrity. Whatever the reason for his anonymity, the list of booksellers on the title page makes Lee's radical associations clear enough. Jordan's name is still there as a bridge between the worlds of popular religion and Thomas Paine, but he is joined by some of the luminaries of radical London bookselling, including Eaton and Spence. The collection is preceded by a note announcing that 'several of the following Poems have suffered much through Omissions and Alterations, which the Fear of Persecution induced the Printer to make, though contrary to the Author's wishes'. Some of these poems had appeared in the second volume of Spence's *Pig's Meat*, others on the playbills and pamphlets bearing the imprint of Citizen Lee. Three of them were also issued separately at some stage in a much cheaper pamphlet form as *The Death of Despotism and the Doom of Tyrants*.[17] Some themes, likely to appeal to a cross-section of dissenting opinion, are carried over from *Flowers from Sharon*, such as 'On the Emancipation of our Negro Brethren in America'. Others are fiercely anti-Catholic as in 'Babylon's Fall or the Overthrow of Papal Tyranny' and 'A Call to Protestant Patriots'. The latter takes government plans for British troops to protect the Vatican against French Republican armies as a sign that the British government is in league with the Beast of Revelation, the traditional symbol for the Papacy in the popular

Protestant imagination. 'Retribution; or the Rewards of Benevolence and
of Oppression' celebrates the 'rich Glories of FREE GRACE' in a levelling
vision of the Judgement Day when 'Monarchs fall beneath thy Frown.'[18]
The zeal of Lee's radicalism was clearly founded on the warmth of his
religious enthusiasm, a fact which caused problems for him with the infidel wing of the radical movement. Most of the poems in *Songs from the
Rock* are characterised by violent language, an unequivocal statement of
divine power and the ability directly to see and feel that power at work
in the world. It is the lack of any ironic disclaimer of the immediacy of
his vision that separates his poetry from most Romantic millenarianism
(for instance, Coleridge's 'Religious Musings'). It was the confidence in
the ability of fleshly eyes to apprehend matters of the spirit which most
appalled Leigh Hunt when he discussed the excesses of popular religious
feeling. This seemed an inflation to such commentators, debasing the
currency of religion by making spiritual enlightenment available at any
time and in any place to people without education or good taste.

Of more immediate influence on the radical movement than these
poems, however, were the broadsides, seldom costing more than 1 or 2d,
which poured from Lee's presses at around the same time. Many combine the violence of the poems of *Songs from the Rock*, sometimes explicitly
invoking divine aid, with a grotesque sense of carnival. In this and other
respects, Lee's work has something of the flavour of the tracts put out
at around the same time by Spence. Spence was an LCS member, but
very much an ultra-radical, looking not only for republican government,
brought about by violent means if necessary, but also redistribution of
land on the basis of parish associations. Often marked by a spirit of fierce
satire, Spence used a variety of media from token coins to political pamphlets to transmit his revolutionary message. *The Happy Reign of George the
Last*, bearing Lee's imprint, argues in favour of Spence's idea of village
associations.[19] Lee probably did not write most of the pamphlets and
broadsides he published, although he sometimes inserted verses which
carried his name, but they were to prove his undoing: the government's
chief concern was to prosecute the publishers rather than the authors of
sedition. The handbill which brought Lee to the government's attention
bore the title *King Killing* (see Figure 2), but it is actually culled from an
essay, 'On Tyrannicide', a discussion of the execution of the French King,
which had appeared at the beginning of 1795 in the first issue of *The Cabinet*. Issued in Norwich by 'a society of gentlemen', *The Cabinet* was devoted
to 'rational reform' and sold in London by Lee's old associate Jordan.
Far from itself advocating king-killing, 'On Tyrannicide' concludes

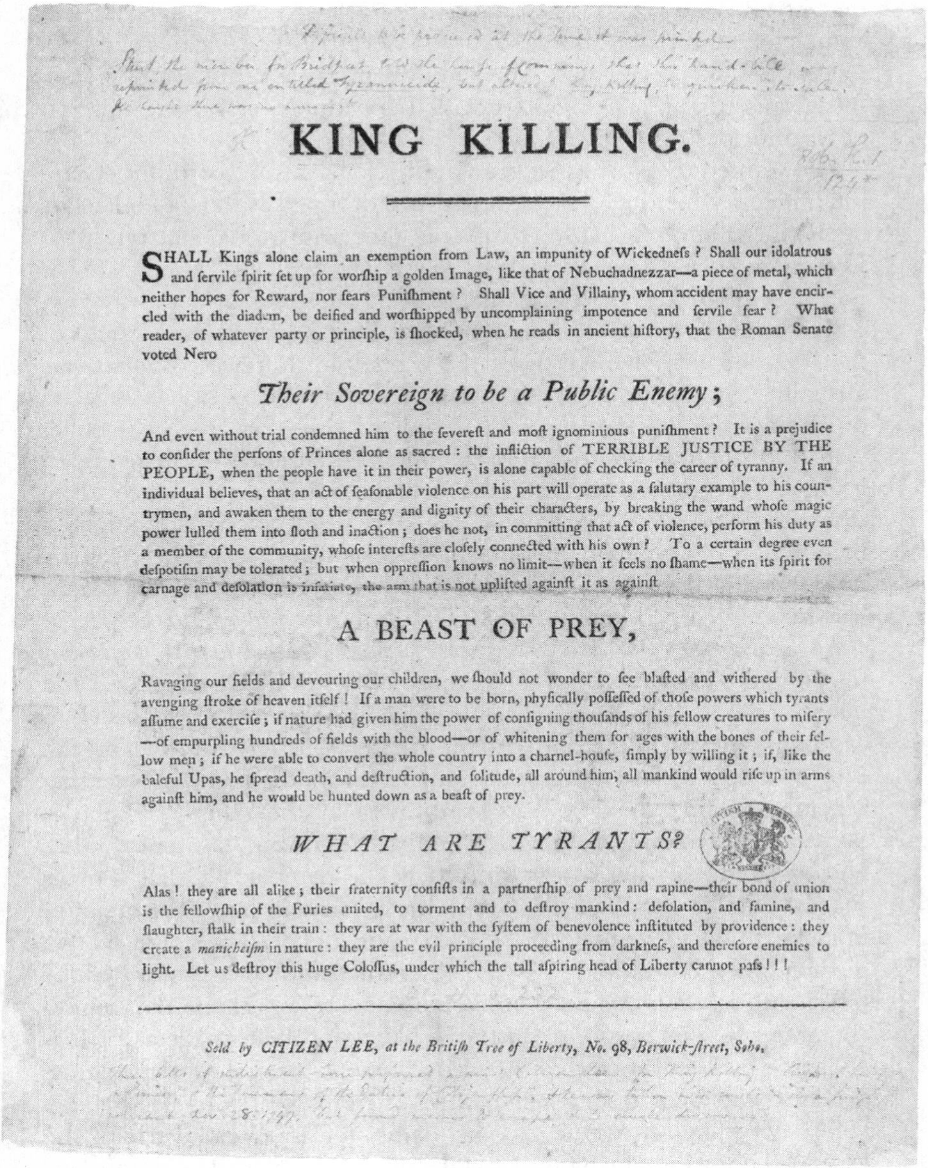

[handwritten notes at top, partially legible]

KING KILLING.

SHALL Kings alone claim an exemption from Law, an impunity of Wickedneſs? Shall our idolatrous and ſervile ſpirit ſet up for worſhip a golden Image, like that of Nebuchadnezzar—a piece of metal, which neither hopes for Reward, nor fears Puniſhment? Shall Vice and Villainy, whom accident may have encircled with the diadem, be deified and worſhipped by uncomplaining impotence and ſervile fear? What reader, of whatever party or principle, is ſhocked, when he reads in ancient hiſtory, that the Roman Senate voted Nero

Their Sovereign to be a Public Enemy;

And even without trial condemned him to the ſevereſt and moſt ignominious puniſhment? It is a prejudice to conſider the perſons of Princes alone as ſacred : the infliction of TERRIBLE JUSTICE BY THE PEOPLE, when the people have it in their power, is alone capable of checking the career of tyranny. If an individual believes, that an act of ſeaſonable violence on his part will operate as a ſalutary example to his countrymen, and awaken them to the energy and dignity of their characters, by breaking the wand whoſe magic power lulled them into ſloth and inaction ; does he not, in committing that act of violence, perform his duty as a member of the community, whoſe intereſts are cloſely connected with his own? To a certain degree even deſpotiſm may be tolerated ; but when oppreſſion knows no limit—when it feels no ſhame—when its ſpirit for carnage and deſolation is infinite, the arm that is not uplifted againſt it as againſt

A BEAST OF PREY,

Ravaging our fields and devouring our children, we ſhould not wonder to ſee blaſted and withered by the avenging ſtroke of heaven itſelf ! If a man were to be born, phyſically poſſeſſed of thoſe powers which tyrants aſſume and exerciſe ; if nature had given him the power of conſigning thouſands of his fellow creatures to miſery —of empurpling hundreds of fields with the blood—or of whitening them for ages with the bones of their fellow men ; if he were able to convert the whole country into a charnel-houſe, ſimply by willing it ; if, like the baleful Upas, he ſpread death, and deſtruction, and ſolitude, all around him, all mankind would riſe up in arms againſt him, and he would be hunted down as a beaſt of prey.

WHAT ARE TYRANTS?

Alas ! they are all alike ; their fraternity conſiſts in a partnerſhip of prey and rapine—their bond of union is the fellowſhip of the Furies united, to torment and to deſtroy mankind : deſolation, and famine, and ſlaughter, ſtalk in their train : they are at war with the ſyſtem of benevolence inſtituted by providence : they create a *manicheiſm* in nature : they are the evil principle proceeding from darkneſs, and therefore enemies to light. Let us deſtroy this huge Coloſſus, under which the tall aſpiring head of Liberty cannot paſs ! ! !

Sold by CITIZEN LEE, *at the Britiſh Tree of Liberty, No.* 98, *Berwick-ſtreet, Soho.*

[handwritten notes at bottom, partially legible]

Figure 2. Citizen Lee's inflammatory 'King Killing' handbill (1795).

that its advocates 'have been dazzled by a few splendid names'. Lee completely distorts his source, omits its view that tyrannicide is 'unlawful, useless, and pernicious', and simply reprints as republican polemic the few paragraphs *The Cabinet* provided as examples of 'the declamation of tyrannicides'.

Lee wanted to reach as wide an audience as possible with his cheap, inflammatory handbill. 'Tyrannicide' was dropped as the title in favour of 'King Killing', 'because the people otherwise would not buy it'.[20] Lee seems to have been hawking *King Killing* with his other wares at the huge LCS rally held in Copenhagen Fields on 26 October 1795, where a hostile crowd shouted anti-Pitt slogans, called for the end of the war and complained about the economic distresses of what was virtually a famine year. On 29 October the king's coach was attacked on the way to the opening of Parliament: either a stone or a bullet passed through a window, and someone in the crowd wrenched open its door. Pitt's government used the incident to move against the radical movement and promulgate the so-called Two Acts, designed to tighten the laws on treasonable, seditious practices and meetings. Lee was the most convenient example of radical extremism; on 17 November Lord Mornington named him in Parliament. Both *King Killing* and *The Happy Reign of King George the Last* were brought before the House to represent the opinions of the LCS.[21] During a brief period of temporary and uneasy co-operation with extra-parliamentary reformers, in order to campaign against the Two Acts, the Foxite Whigs tried to defend the LCS by arguing that Lee was not connected with the society. Presenting a petition against the Two Acts from Sheffield, the Whig MP Charles Sturt rose in Parliament on 23 November to confirm that Lee's mother had told him that her son was no longer a member.[22] Other sources suggest that Lee had fallen out with the leadership over the spread of infidelity in the movement. W. H. Reid claimed that 'Bone and Lee, two seceding members, and booksellers by profession, were proscribed for refusing to sell Volney's *Ruins*, and Paine's *Age of Reason*; and that refusal construed into a censure upon the weakness of their intellects.'[23] It is unclear why Lee was ejected the second time, but significantly the LCS issued a statement distancing themselves from the bookseller the day before Mornington rose to give his name in Parliament. Perhaps the LCS had got wind of what was to take place and threw Lee out to save themselves from being associated with king-killing.[24]

After a year in which there had been no prosecutions for seditious libel in London, the government arrested Lee. *The True Briton* for

1 December 1795 announces: 'At the Westminster Quarter Sessions, held at Guildhall on Saturday, the Grand Jury found three Bills of Indictment against Citizen R. Lee for publishing Seditious Pamphlets.' These were *King Killing, The Rights of Princes* and *A Summary of the Duties of Citizenship.* Lee did not stay in prison long. By 19 December the *True Briton* announced his escape. *The Times* of the same day provided details: 'The escape of Citizen Lee, from the house of the Officer in Bow Street, was thus effected. Three women, or persons in women's cloaths, went to visit him. Their number having been unnoticed by the attendants, four persons in women's cloaths quitted the house. One of these was the person called Citizen Lee, who has not since been heard of.' The spy Powell later claimed that Lee 'made such villainous use of his time as to induce my wife to abscond with him to America at the beginning of March last year'.[25] Lee made for Philadelphia, like many others fleeing from British economic and political oppression. A network of radical exiles there provided important mutual support. Michael Durey has recently listed Lee among those émigrés who contributed to the development of Jeffersonian ideology.[26] Federalists hated their democratic politics, and the Alien and Sedition Acts were in part directed against them. One historian has commented of this period of American politics that 'foreigners seemed to get one sniff of printers' ink and become loyal Jeffersonians'.[27] Lee had already been inhaling deeply at the printing press by the time he emerged in Philadelphia as the editor of the *American Universal Magazine*, a compilation of dissenting religion, radical pro-French politics and help and advice for the recent migrant. Lee was nothing if not a political showman, but he was also deeply committed to the cheap and rapid circulation of knowledge. He quickly became involved in the literary wars between republicans and federalists, made contact with former LCS associates Eaton and Joseph Gales and provoked the bristling ire of Peter Porcupine (William Cobbett), but after June 1797 the *American Universal Magazine* abruptly stopped bearing his imprint. Jane Douglas suggests Lee died, echoing Hardy's claim that Lee fell ill 'soon after' arriving in America, but in 1798 one of Cobbett's frequent streams of abuse against radical exiles paints a mocking picture of him 'comfortably lodged in New-York jail'.[28]

Whatever happened to him subsequently, from 1794 to 1795 'Citizen' Lee shot up like a firework into the firmament of popular print culture, his name briefly flaring in Parliament, before all but disappearing. Print in the eighteenth century was, to adapt Sir Walter's Elliot's comment on the navy, 'the means of bringing persons of obscure birth into undue distinction'.[29] Sir Walter would have regarded what Lee achieved as notoriety, but he did briefly gain honour and distinction among a very different kind of audience. Lee's output as popular writer and publisher assumed the protean quality feared by polite commentators. Lee's radicalisation, we might say, proved the worst fears expressed in such responses. Radical propagandists such as Lee printed from different premises (under threat from church and king thugs), threw together anthologies of other people's writing, inserting their own verses where they were able. They appeared to offer no coherent body of work. They seemed at one moment willing to dispense entirely with the 'author function', cutting up and reassembling whatever was at hand, while at another making shockingly presumptuous claims for the divine basis of their inspiration or grandly styling themselves, as Lee did, 'bookseller to the people'.[30] Faced with the emergence of a popular radical press after the publication of Paine's *Rights of Man* in 1792, the authorities struggled to identify exactly who they were meant to be prosecuting (as the exchange from the Treasury Solicitor's papers with which I began this chapter shows). Dispensing with the author function may have enabled him to elude the government, but Lee had an investment in the process of becoming a part of the radical press beyond the fulfilment of political objectives narrowly defined. 'Reform offered a more practical kind of emancipation or empowerment', as Mark Philp has suggested, 'together with a degree of social mobility.'[31] Lee's religious poetry had also allowed him to express himself. It brought him out of the clerk's office and into the public sphere. *Flowers from Sharon*, at three shillings, looks intended for the patronage of gentlemen and ladies of a methodistical bent: the well-meaning purchasers of the *Evangelical Magazine*. Even the advertisement for the earlier volume in an edition of *Songs from the Rock* pointedly lists a number of eminent clergymen among Lee's patrons. Devotional poetry offered Lee a form of social mobility and an opportunity for self-definition underwritten by the idea of a grace freely available even to the poorest members of society. The explicitly political *Songs from the Rock* was available at 1s 6d, and in a de luxe edition on fine paper at 2s 6d (and it seems he did publish this last volume by subscription). The de luxe edition implies that, even at his most radical, Lee harboured literary as well as purely political ambitions: the collection contains a number of love poems addressed to 'Aminta' as well as the political poems.[32] Powell's bitter account of Lee's celebrity in radical circles suggests that Lee may have struck a figure as a poet of the people in the debating clubs that flourished in the mid-1790s, where anyone was admitted to speak who could pay the weekly subscription and where his songs and poems may well have been read out and even sung.[33]

I am suggesting not that Lee's radical affiliations were simply self-interested, a spectacularly ill-judged species of social climbing, but that he was involved in a kind of self-fashioning, and much the same might be said of the entire popular radical movement.[34] The very word 'conversatione', which Powell claims Thelwall used for his discussion group, suggests something of the awkwardness of the aspirations at stake here. The notion of culture as a polite conversation was ubiquitous in the late eighteenth century, but the nature of 'politeness' and who was to be included in the conversation were continually at issue. Popular radicals wanted to define that politeness in their own terms; in the process they were involved in creating identities in print in the face of persecution and prosecution. Part of the attraction of the movement for the participants was its offering the prospect of their involvement in the public sphere, a fact conservatives eventually acknowledged and contained by offering various models of their own through which the lower orders might consider themselves as contributing to the nation. Michael Durey has suggested that many of those who fled to America had responded to Paine as a meritocrat who opened up the possibility of a more open vision of society. Their radicalism was that of ambitious but socially blocked social classes, he claims, whose resentment was further exacerbated by their dissenting religion.[35] Given that Powell's spy report describes him as a clerk in a London merchant's office, which to the *Evangelical Magazine* meant he was a 'laborious mechanic', Lee fits Durey's categories well. It is not easy to derive an ideology from the kinds of material written and published by Lee, but certainly his showmanship does not correspond to the high-minded tradition of classical republicanism associated with the scholarship of J. G. A. Pocock, nor even Edward Thompson's version of the typical LCS member.[36] Popular radicalism in the period was far from being uniform, corresponding more closely to what Mark Philp has described as a 'fragmented ideology', in which different traditions, reacting to events in France as well as Britain, pragmatically and often with uncertainty responded to a fast developing and novel political situation. Indeed, the fear felt for men like Lee by the upper classes was partly the fear of a society where people claimed the authority to speak from convictions of personal enlightenment rather than any other form of more traditional, institutionalised authority.[37]

The complication is Lee's particular idea of what constituted personal enlightenment. Lee's notion of his right to participate in the public sphere rested not simply on what we might recognise as self-improvement through education, or the universality of private judgement, concepts which modern historians are more disposed to identify with the eighteenth-century Enlightenment, but also on his confidence in the gift of free grace. This should remind us that older religious notions of salvation continued to play an important part in the language of popular politics. Lee's idea of enlightenment, a trope he uses regularly, had its basis in religious experience. Burke had warned of an irrational and dangerous confidence in 'personal self-sufficiency' in his *Reflections*, but it was not simply claims to the self-sufficiency of Reason, derived from the popularisation of Enlightenment freethinking, which inspired the popular radical movement.[38] Burke's phrase is reminiscent of the title of Samuel Cobbler How's *The Sufficiency of the Spirit's Teaching*, the old tub-preacher's pamphlet republished in 1792. Although the adoption of the title 'Citizen' and the celebration of the guillotine led Thompson to see him as an English 'Jacobin', Lee himself described the political poetry of *Songs from the Rock* as an attempt 'to Promote the united cause of God and Man'.[39] Nearly everything he later published continued to affirm the confidence in the sufficiency of his own spiritual illumination over 'unregenerate reason' set out in *Flowers from Sharon*. Not that Lee is simply to be regarded as a throwback to the 1640s. His writing is the product of an interaction between this earlier religious tradition and aspects of late eighteenth-century literary culture. The literary effects of the cult of poetic sensibility, which brought forward so much magazine verse, informs the love poetry included in *Songs from the Rock* and its general valorisation of human feeling and philanthropy. In this sense, he is also the product of what we might call popular Romanticism, the more general cultural movement which facilitated the poetry of Wordsworth and Coleridge (and in reaction against which the two poets to some extent defined themselves).[40] Lee even published a translation of an excerpt from Rousseau's *Emile*, under the title *The Gospel of Reason*. Carefully culled and translated from the confession of faith of the Savoyard Vicar, it presents Rousseau as an advocate of a religion of free grace rather than an Enlightenment *philosophe*: 'I acknowledge ... that the majesty which reigns in the sacred writings, fills me with a solemn kind of astonishment; and that the sanctity of the Gospel speaks in a powerful and commanding language to the feelings of my heart.' The initial reception of Rousseau in England had stressed the 'heat of enthusiasm' in *Emile* and often represented him as a brave (Protestant) defender of religious freedom of conscience. *The Gospel of Reason* goes further, methodising him, and implicitly presenting Rousseau as an apostle of the sufficiency of the spirit's teaching.[41]

Lee's confidence in the voice of God speaking directly to his heart enabled him to publish some of the most incendiary material released by radical presses in the 1790s. He had a faith in what the *Monthly Review* called 'the divine right of republics' as his poem 'The Rights of God' makes clear:

> SOLE KING OF NATIONS, rise! assert thy Sway,
> Thou JEALOUS GOD! thy potent Arm display;
> Tumble the Blood-built Thrones of *Despots* down!
> Let Dust and Darkness be the *Tyrant's* Crown![42]

Although Spence was happy to print 'The Rights of God' in his *Pig's Meat*, such religious warmth caused problems within the radical movement more generally and constantly concerned the leaders of the LCS and associated intellectuals. Their model of enlightenment seemed to be in danger from one in which the emotions of the believer threatened to overwhelm private judgement. Reid certainly believed that the 'warmth' of religious principles such as Lee's made them inherently much more attractive to the lower classes than Priestley's Socinianism. Godwin's anxieties over political associations had its roots in the fear of popular passions, 'propagating blind zeal, where we meant to propagate reason'. Thelwall spent a great deal of time in his lectures trying to distinguish the contemporary radical movement from such 'warmth', contrasting the enlightened principles of the French Revolution with the 'enthusiasm' of the seventeenth-century regicides, a distinction which Lee, for one, flouts.[43] 'Enthusiasm' was a way of naming the dangers of such popular excitement. It could be applied to religious and infidel passions alike by men such as Godwin and Thelwall, not to mention Burke, but its use invoked more than a century of polemic against popular religious enthusiasm. When religious enthusiasm seemed to be manifesting in the heart of the reform movement, it must have seemed to some of its members to be undermining the claim that the LCS represented the true spirit of eighteenth-century Enlightenment.

If one is claiming a right to participate in the public sphere on the basis of the universality of reason, as Thelwall was, it is not very helpful to have as an ally someone claiming to be directly empowered by a divine vision, confirming Burke's worst predictions about popular frenzy and religious dissent. But for modern historians simply to reproduce that discomfort and to regard Lee as a lunatic or an anachronism is profoundly unhistorical. Iain McCalman and Malcolm Chase have recently made much the same point about Spence, arguing that his use of Biblical language and visions are fundamental to his outlook and cannot just be brushed aside as the populist means to a political end. Spence came from a Calvinist background, but Chase suggests that his radicalism became overtly millenarian and visionary only when he submerged himself in London's metropolitan culture of enthusiasm. Lee obviously had a working relationship of some kind with Spence. He may even have been responsible for this shift in Spence's own outlook.[44] The details of their relationship are unclear. What is clear is that enthusiasm such as Lee's continued to be attractive to the uneducated and impoverished as a means of circumventing the invisible barriers of the enlightenment. Anthony J. La Vopa claims that

in Enlightenment discourse, virtue . . . was paired with knowledge rather than with pedigree or inherited property. The implication was that education, in the broadest sense, legitimated the exercise of power. In the meritocratic version of this pairing, everyone is, in principle, equally entitled to highly valued knowledge, though de facto disadvantages – lack of the requisite wealth or of the requisite cultural patrimony – severely restricted the access of the great majority.[45]

Free grace was a means of transcending these worldly disadvantages. Enthusiasm, whether politically inflected or otherwise, was one language by which those outside of the conversation of culture could assert their right to be heard. When it took on a political complexion, it looked to commentators, from both within and without the radical movement, like the terrible return of the sectarianism of the 1640s and 50s, declaring the sufficiency of its own spiritual teaching as a passport to participation in public affairs.[46]

CHAPTER 9

William Cobbett, John Clare and the agrarian politics of the English Revolution

James C. McKusick

William Cobbett (1762–1835) and John Clare (1793–1864) were self-educated agricultural labourers who eventually became professional writers for a largely urban readership. Both were steeped in a deep knowledge of rural traditions, and their understanding of history emerged more from local memory than from reading and archival study. In contrast to their university-educated contemporaries, Cobbett and Clare both remained stubbornly aware of the local contexts of knowledge, and they often explored the subtle ways that landscape affects the contemporary understanding of the past. Conversely, both were aware of the ways that the past remains latent in the rural landscape, deeply buried in folk memory, yet still visible to those who know how to 'read' traces of the almost-forgotten past within the present-day world. For both writers, an essential mode of historical understanding arose from the *archaeology of landscape*: a way of ascribing meaning to landscape by reading traces of the past in its present appearance. Especially for Clare, such a reading of landscape involved archaeology in the literal sense of digging up artefacts from past historical epochs; he was well-acquainted with a local archaeologist, and he once reported the discovery of an antique box that 'containd several farthings from king charles the firsts or seconds reign'.[1]

The English Revolution left many such traces in the visible landscape around Cobbett and Clare, and they both learnt to view contemporary politics through the lens of previous historical events. Of the two writers, Cobbett was much more deeply engaged in the rough-and-tumble of political debate, and his life story can be charted as an intellectual and spiritual journey from his humble origins as a farm-hand at Farnham in Surrey (where he was born in 1762), through a tumultuous military career (1782–91), exile in France (1792) and the United States (1793–1800), to his discovery of a vocation for journalism under the pen-name of Peter Porcupine, ardent defender of the English system of government against the American revolutionaries.[2] Returning to England in 1800, Cobbett found himself lionised by the authorities, and as a loyal government journalist he consorted with cabinet ministers and dined with William Pitt. But Cobbett became increasingly disdainful of the new commercial and industrial order that was overtaking the older agrarian-based economy. In an article of 1806 he sternly denounced the '*paper* system' that was inexorably destroying small farms all over England:

> The taxing and funding, or, in other words, the *paper* system, has . . . drawn the real property of the nation into fewer hands; it has made land and agriculture objects of speculation; it has, in every part of the kingdom, moulded many farms into one; it has almost entirely extinguished the race of small farms; from one end of England to the other, the houses which formerly contained little farms and their happy families, are now sinking into ruins . . . We are daily advancing into that state in which there are but two classes of men, *masters* and *abject dependents*.[3]

Cobbett's growing distaste for the Pitt government and the frenzied pace of commercial activity in London made him increasingly nostalgic for the simple farming life of his childhood. In 1805 he retired to the countryside, purchasing a farm at Botley in Hampshire and seeking a modest, reclusive, self-sufficient way of life.

Cobbett's political allegiance swerved sharply from staunch Toryism towards radical protest in subsequent years, as he became incensed by allegations of corruption among his former political mentors. After serving two years in Newgate Prison (1810–12), Cobbett became the leading voice of the English radical movement, and his *Political Register* became one of the most widely circulated newspapers in the country, particularly after 1816, when it became available in a twopenny edition intended for journeymen and labourers. Exiled once again to the United States for his radical views (1817–19), Cobbett returned to an even greater acclaim among his working-class followers in England. His two-year sojourn in America persuaded him of the practical advantages of its republican form of government, unencumbered by a standing army, tithes, or national debt.

Cobbett's Political Register (1802–35) inaugurated a new style of radical journalism: rabid in its denunciation of official corruption, staunch in its defence of the common people and entertaining in the breadth and variety of its subject-matter, which ranged from casual observation of the English countryside to historical reflection and commentary on current events. A speaker much in demand, Cobbett found occasion to travel throughout England, and his extended sojourns in France and

America enabled him to make incisive comparisons between the social and political institutions of England and those of other nations. Cobbett's finest and most memorable essays were written in the course of his travels on horseback throughout England during the 1820s, and the picaresque essay form proved remarkably congenial to his digressive and historically reflective form of political commentary. These travel essays, gathered in 1830 under the title *Rural Rides*, provide revealing insights into the development of Cobbett's political views.

Rural England in the 1820s presented Cobbett with much evidence of misery, poverty and depopulation, all of which he attributed to a new, capital-intensive mode of agriculture that had arisen as a result of inflated commodity prices during the Napoleonic Wars. After the final defeat of Napoleon, prices for agricultural commodities were held artificially high by the protectionist Corn Laws, which had a devastating effect upon the labouring classes, particularly agricultural labourers, who could no longer afford adequate food for their families. Struck by the brutal juxtaposition of plentiful harvests and starving farm workers, Cobbett accurately predicted the insurrectionary turmoil that would result in the Swing Riots of 1830. Throughout the *Rural Rides*, Cobbett provides his readers not only with telling descriptions of the misery and repression of the rural populace, but also with insightful historical reflections that serve to contextualise their suffering and their struggle.

Cobbett's historical reflections are framed by an overarching contrast between an idyllic past and the miserable and corrupt modern age. His descriptions of the present landscape are frequently compared with the state of the land in bygone eras. Cobbett is especially fond of making ironic comparisons between the 'Dark Ages' and the present 'Enlightenment', usually to the detriment of the latter. Reflecting upon the Enlightenment historiography of Hume, Cobbett remarks:

Hume and other historians rail against the *feudal*-system; and we, 'enlightened' and 'free' creatures as we are, look back with scorn, or, at least, with surprise and pity, to the 'vassalage' of our forefathers. But if the matter were well inquired into, not slurred over, but well and truly examined, we should find, that the people of these villages were *as free* in the days of William Rufus as are the people of the present day; and that vassalage, only under other names, exists now as completely as it existed then.[4]

Cobbett stubbornly interrogates the facile themes of progress and improvement that are uncritically promulgated by 'enlightened' historians.

He continues his critique of what 'we all know' in a reflection upon monasteries:

This town of Reigate had, in former times, a priory, which had considerable estates in the neighbourhood; and this is brought to my recollection by a circumstance which has recently taken place in the town. We all know how long it has been the fashion to take it for *granted* that the monasteries were *bad things*; but of late I have made some hundreds of thousands of good Protestants begin to suspect that monasteries were better than *poor-rates*, and that monks and nuns, who *fed the poor*, were better than sinecure and pension men and women, who *feed upon the poor.*[5]

Cobbett does not claim that the medieval period was a Golden Age of human society; he merely points out the dubious presuppositions that often blind conventional historians to the actual state of affairs in rural England. While rejecting conventional historiography, Cobbett also repudiates the bookish, archival style of historical enquiry pursued in the universities; he embarks upon his journey through England to discover the history embedded within the actual earth beneath his feet, preserved in oral history, local folkways and in traces of the past inscribed in architecture and upon the landscape.

Cobbett's resistance to the implicit progressivism of Enlightenment historiography made him a relatively uncongenial figure to the urban intellectuals of his own era, who deplored his rusticity, his deficient education, and his lack of revolutionary fervour. Cobbett modestly advanced the cause of parliamentary reform, rather than advocating the violent overthrow of the British monarchy, and he harshly denounced corruption and extremism wherever he found it. Although he did speak out boldly for the rights of the common people, he was neither a theorist nor an expounder of revolutionary principles; and his resistance to 'theoretism'[6] (as Mikhail Bakhtin terms the relentless elaboration of abstract principles for their own sake) has made Cobbett an exceedingly problematic figure for cultural commentators of our own time. Raymond Williams, in a sensitive and sustained 1983 study entitled *Cobbett*, devotes a great deal of effort to ascertaining and responding to Cobbett's views on history and politics; but despite much thoughtful analysis, Williams clearly remains disappointed by what he regards as Cobbett's intellectual shortcomings:

It is in thinking about the nature of work that Cobbett is furthest from us. His powerful and necessary respect for physical labour can be too easily translated, in different conditions, into an idealisation of 'hard work'. We have to look at the lights burning late in the offices of political manipulators and the financial schemers to remember how little necessary correlation there may be between

long effort and useful work. Correspondingly, we have to look at 'production'
beyond Cobbett's physical terms.[7]

Evidently, in Williams's view, poor Cobbett was trapped in the world of
the concrete, unable to rise to our own present exalted level of theoretical
abstraction. We are 'enlightened', and Cobbett is not. Such a critique of
Cobbett, however, fails to acknowledge the extent of his actual experience of work, both physical and intellectual. A man who spent several
years of his life as an agricultural labourer, and more than three decades
as a professional journalist, might very well possess a more authentic
conception of the 'nature of work' than even the most advanced cultural
theorist.

Cobbett's imaginative response to the English Revolution is not what
one might predict from the received understanding of his 'radicalism'. He
is very little concerned with the revolutionary ethos of the Interregnum.
He devotes scant attention to the conflicting factions, the enthusiastic
religious sects, or the machinations of the Long Parliament. Nor, despite
his general hostility to monarchs, is he particularly intrigued by the rights
and wrongs of the execution of Charles I. His main interest in the Interregnum centres upon the figure of Oliver Cromwell, whom he regards
as a revolutionary autocrat (precursor to Napoleon) and as a bearer of
a new class identity, specifically as a protagonist of the urban commercial classes, with their Protestant work ethic and their dedication to the
unlimited accumulation of monetary wealth.

Cobbett's most extended commentary on Cromwell occurs in his *History of the Protestant 'Reformation'*, a decidedly unconventional work of historiography that traces all of England's present woes back to the Protestant
Reformation. In Cobbett's view, the 'Reformation' (a word that he always places between inverted commas as a sign of its shameful pedigree)
was only the beginning of a devastating historical process, 'engendered
in lust and brought forth in hypocrisy and perfidy', which had the un-
intended consequence of unleashing the English Revolution and the
Cromwellian Commonwealth, where for the first time the commercial
classes of London succeeded in turning England away from its true
agrarian means of production. Now for the first time in English history,
financial speculation and political adventurism were linked in a bloody
alliance that led by treacherous means to the even more grotesque 're-
formations' of the 'Glorious Revolution' of 1688 which had brought the
National Debt, paper money, the nefarious 'Pitt System' and the present
miserable abjection of the English people. In his introduction to this vast

polemical work, Cobbett writes:

> If you will follow me in this inquiry, I will first show you how this thing called the 'Reformation' began; what it arose out of; and then I will show you its progress, how it marched on, plundering, devastating, inflicting torments on the people, and shedding their innocent blood. I will trace it downward through all its stages, until I show you its natural result, in the schemes of the parson Malthus ... in the present misery indescribable of the labouring classes in England and Ireland, and in that odious and detestable system, which has made Jews and paper-money makers the real owners of a large part of the estates of this kingdom.[8]

In keeping with his understanding of historical process, Cobbett regards the English Revolution as a period of continuity with (rather than a disruption of) the ongoing, sinister process of the Protestant Reformation. The overt anti-Semitism of this passage is fairly typical of Cobbett's political writings, and it bespeaks his need to identify a recognisable scapegoat for the intangible process by which real property has been transformed into an abstract commodity. The main culprits, in Cobbett's view, were the unscrupulous rulers of England who confiscated 'the estates of this kingdom' (particularly those of the monasteries and the landed aristocracy) through an insidious process of 'Reformation'. He claims that Oliver Cromwell, 'though he was tyrannical and bloody, though he ruled with a rod of iron ... was nothing more than the "natural issue", as Elizabeth would have called him, of the "body" of the "Reformation" '.[9]

   Cobbett's method of 'reading' landscape for traces of historical process is particularly apparent in his tour of the countryside near Dover, where he observes Martello towers, trenches and other defensive fortifications along the English seacoast. As relics of the British response to the threat of French invasion, these remnants of a vanished era (already falling into ruin) provide him with an opportunity to reflect upon the unscrupulous motivation that is manifested by these defensive works:

> Simply their object was this: to make the French people miserable; to degrade France, to make the people wretched; and then to have to say to the people of England, Look there: *see what they have got by their attempts to obtain liberty!* This was their object. They did not want Martello towers and honeycombed chalk hills and mad canals; they did not want these to keep out the French armies. The boroughmongers and the parsons cared nothing about the French armies. It was the French example that the lawyers, boroughmongers and parsons wanted to keep out.[10]

In Cobbett's view, the ideology of the French Revolution, and not its military prowess, was the actual cause of terror among the British ruling classes. And yet, considered in historical perspective, the distant prospect of Calais provokes a further reflection on the comparative economic well-being of the English and French farmers:

It is impossible to be upon this honeycombed hill, upon this enormous mass of anti-jacobin expenditure, without seeing the chalk cliffs of Calais and the cornfields of France. At this season it is impossible to see those fields without knowing that the farmers are getting their corn in there as well as here; and it is impossible to think of that fact without reflecting, at the same time, on the example which the farmers of France hold out to the farmers of England . . . The English farmer has to carry on a competition against the French farmer who has *no tithes to pay!* [11]

Cobbett discovers historical significance in the vast relics of 'anti-jacobin expenditure' honeycombed into the Dover cliffs and across the surrounding countryside. In the aftermath of the French defeat, Cobbett still finds reason to sustain his faith in the 'French example': the revolutionary ideals of liberty, equality and freedom from economic oppression.

Cobbett's *Rural Rides* provides a sustained, though hardly systematic, perspective upon the economic plight of the rural working classes, and his frequent allusion to the traces of historical events encoded upon the terrain offers a suggestive means of 'reading' the English landscape. Of all his readers, perhaps none was so deeply affected as John Clare, who wrote in 1832: 'I look upon Cobbett as one of the most powerful prose writers of the age.'[12] Clare was certainly an avid reader of Cobbett's works, not only the *Rural Rides* (which he probably first encountered in the *Political Register*, 1822–6), but also Cobbett's *Grammar of the English Language* (1818), *Cottage Economy* (1822) and *Advice to Young Men* (1830). Clare was somewhat resistant to Cobbett's radical politics (for reasons that I shall discuss later in this chapter); but he was nonetheless deeply impressed by Cobbett's detailed understanding of rural life and culture, and he evidently found much to admire in Cobbett's technique of 'reading' landscape in the *Rural Rides*. Both Clare and Cobbett were conditioned by their personal experience as agricultural labourers to be intensely aware of the ways that historical memory remains latent within the rural landscape, hidden to the casual observer, yet still recorded in the oral tradition of the local community. Especially for Clare, who always sought to remain rooted in the village where he was born, local knowledge of the landscape was an essential element of historical understanding.

John Clare was born in 1793 in the village of Helpston, Northamptonshire, and he spent his early years working in the common fields under a

customary system of open-field agriculture that had changed little since
the Middle Ages. As a young man, however, Clare witnessed dramatic
changes in the familiar landscape of his native village. In 1809, an Act
of Parliament provided for the enclosure of common fields and 'waste'
lands around Helpston. Swamps and marshes were drained, forests and
scrublands were cleared, open fields were enclosed by fences and hedges
and traditional subsistence farming gave way to capital-intensive methods of agriculture. Overlooked in the arcane legal and political process
of enclosure were the traditional grazing and gleaning rights of the poor,
as well as the environmental impact of this drastic change in agricultural
methods. Like Cobbett, Clare deplored the loss of traditional farming
practices, and he was deeply suspicious of the motives behind making
farmland more 'efficient' and 'productive'. Confronted by these destruc-
tive changes in the local landscape, Clare turned to poetry as a medium
in which he could preserve and memorialise the history of the land itself.

Clare embarked on his poetic career with the publication of his first collection, *Poems Descriptive of Rural Life and Scenery* (1820), which forthrightly
denounced the 'improvement' of the local landscape while evoking with
elegiac melancholy the gradual disappearance of the common fields,
marshes and 'waste' lands.[13] Clare's response to the local environment
was more fully developed in his later collections of poetry, entitled *The
Village Minstrel* (1821), *The Shepherd's Calendar* (1827) and *The Rural Muse*
(1835), and in his numerous manuscript poems, letters and journals.
Taken together, all of his writings may be said to constitute an archaeology of landscape; Clare is everywhere attentive to the manifold presence
of the past as it dwells within the tranquil fields and fenlands that sur-
round his native village.

Clare's most extended evocation of local history occurs in a narrative
poem, 'The Village Minstrel', first published in 1821. The eponymous
protagonist of this poem goes wandering amid the ruins of an old castle
near the village of Helpston and although the local shepherds know nothing of 'antiquated books', they are able to recount the latent historical
significance of these ruins, which bear traces of 'old cromwells rage':

> & oft wi shepherds leaning oer their hooks
> Hed stand conjecturing on the ruins round
> Tho little skilld in antiquated books
> Their knowledge in such matters seemd profound
> & they woud preach of what did once abound
> Castles deep moated round old haunted hall
> & something like to moats still swamps the ground

> As neath old cromwells rage the towers did fall
> & bush & ivy creeps the hill & ruin hides it all[14]

As Clare presents it in this poem, the 'profound' knowledge of the shepherds arises not from book-learning, but from their familiarity with local oral tradition, which has recorded events from the time of the English Revolution in legend and song. This episode of local history forms the centrepiece of Clare's extended narrative poem, and it is told in the form of an inset narrative, spoken or sung by a local shepherd using a metrical form (anapestic ballad stanza) that accentuates its status as a traditional oral narrative. The 'framing' narrative, by contrast, is written in the more erudite metrical form of Spenserian stanzas, apparently modelled after those of James Beattie in *The Minstrel* (1770–4).

This local legend describes the doomed efforts of the royalist military officer Michael Hudson to defend Woodcroft Castle 'when charles our unfortunate king / Was disdained by each rebel out law'. This legend is derived from an actual historical event that occurred in June 1648, when Colonel Michael Hudson instigated a short-lived royalist uprising at Woodcroft Castle in Northamptonshire.[15] Clare's opening stanzas present a contrast between the present-day pastoral setting and the scenes of terrible violence that transpired on this very site:

> Tho now ducks & geese they do swim i' the moat
> & the beast at their cribs left to feed
> Tho the tower nows of no other use then a coat
> For the pigeons to roost in & breed
> There once was a day a most terrible day
> When the moat it flowd bloody wi all
> When the top of yon tower saw the midst of the fray
> & the cannons made totter the wall
>
> (stanza 2)

After this ominous prologue, the ballad describes the rebel army marching at dawn toward Helpston from the nearby town of Stamford:

> Twas when dewy morn on the pasture did weep
> From stamford the rebels did roam
> Their tumults no doubt scamperd shepherds & sheep
> & great rout they made as they come
> They rallied thro helpstone ah helpstone I ween
> Thou neer knew a rebel before
> & great consternation no doubt thou wast in
> As the marston chaps were on the moor
>
> (stanza 5)

Figure 3. The death of Michael Hudson. Engraving by William Stukeley, published in a volume of plates to accompany J. Bridges, *History and Antiquities of Northamptonshire* (1791). This engraving depicts the gruesome scene of Colonel Hudson's death in June 1648, following the defeat of his royalist forces at Woodcroft House. Hudson is seen clinging desperately to the roof of the tower while his assailant raises an axe to chop off his right hand. Below, in a subsequent narrative development, Hudson's body is dragged to the edge of the moat and dispatched with a final blow to the head.

The tale presents the moral situation of the town in starkly moralistic terms; the pasture 'weeps' at the onslaught of the Cromwellian horde, and the inset narrator assures us that Helpston 'neer knew a rebel before', in keeping with the staunchly patriotic tone of the ballad. Clare refers to the rebel soldiers as 'the marston chaps', recalling the triumph of Cromwell's army at Marston Moor in 1644, a decisive turning point in the English Civil War.

While the ballad builds to its bloody climax, it takes time out for comic relief, as the local townspeople react with exaggerated terror to the approach of the rebel army. This part of the narrative is related as a further inset tale, derived from local 'gossips':

> Ive heard gossips say when such news spread about
> The maidens near fell into fits

> & old women hearing the rebels were out
> Was a'most scard out of their wits
> The mizer tore slabs up & buried his coin
> & granny she instantly fell
> To hide what she thought the bold rogues woud purloin
> Such as kettles & pots in the well
>
> (stanza 6)

Such panic-stricken efforts at local defence prove needless, as the rebel forces pass through the village to attack Woodcroft Castle, the royalist stronghold.

The ballad reaches its climax in a vivid account of the battle, which ends in the defeat of Michael Hudson and his men, outnumbered by the rebel army 'as thirty to ten':

> But vain are the swords & the deeds of the brave
> When cowards wi numbers oerpower
> As vain hopes the flye to scape fish on the wave
> Or thistle down float in a shower
> They forded the moat & thought conquest was bought
> Ah then came the terrible hour
> When the bold royal captives subdued as they thought
> Pushd again from the top of the tower
>
> Repulse so undaunted – the rebels dismayd
> Offerd quarter for battle to end
> & then was the guardians o woodcroft betrayd
> Ah who woud on cowards depend
> The valiant commander was cowardly flung
> From off the tower top by the foe
> His hand they slashd off on the tower as he hung
> & his body fell bleeding below
>
> (stanzas 9–10)

Despite his valiant defence of the castle, Michael Hudson is defeated by the 'coward' rebels who cruelly slice off his right hand and toss his body into the moat. The right hand is an important motif throughout the ballad; before the battle, all of Hudson's men swear upon their right hands to defend the castle, and Hudson's strength as a swordsman resides in his right hand. As a traditional symbol of fealty to the king of England, the right hand signifies the political ideology of the royalist forces, while the mutilation of Hudson's hand by the rebels provides further evidence of their unscrupulous ambition.

Clare presents this traditional tale through the persona of a simple, unlettered shepherd, and his use of this persona may indicate his desire to distance himself – as an aspirant to the elite status of literate culture – from the simplicity of folk narrative, with its black-and-white morality and its larger-than-life military heroism. Yet we should not assume that Clare implies any criticism of folk narrative as a literary genre; throughout his writings we find many traditional folk songs and patriotic ballads, and it is sometimes difficult to draw the line between what Clare transcribed from local informants and what he personally contributed to that oral tradition. Nor is it tenable to assert that Clare presents the staunch royalist sentiments of this ballad as even faintly questionable; there is no indication that Clare views this local battle as anything other than a clear-cut conflict between right and wrong. Although many commentators have spoken of Clare's 'radical' political views, it seems difficult to reconcile his staunch royalism with the prevailing anti-monarchist sentiments of the urban intellectuals of his era. Like Cobbett, Clare presents himself as a spokesman for the people of rural England, and his political views are quite distinct from those of the urban radical movement.

John Lucas, in a 1994 essay on 'Clare's Politics' and in a subsequent book on Clare, makes what is perhaps the most plausible case to date that Clare is an adherent of 'radicalism', although Lucas is careful to qualify his argument by observing that 'Clare's politics are [not] thought through in a manner that amounts to a programme. Popular radicalism is not like that.'[16] Lucas argues that Clare's underlying radical sentiments 'could be overlaid by or in conflict with that deferential habit which can get into his writing, especially when it is directed at his "betters"'. Thus, in Lucas's view, Clare is merely being obedient to the prevailing opinions of the ruling classes when he expresses royalist sentiments, as he does (for example) in an 1820 manuscript poem entitled 'England', which evokes a past time when 'Laws [were] broke & kings murderd'. According to Lucas, such conventional pieties

are a way of distancing himself from a radicalism that he would naturally have thought dangerous to be identified with just then, not least because he wanted to be acceptable to the London literati. 'England' is then the expression of a need to show Taylor that Clare is not in favour of lawlessness. I suspect that he was covering up.[17]

Although Lucas is certainly correct in finding some fundamental elements of radical thought in Clare's writing, I believe he wrongly seeks to assimilate Clare's political thought to the mainstream of urban radicalism, while discarding as 'insincere' or 'merely deferential' those elements which do not fit. In order to reach an adequate comprehension of Clare's political views, we must interrogate some of our own preconceptions about what constitutes 'radicalism', and we should entertain the possibility that even the most blatant contradictions in his political thought nevertheless felt internally consistent to Clare, within the context of his lifelong experience as an agricultural labourer.

Clare's imaginative response to the English Revolution reveals a consistent pattern of sympathy for Charles I and horror at the prospect of regicide. Clare expresses these views throughout the entire course of his literary career, both in his published works and in his private journals and letters. His interest in the figure of King Charles Martyr is evident from a significant item from his personal library, presently housed at the Northampton Public Library. One of the first books that Clare ever owned, it is entitled *Eikon Basiliké: The Portraicture of His Sacred Majestie in his Solitudes and Sufferings* (1648). This volume is inscribed: 'John Clare / his Book / 1813'. This inscription is particularly significant because Clare only rarely wrote his name in any of the books that he owned. One of the oldest and most valuable items in the Northampton Clare Collection, this book may well be regarded as the Bible of royalism; its text was purportedly written by King Charles himself on the eve of his execution, but it is now generally believed to have been ghost-written by Dr John Gauden (1605–62), Bishop of Exeter. A masterful piece of royalist propaganda, this book is one of the best-known texts of the English Revolution, and it is not surprising that Clare would have known of its existence. What is surprising, however, is that Clare evidently purchased a first edition of this work for his own personal use, at a time when he owned virtually no other books and was earning mere pennies per day as an agricultural labourer. How could Clare possibly have afforded to purchase such a rare and costly book? And why would the personal testimony of a long-dead monarch have inflamed his curiosity?

Clare in 1813 was barely twenty years old; and although he had already tried his hand at poetic composition, he was far from achieving anything like the (fleeting) success that would attend the 1820 publication of *Poems Descriptive of Rural Life*. All evidence seems to suggest that Clare's reading at this early period was driven by his intense aspiration to educate himself, to achieve mastery of the British literary tradition, and eventually to become a professional poet, the peer of Burns, Bloomfield and Byron. Clare's 1813 purchase of *Eikon Basiliké* does not fit smoothly into this set of objectives; the work is hardly an exemplary model of prose style, and it would seem to have very little to teach an aspiring 'Peasant Poet' (as Clare was presented to his readership on the title page of his first book). One may speculate, however, that Clare was fascinated from an early age by the *historical content* of this work, especially in light of the legendary battle of Woodcroft Castle recounted above; Clare may well have been curious to learn more about the 'Solitudes and Sufferings' of King Charles, and to understand how this episode of local heroism fitted into the larger historical process of the English Revolution.

Eikon Basiliké presents an extended justification for the deeds and character of Charles I, and along the way it elaborates a severe indictment against the parliamentary forces who have dared to rebel against the divine right of kings. This book diagnoses the craving for absolute power as an organic disorder which must inevitably prove fatal to the possessor: 'But, I believe, the surfeit of too much Power, which some men have greedily seized on, and now seek wholly to devour, will ere long make the Common-wealth sick both of it and them, since they cannot well digest it; soveraigne Power in Subjects seldome agreeing with the stomacks of fellow Subjects.'[18] This passage exemplifies a pervasive theme of this work: namely, that the king provides the only tenable defence for the common people against the abuse of 'soveraigne Power in Subjects', by which is meant the tyranny of individuals driven by motives of greed and personal aggrandisement. Although such a defence of kingship might not have appealed to the urban radicals of Clare's time, especially in the wake of the French Revolution and the publication of Thomas Paine's *Rights of Man* (1792), nevertheless the notion of the monarchy as a bulwark against tyranny retained much of its currency in rural England, where labourers such as Clare, without official representation in Parliament, had no other recourse against the abuse of power and the wrongful appropriation of common lands by wealthy individuals. In this, as in several other aspects, the political views of rural labourers diverged significantly from those of their urban counterparts.

Clare did not mark up his copy of *Eikon Basiliké*, but he did comment on the character of Charles I in a manuscript fragment that was possibly intended to form part of an essay on religion. This undated fragment was likely composed in the late 1820s, and it indicates that Clare was entirely capable of acknowledging weaknesses and shortcomings in the character of the 'royal martyr': 'The royal martyr as he was called however he might extol himself or be extolled as a christian by others never for got he was a king which has nothing at all to do with the merits of christianity wether he suffered justly or unjustly is not now to be argued.'[19] What interests Clare in the story of Charles I is evidently not the king's supposed saintly qualities: Clare is reluctant to debate whether the king was executed 'justly or unjustly'. Rather, Clare is impressed by the fact that Charles '*never forgot that he was a king*': he suggests that Charles always remained faithful to his role as a monarch, even in extreme adversity. Clare goes on to criticise those who rebelled against the king, since in his view it is never a good idea to overthrow an established system of government, no matter how 'imperfect'.

> tho the weaker party in this case may be said to have triumphed as the race is not always to the swift nor the battle to the strong yet when in power they displayed more insolence & oppression then those of whom they so bitterly & loudly complained & so it is always that the remedy is worse then the disease & thus it ever is that a goverment tho imperfect is better then a new one forced upon its ruins[20]

Clare uses the metaphor of disease, possibly derived from his reading of *Eikon Basiliké*, to epitomise the concept of a disordered state. Despite his acknowledgement of the king's human frailty, Clare argues that the institution of kingship provides an essential stabilising force within the inherently dismal set of possibilities offered by human nature. Whenever a new system of government is 'forced upon [the] ruins' of an old regime, the inevitable result will be even 'more insolence & oppression' than existed before. This is Clare's pessimistic assessment of the consequences of regicide, derived from his critical reading of *Eikon Basiliké* and his local knowledge of the events of the English Revolution. Although such attitudes may not be consistent with those of the urban radicals of Clare's era, I believe they are typical of a broad sector of the rural working class. The Luddites and the Swing rioters did not accurately represent the aspirations of the 'silent majority' of rural folk during the 1820s, many of whom desperately hoped to be able to retain what meagre subsistence they still possessed. Few rural labourers of this period were truly interested in revolutionary adventures. Clare, like Cobbett, had no taste for violent revolution; the modest political objective of both writers could be summarised in the word 'reform'.

In 'The Village Minstrel', Clare seeks to indicate how the traditional ballad of Woodcroft Castle is related to his present-day political concerns. As we have seen, Clare tells this story in a 'primitive' way that heightens the heroism of the royalists and accentuates the brutality of the rebels. When he returns to the 'framing' narrative, Clare suggests that the murderous violence of the Civil War is akin to the process of parliamentary enclosure currently underway in the vicinity of Helpston:

> But who can tell the anguish of his mind
> When reformations formidable foes
> Wi civil wars on natures peace combind

> & desolation struck her deadly blows
> As curst improvment gan his fields inclose
> O greens & fields & trees farwell farwell
> His heart wrung pains his unavailing woes
> No words can utter & no tongue can tell
> When ploughs destroyd the green when groves of willows fell
>
> (stanza 103)

Clare articulates a provocative analogy between the senseless violence of the English Revolution and the war against nature perpetrated by agents of 'improvement' in his native village. Clare regards the process of enclosure as only the latest episode of a 'reformation' that has been in progress for centuries; like Cobbett, he is sceptical of any supposed 'reformation' that devastates the countryside and neglects the rights and privileges of the common people.

Both Cobbett and Clare stubbornly resist the tyranny of progress. Through their reading of landscape and their habit of listening attentively to the voices of the dispossessed, both of these writers evince an understanding of historical process that is quite distinct from the more 'enlightened' and 'progressive' views of the contemporary urban radical movement. Both Clare and Cobbett regarded the English Revolution as an episode of senseless violence that succeeded only in establishing a tyranny that proved worse than the monarchy it overthrew. Clare's historical imagination leads him to regard the process of enclosure as a violent political and ecological disruption that re-enacts the most ruthless episodes of the English Revolution, destroying for ever the pastoral harmony that once prevailed between the masters and the men. Such an evidently conservative stance should not be dismissed as mere reactionary dogma, since it likewise embodies an inherently radical resistance to the 'improvement' of landscape and the 'reformation' of agricultural production. The radical conservatism of Cobbett and Clare emerges from their deeply ambivalent response to the historical experience of the English Revolution.

CHAPTER 10

'Not a reforming patriot but an ambitious tyrant': representations of Cromwell and the English Republic in the late eighteenth and early nineteenth centuries

Peter J. Kitson

The impact of the thinkers and activists of the English Revolution upon the participants in the political debate begun by the French Revolution is still largely unexplored. There have been several studies of the impact of Milton's thought upon Wordsworth, Coleridge and Blake and a few others have investigated the influence of Harringtonian ideas about property and the constitution upon Coleridge, but the wider expanses of seventeenth-century political thought and its various influences on writing of the Romantic period has still to be charted.[1] Our views of this relationship between the debates of the two revolutions are too constricted by an overly canonical concern with Milton, Wordsworth, Coleridge and Blake. This is regrettable since it is clear that writings and examples of the panoply of reformers and radicals that historians in the wake of Christopher Hill have popularised were accessible to the writers of the 1790s in various histories and their reprints. William Godwin's great *History of the Commonwealth of England* (1824–8), although published late in the Romantic period, demonstrates a first-hand knowledge, not just of the lives and works of the Commonwealthsmen – Henry Vane, Major-General Thomas Harrison, John Bradshaw, Henry Marten, James Harrington and Algernon Sidney who were his political idols – but also an awareness of the writing and activities of Edward Sexby, James Nayler and George Fox, the Fifth Monarchy Men, the Diggers, the Ranters, Lodowicke Muggleton and others who famously attempted to turn the world upside-down. Godwin's *History* uses sources such as Marchamont Nedham's *Mercurius Politicus* and Thurloe's *State Papers* which were available to the late eighteenth- and early nineteenth-century reader mediated through a series of histories, such as Joshua Toulmin's 1793 edition of Daniel Neal's *History of the Puritans* (1735), Isaac Kimber's *The Life of Oliver Cromwell* (1725) and John Banks's *A Short Critical Review of the Political Life of Oliver Cromwell* (1739), all three the work of dissenters. In addition to these were a number of studies of Cromwell of varying seriousness appearing in the early nineteenth century, M. Villemain's *Histoire de Cromwell* (1819), Oliver Cromwell's (a descendant) *Memoirs of the Protector* (1820), Thomas Cromwell's *Oliver Cromwell and his Times* (1821) and George Brodie's *History of the British Empire from the Accession of Charles the First to the Restoration* (1822). Although several of these, like the earlier Mark Noble's *Lives of the English Regicides* of 1798 and the anonymous *Cromwelliana* (1810), were primarily of antiquarian concerns, they did show evidence of a continuing interest in the Protector's work. In fact Godwin's knowledgeable and informed account of the Interregnum pre-empts that of Hill's seminal studies, *The World Turned Upside Down* (1972) and *Milton and the English Revolution* (1978), in its awareness of the radical dissenting milieu of the Revolution. As John Morrow puts it, Godwin 'attempted to establish the English commonwealth as a ground for serious theoretical speculations on government, one that outlived the politically significant but otherwise facile analysis that characterized many contemporary treatments of the Revolution'.[2] Godwin was not the only one with such historical knowledge. Robert Southey also demonstrated a similar, if less sympathetic, grasp of radical and dissenting histories in essays for the *Quarterly Review* of 1815 and 1821.

The subject of this chapter concerns the portrayal in the Romantic period of the Lord Protector, Oliver Cromwell. Received wisdom has always stressed the negativity of views of Cromwell, prior to Carlyle's great edition of *Oliver Cromwell's Letters and Speeches with Elucidations* of 1845. Carlyle gave his audience the inner workings and troubled conscience of a Christian hero who would speak to the increasing predominance of Nonconformity in Victorian England. Thus began the Victorian historiographical revolution after which Cromwell and English Puritanism would come to be regarded as important moral forces, representing the spirit of their age. Congregationalists, Baptists, Unitarians and Presbyterians invariably traced their origin back to seventeenth-century dissent. Like middle-class reformers, working-class radicals were also to praise Cromwell's direct action, especially the 'Physical Force' wing of the Chartist movement of the 1840s. After Godwin's and Carlyle's works other major histories were written by dissenters, such as Robert Vaughan and John Forster, which were able to accommodate seventeenth-century Nonconformity in the sectarian diversity of a liberal England no longer dominated by an Anglican hierarchy. This process reached its apogee, perhaps, in Samuel Rawson Gardiner's monumental histories of the Civil Wars and Interregnum of the late nineteenth

century. In such works Cromwell becomes an almost Gladstonian figure, a religiously inspired politician attempting to fashion a society out
of the principles of civil liberty and religious toleration. Before Carlyle,
however, Cromwell, it is usually claimed, was regarded with equal hostility and derision by Tory, Whig and Radical alike. Typical of this view
is Timothy Lang's recent comment:

Even the radicals, whose distrust of the crown and attraction to republicanism
might have led them to look more favourably on the Puritan past, hurled some
of the most bitter invective at the Protector. It was Cromwell, after all, who
turned against the Commonwealth in order to satisfy his own ambitions, thus
terminating prematurely England's republican experiment. No one, in the late
eighteenth and early nineteenth centuries, was prepared to utter a good word
in defense of Cromwell and the Puritans.[3]

This is not entirely true, as Lang himself goes on to show. Although the
leading tenor of late eighteenth- and early nineteenth-century comment
on Cromwell is negative, there are other, positive views as well as more
ambiguous discussions of his rôle in English politics. Jeremy Bentham,
for instance, while praising the law reform of Bonaparte, 'the *Cromwell
of France*', could also celebrate Cromwell's intended legal reforms which
rank 'that wonderful man higher than anything else that I ever read of
him'.[4] Moreover, the English Revolution of the 1640s and 1650s came
to be seen as a precedent and a means of understanding the French
Revolution of the 1790s and Cromwell's rôle in the former was often
to serve as a warning for the drift from freedom to military despotism.
Cromwell became a filter through which to view first Robespierre, then
Bonaparte. For the radicals and reformers he demonstrated the dangers
of a despotic ambition that would stifle liberty, and for Burkeian conservatives he was the prior example of the logic of inevitability that operates
in political revolutions when obedience is replaced by anarchy. Nevertheless Cromwell was not Bonaparte and English Puritanism was not,
despite its similarities, Jacobinism, as some of the more incisive commentators of the time point out. In the 1790s a religious radicalism akin to
seventeenth-century Puritanism still flourished and, if anything, was the
leading strand of radical thought. However, other, more secular, ideologies of opposition based on Painite principles of natural rights and
Benthamite utilitarianism were gaining ascendancy. The rôle of religious
motivation in effecting political change came under increasing scrutiny.
The extent to which the radicals and reformers of the 1790s could be
compared to seventeenth-century Puritans was one of the key issues in

the debates between Burke and Priestley.[5] More than this, Cromwell's example raised the question that haunted the radicals and reformers of the period, such as the much-persecuted John Thelwall and the oft-reviled William Godwin, as it had troubled Milton: how could a libertarian and democratic political ideology maintain itself when a majority of the people preferred the bondage of kings and lords, and what therefore was the role of violence and exclusion in a democratic republic? In some ways Cromwell's demonisation in the period functioned as the return of the repressed from the political unconscious, a figure loaded with displaced political anxieties and fears to be ritualistically denounced and exorcised, a dangerous political *Doppelgänger* of the writer's preferred ideal.

EIGHTEENTH-CENTURY SOURCES

Views of Cromwell were mediated through a variety of sources: images, histories, political debates, literary recreations and verbal traditions. A number of histories took up the subject of the Civil War and Republic. Most historians regard David Hume's portrayal of Cromwell and seventeenth-century Puritanism as most influential in the later period. Lang argues that no historian would 'alter significantly Hume's characterization of Oliver Cromwell as an ambitious and hypocritical fanatic' and Peter Karsten claimed that 'the Lord Protector had been in the darkness for well over a century before his nineteenth-century resurrection'.[6] Hume's *History of Great Britain* (1754–61) attempted to provide a justification for both sides in the Civil War as a means to create a consensus for the Hanoverian succession. As such, Hume reserved his most trenchant criticism for Puritan enthusiasm which triumphed over constructive and moderate political reform. His treatment of Cromwell was extremely hostile: Cromwell was 'a most frantic enthusiast ... the most dangerous of hypocrites ... who was enabled after multiplied deceits to cover, under a tempest of passion, all his crooked schemes and profound artifices'.[7] Although opposed to Hume's defence of the Hanoverian constitution, the Republican historian Catharine Macaulay found Cromwell equally objectionable:

[H]e deprived his country of a full and equal system of liberty, at the very instant of fruition; stopped the course of her power in the midst of her victories; impeded the progress of reformation by destroying her government and limiting the bounds of her empire; and by a fatal concurrence of circumstances was enabled to obstruct more good and occasion more evil than has been the lot of any other individual.[8]

Macaulay, responding to Burke's *Reflections* in 1790, blames Cromwell for rendering the 'Revolution and the Revolutionists odious' because of the 'general detestation which men conceived of his *treachery* and *tyranny*', thus paving the way for the 'restoration of the old government'.[9] Most Whig and republican sympathisers in the period followed Macaulay's lead in blaming Cromwell for the ruination of representative government. The Scottish Whig theorists and republican sympathisers John Millar and James Burgh, while praising the tolerance of the Independents, found Cromwell to be a hypocritical and ambitious villain who tragically destroyed England's best chance for a representative republican government. Millar described him as 'an extraordinary genius, utterly devoid of all principle' who manufactured 'an odious species of despotism', and Burgh castigates 'the villainous *Cromwell*' for demolishing the 'true government by representation' of the Rump Parliament.[10] However, other voices are still to be heard. The Independent minister and dissenting historian Daniel Neal, who published his influential and rarely discussed *History of the Puritans* between 1732 and 1738, presents a more positive portrait of Cromwell for a liberal and dissenting audience. Although even Hume had to admire grudgingly the Protector's energy and ability, Neal goes a great deal further. Commenting on Cromwell's installation as Lord Protector, he enthuses:

Thus did this wonderful man, by suprising management, supported only by the sword, advance himself to the supreme government of the three kingdoms without consent of parliament or people. His birth seemed to promise nothing of this kind; nor does it appear that he had formed the project, till after the battle of Worcester, when he apprehended the parliament had projected his ruin by disbanding the army, and perpetuating their authority among themselves: which of the two usurpations was most eligible, must be left with the reader; but how he brought the officers into his measures, and supported his sovereignty by an army of enthusiasts, Anabaptists, fifth monarchy men, and republicans will be the admiration of all posterity; and though by this adventurous act he drew upon himself the plots and conspiracies of the several factions in the nation, yet his genius and resolution surmounted all difficulties, his short empire being one continued blaze of glory and renown to the British isles, and a terror to the rest of Europe.[11]

Neal admires Cromwell's policies of toleration and justice, but it is his foreign policy which excites him most. His Cromwell 'to the supreme government of these nations, appeared on a sudden like a comet or blazing star, raised up by providence to exalt this nation to a distinguished pitch of glory, and to strike terror into the rest of Europe'. Under Cromwell justice 'was restored to its ancient splendour', manners were reformed, 'trade flourished and the arts of peace were cultivated throughout the whole nation'. Neal is suspicious of Cromwell's usurpation, suspecting ambition, but he applauds the dismissal of the Rump and concludes that 'Oliver Cromwell had no other choice, but to abandon the state, or to take the administration upon himself; or put it into the hands of some other person who had no better title.' Nor is Neal's portrait of Cromwell simply that of the consummate statesman. His Cromwell is a generous, jocular, intelligent and pious man. Cromwell's faults were those of his enthusiasm and his not deriving his religion from rational principles, in the manner of the eighteenth-century rational dissenter. Ambition also 'might sometimes lead him aside' especially when he imagined himself as the 'second Phineas, raised up by providence to be the scourge of idolatry and superstition'. The negativity which surrounds his reception is easily explained by Neal in the hostility of Royalists, Prebyterians and Republicans.[12] In Neal's Independent defence of Cromwell we have a strong anticipation of Carlyle's Christian hero. In 1793 Neal's *History* was edited and enlarged by the Unitarian minister at Taunton, Joshua Toulmin. Toulmin was also a friend of the young Unitarian radical S. T. Coleridge. His influence on the radical dissenters of the 1790s and beyond was not inconsiderable.[13]

That there existed a strong, if underground, dissenting tradition that favoured the Protector is also suggested by other evidence. The independent Presbyterian minister James Murray, who established a chapel in Newcastle in 1764, was perhaps typical of numerous dissenting ministers who applauded the English Revolution. In 1778 he published a warning to George III in opposition to his policy in America, entitled EIKON BASILIKÉ. Murray, like many dissenters, celebrated the events of the Puritan Revolution and applauded Cromwell's example in his *Finishing Stroke*.[14] More soberly, George Crabbe depicted a dissenting, Independent family in his 'The Frank Courtship', from the *Tales* of 1812. He poignantly describes the group for whom '*Cromwell* was their Saint, and when they met / They mourn'd that the Saints were not their Rulers yet'. In the plain and orderly sitting room of the dissenter's house is a 'small Recess' containing 'pencil'd ware'. This china is turned:

> by chosen friends, and there appear'd
> His stern, strong features, whom they all rever'd;
> For there in lofty air was seen to stand,
> The bold Protector of the conquer'd land;
> Drawn in that look with which he wept and swore,

Turned out the Members and made fast the door,
Ridding the House of every knave and drone,
Forc'd, though it griev'd his soul, to rule alone.
The stern still smile each Friend approving gave,
Then turn'd the view, and all again were grave.[15]

It seems fair to assume that there was, as Roger Howell Jr suggests, 'an underground tradition favourable to Cromwell . . . from the time of the Restoration, especially among dissenters and radicals'.[16] Dissenters and Nonconformists marked the anniversary of Charles I's execution not with the prescribed fast day but rather with celebrations. Howell points to more positive appreciations of Cromwell's career in Isaac Kimber's *The Life of Oliver Cromwell* (1725) and John Banks's *A Short Critical Review of the Political Life of Oliver Cromwell* (1739), both written by dissenters.[17] Of course there were also strong oral traditions and folk memories of the Protectorate, many favourable to Cromwell.[18] John Clare's haunting lines from an untitled sonnet on Woodcroft Castle may be a part of this folk tradition with its evocation of 'The locked up room where superstition sleeps / & cromwells memory in dread mystery keeps'.[19] It seems certain that within the confines of the dissenting academies and Nonconformist circles, as well as in the oral histories of the lower classes, there existed deep-rooted traditions of admiration for the works of the Protector.

CROMWELL IN THE FRENCH REVOLUTION DEBATE

The British reformers and radicals of the 1790s often saw themselves in the context of the English Revolution and they were frequently represented by their opponents as the true heirs of the regicides of the 1640s. This process of identification receives its fullest investigation in Godwin's *History of the Commonwealth*, a work which attempts to reassess the tradition of English republican thought. The general tenor of hostility towards Cromwell in the period prior to the late 1820s is thus understandable. When Edmund Burke sought to discredit Richard Price's millenarian enthusiasm for the French Revolution in his *Discourse on the Love of our Country* (1789), he linked Price's political and religious rhetoric with that of Cromwell's chaplain Hugh Peter. Price, Burke claimed in his *Reflections on the Revolution in France* (1790), had uttered thoughts in a manner not heard 'since the year 1648, when a predecessor of Dr Price, the Rev. Hugh Peter, made the vault of the king's own chapel at St James's ring with the honour and privilege of the saints'. Burke disliked the radical Protestant equation of politics and religion: 'politics and the pulpit' were for him 'terms which have little agreement'.[20] He thus attempted to reclaim the Revolution of 1688 from the hands of the Protestant dissenters whose true ancestors he believed to be the enthusiasts of the 1640s, a pedigree confirmed as much by rhetoric as ideology. In so doing Burke encouraged the reformers and dissenters to investigate their own historical ancestry to see where their true origins lay. Burke himself was ambiguous about Cromwell's status. He saw him as 'one of the great bad men of the old stamp', a sublime 'destroying angel' who 'smote the country' and whose virtues were corrective to his faults.[21] In *A Letter to a Member of the National Assembly* (1791) he contrasted the Protector favourably with the 'philosophic usurpers' who chose to follow him. Cromwell 'was a man in whom ambition had not wholly suppressed, but only suspended the sentiments of religion', and 'the love . . . of a fair and honourable reputation', who sought to legitimise his usurpation by upholding not remaking the law, delivering 'England from anarchy'.[22]

In the bitter political debate that Burke began, Cromwell often served as the dissenter's limiting case and thus became the recipient of hostility. Although there did exist a positive dissenting view of Cromwell well before Carlyle, most of Burke's opponents demonised the Protector as the signifier of all those things alien to their own beliefs. Joseph Priestley, for instance, in his *Lectures on History* of 1788, denounced the Interregnum as a time of 'absolute anarchy and confusion', especially blaming Cromwell, 'the man, who at the head of an army of Enthusiasts and Fanatics, passionately devoted to their leader, effected the subversion of the Constitution'.[23] Although radicalised by his millenarian expectations of the French Revolution a few years later, Priestley could still, in his *Familiar Letters Addressed to the Inhabitants of Birmingham* (1790), dissociate himself from Cromwell and his Independents, the true king-killers, and claim an ancestry for his Unitarianism back to the Presbyterian opponents of Cromwell. Nevertheless Priestley sneaks a justification of the regicide into his argument. '*Cromwell*, and the rest' executed Charles I for 'their *safety* and *ambition*'.[24]

Charles James Fox, the parliamentary leader of the Whigs during the 1790s, similarly wished to dissociate himself from Cromwell and radical Puritanism. His posthumously published *History of the Early Part of the Reign of James the Second* (1808) served as a statement of his brand of Whig politics. Fox blamed Cromwell for the excess of the 1640s and beyond, denying the Burkeian equation of 1649 and 1789. For Fox, Cromwell was 'too odious ever to be the object of praise or imitation'.[25] Despite this, Fox

Figure 4. James Sayers, *The Mirror of Patriotism* (1784).

himself was caricatured by his enemies as a potential Cromwell. A print
of 1783 by William Dent represents Fox preaching below a bust of the
Protector. Most famously James Sayers's print 'The Mirror of Patriotism'
depicts Fox in the act of practising his speech in front of a mirror which un-
cannily reflects back Oliver Cromwell from Fox's political unconscious.
James Gillray also associated Fox with Cromwell after the politician's

death in a print of 1807, *Charon's Boat*.[26] Most of the replies to Burke, when they do allude to Cromwell, are dismissive. John Scott granted 'that the despotism of the long Parliament, and of Cromwell, was more grinding than the milder tyranny of the First Charles' but claimed that 'we owe our present happy constitition', which was cemented by 1688, to the resistance of 'those days'. The fiery radical Henry Redhead Yorke despised alike 'the Despot Charles' and 'the Tyrant Cromwell'. Partisans of Burke, by and large, did not share their mentor's sneaking admiration for the 'great bad man'. The unknown author of *Remarks on Mr Paine's Pamphlet* (1791) referred to 'that late and disgraceful period of national delerium when the title of a Commonwealth sanctioned the eversion [*sic*] of the constitution' and the 'usurper declined that blood-stained crown which would have sate uneasily on his head'. William Sewell denounced '*Cromwell . . . that* Arch-Cheat! that ruthless *Tyrannus Tyranno-rum*'; and Charles Harrington Elliot accorded him the 'eternal infamy of a traitor and tyrant'. Thomas Hearn in 1793 claimed that Cromwell 'exercised a higher prerogative, and was more arbitrary than any king'.[27]

All these references, however, tend to be historical and polemical asides. Burke's challenge to the dissenters to reappraise their levelling past is not taken up for several years. A serious historical discussion of the similarities and differences of the English and French Revolutions is, however, attempted by the English Jacobin, John Thelwall. Thelwall's work shows a sustained attempt to ground his own political ideology on a historical basis, a venture which stood him in good stead when he was prevented from lecturing on political subjects by the 'gagging acts' of 1795. Thelwall, a materialist, saw himself as the heir to the English Parliamentarians and Republicans, particularly admiring the two patriot heroes John Hampden and Algernon Sidney, after whom he named his two sons. Having little grasp of revolutionary Puritan thought, he does not wish to claim a similarity for the French and English Revolutions, but rather to argue that the French is infused by a spirit of liberty whereas the English was mainly the result of fanaticism, thus breaking the link forged by Burke between the two. Significantly Thelwall doubles Cromwell with the Leveller activist Colonel John Lilburne, who suffered similar persecution for his political views as he himself was to experience. In 1794 Thelwall was tried for High Treason just as Lilburne had been, a century and a half or so earlier, and both men had been acquitted. The materialist Painite lecturer was able to find in Lilburne a more congenial precedent for his political activity than Presbyterians or Independents. The 'virtuous and gallant patriot Lillburne' shows the opposite example to the 'usurping tyranny of an Oliver Cromwell'.[28] In his important two lectures on the 'UNFORTUNATE RESTORATION of the HOUSE of STUART delivered on 29 May and 3 June 1795', Thelwall targeted not Charles I as the main enemy of religious and political freedom but, instead, the Protector: '*Oliver Cromwell*; who, though he set out perhaps with as large a portion of the love of liberty as was possible for a hypocritical fanatic, yet undoubtedly in the end proved himself to be, not a reforming patriot, but an ambitious usurper'. This 'hypocritical pretender to divine inspiration could lead a larger portion of the people with him' than those 'whose pure and enlightened spirit was dictated by the philosophic principles of liberty and universal justice'.[29] Thelwall's portrayal of Cromwell is one of the first mature considerations of the politics of Robespierre's Terror of 1793–5, a political philosophy which would trouble him for the rest of his career. Cromwell provided a framework within which to investigate Robespierre's usurpation of power and the phenomenon of the Terror in an anticipation of Trotskyist denunciations of Stalin's 'Cult of Personality':

Thus the *Protectorate*, or, as it is called the Republic, continued as long as he lived, because of the superior activity of his mind, the terror of his name, and that sort of fanatic eloquence which he possessed, kept all other persons in awe and, so long as the architect remained, the pillars of the revolution appeared to be secure, whatever change might take place in particular parts of the building ... everything rested, not upon digested principles, which are permanent and durable; but merely upon his shoulders; therefore, of course, no sooner did he fall, than anarchy and debility were exhibited in every part of the state; and the nation destitute of able and popular leaders, and wearied with incessant fluctuations, was driven to seek repose again in its ancient despotism.[30]

Thelwall's depiction of a charismatic fanatic obsessed with his own power and ambition is as relevant to a Robespierre as to a Cromwell, not known in the period for the 'fanatic eloquence' of the French Jacobin. Anxieties haunt this lecture. Whereas the French Revolution, which proceeds from a nation undergoing a collective enlightenment, must succeed, the Commonwealth, which sprang from the fanaticism of a small number of Puritans, inevitably failed. Thelwall reassures himself that despite Robespierre's Terror, 'the causes which enabled *Oliver Cromwell* to usurp a tyranny over this country, and make himself Protector, do not exist, nor ever have existed, at any period of the French Revolution'.[31] Thelwall's optimism was no doubt partially a response to Robespierre's fall in July 1795 (news of Robespierre's fall began to be circulated in London from

14 August onward, after the Lectures were delivered but before they were published in 1796). But this optimism was short-lived. Thelwall was to find out himself, after leaving London, that his enlightened principles were no more shared by the majority of the British nation than Cromwell's beliefs had been in his time.[32]

The polyvalency of Cromwell in political discourse made him capable of representing the 'Oliverism of that cold-blooded monster' Pitt for Richard Carlile[33] as well as encompassing the despotism of what Coleridge and Southey refer to in *The Fall of Robespierre* (1794) as 'This worse than Cromwell / The Austere, the self denying Robespierre'.[34] Like Thelwall, the dissenting Coleridge of the 1790s saw Robespierre in terms of the Puritan ruler. He planned to give in a series of six historical lectures 'a Comparative View of the English Rebellion under Charles the First and the French Revolution' in June 1795, the fifth of which was to consider 'Oliver Cromwell and Robespierre'.[35] Like Thelwall, Coleridge was keen to ground his radical dissent in a serious engagement with Commonwealthsman ideology.[36] As Coleridge moved towards his later conservatism he often returned to the issue of single-person rule, filtered through the experience of Bonapartism. In 'Letters on the Spaniards. v' for *The Courier* of 20 December 1809 he argues for the importance of representative institutions as a check on personal ambition:

Under extraordinary circumstances of national terror, Robespierre indeed used the frenzy of the Parisian populace to terrify and enslave the National Assembly: but he was sacrificed to public vengeance before he had disclosed any plan of permanent usurpation, and at this hour it remains uncertain whether the Monster died a fanatic or impostor . . . Cromwell would never have been Protector if the Parliament had been the sole scene of his hypocrisy: he found the mock Parliaments of his own election unmanageable tools. Neither the victories, nor the oaths, nor the bombastic harangues of Bonaparte, nor even the more powerful presidential authority of his brother Lucien, would have saved him from the sentence of the Legislature, or the hastier daggers that leapt forth to avenge its insulted Majesty, had not his dragoons protected him, and the army joined the conspiracy against freedom.[37]

Coleridge here introduces Cromwell as a third term into a political discourse which is essentially about Bonaparte's career, a phenomenon which had substantial implications for his ideas about genius, both artistic and worldly. For Coleridge, Cromwell could stand for the spirits of both Bonapartism and Jacobinism. In *The Friend* (1811) he remarks how he remembered 'that when the examples of former Jacobins, Julius Caesar, Cromwell, &c. were adduced in France and England' to gloss the First

Consul's ambitions, they were dismissed as unthinkable in the enlightened eighteenth century.[38] Coleridge argues that Cromwell has an affinity for Robespierre and Bonaparte, as they are all, in some ways, the children of Jacobinism. What is most suprising, perhaps, is that in an age which privileged genius, Cromwell is never allowed to represent either republican or Romantic idealism in any form. Emblematic of this situation is the case of that heir of the revolutionary and republican tradition, Percy Bysshe Shelley. In his unfinished tragedy *Charles the First*, it is clear that John Hampden is to represent republican (and thus Romantic) idealism rather than Oliver, who is dramatically silent and strangely marginal to the action of what we have of the play.[39]

SOUTHEY'S CROMWELL AND OTHER PERSPECTIVES OF THE 1820s

In many ways, one of the most sustained discussions of Cromwell's rôle in British history in the early decades of the nineteenth century, prior to Godwin, is found in the writings of the arch-Tory Anglican Robert Southey. Southey, although an inveterate enemy of sectarianism, was fascinated by the lives and activities of the dissenters of the 1640s and 1650s. No longer the Godwinian radical who in 1797 could praise the 'ardent mind' and 'goodliest plans of happiness on earth' of the republican and regicide Henry Marten, he could nevertheless find good copy in the activities of James Nayler, George Fox, Mary Fisher, and the Quakers, Ranters and Seekers.[40] Southey was concerned to defend the inclusiveness of the nineteenth-century national Anglican church against what he perceived to be the fragmentation and divisiveness of the spirit of sectarianism in the face of the growing strength of Nonconformity. In his review of three recent publications on the history of dissent (including Edward Parsons's two-volume abridgement of Neal's *History* of 1812) for the *Quarterly Review* in 1813, Southey condemns its adherents for their intolerance of others. He seeks to confront the respectable contemporary dissenters with the extravagancies and excesses of their schismatic forefathers, returning their dissent to its less than respectable origins. Arguing that 'sectarianism ... contains in itself the seeds of schism in infinite series' and claiming that Puritanism has always been a religion of intolerance, he instances the Presbyterian Thomas Edwards's *Gangraena* (1645) as descriptive of its endless schisms and its author himself as representative of its true, persecuting spirit. In the failure of the Puritans and their latter-day historians to show compassion and sympathy for the

broken Archbishop Laud and their exclusive concern with the suffering
of their own brethren, Southey detects their main error, the inability to
appreciate 'that all the virtues are not on one side, and all the vices on the
other'. It is in the extravagancies of the sects of the 1650s that Southey
detects a warning for his own age when, confronted by the breakdown
of established forms of belief, people 'found themselves astray like sheep
when the fold has been broken down'. The early Quakers with their
principles of the inner light and of private judgement were particularly
dangerous. Among dissenters 'the right of private judgment is so inju-
diciously inculcated' that they 'despise all judgment except their own'.
The spirit of dissent itself is 'evil'. It breaks down the national consensus
as those it inflicts ally themselves with enemies of the nation, such as
the American and French Revolutionaries. It is this 'moral expatriation'
which is dangerous and threatens anarchy and confusion in the body
politic.[41]

It was in the context of the dissenting campaign to repeal civil disabili-
ties that Southey wrote to warn his audience of the potential anarchy that
would ensue were the national church to be disturbed. His neglected 'Life
of Cromwell' for the *Quarterly Review* of July 1821 continues this theme.
Reviewing a series of recent works about Cromwell, Southey puts together the life of a dissembling Puritan hypocrite. His 'Life' is notable
for its strong sympathy for the 'unambitious and conscientious spirit'
of Charles I, unusual even in inveterate Cromwell-haters of the period.
Southey follows Clarendon in applauding the success of Charles's personal rule and he accepts the authenticity of *Eikon Basiliké*, from which he
frequently quotes.[42] For Southey, Cromwell was not a naturally wicked
man and, 'in private life', he showed many good qualities. He is certainly preferable to the severe republicans of the Long Parliament and
the 'thorough fanatic' Henry Vane. What damns him is the 'fanatical constitution' that Southey detected in all dissenters. The English Revolution,
like the French, was the result of the activities of schismatics and unbeliev-
ers who had 'determined to overthrow the existing government in church
and state'. It was in Cromwell's power to restore monarchy and peace
after the first Civil War: 'In the movements of the revolutionary sphere
his star was rising, but it was not yet lord of the ascendant; and, in raising
himself to his present situation, he had, like the unlucky magician in
romance, conjured up stronger spirits than he was yet master enough
of the black art to control.'[43] Once having attained power by sinister
means, Cromwell was unable to govern 'equitably and mercifully' as he
would have wished. 'In spite of himself' he 'was compelled to govern

tyranically'. Ultimately for Southey, Cromwell was 'this most fortunate and least flagitious of usurpers' who left an 'imperishable name so stained with reproach . . . it were better for him to be forgotten than to be so remembered'.[44]

If Neal's *History*, repackaged by Toulmin, anticipated the later nineteenth-century rehabilitation of Cromwell, then Southey's Tory apologia for church and state looked back to Hume's defence of the Hanoverian succession. By and large Toulmin's party were to win the day. Although Henry Hallam's Whiggish *Constitutional History of England* (1818–27) could remain hostile to the usurping Cromwell, preferring, instead, to depict the Long Parliament as an anticipation of 1688, it was Thomas Babington Macaulay's panegyric to Cromwell that would firmly set the tone for the coming Victorian age.[45] Hallam's view of the Civil Wars, like Southey's, looked back to an inclusive Anglican settlement at risk from Cromwellian or Bonapartist predators, whereas Macaulay's liberal England prided itself on being tolerant and sectarian. In his essay 'Milton' for the *Edinburgh Review* of 1825 Macaulay praised Cromwell as a sincere and enthusiastic supporter of Parliament until it reneged on its duty: 'Cromwell was evidently laying . . . the foundations of an admirable system. Never before had religious liberty and the freedom of discussion been enjoyed in a greater degree.'[46] Macaulay stressed Cromwell's Whiggish and Republican virtues rather then the deep introspective Protestant heroics which would later find favour with Carlyle. Nevertheless, by the time he was writing, Cromwell's career and character were becoming more palatable to an age freeing itself from the political consequences of the French Revolution.

GODWIN'S *HISTORY OF THE COMMONWEALTH*

In many ways it is William Godwin's remarkable *History of the Common-wealth* (1824–8) which stands as a coda to the appreciations of Cromwell and the English Republic in the pre-Carlyle era. Godwin had a long-standing interest in the Commonwealth period, having already written a tragedy, *Faulkener*, set in 1669 (1807).[47] In 1828 the repeal of the Test and Corporation Acts removed the barriers against both the dissenters and Catholics from participating in the national politics of the country. Godwin's *History* can be seen as an attempt to re-examine the British republican tradition in the light of this forward motion. Godwin's own political thought was derived from his dissenting Sandemanian back-ground and although he had soon dispensed with the religious aspect of this belief, he was committed to its espousal of notions of reason and private judgement.[48] Godwin's *History* shows an excellent knowledge of the primary materials available at the time. He perused contemporary tracts in the British Museum and consulted the journals of the Houses of Parliaments.[49] In the *History* Godwin attempted a defence of Republican thought. The Commonwealth failed in seventeenth-century Britain because the country was not advanced enough to support an enlightened government. As part of this defence Godwin argues for the importance of Puritanism as a moral force meant to shape men into subjects capable of sustaining the republic. In particular Godwin identifies republicanism with the Independents who desired a broad and 'generous spirit of toleration'. For Godwin, a republic propagated freedom of thought and encouraged men to be rational agents. The 'determined republicans' of the time wished to found a 'pure commonwealth, with no court, and no master; but where every citizen should know himself the equal of every other citizen, and feel convinced that the highest elevation of the state was open to everyone, whose virtues and talents might qualify him to fill it'. Godwin understood that the aim was essentially doomed as this vision was not shared by the multitude of the people and the Republic was deprived of the time necessary to inculcate its values in the populace. Godwin is dismissive of the royalists, Presbyterians and Levellers and reserves his praise for the period 1639 to 1653, when Cromwell's *coup d'état* effectively ended the Republic. This five-year period is equal to any time in English history for 'the glory of its rule, and perhaps in the virtue and disinterestedness of its most distinguished leaders'.[50]

The leading ideas of Godwin's *History* have been expertly discussed by John Morrow, but here I want to concentrate on the fourth volume of the *History*, subtitled *Oliver, Lord Protector*, which contains Godwin's mature view of Cromwell.[51] The object of the preceding volumes of the *History*, Godwin explains, was to 'describe the unavailing efforts of virtuous and magnanimous men in the perhaps visionary attempt to establish a republic in England', whereas the business of the final volume is to 'delineate the reign of a usurper, who seems to have had the idea of becoming a public benefactor'. Godwin's Cromwell is a superlative statesman and an extraordinary man. He is a man who desires the public good and who believes he is 'an instrument in the hands of God for accomplishing great things for a chosen generation of men'. He is a man possessed of 'philanthropy and patriotism', yet he failed to establish a lasting settlement because his plan did not 'include the personal element of every individual in the soil of England' which was necessary to encourage personal independence. Vane, on the contrary, desired a republic in which 'every Englishman should be a king . . . that none of his country-men should have a master'. Cromwell's project of a single-person gov-ernment stood little chance of success, whereas it was conceivable that the Republic could have survived to mould the characters of its citizens to civic virtue. It was thus Cromwell's unbounded ambition 'to build up a new race of kings in himself' that was his failing, and once he dismissed the Rump the Rubicon was inevitably crossed. Nevertheless Godwin finds in his hero-villain a 'truly astonishing' friend of toleration and one whose reign benefits education, science and law and substan-tially enhances England's status as a European power. It is even possible that there is an element of the self-identification of the historian with his subject when the Protector is imaged standing, despised but undaunted, as he himself had stood during his vilification of the mid-1790s: 'Plots and conspiracies, pistols and daggers, had been prepared to destroy him. In the midst of these things he stood, as a man of true magnanimity al-ways does, uncorrupted, unsoured, free from the smallest intermixture of spleen and misanthropy. He knew mankind; and, in the result of his knowledge, he felt impelled to trust and confide in them.'[52] If this in-deed be Godwinian self-projection it is the first time we have witnessed this process in all the representations of the Protector we have discussed. Although Cromwell was, for Godwin, guilty of the most 'flagrant usurpa-tion' in 'the records of the history of any country', it was clear that once the Rump was dismissed his government was necessary for, 'if he, the binding piece that held together the machine, were taken away, presby-terians and independents, anabaptists and fifth-monarchy men, would fall to the tearing of each other to pieces'. Ultimately for Godwin, legal-ity and parliamentary democracy were not crucial factors in estimating the worth of any government and 'England was governed in a more generous spirit, with more virtue, regard for the public, and elastic and healthful tone of administration' than under the House of Stuart.[53]

Godwin's sophisticated and detailed appraisal of a virtuous Cromwell who loved power too much marks the end of the period where demon-isations and vilifications of the Protector were predominate. Godwin frees his subject from stilted political comparisons and pejorative jibes and releases him into the mainstream of nineteenth-century historical thought. So too does Godwin's treatment begin the serious reconsid-eration of English Puritanism as a moral and political force, capable of motivating men and women to revolutionary actions. The figure of the Puritan hypocrite was less easy to sustain after Godwin. Even more importantly we should note that many of the various representations of Cromwell in the period from Burke to Godwin demonstrate that there was a substantial and knowledgeable awareness of the nuances, factions, sects and groupings of the participants in the English Revolution among the equally diverse radical and reforming supporters of the revolution of the 1790s.

Afterword: the republican prompt: connections in English radical culture

Paul Hamilton

I want to argue that a reasonable speculation invited by the foregoing chapters and the project of the book they contribute to is this. The supposed vagueness of the aims of the English republicans after 1649 connects them to the wider agenda of social reform advocated at the end of the eighteenth century. In between comes the construction of a domain where are discussed the kinds of issue which, in the event, had been excluded from the policies of the Commonwealth and Protectorate. This public sphere, most influentially theorised by Habermas, had a political dynamic, but one continually attenuated by conservatives not wishing its radical destination to be reached. They foreshortened the trajectory of the public sphere by praising its institutional self-sufficiency, granting its opinions an autonomous value obviating the need for further political exemplification. Many writers in the late eighteenth century can be seen to resist this Romantic sublimation, recovering in the process that sublimely open-ended moment after 1649 before what was to count as politics rigidified into set, and no doubt more manageable, patterns. But classical republican theory allows for this reconceptualisation of a constitution in line with actual historical need. While Machiavelli could never have envisaged 'the people' on the scale momentarily entertained by English revolutionary debate, his historicism leaves the door open to the possibility of its meaningful political participation. Comparably, Romantic sublimations are now often too hastily quarantined by much criticism as an ideology which too long has infected historical judgements on Romanticism. Their aesthetic character, though, also pronounces them characteristically self-conscious enough to be able to *say* and make it part of their meaning that they are just one way of dealing with radical impulses which could be deployed by different discursive functions to devastating effect.

English republicanism, many commentators have decided, was a consequence of regicide, not its motive. In Blair Worden's succinct summary of the dilemma, they 'cut off King Charles' head and wondered what to do next'.[1] Of those who subsequently wondered, Milton's has become the canonical view about the implications of regicide for the tenure of kings and magistrates. Milton was unequivocal about the absolute right of a society to cashier its elected leaders, a right which the heroic rectitude of regicide had revealed. His targeting of tyrants rather than kings in his pamphlet of 1649, *The Tenure of Kings and Magistrates*, can have deceived no one as to his scepticism of monarchism. His readers must have seen in his later characterisation of his preferred leaders, in *The Ready and Easie Way*, as 'perpetual drudges and servants' of a 'free Commonwealth', the obvious conclusion to be drawn from his earlier pamphlet: the indefeasible answerability of those in power to 'the people'. But *The Tenure*'s main emphasis is arguably less on the rightness or wrongness of various constitutional forms and more on getting its readers to believe in the sheer practicability of change. If not recommending perpetual revolution, the pamphlet makes clear that a people should continually reframe their constitution in their own changing historical image. Correspondingly, rulers should willingly step down when their policies no longer implement the providential force shaping the times. Milton could have found support for this historicism in Machiavelli, whom, as we know from his commonplace book, Milton read carefully. But the greater generosity of Milton's conception of a people in all its historical variety perhaps necessitated the varied registers of poetic expression, the nuance or mutual inflection of both sympathy and disapproval, inadvisable in discursive polemic but a rich resource in *Paradise Lost*. Nevertheless it is significant that his epic's adequacy to the diversity of opinion in the Interregnum has, as I shall try to substantiate, a republican prompt. As a result, while we should continue to accept Worden's dismissal of republican motives for constitutional change in 1649, we should perhaps not throw out the idea that republican theory might help explain what happened, although it historicises itself in the process.[2]

A definition of English republicanism that works must pay attention to the European opposition to the growth of absolute monarchies during the early modern period. It must also respect the local English narrative into which it fits. It is successful in proportion as it is flexible, or, to put it bluntly, vague. Transposed to poetry and imaginative discourse, as I have just suggested, this vagueness can be transvalued to read as licenced generosity or adequacy to diversity. English republicanism can describe anything from a constitutional monarchy, a Polybian mixed constitution, a free state or commonwealth, another revival of a

Roman model, a staging-post on the road to Whiggery. Even outside poetry, however, vagueness ceases to disadvantage historical recollection to the degree that it becomes true to the breadth of opportunity open to contemporary interpreters of the political future created by 1649. Some form of non-monarchical government ensued, certainly, after the beheading of Charles I. But it was simultaneously surrounded by an unprecedented number of accounts both of what should have happened but did not, and of what ought to happen as a result. The first critical grouping might be described as writing from outside the Commonwealth, and from still further outside the Protectorate; it would have to include Cromwell's sectarian and Levelling opponents. The second grouping, in which Government publicists like Milton and Marchamont Nedham showed prominently, tried conspicuously to affect developments from within.

But this balanced overview is in danger of underplaying the extraordinariness of the opportunity for political originality the moment presented. What was on the political agenda, what, in fact, might constitute a political agenda, was open to discussion in unparalleled fashion. I want to suggest that it is in this latter kind of political imagining that continuities between the radical cultures of the mid-seventeenth and late eighteenth centuries lie. The chance fundamentally to reconceptualise politics, resituating differences between high and low, public and private, was on offer in the earlier period. In David Norbrook's phrase, 'the political horizon was bafflingly open'.[3] The fact that the moment was lost perhaps obscures later attempts to recreate it by obtruding domestic, sectarian and other regional concerns on a central political agenda which by then appeared to exclude their valid representation as a matter of definition. Hence arise such paradoxes as those identified in this book by Timothy Morton and Nigel Smith whereby the radicalism of the English Revolution is being drawn on to create possibilities other than mere reformism (Introduction, pp. 6–7).

Although such liberalisation of politics did not happen in the 1650s, we have two main indications that it could have taken place. One is the number of different agenda proposed; another is the hesitancy and express sense of beginning *ab initio* used to describe and plan the new dispensation which actually was put in place. It is easy to lose sight of the continuity between these two kinds of creative political thinking; the difficulty is the same as that of keeping visible the continuities across historical periods which this book addresses. The later radicalism often sounds alternative, even underground, in a fashion irrevocably separated from any accredited political programme. It appears to preserve the lost agenda, sceptical of politics entirely, regarding its own causes as ruled out of court by the terms of parliamentary discussion. It can see itself as possessing all the more momentous constitutional importance for that reason. The later period accordingly produces a vocabulary which denies radical complaint the language of effective political advocacy it wants to speak, but contrives this disadvantage paradoxically by putting it in a higher rather than a lower court. Aesthetic, religious, civic and cultural discourses of all kinds do not diminish but amplify radical voices as part of an exercise of containment. The dominance the aesthetic comes to occupy in this exercise has recently been one influential way of describing Romanticism. But the radical voices themselves of course reject this repressive tolerance. In so doing, they recover that originary moment in which they reveal what gets politics going in the first place. They expose the arbitrariness of current constituencies, the accident of hereditary and traditional authority, the possibility that things might be completely different.

Such explanations of the republican moment as one of unusual potential for political innovation are not confined to exploring the the infiltration of the high by the low. No doubt the most obvious chances for a new start arise when all are momentarily disenfranchised as the boundaries of political citizenship are redrawn. All can then press their claims. Retrospectively, the conclusion can seem foregone, but at the time, at points in, say, the Putney debates, the freedom with which an interest in the state is debated leaves the outcome unforeseeable. But, returning now to my earlier remarks on Milton and Machiavelli, even in pure versions of unrepentantly 'high' republican theory in the Machiavellian tradition, which understands itself within a learned history of ideas from the ancients through the medieval Schoolmen to the moderns, comparably unpredictable possibilities appear as part of its republican texture.

Quentin Skinner's article, 'The Republican Ideal of Political Liberty', which concludes the collection *Machiavelli and Republicanism*, confirms this impression. Skinner summarises the tradition that he believes that book's discussions of Machiavelli have revealed by distinguishing republican liberty from two other kinds of freedom. One freedom emerges from a positive, largely Aristotelian tradition in which liberty is defined as an exercise only possible in an environment conducive to human flourishing. Action in the public interest to ensure that such fulfilment takes place may appear more like social drudgery than personal expression. But thought of in this way, freedom may, without contradiction, be enjoined upon the individual as the duty of maintaining the habitat required for him or her to continue to be free. Republicanism similarly endorses this priority of duty over right in the specification of what is to count as liberty. What Machiavelli and his followers dispense with in this account of liberty is its grounding in Aristotelian ethics. Political liberty need not be commensurate with *eudaimonia*, or an Aristotelian understanding of the meaning and purpose of being human. Skinner regards Hannah Arendt, Alasdair MacIntyre and Charles Taylor as commendably anti-individualistic, but too prescriptive in a neo-Aristotelian manner. Machiavelli's republicanism opposes their positivism by emphasising the right to choose one's political environment, even if that is an unhappy one, according to circumstances and desires rather than moral essence.[4] He still agrees that the duty of supporting the institutions facilitating this right takes precedence over the exercise of the right.

This seems only rational. Skinner, though, is equally careful to differentiate his republicanism from Kantian rationalism. The creative space he has preserved from Aristotelian or Thomist positivism has also to be safeguarded from other forms of universalism. Relativism, pragmatism, reasons of state, all the expected precepts for which Machiavelli has so often been adjudged immoral are here described as respect for 'the variety of human aspirations and goals'. For a Kantian, of course, these constitute impediments to our moral functioning just insofar as they embody desires rather than the categorical imperatives of pure reason. For a Machiavellian republican, by contrast, the shifting historical character of the political universals enabling individual freedom reflects changes in desire which it is only logical to take into account. At signal historical moments, it is on the model of Kantian aesthetics, rather than ethics, that the members of each particular grouping have to judge or negotiate amongst themselves the common framework of laws which would most justly bind them together in a state. It is rational, in other words, to undertake public service to secure personal liberty. This remains true for the different desires such liberty might fulfil, provided they are not desires for the breakdown of precisely that kind of practical reasoning. Such individualism would indeed be self-contradictory. And in the respect paid to differences of desire lies that honouring of human variety redescribing Machiavellian opportunism.

Nevertheless, 'variety' remains a surprising word to use in this context. Its connotations of pluralism sound anachronistic. One might argue that Machiavelli's idea of variety in politics is still exhausted by Aristotle's or Polybius' preference for a mixed constitution, a liberality more often used to keep people in characteristic rôles, not to encourage diversification or originality. But Skinner's choice of word is surely true to Machiavelli's modern break with medieval tradition, a rupture typified by the historicism rationalising the *Discorsi*'s applications of Livy, or *Il Principe*'s commendation of *virtù* as a leader's adequacy to the indeterminacies of Fortune, discontinuities his innovatory leadership may have incited, and not his attunement to a determinate human essence. A republicanism so characterised (or a Machiavellianism so exonerated from the Elizabethan and Jacobean demonising which would have rung in Milton's literary ears) is almost entirely defined by its sensitivity to change, by its unprecedented willingness to recast politics to fit the times. There lies its partial compatability with forms of radicalism emanating from outside any received political agenda.

Other 'turns' to Machiavelli similarly use historicism to equivocate between calculated pragmatism and welcoming pluralism, *Realpolitik* and new forms of social flourishing. The German philosopher, Johann Gottlieb Fichte, Kant's immediate successor and in so many ways *the* transitional figure between Enlightenment and Romanticism, is a striking instance of this continuity. Some commentators (Kuno Fischer and Wilhelm Windelband are examples) stress the consistency between Fichte's early cosmopolitanism and later patriotism. But the *Addresses to the German Nation* delivered from 1807 onwards root the understanding of a universal human mission firmly in German soil and destiny. Such confidence in the power of the particular to embody the universal has primarily Romantic justifications, from the writings of Herder on the cultural specificity of language to the many formulations of a symbolism fundamental to the poetic form of writing characteristically privileged within Romanticism. Yet Fichte had also been reading Machiavelli, and had just written an extended essay on him.[5] Machiavelli's lack of scruple in using force for reasons of state obviously appealed to the member of another defeated party, this time keen to enforce national unity in the struggle against Napoleonic rather than French or Papal hegemony. It impressed 'the despot in Fichte', as Friedrich Meinecke wrote.[6] But Machiavelli also provided Fichte with a historicism justifying the German right to regard the German people as the temporary representative of humanity in general. Otherwise Fichte's Romanticising of the *Volk* is overlaid for us with retrospective knowledge of its barbaric twentieth-century distortion. Alain Renaut, though, can gloss Fichte's position with a straightforwardly Machiavellian vocabulary: 'The political understanding, knowing that human reason is in no way in command of the times [*maîtresse du temps*], includes a prudential dimension, an openness to the 'occasion' and to the 'time' which in no way cancels the necessity for it to be founded on a 'knowledge' [*Wissenschaft*].'[7] The effective politician, in being equal to all reversals, all unpredictable historical *bouleversements*, shows the universal quality of his historical adaptability. Continuity between the general theory of knowledge of the *Wissenschaftslehere* and the relativism of Fichte's later patriotism is thus established via Machiavellian virtuosity.

In the absence of the requisite political community, at a time when Fichte could have no model for the German nationalism he tried to inspire, Machiavelli offers him a way of thinking a possible political agenda. Friedrich Meinecke sees this precisely as Fichte's idealism at work. Fichte's affinity with Machiavelli lies simply in his belief in the badness of men. Utopianism, in Meinecke's view, weakens Fichte's nationalism: his ideas 'on the nation and the national state seem more modern and historical to us than they really are' because, at bottom, they signify a demand for moral autonomy, a freedom unconditioned by circumstance.[8] But the Machiavellian context may instead expose Fichte's typically Romantic continuities with before and after. The turn to Machiavelli, as the English use of his republican theory shows especially, can provide a most practical resource in revolutionary or extreme political situations where precedents are lacking and creative action is imperative.

Even when conservative thinkers try to contain this creative effervescence its idiom seems to break through their most careful demurrals. David Hume is a case in point. In an early essay of 1741, 'That politics may be reduced to a science', Hume launches a two-pronged attack on the highly inventive thinking of the Tory rebel, Henry St John, Viscount Bolingbroke. Bolingbroke, he first claims, contradicts himself by defending an abstract principle – the indigenous, patriotic representativeness of the British constitution – in the course of attacking a government minister (Walpole) who has with apparent ease made it serve his selfish purposes. But, Hume points out, the constitution cannot be both incorruptible and corruptible. Secondly, Hume attacks the other main strain in Bolingbroke's thought: a political idealism which, in consequence of the foregoing contradiction, in fact dismisses a constitution corrupted by the current administration and imagines what a truly patriotic one would look like. This, argues Hume, is just to leave the present conduct of public affairs in confusion; 'and the zeal of *patriots* is in that case much less requisite than the patience and submission of *philosophers*'.[9] Curiously, though, Hume does publish in 1752 a speculative political essay sketching his own 'Idea of a perfect commonwealth', this time largely as a response to Harrington rather than to Bolingbroke.

How does this fit with his scorn for 'any fine imaginary republic' and his pragmatic leaning towards absolute monarchy rather than republicanism as the lesser of the two evils between which actual politics under the Hanoverians steers a middle way? His exposition of the 'subject of speculation' contradicts his Tory empiricism, unless it is somehow a separate activity altogether, intellectual as opposed to practical, just as his epistemological scepticism concerning personal identity apparently leaves his stout moral naturalism intact.[10] We might have expected this flexibility, remembering that more famous occasion where Hume's ostensible doubt as to whether an 'ought' can ever be derived from an 'is' does not get in the way of his overpowering demonstration that if human nature is of a certain kind, then 'oughts' of a particular sort habitually follow. But the 'commonwealth' idiom in which he imagines 'what is most perfect in the kind' of government is perhaps embarrassing enough to provoke him to a bit of bridge-building between theory and practice. Again, Machiavelli is the key to Hume's precarious consistency. Echoing Bacon in *De Augmentis*, he cites Machiavelli's belief that 'a government must often be brought back to its original principles' to distinguish his own scheme from Harrington's.[11] So we can either conclude, conservatively with Hume, that a Commonwealth has nothing to add to Toryism perfected over time, or, radically, that Toryism, reduced to first principles, implies something different, a Commonwealth.

It all depends on what custom and habit lead one to believe. From Kant onwards Hume's philosophy has frequently been described as a philosophy of belief, a psychology rather than a logic. Similarly, in his political thought, his explanation of what actually happens as opposed to what ideally should happen refers us to public opinion. When he writes 'Of the first principles of government' he is unequivocal on this point: 'governors have nothing to support them but opinion. It is therefore on opinion only that government is founded; and this maxim extends to the most despotic and most military govenments, as well as to the most free and most popular.'[12] When he considers 'Whether the British government inclines more to absolute monarchy, or to a republic', he claims that in his own time opinion was turning in favour of monarchy after a period favouring popular government. But he has inadvertently left open the door to the possibility that were public opinion to reason philosophically, it might see where its true interests lay. He has also made a form of government, monarchy, whose legitimacy has been the subject of civil war and the foundation of religion, into a historical accident of belief, a matter of how people misinterpret their interests at a particular time.

Here, his irony resembles that of his contemporary, Edward Gibbon, a historian of comparably sceptical temperament. In chapter 15 of *The History of the Decline and Fall of the Roman Empire*, Gibbon imagines Galerius Maximus persuading the emperor Diocletian to persecute the Christians. He has Galerius conjuring up a vision of Christians as an association in the public sphere threatening to realise its political potential: 'Christians (it might speciously be alleged) in renouncing the gods and institutions of Rome, had constituted a distinct republic.'[13] Specious such allegations may have been, but Gibbon had already described the early church's coming to self-consciousness as a return to republicanism.[14] The Christians' 'separate society' inspired 'a spirit of patriotism, such as the first of the Romans had felt for the republic'.[15] From this simplicity the church declined into more and more authoritarian forms of government, like Rome itself, until, appropriately, the two societies, Christian and imperial, merged. But the originally republican outlook of the early church was historicist rather than prescriptive. Again we find the connection made, this time in Gibbon's mind, between seeing a community, here the early Christians, as 'a free people' and seeing them as preserving 'the liberty of varying their forms of ecclesiastical government according to the changes of time and circumstance'.[16]

Augustine had famously likened Christian community to the *res publica* defined by Cicero through his mouthpiece Scipio in *De Republica*, a state of justice to which Augustine thought the Romans aspired but never acceded because of their paganism.[17] No doubt with calculated irony, Gibbon manipulates Augustine's idiom so as to treat the history of religion as one of primarily political rather than theological debate, a history of ecclesiastical government. He shows in the monumental example of Rome that future forms of government could be plotted in a public space aside from the actual political arena. The trajectory leads to the Holy Roman Empire, but Gibbon could have plotted this progress still further. Ecclesiastical authoritarianism arguably led to the absolute monarchies and ecclesiastical polities subsequently rationalised in England by Filmer, Hooker and Divine Right theorists generally; early church republicanism led to the Commonwealth of the Independents. As Justin Champion shows us, it is too simple to call the later stages of the process, from 1650 onwards, a process of secularisation. Polemicists such as John Toland anticipate Gibbon in insisting that it always went on, even in periods of pristine religious commitment. Again, as Champion so astutely demonstrates, the consciousness of what was at stake in opting for church history rather than the history of theology became increasingly sophisticated in eighteenth-century writers. Bacon, following Machiavelli, had already valued religion for its political effects. Once religion was distinguished for its political desirability rather than its doctrinal truth, any attitude towards religion, however irreligious, could be defended. Unlike superstitious people, for example, atheists were 'no reformers'.[18] Disingenuously, Bacon displaces theology with politics, sidestepping the question of belief and creating an acceptable parallel in which to debate political experiment. Toland, in Champion's examples, can treat religious prophets as 'really political legislators adapting their religious institutions to national and historical circumstances' (chapter 1, p. 41). Properly understood, religious beliefs are not only relative to their time, in need of reinterpretation as was to be shockingly argued later in the eighteenth century by the 'higher criticism' of Herder and his successors. The history of religious beliefs evinces strategies for restructuring a society in response to changed times. To talk politics by talking religion could thus have an inbuilt radical meaning, foregrounding the need to reform, but without reviving the convictions of the godly in the 1640s and 1650s that religious causes are the same as political ones. In the institutional histories of religion, religion is taken both more and less seriously: it may no longer be providential, but its story now instructs us in how to adapt and organise in response to altered circumstances in a manner setting a pattern for political reform.

Religious dissent too radical to stay on the Commonwealth agenda recrudesces in a public sphere of discussion. There, its political significance can be supported not only directly by outright radicals but also indirectly by conservative sceptics. They share a historicism which justifies changing religious establishments; and the political activity involved can show that the Houses of Parliament need not necessarily hold a monopoly on what is to count as politics. As David Womersley points out in his excellent Introduction to the new Penguin edition of Gibbon's *History*, Gibbon commends policy which acts on Sallust's precept, 'that empire must be acquired and defended by the same arts'.[19] In support of Gibbon's historicism Womersley could have quoted instead the last two lines of that most Machiavellian of poems, Andrew Marvell's 'An Horatian Ode Upon Cromwell's Return From Ireland': 'The same arts that did gain /A power must it maintain.' Marvell's poem is outspoken in the deference it pays to political opportunism exercised in response to *Fortuna*. The poem carries this endorsement to the extent of simulaneously modelling a new beginning for its own art, the art of poetry, which now, sharing or even anticipating the risks of Cromwell's modern heroism, must forsake received standards of authority and assay a new kind of discourse, questionable and paradoxical as it might at first appear:

> The forward youth that would appear,
> Must now forsake his Muses dear,
> Nor in the shadows sing
> His numbers languishing . . . [20]

Time and time again, commentators in this book have found it appropriate to search for comparable discursive remouldings. They pick out extra-parliamentary forms of representation or groupings which increasingly provide an alternative politics rather than an alternative to politics. Fear of this happening is raised by Burke at the start of *Reflections upon the Revolution in France*, when he attacks the presumption of Richard Price, 'the Constitutional Society and the Revolution Society' for taking upon themselves 'a sort of public capacity' to send English congratulations to the infant French republic.[21] When Hazlitt, over thirty years later, calls Cobbett and his *Political Register* 'a kind of *fourth estate* in the politics of the country', his comic improvement on the *tiers état* which Burke declared politically incompetent is a calculated tactic and a measured rebuff.[22] Cobbett's kind of radicalism is dramatised as the fears of Burke realised again. Cobbett, after all, consistently takes up stances antithetical to Burke. Burke's unwavering parliamentarianism leads him to oppose George III's use of the royal prerogative in the American War of Independence. It also makes him support the monarchy against those new forms of government abroad in the 1790s which he takes to be alternatives to the British constitution and particularly Parliament's allotted rôle within it. Cobbett, on the other hand, was against the Americans, and so no supporter of parliamentary independence; his subsequent opposition to government is primarily motivated by a hatred of centralism, London, the 'Wen', and is expressed through passionately inventive readings of provincial landscape. This 'archaeology', as James McKusick calls it, registers political interests unassimilable by London bureaucracy. As McKusick also shows, Cobbett's devolutionary activities resist Whig interpretations of history and assert customary rights and duties which have diminished under 'the tyranny of Progress' (chapter 9, p. 182). This can seem to align Cobbett with a 'country' interest, one unembarrassed by his railing against Jews, jobbers and rentier culture. G.K. Chesterton's formidable Cobbett hoves into sight:

> I saw great Cobbett riding,
> The horseman of the shires,
> And his face was red with judgement,
> And a light of Luddite fires.[23]

The plausibility of Cobbett as the ebullient champion of reaction perhaps explains the reservations qualifying Raymond Williams's approval of him. Yet the radical provocation of his rural rides, the political mobilisation represented by this *rosbif* who can stalk the shires as if they were his own policies, because he knows their labour history better than anyone else, is undeniable.

One might explain the phenomenon of Cobbett in more general terms as one more in a line of continuous attempts throughout the long eighteenth century to exploit the political possibilities of the public sphere. Perhaps 'attempts' is too intentional a term, since the inner dynamic of this public domain itself translates opinion into lobbying or pressure groups with their own impetus for political change. But Michael Scrivener, for example, writes convincingly above of John Thelwall's 'commitment to expanding the public sphere'.[24] Habermas's description of the radical impulse and its containment within bourgeois culture is no longer the blunt instrument of his first analysis. It has now diversified under the scrutiny of his critics and followers. The cultural narratives recounted in this book suggest that the history of the public sphere describes two things. First of all it looks like an alternative to the story of executive decisions or big events in national life. It documents something other than political history, telling instead of a forum for communicative exchanges now recognised as possessing an importance of their own worthy of independent record. If one thinks of the example of women's history and feminism, this abstract formulation becomes more convincing. Consistent with the Romantic practice I have defined above is to keep such concerns in the public sphere, to deny them political agency and to think them all the more important for that. And this takes me to the second movement recorded in the history of the public sphere. Charlotte Sussman's chapter shows orthodox politics losing the power to exclude public concerns which, like the abolition of slavery, have become so important that a political agenda which does not take them on board risks losing credibility. In some cases, politics must get in tune with 'the way women were able to imagine their own political agency' (chapter 7, p. 149), here through the good works and agitation typical of feminine evangelical circles around Wilberforce, in order to represent public opinion. But then to continue to exclude the feminine source of such political sea-changes from the franchise, this dynamic accurately implies, is to perpetuate a dishonesty which, in its turn, will have to go if the political executive is to go on plausibly connecting with its constituency.

Jon Mee's account of the publishing career of Citizen Lee telescopes the complex variations of this movement into an individual case. Lee's outrageous radical bricolage, by which he turns excerpts from other writings against the sense of their original context to furnish him with the treasonable opinions he wants, certainly propels him into the public sphere. He even completes its ultimately political trajectory by getting himself named in Parliament. But the instability of his eclectic authorial identity and its *ersatz* productions both helps him elude censorious definition and renders him ineffective. Beckoning from the wings, however, is the more polite acceptance of his religious enthusiasm in print open to him under the patronage of the Rev. Thomas Grove and the Evangelical Magazine (chapter 8, pp. 152–5). Although less directly political, clearly, than the tyrannicide pamphlets, Lee's devotional verses may, Mee suggests, have had more practical effect. His success here raised his status in radical circles and allowed him the opportunity of fashioning a social voice which would be listened to but which was still to some extent formed out of visibly impolite elements, radical elements normally excluded from the cultural conversation. Such are the indirections by which print culture finds directions out. And such, still following Habermas, are the ways in which the models by which the public sphere assigns disruptive political aspirations a higher (aesthetic, religious) vocation contain the seeds of their own dissolution.

Whatever the reasons – censorship, anti-theoretical prejudice, the unreflective character of the idiom of the 'Good Old Cause' – the clearly oppositional languages of the public sphere have until recently obscured the radical tendency towards political consummation of that sphere itself. Victoria Kahn's rich study of the uses of Machiavellian rhetoric uncovers, amongst many other things, a characteristically English assimilation of continental theory to linguistic practices constituting the parallel but oppositional play of the public sphere which I have been tracing. I shall try to clinch my argument with the help of her fine book.[25] In the period, from the Counter-Reformation to Milton, which she studies, English rhetoric

absorbed political theory and became charged with Machiavellian
potential as a consequence. In Romantic period writing, theories of
imagination, irony and rhetorical reserve, which English savants like
Coleridge conspicuously failed to theorise convincingly, are what energise writings calling out for their hidden rationale to be voiced. This occulted theory, in its turn, might, if properly expounded in all its Fichtean
sensitivity to a Machiavellian heritage, have *recovered* not alienated that native, domestic, republican sublime whose absence from our postmodern
understanding of Romanticism David Norbrook has rightly lamented.[26]
Kahn shows that performative or practical understanding of Machiavelli
in the English Renaissance originally enacted his ideas in the rhetorical
expertise those ideas advocated, a skill in which casuistry and historicism worked together. Kahn's more mainstream examples of rhetorical
casuistry include Roger Ascham, ambiguous villains and heroes
of Marlowe and Shakespeare, and George Puttenham's argument in
The Arte of English Poesie (1589) that

> it may come to passe that what the Grammarian setteth downe for a viciositee
> in speach may become a vertue and no vice, contrariwise his commended figure
> may fall into a reproachful fault; [thus with] a speciall regard to all circumstances
> of the person, place, time, cause and purpose he hath in hand . . . [the poet]
> maketh now and then very vice goe for a formal vertue in the exercise of this
> arte.[27]

Here, the distinction between virtue and vice is made subject to *occasion* – 'person, place, time, cause and purpose'. To demonstrate that the
genre of poetry owns a special propriety, Puttenham effectively equates
poetic licence with Machiavellian historicism. Poetic topicality and political opportunism share the same rhetorical justification for bending the
rules of literal truth or grammatical reality so as to make good evil, evil
good. Near contemporary defences of poetry, such as Sir Philip Sidney's,
lose some of their Neoplatonic high-mindedness in this context. The exemplary quality of poetry, taken up of course by Romantic manifestos,
exceeds prescription; in the same way it is only recipes for coping with
unforeseen contingencies, with the irregularities of *fortuna*, that examples
from history provide. The autotelic realm Sidney carves out for the poet
who plays in 'the zodiac of his own wit' exceeds Castiglione's graceful
courtly realism or display of *sprezzatura* and lets the poet represent or
figure an absolute right to self-determination in response to individual
circumstances. A Protestant tradition is encoded in this historicism which

extends, as Blair Worden has recently described, via the Essex circle, Sir Walter Ralegh and Francis Bacon to Milton, all people profoundly interested in Machiavelli.[28]

When William Blake notoriously calls Bacon's essays 'Good Advice for Satan's Kingdom', his angry opposition to Bacon should perhaps be taken as the flip-side of his true friendship for a clued-up inhabitant of 'Ulro' or the fallen world of generation.[29] In this Urizenic, systematised, ideologically constructed world, though, redemption only comes through an advancing of particular circumstances beyond the rules of accepted generalisation. Beyond the idiocy which cannot see a providence in the fall of a sparrow or infinity in a grain of sand lies the vision which alike spurned *Hamlet*'s clapped-out Elizabethan court in the wake of the Essex rebellion and the execrable political hegemony of Blake's own day. But such electric connections lie in the domestic sublimity of the language which is where, in English writing, they so often are.

Notes

INTRODUCTION

1 Published in 1792; for a further discussion, see Terence Hoagwood, 'Gillray, Cromwell, and the Problem of Representation', *The Wordsworth Circle*, 25.3 (1994), 134–8.
2 Craig Rose, *England in the 1690s* (Oxford and New York: Oxford University Press, 1999), 259–62; see also Laura Lunger Knoppers, 'The Politics of Portraiture: Oliver Cromwell and the Plain Style', *Renaissance Quarterly*, 51.4 (1998), 1283–319.
3 See Sean Kelsey, *Inventing a Republic: The Political Culture of the English Commonwealth 1649–1653* (Manchester: Manchester University Press, 1997), 55–6.
4 Gillray's representation of the miniature bears no relation to any of Cooper's four miniatures of Cromwell. Cooper's Cromwell never has eyes that look at the viewer; the Gillray version bears a passing resemblance to Cooper's miniature of Henry Ireton (1611–51), Cromwell's son-in-law, Lord Deputy of Ireland, and a prominent Parliamentary commander, and his miniature of Colonel Robert Lilburne (1613–65), brother of the Leveller John, Parliamentary commander and regicide.
5 Annabel Patterson, *Early Modern Liberalism* (Cambridge and New York: Cambridge University Press, 1997), chapters 1 and 8.
6 Percy Shelley, *The Letters of Percy Bysshe Shelley*, ed. Frederick L. Jones, 2 vols. (Oxford: Oxford University Press, 1964), II:219–20.
7 *Ibid.*, II:372.
8 *Ibid.*, II:388.
9 Mary Shelley, *Frankenstein: Or the Modern Prometheus; the 1818 Text*, ed. Marilyn Butler (Oxford and New York: Oxford University Press, 1994), 133–4; for a strong analysis of Victor's egotism and the reactionary science in which he invests, see the Introduction, especially xv–xxi. We have substituted the correction 'Goring' for 'Gower' (this error appeared in the 1818 text and was revised in 1823 at Percy Shelley's bidding).
10 Percy Shelley, *Letters*, II:21.
11 *Ibid.*, II:294.
12 We are grateful to Nora Crook for helping us with this.
13 *Dictionary of National Biography*, 'Leighton, Alexander'. See also Stephen Foster, *Notes from the Caroline Underground: Alexander Leighton, the Puritan*

Triumvirate and the Laudian Reaction to Nonconformity (Hamden, CT: Archon, 1978).

14 Thomas Medwin, *The Life of Percy Bysshe Shelley*, 2 vols. (London: Thomas Cautley Newby, 1847), ii:164–65.

15 Percy Bysshe Shelley, *Poetical Works*, ed. Thomas Hutchinson (London and New York: Oxford University Press, 1970), 490.

16 For a further discussion, see Timothy Morton, *Shelley and the Revolution in Taste: The Body and the Natural World* (Cambridge and New York: Cambridge University Press, 1994, 1998), chapter 3.

17 Walter Benjamin, *One-Way Street and Other Writings*, trans. E. Jephcott and K. Shorter (London: Verso, 1979; paperback, 1985), 359.

18 Shelley, *A Vindication of Natural Diet*, in *Shelley's Prose: or the Trumpet of a Prophecy*, ed. David Lee Clark (London: Fourth Estate, 1988), 88.

19 J. G. A Pocock, 'Criticism of the Whig Order in the Age between Revolutions', in Margaret Jacob and James C. Jacob, eds., *The Origins of Anglo-American Radicalism* (London and Boston: Allen and Unwin, 1984), 33–57 (37).

20 John Brewer, *Party Ideology and Popular Politics at the Accession of George III* (Cambridge: Cambridge University Press, 1976); H. T. Dickinson, *The Politics of the People in Eighteenth-Century Britain* (London: Macmillan and New York: St Martin's Press, 1995).

21 The information in this paragraph is indebted to an important article by H. T. Dickinson, 'The Precursors of Political Radicalism in Augustan Britain', in Clyve Jones, ed., *Britain in the First Age of Party 1680–1750: Essays Presented to Geoffrey Holmes* (London: Hambledon Press, 1987), 63–84.

22 *Ibid.*, 81.

23 See Blair Worden, 'Wit in a Roundhead: The Dilemma of Marchmont Nedham', in Susan D. Amussen and Mark A. Kishlansky, eds., *Political Culture and Cultural Politics in Early Modern England: Essays Presented to David Underdown* (Manchester and New York: Manchester University Press, 1995), 301–37; Nigel Smith, 'Popular Republicanism in the 1650s: John Streater's "Heroick Mechanicks"', in David Armitage, Armand Himy and Quentin Skinner, eds., *Milton and Republicanism* (Cambridge and New York: Cambridge University Press, 1995), 137–55; Kathleen Wilson, *The Sense of the People: Politics, Culture and Imperialism, 1715–1785* (Cambridge and New York: Cambridge University Press, 1995, 1998), chapters 1 and 2; also below, pp. 201–2, 204–15.

24 As discussed by Olivia Smith, *The Politics of Language, 1791–1819* (Oxford and New York: Oxford University Press, 1984).

25 John Barrell, *Imagining the King's Death: Figurative Treason, Fantasies of Regicide 1793–96* (Oxford and New York: Oxford University Press, 2000), 1–46.

26 Abraham Rees, *The Cyclopaedia; or, Universal Dictionary of Arts, Sciences, and Literature*, 41 vols. (Philadelphia: Samuel Bradford, Murray, Fainman and Co., 1810–24), Hhv.

27 J. G. A. Pocock, 'Post-Puritan England and the Problem of Enlightenment', in P. Zagorin, ed., *Culture and Politics: From Puritanism to the Enlightenment* (Berkeley: University of California Press, 1980), 91–112.

28 J. A. I. Champion, *The Pillars of Priestcraft Shaken: The Church of England and its Enemies 1660–1730* (Cambridge and New York: Cambridge University Press, 1992). See also Christopher Hill, 'Freethinking and Libertinism: The Legacy of the English Revolution', in Roger D. Lund, ed., *The Margins of Orthodoxy: Heterodox Writing and Cultural Response 1660–1750* (Cambridge and New York: Cambridge University Press, 1995), 54–70.

29 See for example the essays by Gordon Schocket, Jeffrey F. Chamberlain and Joseph M. Levine in Lund, ed., *The Margins of Orthodoxy* (119–48, 195–215, 219–39); see also below, Jane Shaw, 'Fasting Women: the Significance of Gender and Bodies in Radical Religion and Politics, 1650–1813' (pp. 101–15).

30 See Roger D. Lund, 'Irony as Subversion: Thomas Wollaston and the Crime of Wit', in Lund, ed., *The Margins of Orthodoxy*, 170–94.

31 See Mark Jenner, 'Bathing and Baptism: Sir John Floyer and the Politics of Cold Bathing', in Kevin Sharpe and Steven Zwicker, eds., *Refiguring Revolutions: Aesthetics and Politics from the English Revolution to the Romantic Revolution* (Berkeley and Los Angeles: University of California Press, 1998), 197–216.

32 Nigel Smith, 'Enthusiasm and Enlightenment: Of Food, Filth and Slavery', in Gerald MacLean, Donna Landry and Joseph P. Ward, eds., *The Country and the City Revisited: England and the Politics of Culture, 1550–1850* (Cambridge and New York: Cambridge University Press, 1999), 106–18; see also below, pp. 70–5.

33 Andy Wood, 'Custom, Identity and Resisitance: Engish Free Miners and their Law *c.* 1550–1800', in Paul Griffiths, Adam Fox and Steve Hindle, eds., *The Experience of Authority in Early Modern England* (New York: St Martin's Press, 1996), 249–85. See also Andy Wood, *The Politics of Social Conflict: The Peak Country, 1520–1770* (Cambridge and New York: Cambridge University Press, 1999).

34 J. G. A. Pocock's *Barbarism and Religion*, vol. I, *The Enlightenments of Edward Gibbon, 1737–64* (Cambridge and New York: Cambridge University Press, 1999) seeks to address this issue.

35 But see the essays in Knud Haakonssen, ed., *Enlightenment and Religion: Rational Dissent in Eighteenth Century Britain* (Cambridge and New York: Cambridge University Press, 1996); see now also Isabel Rivers, *Reason, Grace and Sentiment. A Study of the Language of Religion and Ethics in England, 1660–1780*, vol. II, *Shaftesbury to Hume* (Cambridge and New York: Cambridge University Press, 2000).

36 James A. Epstein, *Radical Expression: Political Language, Ritual, and Symbol in England, 1790–1850* (New York and Oxford: Oxford University Press, 1994), 150.

37 Peter Stansky, *From William Morris to Sergeant Pepper: Studies in the Radical Domestic* (Palo Alto, CA: The Society for the Promotion of Science and Scholarship, 1999), vii–viii. The term was coined by Christopher Reed.

38 Jon Mee, 'The Strange Career of Richard "Citizen" Lee', below, p. 163.

39 In *Reading Revolutions: The Politics of Reading in Early Modern England* (New Haven and London: Yale University Press, 2000), Kevin Sharpe examines in detail the reading habits, annotations and changing perceptions of the seventeenth-century lawyer Sir William Drake.

40 The allusion in Wordsworth is in *Tintern Abbey*, lines 122–4: 'And this prayer I make, / Knowing that Nature never did betray / The heart that loved her.' Cf. Samuel Daniel, *The Civil Wars*, II.225–6: 'Here have you craggy rocks to take your part, / That never will betray you.' William Wordsworth, *William Wordsworth*, ed. Stephen Gill (Oxford and New York: Oxford University Press, 1984; repr. 1987). See Duncan Wu, ed., *Romanticism: An Anthology*, 2nd edn (Oxford: Blackwell, 1998), 268. The passage in De Quincey performs a similar operation of internalisation: 'I shall be charged with mysticism, Behmenism, quietism, &c. but *that* shall not alarm me. Sir H. Vane, the younger, was one of our wisest men; and let my readers see if he, in his philosophical works, be half as unmystical as I am'; see Anne K. Mellor and Richard E. Matlak, *British Literature 1780–1830* (London and New York: Harcourt Brace, 1996), 858.

41 We are grateful to Nanora Sweet and Hugh Roberts for pointing this out; Lord George Gordon Byron, *The Complete Poetical Works*, ed. Jerome McGann, 5 vols. (Oxford: Clarendon Press, 1980–6); Felicia Hemans, *The Works of Mrs Hemans*, 7 vols. (London: Thomas Cadell and Edinburgh: William Blackwood and Sons, 1839).

42 Robert J. Griffin, *Wordsworth's Pope: A Study in Literary Historiography* (Cambridge and New York: Cambridge University Press, 1995), 10.

43 J. G. A. Pocock, 'The Varieties of Whiggism', in *Virtue, Commerce, and History: Essays on Political Thought and History, Chiefly in the Eighteenth Century* (Cambridge: Cambridge University Press, 1985), 232; see Griffin, *Wordsworth's Pope*, 11.

44 David Norbrook, *Writing the English Republic: Poetry, Rhetoric and Politics 1627–1660* (Cambridge and New York: Cambridge University Press, 1999), 140–1. *The Wordsworth Circle*, 25.3 (Summer 1994) is entitled 'Cavaliers and Roundheads First: Interdisciplinary Essays on Romantic and Victorian Recuperations of the English Civil War', and contains, among others, a foreword by Kenneth R. Johnston; Terence Hoagwood on Gillray's cartoon (discussed above); Greg Kucich, 'Inventing Revolutionary History: Romanticism and the Politics of Literary Tradition', 138–45; Thomas Prasch, 'The Making of the English Working Past: The Rediscovery of Gerrard Winstanley and Late Victorian English Radicalism', 166–72.

45 John Mullan, *Sentiment and Sociability: The Language of Sensibility in the Eighteenth Century* (Oxford and New York: Oxford University Press, 1988).

46 See John Barrell, 'Sad Stories: Louis XVI, George III, and the Language of Sentiment', in Sharpe and Zwicker, eds., *Refiguring Revolutions*, 75–98.

47 Paul Hamilton, 'The Republican Prompt', below, p. 214.

48 Henry Brougham, quoted in Epstein, *Radical Expression*, 16.

49 Mark Philp, 'English Repubicanism in the 1790s', *The Journal of Political Philosophy*, 6.1 (1998), 1–28.

50 For an instance of this approach, see Marilyn Morris, *The British Monarchy and the French Revolution* (New Haven and London: Yale University Press, 1998).

51 For an example of the intersection between African-American culture and political discourse, see Houston A. Baker, Jr., *Black Studies, Rap, and the Academy* (Chicago and London: University of Chicago Press, 1993).

52 Hamilton, 'The Republican Prompt', below, p. 207.

53 Peter Linebaugh and Marcus Rediker, *The Many-Headed Hydra: Sailors, Slaves, Commons, and the Hidden History of the Revolutionary Atlantic* (Boston: Beacon Press, 2000).

54 Epstein, *Radical Expression*, 122.

55 *Ibid.*, 112.

56 Jacques Derrida, *Of Grammatology*, trans. Gayatri Chakravorty Spivak (Baltimore and London: Johns Hopkins University Press, 1987), 168.

57 Mee, 'The Strange Career of Richard "Citizen" Lee', below, pp. 151–2.

58 Epstein, *Radical Exression*, 35.

59 *Ibid.*, 39, 55.

60 Derrida, *Of Grammatology*, 85–6.

61 See Brian Young, *Religion and Enlightenment in Eighteenth-Century England: Theological Debate from Locke to Burke* (Oxford and New York: Oxford University Press, 1998).

62 See Brian J. Gibbons, *Gender in Mystical and Occult Thought: Behmenism and its Development in England* (Cambridge and New York: Cambridge University Press, 1996), 173–9.

63 Edward Hyde, Earl of Clarendon, *The History of the Rebellion* (Oxford, 1720), vol. III, pt. 1, Bk. XI, 250–74.

64 Hamilton, 'The Republican Prompt', below, p. 204.

65 *Ibid.*, p. 207.

1 'MAY THE LAST KING BE STRANGLED IN THE BOWELS OF THE LAST PRIEST': IRRELIGION AND THE ENGLISH ENLIGHTENMENT, 1649–1789

1 W. H. Reid, *The Rise and Dissolution of the Infidel Societies in the Metropolis: Including, the Origin of Modern Deism and Atheism; the Genius and Conduct of those Associations; their Lecture-Rooms, Field-Meetings, and Deputations; from the Publication of Paine's Age of Reason till the Present Period* (London: n.p., 1800), iii–v, 3–8, 10–13, 16. Both Mirabeau and d'Holbach are represented on Robert Darnton's listing of best-selling 'forbidden' books; see 'The Forbidden Books of Pre-Revolutionary France', in Colin Lucas, ed., *Rewriting the French Revolution* (Oxford and New York: Oxford University Press, 1991), 1–32; see Tables 1 and 2 for a listing of most popular titles.

2 For discussion of English radical political culture, see Iain McCalman, *Radical Underworld: Prophets, Revolutionaries and Pornographers in London, 1795–1840* (Cambridge: Cambridge University Press, 1988); Jon Mee, *Dangerous Enthusiasm: William Blake and the Culture of Radicalism in the 1790s* (Oxford:

Clarendon Press, 1992). A work exploring the continuities of English traditions is E. P. Thompson, *Witness Against the Beast: William Blake and the Moral Law* (Cambridge and New York: Cambridge University Press, 1993).

3 For a useful survey see M. S. Anderson, *Historians and Eighteenth-Century Europe 1715–1789* (Oxford: Clarendon Press, 1979), 64–119.

4 See for example: George S. Rousseau and Roy Porter, eds., *Exoticism in the Enlightenment* (Manchester: Manchester University Press, 1990) and *Sexual Underworlds of the Enlightenment* (Manchester: Manchester University Press, 1987); also P. Hulme and L. Jordanova, *The Enlightenment and its Shadows* (London: Routledge, 1990) and M. C. Jacob, *Living the Enlightenment: Freemasonry and Politics in Eighteenth-Century Europe* (Oxford: Oxford University Press, 1991).

5 See J. G. A. Pocock, 'Post-Puritan England and the Problem of the Enlightenment', in P. Zagorin, ed., *Culture and Politics: From Puritanism to the Enlightenment* (Berkeley: University of California Press, 1980), 91–112, (91, 106); see also J. G. A. Pocock, 'Clergy and Commerce: The Conservative Enlightenment in England', in R. Ajello, E. Contense and V. Piano, eds., *L'Età dei Lumi: Studi Storici sul Settecento Europeo in onore di Franco Venturi* (Naples, n.p., 1985), 1:523–62. For an excellent overview sharing many of the arguments of this piece, see M. A. Goldie, 'Priestcraft and the Birth of Whiggism', in N. Phillipson and Quentin Skinner, eds., *Political Discourse in Early Modern Britain* (Cambridge: Cambridge University Press, 1993), 209–31.

6 See Roy Porter and M. Teich, *The Enlightenment in National Context* (Cambridge: Cambridge University Press, 1981); J. Gascoigne, *Cambridge in the Age of Enlightenment* (Cambridge: Cambridge University Press, 1989).

7 See T. Harris, *Politics under the Later Stuarts* (London: Longman, 1992).

8 See Paul Langford, *A Polite and Respectable People: England 1727–1783* (Oxford and New York: Oxford University Press, 1989), *Public Life and Propertied Englishmen 1689–1798* (Oxford and New York: Oxford University Press, 1991); L. Colley, *Britons: Forging the Nation 1707–1837* (New Haven: Yale University Press, 1992); E. P. Thompson, *Customs in Common* (London: Merlin Press, 1993).

9 Colley, *Britons*, 11–54; Thompson, *Customs in Common*, 49–50, 56, 64.

10 Thompson, *Customs in Common*, 86–7. For an examination of the material infrastructure of the eighteenth-century state see John Brewer, *The Sinews of Power: War, Money and the English State, 1688–1783* (London: Unwin and Hyman, 1989).

11 Thompson, *Customs in Common*, 50; see also Paul Langford, *Public Life and the Propertied Englishman* (Oxford and New York: Oxford University Press, 1991), 430.

12 See John Walsh, C. Heydon and S. Taylor, eds., *The Church of England c. 1689–1833: From Toleration to Tractarianism* (Cambridge and New York: Cambridge University Press, 1993); Knut Haakonssen, ed., *Enlightenment and Religion:*

Rational Dissent in Eighteenth-Century Britain (Cambridge and New York: Cambridge University Press, 1996). See also W. M. Jacob, *Lay People and Religion in the Early Eighteenth Century* (Cambridge and New York: Cambridge University Press, 1996).

13 See Michel de Certeau, 'La formalité des practiques. Du système religieux à l'éthique des lumières (XVIIe–XVIIIe)', translated into English in *The Writing of History* (New York: Columbia University Press, 1988), 147–206, 166.

14 See R. Hole, *Pulpits, Politics and Public Order in England 1762–1832* (Cambridge and New York: Cambridge University Press, 1989).

15 Margaret C. Jacob, *The Radical Enlightenment: Pantheists, Freemasons and Republicans* (London: Allen and Unwin, 1981); Franco Venturi made similar suggestions in *Utopia and Reform in the Enlightenment* (Cambridge: Cambridge University Press, 1971), 47–69. For a survey of the historiography see J. E. Force, 'The Origins of Modern Atheism', *Journal of the History of Ideas*, 50 (1989), 153–162.

16 Alexis de Tocqueville, *The Old Regime and the French Revolution* (London: J. M. Dent and Sons, 1988), 155.

17 *Ibid.*, 151.

18 *Ibid.*, 152.

19 *Ibid.*, 153–4.

20 D. Mornet, 'Les enseignements des bibliothèques privées (1750–1780),' *Revue d'histoire littéraire de la France*, 17 (1910), 449–96 and *Les origines intellectuelles de la Révolution Française 1715–1789* (Paris: Armand Collin, 1938). For a useful discussion of Mornet see Robert Darnton, *The Literary Underground of the Old Regime* (Cambridge, MA: Harvard University Press, 1982), 167–8, 176–82.

21 K. M. Baker, *Inventing the French Revolution* (Cambridge and New York: Cambridge University Press, 1990) and R. Chartier, *The Cultural Origins of the French Revolution* (Durham: Duke University Press, 1991).

22 See K. M. Baker, *Inventing the French Revolution*, 12–31; and 'Enlightenment and Revolution in France: Old Problems, Renewed Approaches', *Journal of Modern History*, 53 (1981), 281–303, and 'On the Problem of the Ideological Origins of the French Revolution', in D. La Capra and S. L. Kaplan, eds., *Modern European Intellectual History: Reappraisals and New Perspectives* (Ithaca: Cornell University Press, 1982). For some very cogent criticisms of Baker's arguments see J. Horns, 'The Revolution as Discourse', *History of European Ideas*, 13 (1991), 628–30.

23 See Darnton, *The Literary Underground*, and 'Forbidden Books', Tables 1 and 2.

24 Chartier, *Cultural Origins*, chapter 4, 'Do Books Make Revolutions?' especially 81–91. For a useful discussion of Chartier's work see D. Goodman, 'Public Sphere and Private Life: Towards a Synthesis of Current Historiographical Approaches to the Old Regime', *History and Theory*, 31 (1992), 1–20. See Jürgen Habermas, *The Structural Transformation of the Public Sphere: An Inquiry into a Category of Bourgeois Society* (Cambridge, MA: MIT Press, 1989).

25 See de Certeau, *The Writing of History*.

26 Chartier, *Cultural Origins*, 136.
27 *Ibid.*, 68.
28 The exceptions are the works of F. Venturi and M. Jacob. See also A. C. Kors and P. J. Korshin, *Anticipations of the Enlightenment in England, France and Germany* (Philadelphia: University of Pennsylvania Press, 1987).
29 See for example J. Texte, *Jean-Jacques Rousseau et les origines du cosmopolitanisme littéraire* (Paris: Hachette, 1895); A. C. Hunter, *J-B Suard: un introducteur de la littérature anglaise en France* (Paris: Champion, 1925); H. J. Reesink, *L'Angleterre et la littérature anglaise dans les trois plus anciens périodiques français de Hollande de 1684 à 1709* (Paris: Libraire Ancienne Honoré Champion, 1931); G. Bonno, *La Culture et la civilisation britanniques devant l'opinion française de la paix d'Utrecht aux lettres philosophiques (1713–1734)* (Philadelphia: University of Pennsylvania Press, 1948). See also C. A. Rochedieu, *Bibliography of French Translations of English Works 1700–1800* (Chicago: Chicago University Press, 1948). For a more recent assessment of the relations between English and French freethought see C. B. O'Keefe, *Contemporary Reactions to the Enlightenment* (Geneva: Bibliothèque de Littérature Comparée, 1973); J. Grieder, *Anglomania in France 1740–1789: Fact, Fiction and Political Discourse* (Geneva: Libraire Droz, 1985).
30 See for a useful survey of the older literature I. O. Wade, *The Structure and Form of the French Enlightenment*, 2 vols. (Princeton: Princeton University Press, 1977), I:120–71 (citation at 136).
31 See Darnton, 'Forbidden Books', Table 2: both Voltaire and d'Holbach topped the best-sellers list of illegal books.
32 On Voltaire see N. L. Torrey, *Voltaire and the English Deists* (New Haven: Yale University Press, 1930); on d'Holbach see P. Naville, *D'Holbach et la philosophie scientifique au XVIIIe siècle* (Paris: VRIN, 1967). D'Holbach seems particularly interested in the writings of John Toland (1670–1722): the *Catalogues des Livres de feu M. le Baron d'Holbach* (Paris, 1789) show that he owned an almost complete collection of Toland's writings, many of which he translated anonymously or as composed under his own name. See also J. Vercruysse, *Bibliographie descriptive des écrits du Baron d'Holbach* (Paris: Press Université de France, 1971) for translations from John Trenchard and Thomas Gordon.
33 See Miguel Benitez, *La Face cachée des lumières* (Paris: Universitas, 1996), 32–60.
34 J. G. A. Pocock, 'Introduction', *Edmund Burke: Reflections on the Revolution in France* (Indiana: Hackett, 1987), xi.
35 See Christopher Hill, *Some Intellectual Consequences of the English Revolution* (Madison: University of Wisconsin Press, 1980) and 'Freethinking and Libertinism' in Roger D. Lund, ed., *The Margins of Orthodoxy: Heterodox Writing and Cultural Response 1660–1750* (Cambridge and New York: Cambridge University Press, 1995), 54–70.
36 See J. C. D. Clark, *English Society 1688–1832* (Cambridge: Cambridge University Press, 1985). See also 'England's *ancien régime* as a Confessional State', *Albion*, 21 (1989), 450–74; for a massive revision of the eighteenth century see *The Language of Liberty: Political Discourse and Social Dynamics in the Anglo-American*

World 1660–1800 (Cambridge and New York: Cambridge University Press, 1993).

37 See T. Harris, P. Seaward and M. A. Goldie, *The Politics of Religion in Restoration England* (Oxford: Blackwell, 1990).

38 See Horns, 'Revolution as Discourse', 626.

39 For some suggestive remarks see J. G. A. Pocock, 'Edmund Burke and the Redefinition of Enthusiasm', in François Furet and Mona Ouzouf, eds., *The French Revolution and the Creation of Modern Political Culture 1789–1848*, 4 vols. (Oxford and New York: Pergamon Press, 1989), III:19–43 (citation at III:23).

40 See P. Rétat, ed., *Le Traité des trois imposteurs et l'esprit de Spinoza 1678?–1768* (Paris: Universitas, 1998), 7; there were editions in 1775, 1776, 1777, 1793, 1796. For an overview of the state of scholarship on the *Traité*, see S. Berti, F. Charles-Daubert, R. H. Popkin, eds., *Heterodoxy, Spinozism, and Freethought in Early Eighteenth-Century Europe* (Dortrecht: Klewer, 1996). See also O. Bloch, ed., *Le matérialisme du XVIIIe siècle et la littérature clandestine* (Paris: VRIN, 1982). The most comprehensive work is now F. Charles-Daubert, ed., *Le Traité des trois imposteurs et l'esprit de Spinoza, philosophie clandestine entre 1678 et 1768* (Oxford: Voltaire Foundation, 1999).

41 See Ira Owen Wade, *The Clandestine Organization and Diffusion of Philosophic Ideas in France from 1700 to 1750* (Princeton: Princeton University Press and London: H. Milford and Oxford University Press, 1938); J. Spink, *French Freethought from Gassendi to Voltaire* (London: Althone Press, 1960); D. C. Allen, *Doubt's Boundless Sea* (Baltimore: Johns Hopkins University Press, 1964).

42 Rétat, *Traité*, 'Introduction', 12. For full details of the extant manuscript tradition see M. Benitez, *La Face cachée des lumières*, 51–2. An English translation of the 1777 version of the *Traité* is available edited by A. Anderson, *The Treatise of the Three Impostors and the Problem of the Enlightenment* (Lanham: Rowman and Littlefield, 1997). F. Charles-Daubert, *Le Traité des trois imposteurs* provides transcriptions of the major manuscript traditions and variations.

43 Rétat, *Traité*, 'Tables des Matières'.

44 See Sylvia Berti, 'Jan Vroesen, autore del *Traité des Trois Imposteurs*?', *Rivista Storica Italiana*, 103 (1991), 528–43.

45 *Ibid.*, 539.

46 M. Benitez, 'La coterie hollandaise et la réponse à m. de la Monnoye sur *le Traité des trois imposteurs*', *Lias*, 21 (1994), 71–94. My own work on Toland and the *Traité* is forthcoming in *Republican Learning: John Toland and the Crisis of Christian Culture 1680–1722* (Manchester: Manchester University Press).

47 See J. Morrill, *The Nature of the English Revolution* (London: Longman, 1993), especially Part One, 'England's Wars of Religion', 31–176; J. C. Davis, 'Religion and the Struggle for Freedom in the English Revolution', *The Historical Journal*, 35 (1992), 507–30. See also J. A. I. Champion, ' "Religion's safe, with priestcraft is the war": Augustan Anticlericalism and the Legacy of the

English Revolution, 1660–1720', *The European Legacy*, 5 (2000), 553–67;
C. Hill 'Freethinking and Libertinism: The Legacy of the English Revolution', in Lund, ed., *The Margins of Orthodoxy*, 54–70.

48 For a general account see J. A. I. Champion, *The Pillars of Priestcraft Shaken: The Church of England and its Enemies 1660–1730* (Cambridge and New York: Cambridge University Press, 1992); see also M. A. Goldie, 'Priestcraft and the Birth of Whiggism' and 'Ideology' in J. Farr, T. Ball and T. Hanson, eds., *Political Innovation and Conceptual Change* (Cambridge and New York: Cambridge University Press, 1989), 209–31. See also P. N. Miller, ' "Freethinking" and "Freedom of Thought" in Eighteenth-Century Britain', *Historical Journal*, 36 (1993), 599–617.

49 For an extended discussion see J. A. I. Champion, ed., *John Toland Nazarenus* (Oxford: Voltaire Foundation, 1999).

50 For a general account of English attitudes towards the status of Revelation and the Biblical text see Christopher Hill, *The English Bible and the Seventeenth-Century Revolution* (London: Allen Lane, 1993). For a broader overview see R. A. Muller, *Post Reformation Reformed Dogmatics. Volume II, Holy Scripture: The Cognitive Foundations of Theology* (Grand Rapids, MI: Baker Books, 1993).

51 See Rochedieu, *Bibliography of French Translations*: translations were published in Berlin in 1774 and Amsterdam in 1779.

52 The best account of these contributions is M. P. McMahon, *The Radical Whigs, John Trenchard and Thomas Gordon: Libertarian Loyalists to the New House of Hanover* (Lanham: University Press of America, 1990).

53 See J. A. I. Champion, 'Legislators, Impostors, and the Politic Origins of Religion: English Theories of "Imposture" from Stubbe to Toland', in Berti, Charles-Daubert and Popkin, eds., *Heterodoxy*, 333–56.

54 See J. A. I. Champion and R. H. Popkin, 'Bibliography and Irreligion: Richard Smith's "Observations on the Report of a Blasphemous Treatise" ', *The Seventeenth Century*, 10 (1995), 77–99.

55 See Michel Vovelle, 'The Adventure of Reason or From Reason to the Supreme Being' in Colin Lucas, ed., *Rewriting the French Revolution*, 132–50. See Champion, *Pillars of Priestcraft Shaken*, chapter 7.

56 See Rochedieu, *Bibliography of French Translations*.

57 See C. J. Sommerville, *The Secularisation of Early Modern England* (Cambridge and New York: Cambridge University Press, 1992).

58 The material is substantial for a major study of the cultural significance of book ownership and the European diffusion of ideas. Following in the traditions of Mornet and Chartier, the starting point would be a comparison of the *c*.3,000 surviving sales catalogues of private book collections with the literary journals. For a listing see A. N. L. Munby and L. Coral, *British Book Sale Catalogues 1676–1800* (London: Mansell, 1977) and R. S. Crane and F. B. Kaye, *A Census of British Newspapers and Periodicals 1620–1800* (Chapel Hill, NC: University of North Carolina Press and London: Cambridge University Press, 1927).

59 For a discussion see Benitez, 'Lumières et élitisme dans les manuscrits clan-destins', in *La Face cachée des lumières*, 199–211.

60 For a useful cross-cultural comparision of the popular press see Stephen Botein, Jack Censer and Harriet Ritvo, 'The Periodical Press in Eighteenth-Century English and French Society', *Comparative Studies in Society and History*, 23 (1981), 464–90. See also R. H. Popkin, 'Periodical Publication and the Nature of Knowledge in Eighteenth-Century Europe', in D. H. Kelly and R. H. Popkin, eds., *The Shapes of Knowledge from the Renaissance to the Enlightenment* (Dortrecht and Boston: Kluwer, 1991). For older work on French periodical literature see J. de la Harpe, 'Le journal des savants et l'Angleterre 1702–1789', *Modern Philology*, 20 (1937–41), 289–520: 'L'importance du rôle de l'Angleterre dans la formation de la pensée française du XVIII siècle est, à cette heure, un fait acquis' (289).

61 See B. W. Young, *Religion and Enlightenment in Eighteenth-Century England: Theological Debate from Locke to Burke* (Oxford: Clarendon Press, 1998).

2 RADICALISM AND REPLICATION

1 N. H. Keeble, *The Literary Culture of Nonconformity in Later Seventeenth-Century England* (Leicester: Leicester University Press and Athens, GA: University of Georgia Press, 1987), especially chapters 2, 6 and 7.

2 *Ibid.*, chapter 9; Mark Goldie, 'The Revolution of 1689 and the Structure of Political Argument: An Essay and an Annotated Bibliography of Pamphlets on the Allegiance Controversy', *Bulletin of the Institute of Historical Research*, 83 (1980), 473–564.

3 Keeble, *Nonconformity*, 283–5.

4 See Maureen Bell, 'Elizabeth Calvert and the "Confederates"', *Publishing History*, 32 (1992), 5–49; '"Her Usual Practices" : The Later Career of Elizabeth Calvert, 1664–75', *Publishing History*, 35 (1994), 5–64.

5 See Maureen Bell, 'Women and the Opposition Press after the Restoration', in John Lucas, ed., *Writing and Radicalism* (London and New York: Longman, 1996), 39–60.

6 See George Fox, *The Journal*, ed. Nigel Smith (Harmondsworth: Penguin, 1998), 273.

7 Anon., *Mirabilis Annus Secundus* (1662), 8–9.

8 Elizabeth Clarke, 'Tinker, Tailor, Soldier, Poet: Popular Cultures of Early Whiggism', unpublished paper given at the conference, 'Varieties of Whiggism', Jesus College, Oxford University, 28–30 March 2000.

9 Indictments for the printing of seditious ballads are registered in Corporation of London Record Office, Common Council, Sessions File 205.

10 See Blair Worden, 'Wit in a Roundhead: The Dilemma of Marchmont Nedham', in Susan D. Amussen and Mark A. Kishlansky, eds., *Political Culture and Cultural Politics in Early Modern England: Essays Presented to David Underdown* (Manchester and New York: Manchester University Press, 1995), 301–37.

11 Ralph Wallis, *Room for the Cobler of Gloucester* (1668), 4.

12 See Tim Harris, 'The Bawdy House Riots of the 1668', *Historical Journal*, 29 (1986), 537–56.
13 *Ibid.*, 5.
14 *Ibid.*, 33.
15 See below, pp. 151–66.
16 Jonathan Scott, *England's Troubles* (Cambridge and New York: Cambridge University Press, 2000), 388.
17 Mark Knights, *Politics and Opinion in Crisis, 1678–81* (Cambridge and New York: Cambridge University Press, 1994).
18 See also [John Toland], *Clito* (1700); Edward Sexby's call for Cromwell's assassination as an act of political virtue, *Killing no Murder* (1657) was republished in 1689.
19 See Abigail Williams, 'The Making of Williamite Panegyric: Poetry, Politics and Patronage, 1688–1702' (unpublished M. Phil. thesis, University of Oxford, 1997).
20 The Bodleian copy, from the Malone collection (Mal. 116 (6)), has 'Mr Southly' written on the title page.
21 The common source is Plutarch's Life of Timoleon. Laurence Kennedy, 'Standing Armies Revisited (1697–1701): Authorship, Chronology and Public Perception', *Notes and Queries*, n.s. 43 (1996), 287–90, describes the play as Machiavellian, presumably in the light of the positive reference to the *Discorsi* in the dedicatory epistle (sig. A2r), which mentions the story of Cincinnatus, very much a parallel to that of Timoleon. The preface's call for moral reformation of drama recalls the sentiments of several 1650s republicans, including Milton, Harrington and Streater (see Nigel Smith, 'Popular Republicanism in the 1650s: John Streater's "Heroick Mechanicks"', in David Armitage, Armand Himy and Quentin Skinner, eds., *Milton and Republicanism* (Cambridge and New York: Cambridge University Press, 1995), 137–55; David Norbrook, *Writing the English Republic: Poetry, Rhetoric and Politics 1627–1660* (Cambridge and New York: Cambridge University Press, 1999), 363–4).
22 See the discussion in Derek Hughes, *English Drama, 1660–1700* (Oxford and New York: Oxford University Press, 1996), 430–1.
23 *Timoleon: Or, The Revolution* (1697), 78
24 Smith, 'Popular Republicanism', 146.
25 *Timoleon*, 79.
26 *Ibid.*, 78.
27 *Ibid.*, 79.
28 *Ibid.*
29 *Ibid.*
30 The play is sufficiently close to *Clito* and Toland's extreme republican expressions at this time, that his own involvement in this text cannot be discounted. Cf. Nigel Smith, 'The English Revolution and the End of Rhetoric: John Toland's *Clito* (1700) and the Republican Daemon', *Essays and Studies* (1996), 'Poetry and Politics', 1–20.

31 *Timoleon*, 74.
32 *Ibid.*, sig. A2ʳ.
33 Smith, 'The English Revolution and the End of Rhetoric', 8–10.
34 See Justin Champion, unpublished paper given at the conference, 'Varieties of Whiggism', Jesus College, Oxford University, 28–30 March 2000.
35 See Don Herzog, *Happy Slaves: A Critique of Consent Theory* (Chicago: University of Chicago Press, 1989).
36 Gary S. de Krey, 'Political Radicalism in London after the Glorious Revolution', *Journal of Modern History*, 55 (1983), 585–617; Gary S. de Krey, *A Fractured Society: The Politics of London in the First Age of Party 1688–1715* (Oxford and New York: Oxford University Press, 1985), especially chapters 3 and 4.
37 See above, pp. 13–20.
38 Brean S. Hammond, *Professional Imaginative Writing in England, 1640–1740: 'Hackney for Bread'* (Oxford and New York: Oxford University Press, 1997), especially chapter 1.
39 Edmund Ludlow, *A Voyce from the Watchtower. Part Five: 1660–1662*, Camden Fourth Series, ed. A. B. Worden (London: Royal Historical Society, 1978), Introduction, 39–55; see also Worden, 'Republicanism and the Restoration, 1660–1683', and M. M. Goldsmith, 'Liberty, Virtue and the Rule of Law, 1689–1770', in David Wootton, ed., *Republicanism, Liberty and Commercial Society, 1649–1776* (Stanford, CA: Stanford University Press, 1994), 197–232.
40 Worden, in Ludlow, *A Voyce*, 40–1.
41 Michael Foot, *The Pen and the Sword: Jonathan Swift and the Power of the Press* (London: MacGibbon and Kee, 1957; 3rd edn, 1984); H. T. Dickinson, 'The Precursors of Political Radicalism in Augustan Britain', in C. Jones, ed., *Britain in the First Age of Party 1680–1750: Essays Presented to Geoffrey Holmes* (London: Hambledon Press, 1987), 63–84.
42 Paul Monod, *Jacobitism and the English People, 1688–1788* (Cambridge and New York: Cambridge University Press, 1988, 1993).
43 Linda Colley, 'Eighteenth-Century English Radicalism before Wilkes', *Transactions of the Royal Historical Society*, 5th series, 31 (1981), 1–19.
44 See Richard Franck, *Northern Memoirs* (London, 1694); Richard Franck, *Northern Memoirs*, ed. Sir Walter Scott (Edinburgh, 1821); Kathryn Sutherland, 'Travel Books, Fishing Manuals, and Scott's *Redgauntlet*', *Scottish Literary Journal*, 13 (1986), 20–30; Nigel Smith, *Literature and Revolution in England, 1640–1660* (New Haven and London: Yale University Press, 1994), 330–6.
45 The tract is unsigned; internal evidence suggests strongly that Franck was the author.
46 Richard Franck, *The Admirable and Indefatigable Adventures of the Nine Pious Pilgrims* (London, 1707), sig. A3ᵛ.
47 *Ibid.*, sig. A6ʳ.
48 *Ibid.*, 5.
49 *Ibid.*, 107–8.

50 *Ibid.*, 110.
51 *Ibid.*, 112.
52 Nigel Smith, ' "Naked Space": Cultural Boundaries in the Leveller Republic', in Peter Lake and Steven Pincus, eds., *The Public Sphere in Early Modern England* (Manchester, forthcoming).
53 Franck, *Admirable and Indefatigable Adventures*, 154.
54 *Ibid.*, 111.
55 *Ibid.*, 142–58.
56 See Ovid, *Metamorphoses*, 5.376–571. The Ovid edition I used is *Ovid in Six Volumes*, III *Metamorphoses*, English translation by Frank Justis Miller, 2 vols. (Cambridge, MA: Harvard University Press, 1916; 3rd edn 1977; reprinted 1984), I: 264–77.
57 Franck, *Admirable and Indefatigable Adventures*, 106.
58 *Ibid.*, 163–4.
59 See Clarke, 'Tinker, Tailor, Soldier, Poet'.
60 Gregory Claeys, ed., *Utopias of the British Enlightenment* (Cambridge and New York: Cambridge University Press, 1994), xii.
61 See below, pp. 58, 64–6, 68, 70–83, 96.
62 See Brian J. Gibbons, *Gender in Mystical and Occult Thought: Behmenism and its Development in England* (Cambridge and New York: Cambridge University Press, 1996), 143–62.
63 *The Ascent to the Mount of Visions* (London, 1699), 25.
64 *Ibid.*, 27.
65 *Ibid.*, 218.
66 See Paula McDowell, *The Women of Grub Street: Press, Politics and Gender in the London Literary Market Place 1678–1730* (Oxford: Clarendon Press, 1998), 171–8, 197, 199–201, 287–8.
67 I am most grateful for a discussion wih Daniel Carey on this issue.
68 Smith, *Literature and Revolution in England*, chapter 5.
69 See John Bellers, *John Bellers His Life, Times and Writings*, ed. George Clarke (London and New York: Routledge, 1987).
70 See John Bellers, *Essays about the Poor, Manufactures, Trade, Plantations, and Immorality* (London, 1699).
71 John Bellers, *Proposals for Raising a Colledge of Industry of all Useful Trades and Husbandry* (London, 1696); John Bellers, *An Essay Towards the Improvement of Physick* (London, 1714), esp. 35, 47.
72 See John Bellers, *An Abstract of George Fox's Advice and Warning* (London, 1724).
73 Bellers, *Proposals*, 23.
74 *The Sophick Constitution* (1700), 21.
75 The one exception was the hiring of actors to perform Shakespeare's *Richard II* on the eve of the Essex Rebellion in 1602. But by being hired, were the players acting in the rebellion itself?
76 The portrait is by John Michael Wright, and is currently in the Royal Collection, but a reproduction is printed on the dustjacket of Hughes, *English Drama, 1660–1700*. For Lacy, see *Dictionary of National Biography*.

77 Paula R. Backscheider, *Spectacular Politics: Theatrical Power and Mass Culture in Early Modern England* (Baltimore and London: Johns Hopkins University Press, 1993).

78 Mark Goldie, 'The Hilton Gang and the Purge of London in the 1680s', in Howard Nenner, ed., *Politics and Imagination in Later Stuart Britain* (Rochester, NY: University of Rochester Press, 1997), 43–73.

79 Clarke, 'Tinker, Tailor, Soldier, Poet'.

80 John Toland, Preface to *Christianity not Mysterious* (London, 1696); see Ronald Paulson, *The Beautiful, Novel, and Strange: Aesthetics and Heterodoxy* (Baltimore and London: Johns Hopkins University Press, 1996), 7–8, 24, 336.

81 Donna T. Andrew, 'Popular Culture and Public Debate: London 1780', *Historical Journal*, 39 (1996), 405–23. See also Andrew, *London Debating Societies, 1776–1799*, 30 (1994). See also Peter Clark, *British Clubs and Societies c. 1580–1800: The Origins of an Associational World* (Oxford and New York: Oxford University Press, 2000).

82 John Barrell, *Imagining the King's Death: Figurative Treason, Fantasies of Regicide 1793–96* (Oxford and New York: Oxford University Press, 2000), 1–46.

83 Richard Ashcraft, *Revolutionary Politics and Locke's Two Treatises of Government* (Princeton: Princeton University Press, 1986); John Marshall, *John Locke: Resistance, Religion and Responsibility* (Cambridge and New York: Cambridge University Press, 1994), 76–8, 128n., 240n., 243–7, 250–2, 262–5, 280–3; and Gerald Aylmer, 'Locke no Leveller', in Ian Gentles, John Morrill and Blair Worden, eds., *Soldiers, Writers and Statesmen of the English Revolution* (Cambridge and New York: Cambridge University Press, 1998), 304–22.

84 Melinda Zook, 'Violence, Martyrdom, and Radical Politics: Rethinking the Glorious Revolution', in Nenner, ed., *Politics and Imagination in Later Stuart Britain*, 75–95; see also Melinda Zook, *Radical Whigs and Conspiratorial Politics in Late Stuart England* (University Park, PA: Penn State University Press, 1999).

3 THE PLANTATION OF WRATH

1 See Timothy Morton, *Shelley and the Revolution in Taste: The Body and the Natural World* (Cambridge and New York: Cambridge University Press, 1994; repr. 1998).

2 Nigel Smith, *Literature and Revolution in England, 1640–1600* (New Haven and London: Yale University Press, 1994), 320–36; the quotation is from 333.

3 *Dictionary of National Biography*. I am grateful to Daniel White for helping me with this information.

4 Smith, *Literature and Revolution in England, 1640–1600*, 97.

5 Bernard de Mandeville, *The Fable of the Bees: or, Private Vices, Publick Benefits. The Second Edition, Enlarged with many Additions. As also an Essay on Charity and Charity-Schools. And a Search into the Nature of Society* (London, 1723; first edn, 1714), 185–97.

6 This is the copy in the Harry Ransom Center at the University of Texas at Austin, number An/Sh 44/Zz802r/Rare/Books/Col.

7 Smith, *Literature and Revolution in England, 1640–1600*, 362.

8 Timothy Morton, ed., *Radical Food: The Culture and Politics of Eating and Drinking, 1780–1830*, 3 vols. (London and New York: Routledge, 2000) 1:60.

9 See Keith Thomas, *Man and the Natural World: Changing Attitudes in England 1500–1800* (London: Allen Lane, 1983; repr. Penguin, 1984), 296. The Vegetarian Society had close connections with this church: see W. E. A. and E. Axon, *Ninety-Two Years of the Vegetarian Society* (Manchester: The Vegetarian Society, 1939), 4. See Joseph Brotherton, *The First Teetotal Tract. On Abstinence from Intoxicating Liquor. First Published in 1821* (Manchester: 'Onward' Publishing Office and London: S. W. Partidge, 1890), for the way in which vegetarianism could easily be linked to abstinence from alcohol.

10 Nigel Smith, 'Enthusiasm and Enlightenment: Of Food, Filth, and Slavery', in Gerald MacLean, Donna Landry and Joseph P. Ward, eds., *The Country and the City Revisited: England and the Politics of Culture, 1550–1850* (Cambridge and New York: Cambridge University Press, 1999), 116.

11 Jacob Boehme, *Essential Readings*, ed. Robin Waterfield (Wellingborough, Leicestershire: Crucible, 1989), 26.

12 *Ibid.*

13 *Ibid.*, 27.

14 *Ibid.*

15 Andrew Weeks, *Boehme: An Intellectual Biography of the Seventeenth-Century Philosopher and Mystic* (Albany: State University of New York Press, 1991), 139. See Smith, 'Enthusiasm and Enlightenment', 109–11.

16 Boehme, *Essential Readings*, 49.

17 Weeks, *Boehme*, 2.

18 Boehme, *Essential Readings*, 31. Percy Shelley, 'A Vindication of Natural Diet', in *Shelley's Prose: or the Trumpet of a Prophecy*, ed. David Lee Clark (London: Fourth Estate, 1988), 83.

19 Weeks, *Boehme*, 33.

20 Boehme, *Essential Readings*, 37.

21 *Ibid.*, 120.

22 Weeks, *Boehme*, 151.

23 *Ibid.*, 170.

24 Jacob Boehme, *Signatura Rerum: or the Signature of All Things: Shewing the Sign, and Signification of the Severall Forms and Shapes in the Creation: and what the Beginning, Ruin, and Cure of Every Thing is; it Proceeds out of Eternity into Time, and again out of Time into Eternity, and Comprizeth All Mysteries*, trans. J. Ellistone (London, 1651), 42.

25 *Ibid.*, 57.

26 Thomas Tryon, *Pythagoras His Mystic Philosophy Revived; or, the Mystery of Dreams Unfolded. Wherein the Causes, Natures, and Uses, of Nocturnal Representations,*

and the Communications both of Good and Evil Angels, and also Departed Souls, to Mankind, are Theosophically Unfolded; that is, According to the Word of God, and the Harmony of Created Beings. To which is Added, a Discourse of the Causes, Natures, and Cure of Phrensie, Madness or Distraction (London, 1691), 105 and throughout.

27 George Cheyne, *An Essay on Regimen. Together with Five Discourses, Medical, Moral, and Philosophical: Serving to Illustrate the Principles and Theory of Philosophical Medicin, and Point out Some of its Moral Consequences* (London, 1740), 26, 146–7, 29.

28 *Ibid.*, 56–9.

29 *Ibid.*, 145.

30 Richard Brothers, *Prophetical Passages, Concerning the Present Times, in which the Person, Character, Mission, &c. &c. of Richard Brothers, is Clearly Pointed at as the Elijah of the Present Day, the Right Star to Guide the Hebrews, &c. Selected from the Writings of Jacob Behmen, C. Poniatnia, Kotterus, Salizarus, B. Keach, &c. also, the Remarkable Prophecy of Humphrey Tindal, Vicar of Wellington, to which is Added (by Permission) Some Letters which have been Sent to Mr Brothers* (London, 1795), 3.

31 *Ibid.*, 4.

32 *Ibid.*, 20–1.

33 Iain McCalman, *Radical Underworld: Prophets, Revolutionaries and Pornographers in London, 1795–1840* (Cambridge: Cambridge University Press, 1988), 61.

34 Richard Brothers, *A Letter to Subscribers for Engraving the Plans of Jerusalem, the King's Palace, the Private Palaces, College-Halls, Cathedrals, and Parliament-Houses* (London: printed by E. Spragg, 1805), 18–19.

35 Timothy Morton, *The Poetics of Spice: Romantic Consumerism and the Exotic* (Cambridge and New York: Cambridge University Press, 2000), 90–2.

36 See Alan Richardson, *A Mental Theater: Poetic Drama and Consciousness in the Romantic Age* (University Park: Pennsylvania State University Press, 1988).

37 Thomas Tryon, *Friendly Advice to the Gentlemen-Planters of the East and West Indies. In Three Parts* (London, 1684), 75ff.

38 *Ibid.*, 75–6.

39 Morton, *Shelley and the Revolution in Taste*, 128.

40 John Field, *The Absurdity & Falsness of Thomas Trion's Doctrine Manifested, in Forbidding to Eat Flesh, Contrary to the Command of God, the Example of Angels, Christ Jesus, and the Holy Apostles: and Proved to be Doctrine of Devils, by the Testimony of Holy Scriptures: in a Few Queries Thereon, as Laid Down in His Books, – One Intituled, The Way to Health, Long Life and Happiness; the Other, The Way to Make all People Rich: Subscribed Phylotheos Physiologus. Also, His Great Errour in Affirming, that Killing the Creatures for Food, is from the Fierce Wrath of God, and Hellish Nature in Man, and a Fruit of Hell. And, the Lawfulness of Eating both Flesh of Fowls and Fish, &c. in the Fear of God, Being Received with Thanksgiving, Proved by Scripture, and the Example of Christ and His Apostles. Together with Some Remarks on the Verses, Printed as a Preface to His Book Entituled, The Way to Make All People Rich, &c. In which Verses it is said: 'Not He that bore the*

Almighty Wand could give / Diviner Dictates how to Eat and Live' than *Thomas Trion*
(London, 1685), 14.

41 Smith, *Literature and Revolution in England*, 2–3, 218–23 ('Creating Interiority').

42 Tryon, *Friendly Advice*, 76–7.

43 *Ibid.*, 77.

44 *Ibid.*, 79–80.

45 *Ibid.*, 145.

46 *Ibid.*, 88–9.

47 *Ibid.*, 109.

48 *Ibid.*, 142.

49 *Ibid.*, 146ff.

50 *Ibid.*, 151–2.

51 *Ibid.*, 162.

52 *Ibid.*, 89.

53 *Ibid.*, 91.

54 *Ibid.*, 96.

55 Robert Wedderburn, *The Horrors of Slavery, and Other Writings*, ed. Iain McCalman (Edinburgh: Edinburgh University Press, 1991), 6.

56 *Ibid.*, 7.

57 *Ibid.*, 3.

58 McCalman, *Radical Underworld*, 71

59 Wedderburn, *The Horrors of Slavery*, 97.

60 *Ibid.*, 100–1. Wedderburn is quoting from Robert Merry, 'The Slaves. An Elegy', in Edward Topham, ed., *The Poetry of the World*, 2 vols. (London, 1788), vol. I. My thanks to Kevin Binfield for pointing this out.

61 Smith, 'Enthusiasm and Enlightenment', 116.

62 Richard Holmes, *Coleridge: Early Visions* (London and New York: Viking, 1990), 82–3, 89.

63 McCalman, *Radical Underworld*, 71.

64 Wedderburn, *The Horrors of Slavery*, 133–4.

65 *Ibid.*, 81.

66 Morton, 'Blood Sugar', *The Poetics of Spice*, chapter 4.

67 *Ibid.*, 82.

68 *Ibid.*, 86.

69 Thomas Tryon, *The Way to Make All People Rich: or, Wisdom's Call to Temperance and Frugality. In a Dialogue between Sophronio and Guloso, One a Lover of Sobriety, the Other Addicted to Gluttony and Excess* (London, 1685), 21–2.

70 *Ibid.*, 46.

71 *Ibid.*, 31.

72 Orrin Wang, 'Romantic Sobriety', *Modern Language Quarterly*, 60.4 (December 1999), 469–93.

73 John Evelyn, *Acetaria: A Discourse of Sallets* (London, 1699), before A1 v. (np). On the Golden Age, see 146.

74 *Ibid.*, 138–9.

75 *Ibid.*, 179.
76 *Ibid.*, 86.
77 *Ibid.*, 137.
78 *Ibid.*, 154–5.
79 *Ibid.*, 156.
80 *Ibid.*, 164–5.
81 *Ibid.*, 185–6.
82 *Ibid.*, 180.
83 *Ibid.*, 180–1.
84 *Ibid.*, 192.
85 Field, *The Absurdity & Falsness of Thomas Trion's Doctrine Manifested*, 23.
86 Cheyne, *Essay on Regimen*, 1 (title page).
87 William Law, *Remarks upon a Late Book, Entitled, The Fable of the Bees, or Private Vices, Publick Benefits. In a Letter to the Author. To which is Added, a Postscript, Containing an Observation or Two upon Mr Bayle*, 3rd edn (London, 1726), 54, 91.
88 *Ibid.*, 155–6.
89 *Ibid.*, 182.
90 See Morton, *Shelley and the Revolution in Taste*, chapters 1 and 2, especially 26–8, 152–7.
91 Joseph Ritson, *An Essay on Abstinence from Animal Food, as a Moral Duty* (London: Richard Phillips, 1802), 82–3, 220–2.
92 *Ibid.*, 81.
93 *Ibid.*, 89, 101, 184–5.
94 Robert D. Arner, 'Politics and Temperance in Boston and Philadelphia: Benjamin Franklin's Journalistic Writings on Drinking and Drunkenness', in J. A. Leo Lemay, ed., *Reappraising Benjamin Franklin: a Bicentennial Perspective* (Newark: University of Delaware Press and London and Toronto: Associated University Presses, 1993), 52–77 (72).
95 Benjamin Franklin, *Works of the Late Doctor Benjamin Franklin: Consisting of His Life, Written by Himself, together with Essays, Humorous, Moral & Literary, Chiefly in the Manner of The Spectator* (Dublin, 1793), 12.
96 *Ibid.*, 19–20.
97 Sacvan Bercovitch, 'The Ritual of American Autobiography: Edwards, Franklin, Thoreau', *Revue Française d'Etudes Americaine*, 7:14 (May 1982), 140, 142–3. See R. C. De Prospo, 'Humanizing the Monster: Integral Self Versus Bodied Soul in the Personal Writings of Franklin and Edwards', in Barbara B. Oberg and Harry S. Stout, eds., *Benjamin Franklin, Jonathan Edwards, and the Representation of American Culture* (Oxford and New York: Oxford University Press, 1993), 204–17.
98 *Ibid.*, 145–8.
99 A. Owen Aldridge, 'The Alleged Puritanism of Benjamin Franklin', in Lemay, ed., *Reappraising Benjamin Franklin*, 362–71.
100 Franklin, *Life*, 45–46.

101 David Levin, 'Reason, Rhythm, and Style', in Oberg and Stout, eds., *Benjamin Franklin, Jonathan Edwards, and the Representation of American Culture*, 171–85; the quotation is from 172.
102 Leigh Hunt, review of *The Revolt of Islam*, *The Examiner* (10 October 1819), 652–3, 636.
103 John Taylor Coleridge, review of *The Revolt of Islam*, *Quarterly Review*, 21 (April 1819), 460–71; the citation is from 467.
104 McCalman, *Radical Underworld*, 28.
105 *The Republican*, 1 (27 August 1819 – 7 January 1820), 213; *The Republican*, 5 (January–May 1822), 148.
106 McCalman, *Radical Underworld*, 28.

4 THEY BECAME WHAT THEY BEHELD: THEODICY
AND REGENERATION IN MILTON, LAW AND BLAKE

1 Acts 17:27. Unless specified, all quotations of Blake are from *The Complete Poetry and Prose of William Blake*, ed. David V. Erdman, commentary by Harold Bloom (Berkeley: University of California Press, 1982). I have retained Blake's spelling, punctuation, etc., as it appears in Erdman's text. In these notes, 'E' denotes this edition; here, E146.
2 And this is why, *pace* William Kerrigan, eighteenth-century optimism was not Milton's main theodical competition. Had there *not* been other 'larger' approaches to theodicy, Kerrigan's Blake would have gone mad. Dennis Danielson, ed., *The Cambridge Companion to Milton* (Cambridge: Cambridge University Press, 1989), 268, 269.
3 All Scripture quotations are from the Authorised Version.
4 John Locke, *An Essay Concerning Human Understanding*, ed. Peter Nidditch (Oxford: Clarendon Press, 1988), II.xxiii.33. Working within revealed religion, writers softened such divine attributes as implacability and impassibility through either new translations or paraphrases of Scripture, or by restricting their exegeses of the Bible to books featuring a more *humane* God. In the main, rational or natural theology relied on anthropomorphism. Yet, for Hume, anthropomorphism was the Trojan horse that his rationalist, Cleanthes, drags into the midst of the whole theodicean enterprise. Michael Prince persuasively argues that in the *Dialogues Concerning Natural Religion*, Hume intentionally, and with a well-considered knowledge of the genre, sabotaged philosophical dialogue as a means of exploring issues in natural religion, especially theodicy (*Philosophical Dialogue in the British Enlightenment: Theology, Aesthetics and the Novel* (Cambridge and New York: Cambridge University Press, 1996), 136–60).
5 E3; John Calvin, *Institutes of the Christian Religion* (Grand Rapids: W. B. Eerdmans, 1966). Having pummeled Osiander for introducing a 'monstrosity termed *essential righteousness*... desiring to transfuse the divine essence into man... [and its concomitant notion]... that Adam was formed in the

image of God, because even before the fall Christ was destined to be the
model of human nature' – bk. III, ch. xi, par. 5 – Calvin has a short-lived
concern that he had made righteousness too unreal, bk. III, ch.xiv, par. 5. '*Si
les pecheurs tant seulement sont introduictz a salut; qu'est-ce que nous y cerchons entrée
par noz justices contrefaictes?* (1541); '*Si soli peccatores admittuntur, quid per fictitias
iustitias aditum quaeramus?*' (1559).

6 John Scott, *The Christian Life from its Beginning to its Consummation in Glory*, 6th
edn corrected (London, 1694), 5.

7 *Ibid.*; David Bogue, *The Importance of Having Right Sentiments in Religion* 2nd
edn (London, 1789), 11. Tom Paine, a self-proclaimed deist, makes the
crucial point: 'It is from the Bible that man has learned cruelty, rapine, and
murder; *for the belief of a cruel God makes a cruel man.*' M. C. Conway, ed., *The
Writings of Thomas Paine*, 4 vols. (New York: AMS Press, Inc., 1967), IV:186,
190, 198, emphasis added. Though the theologies of Scott, Bogue, Paine
and Law differed (widely at points), the identity-shaping power of one's
conception of God emerges as a point held in common between writers of
various persuasions.

8 See note 52 and Keith Thomas, *Man and the Natural World: Changing Attitudes
in England 1500–1800* (London: Allen Lane, 1983; repr. Penguin, 1984),
149–50, 173–81.

9 E691.

10 This diagram's truth is nowhere more clearly illustrated than in the fact that
Law's evangelical critics' – old and new – first point of attack is that emanation, as opposed to *ex nihilo* creation, so redefines as to eliminate the very
wrath of God that underpins forensic soteriology. See Martin Madan, 'A Full
and Compleat Answer to the Capital Errors, Contained in the Writings of the
Late Rev. William Law' (London: Edward Duffy, 1763), especially vi–ix. John
Wesley, 'A Letter to the Reverend Mr Law: Occasioned by Some of His Late
Writings' (London, 1756), 13–21, 39ff. And more recently, 'Law's . . . desire
for an ultimate unity is nowhere more conspicuous than in his treatment of
the wrath of God' (J. Brazer Green, *John Wesley and William Law* (London:
The Epworth Press, 1945), 114.

11 *Prometheus Unbound*, 1.450, in *Shelley's Poetry and Prose*, ed. Donald Reiman and
Sharon B. Powers (New York: W. W. Norton, 1977).

12 Lactantius, *A Treatise on the Anger of God*, trans. William Fletcher, in *The Ante-
Nicene Fathers*, ed. A. Roberts and J. Danielson (Grand Rapids: Eerdmans,
1957), VII.271.

13 A. D. Nuttall, *Pope's Essay on Man* (London: George Allen and Unwin, 1984),
207–8, emphasis added.

14 William Law, *The Spirit of Prayer* (1749), 8–11, emphasis added. Citations
from Law are from *William Law: The Works*, ed. G. B. Morton, 3 vols. (New
York: Georg Olms Verlag, 1974).

15 Mark Kaplan aptly distinguishes between androgyny and hermaphroditism
in Blake. Despite Blake's sexual bravado, androgyny is essential to his myth:

'in *Milton*: individuals pass through States, but must avoid total identification with any single State. To identify with a State is to freeze ourselves into a fixed, immutable Selfhood and to lose touch with our total humanity. Gender is one of these States...' See Kaplan's 'Jerusalem and the Origins of Patriarchy', *Blake: An Illustrated Quarterly*, 30:3 (Winter 1996/7), 80–1. Regarding Boehme, Brian J. Gibbons observes, 'The duality of gender is itself a principle of death; life can only be lived fully when this duality is transcended spiritually' (*Gender in Mystical and Occult Thought: Behmenism and its Development in England* (Cambridge and New York: Cambridge University Press, 1996), 97.

16 Law, *An Appeal to All that Doubt, or Disbelieve the Truths of the Gospel, whether they be Deists, Arians, Socinians, or Nominal Christians* (London, 1740), 134–5, my emphasis. Significant differences exist between Law (a clergyman and writer of devotional and polemic theological prose, living with two women, albeit not in a Swedenborgian way) and Blake (a streetwise Londoner, an engraver and composite artist). But careful readers will note broad similarity. Law's rigorism just may be a version of Blake's energetic denial of the vegetative world, and so on.

17 A phrase, 'the dream of life', appears throughout Law's writings, representing the fall into the senses and a loss of Sophia, the divine influx. We are born 'in the dregs of time... Is there any dream like the dream of life?', *Serious Call* (London, 1729), 25–6. Law's emphasis. Also, Shelley: 'he is not dead... / He hath awakened from the dream of life /... From the contagion of the world's slow stain / He is secure' (*Adonais*, lines 343–57). William Law, *A Serious Call to a Devout and Holy Life*, and *The Spirit of Love*, ed. Paul G. Stanwood (New York, Ramsey, Toronto: The Paulist Press, 1978).

18 *The Spirit of Prayer*, 3–8, Law's emphasis.

19 *An Appeal*, 60–1, Law's emphasis.

20 Jacob Boehme, *The Second Book Concerning the Three Principles of the Divine Essence*, trans. J. Sparrow (London, 1648), 1.2.

21 Law, *The Spirit of Love*, 7.

22 E 584, 635; *A Serious Call*, (1729), 262; *An Appeal* (1740), 58–9.

23 Emanuel Swedenborg, *True Christian Religion: Containing the Universal Theology of the New Church* (London: R. Hindmarsh, 1795), par. 76.

24 E563.

25 E565.

26 E554.

27 E705.

28 Northrop Frye, *Fearful Symmetry: A Study of William Blake* (Princeton: Princeton University Press, 1974), 256–7.

29 E171.

30 E565.

31 E27.

32 E153, 201.

33 E3.

34 E146, 184.

35 E113.

36 E212. Such a rationalist critique would be, 'Nothing is more repugnant to free forgiveness, than full satisfaction. For the creditor which is satisfied... cannot be truly said to have freely... forgiven the debt' (Valentine Schmalz and Johannes Völkel, *The Racovian Cathechisme*, trans. J. Biddle (Amsterdam, 1652), 127).

37 Law, *Some Animadversions Upon Dr Trapp's Late Reply* (Appended to Law's *An Appeal*), 203, Law's emphasis.

38 Law, *An Humble, Earnest, and Affectionate Address to the Clergy* (London, 1761), 53, Law's emphasis. Law's editor points the reader to Milton's 'Enormous Bliss' (*Paradise Lost* V:297).

39 Unless otherwise specified, quotations from Milton are taken from: *Paradise Lost*, ed. Alastair Fowley (London and New York: Longman, 1968, 1971); *John Milton: Complete Shorter Poems*, ed. John Carey, 2nd edn (London and New York: Longman, 1968, 1971); *Christian Doctrine* is from *The Complete Prose Works of John Milton, vol. vi ca. 1658–1660*, ed. Don. M. Wolfe (New Haven and London: Yale University Press, 1971), vol. VI.

40 Dennis R. Danielson's *Milton's Good God: A Study in Literary Theodicy* (Cambridge: Cambridge University Press, 1982) is well known for its erudite exploration of Milton's theodicy. For Danielson, Milton's theodicy is strongly anchored in Arminianism – as opposed to *felix culpa*, the latter of which downplays human freedom. Unfortunately, Danielson's argument for the concept of 'soul-making' – which has such immense theodicean appeal – does not get us very far. *Paradise Lost* V:498 ff. and VII:157 ff. do not come close to suggesting the arousal of an ontological bond between Creator and creature; instead 'passions tried' lead to what Blake decried as 'moral virtue'; and, for Blake, 'If Morality was Christianity Socrates was The Saviour' (E667). Blake would make the same critique of modern reader-response criticism, i.e. if soul-making takes place in the reader, it is of the same order as that which Adam and Eve experience.

41 Stanley Fish, *Surprised by Sin*, 2nd edn (Cambridge, MA: Harvard University Press, 1997); Marshall Grossman, *'Authors to Themselves': Milton and the Revelation of History* (Cambridge: Cambridge University Press, 1987). William Empson, *Milton's God*, revised edn (London: Chatto and Windus, 1965).

42 Irene Samuel, 'The Dialogue in Heaven: A Reconsideration of *Paradise Lost*, III.1–417', *PMLA*, 72 (1947), 601. Milton's Arianism (as opposed to subordinationism) is persuasively demonstrated by Rumrich in Stephen B. Dobranski and John Rumrich, eds., *Milton and Heresy* (Cambridge and New York: Cambridge University Press, 1998), 75–92.

43 Margaret L. Bailey, *Milton and Jacob Boehme: A Study of German Mysticism in Seventeenth-Century England* (New York: Haskell House, 1964), 144.

44 *Ibid.*, 156.

45 *Ibid.*, 157–8.
46 John Milton, *Christian Doctrine. Ibid.*, 208–12; 262–5; *Paradise Lost* III:243–4.
47 Milton, *Christian Doctrine*, note 15, 135, 213.
48 *Ibid.*, 118. The tension between 'the conceptual bounds imposed by Protestant exegetes' and Boehme in Milton's mind is briefly and best summarised by James G. Turner, *One Flesh: Paradisal Marriage and Sexual Relations in the Age of Milton* (Oxford: Clarendon Press, 1993), 154–6.
49 Daniel Watkins, in Nicholas Roe, ed., *Keats and History* (Cambridge and New York: Cambridge University Press, 1995), 96, my emphasis.
50 It is remarkable how Behmenist theology circulated among individuals who were aligned to vastly different religious traditions. In 1749, the Countess of Huntingdon, whose one-time chaplain was George Whitefield, reprinted the first part of Law's *Spirit of Prayer*, the most radical of Law's critiques of evangelical soteriology in general and *creatio ex nihilo* in particular. See Edwin Welch, *Spiritual Pilgrim: A Reassessment of the Countess of Huntingdon* (Cardiff: University of Wales Press, 1995), 67. Thomas Hartley (friend of Whitefield, Hervey, Law and translator of Swedenborg), in the presence of the Countess of Huntingdon, criticised a manuscript copy of James Hervey's *Theron and Aspasio* for its defence of imputed righteousness. Hervey blamed Hartley for the Countess's refusal to be the book's dedicatee. Peter Lineham, 'The English Swedenborgians' (Ph.D. thesis, University of Sussex, 1978), 13–30, and my entry for 'Hartley', in J. Yolton, ed., *Dictionary of Eighteenth-Century British Philosophers* (Bristol: Thoemmes Press, 1999); John Byrom, *Private Journal and Literary Remains*, ed. Richard Parkinson, 2 vols. (Manchester: The Chethem Society, 1854–7); *The Correspondence of Henry Brooke* (Walton MS. 1.1.43. London: Dr Williams's Library).
51 *Christian Doctrine*, 174.
52 *Ibid.*, 187.
53 *Ibid.*, 185–6.
54 The phrase is Andrew Weeks's (*Boehme: An Intellectual Biography of the Seventeenth-Century Philosopher and Mystic* (Albany: State University of New York Press, 1991, 146), referring to such Behmenist warnings as: 'O! what a great misery it is that we are ignorant in what soil we grow, and what essences we draw to us, seeing our fruit shall be tasted, and that which is pleasant shall stand upon God's table; and the other shall be cast to the devil's swine'. Boehme, *The Second Book*, 27.3.
55 See John Carey's summary of Milton's views in *ibid.*, 91–5. Milton is uncertain whether this earth will be conflagrated or renovated, *ibid.*, 627, 632. It is a small point, but contemporary theodicists argue that an author's commitment to the notion of Purgatory as being a very different annex to life in this world, or to a belief in the destruction of this world – as opposed to non-retributive reincarnation – acts as a barometer to a given author's confidence in this world as an adequate soul-making atmosphere. See Michael

Stoeber, *Evil and the Mystics' God* (Toronto: University of Toronto Press, 1992), 165–87.

56 E610–11.

57 Law, *Divine Knowledge*, 175ff.

58 Law, *Address to the Clergy*, 91, Law's emphasis.

59 *Ibid.*, 90, Law's emphasis. This work immediately followed Law's critique of vicarious atonement, justification by faith in Christ's imputed righteousness (*Of Justification by Faith and Works* (London, 1760)).

60 E2, 3.

61 'Mr Law said he owed it to [Malebranche] that he kept his act at Cambridge upon *"Omnia videmus Deo"*' (Byrom, *Private Journal and Literary Remains*, vol. 1, pt. 2, 337). Like Berkeley, Law would have been drawn to Malebranche for his Representationalism, i.e. 'seeing all things in God', (the three writers make heavy use of Acts 17:28) and not the full-blown occasionalism. A. A. Luce, *Berkeley and Malebranche* (Oxford: Clarendon Press, 1967), 76–86, 89–91. When Law repeatedly says that God can only love that which is lovable, he is not making a rigorist behaviour judgement, but an ontological one, as per Malebranche: '[God] cannot prevent Himself from loving things in proportion as they are lovable . . . This is not because sinners offend God . . . nor because God punishes them out of . . . vengeance.' Nicholas Malebranche, *Dialogues on Metaphysics and on Religion*, ed. Nicholas Jolley (Cambridge and New York: Cambridge University Press, 1997), 145–6. Because of Malebranche's use of Acts 17:28, Jolley terms Malebranche's scheme, 'Pauline Cartesianism', xxii.

62 See A. Keith Walker, *William Law: His Life and Thought*, (London: SPCK, 1973), 235–6.

63 Law, *Spirit of Prayer*, 104, 110–43.

64 Lewis F. Hite, *Ultimate Reality* (London: Swedenborg Society, 1936), 34–6.

65 E584.

66 E336–8.

67 E97.

68 E177.

69 *Ibid.*

70 E178.

71 E179.

72 E217.

73 E218–19.

74 E78.

75 E132.

76 Emanuel Swedenborg, *A Treatise Concerning the Last Judgment and the Destruction of Babylon* (London, 1788), para. 25.

77 With reference to Keats's description of 'soul-making' a key phrase must be kept in mind: 'thus does God make individual beings, Souls, Identical Souls of *the sparks of his own essence*' (*The Letters of John Keats*, ed. M. Forman (Oxford: Oxford University Press, 1948), 335–6, emphasis added).

5 FASTING WOMEN: THE SIGNIFICANCE OF GENDER AND
BODIES IN RADICAL RELIGION AND POLITICS, 1650–1813

1 Joan Jacobs Brumberg generally relies on the secularisation thesis (though in a sophisticated way) in her *Fasting Girls: The History of Anorexia Nervosa* (New York: Plume, 1989). For a discussion and critique of Blumberg's assumptions about the changing meanings of fasting women and secularisation, see Michelle Lelwica, *Starving for Salvation: The Spiritual Dimensions of Eating Problems Among American Girls and Women* (Oxford and New York: Oxford University Press, 1999).

2 Veronika E. Grimm, *From Feasting to Fasting. The Evolution of a Sin: Attitudes to Food in Late Antiquity* (London and New York: Routledge, 1996), 3.

3 See Henry Cadbury's Introduction to his edition of *George Fox's 'Book of Miracles'* (Cambridge: Cambridge University Press, 1948).

4 This has been especially well demonstrated by Phyllis Mack in her *Visionary Women: Ecstatic Prophecy in Seventeenth-Century England* (Berkeley and Los Angeles: University of California Press, 1992); see especially chapter 3.

5 Anna Trapnel, *The Cry of a Stone* (London, 1654), 2,3,5 and 7.

6 Henry Jessey, *The Exceeding Riches of Grace Advanced* (London, 1647), 27–30.

7 Trapnel, *Report and Plea: Or, a Narrative of the Journey from London into Cornwal, the Occasion of it, the Lord's Encouragement to it, and Signal Presence with Her in It* (London, 1654), 6–7. In this regard, Trapnel has more in common with the medieval and early modern mystics who survived on the host discussed by Caroline Walker Bynum in *Holy Feast and Holy Fast: The Religious Significance of Food to Medieval Women* (Berkeley and Los Angeles: University of California Press, 1987).

8 Nigel Smith, *Perfection Proclaimed: Language and Literature in English Radical Religion 1640–1660* (Oxford: Clarendon Press, 1989), 50.

9 Martha Taylor died in 1684, according to the Parish Register, but whether she continued fasting beyond the year recorded and discussed by the various pamphlet writers is not known. See John Pendleton, *A History of Derbyshire* (London: Elliott Stock, 1886), 100.

10 Thomas Robins, *The Wonder of the World* (London, 1669), 11.

11 H. A., *Mirabile Pecci: Or the Non-Such Wonder of the Peak in Derbyshire* (London, 1669), 31. While appearing anonymously under the initials H. A., this pamphlet was in fact published by the Presbyterian stationer, Thomas Parkhurst.

12 *Ibid.*, Preface (n.p.).

13 See Bynum, *Holy Feast and Holy Fast*.

14 H. A., *Mirabile Pecci*, 29.

15 Trapnel, *The Cry of a Stone*, 3

16 Trapnel, *Report and Plea*, 19, 21, 22.

17 H. A., *Mirabile Pecci*, 16.

18 John Reynolds, *A Discourse Upon Prodigious Abstinence Occasioned by Twelve Months Fasting of Martha Taylor, The Famous Derbyshire Damsell: Proving that Without any Miracle, the Texture of Human Bodies may be so Altered that Life may*

be Long Continued Without any Supplies of Meat and Drink (London, 1669). John Reynolds was also a Presbyterian minister who had been ejected from his living at the Restoration.

19 Thomas Robins, *News from Darby-shire, or the Wonder of all Wonders* (London, 1668), 3.

20 H. A. *Mirabile Pecci*, Preface to the Reader.

21 For a much fuller discussion of this, see Steven Shapin, *A Social History of Truth. Civility and Science in Seventeenth-Century England* (Chicago: University of Chicago Press, 1994).

22 Henry Jessey, *Exceeding Riches*, Postscript to the Reader.

23 For a more detailed discussion of this aspect of Taylor's case, see Simon Schaffer, 'Piety, Physic and Prodigious Abstinence', in Ole Peter Grell and Andrew Cunningham, eds., *Religio Medici: Medicine and Religion in Seventeenth-Century England* (Aldershot: Scolar Press, 1996), and Brumberg, *Fasting Girls*, 50.

24 Barbara Ritter Dailey, 'The Visitation of Sarah Wight: Holy Carnival and the Revolution of the Saints in Civil War London', *Church History*, 55:4 (1986), 438–55.

25 Trapnel, *Cry of a Stone*, 4.

26 Reynolds, *A Discourse Upon Prodigious Abstinence*, 36.

27 H. A., *Mirabile Pecci*, 25, 29.

28 Trapnel, *Report and Plea*, Preface to the Reader.

29 Barbara Ritter Dailey has argued that Jessey's account of Wight closely reflected the *ars moriendi* tradition. See her 'The Visitation of Sarah Wight'.

30 See Richard Morton, *Phthisologia, or a treatise of consumption* (London, 1694).

31 Brumberg, *Fasting Girls*, 55–6.

32 *Ibid.*, 55.

33 Legh Richmond, *A Statement of Facts, relative to the supposed abstinence of Ann Moore, of Tutbury, Staffordshire* (Burton-on-Trent: J. Croft, 1813), 1.

34 *The Life of Ann Moore: her Wonderful Existence without Food* (Leeds: G. Wilson, c.1810), 5.

35 Richmond, *A Statement of Facts*, 3–4.

36 J. F. C. Harrison, *The Second Coming: Popular Millenarianism 1780–1850* (London: Routledge and Kegan Paul, 1979), 115.

37 Joanna Southcott, *The True Explanations of the Bible, Part VII . . . With an account of Ann Moore* (London: printed by Galabin and Marchant, 1810), 608–9.

38 *Ibid.*, 609.

39 Joanna Southcott, *A Warning to the World* (London: printed by Galabin and Marchant, 1804), 3–4.

40 *Ibid.*, 5–6.

41 Southcott, *True Explanations*, 610, 611, 613.

42 For the place of Southcott in this radical tradition, see especially James K. Hopkins, *A Woman to Deliver Her People: Joanna Southcott and English Millenarianism in an Era of Revolution* (Austin: University of Texas Press, 1982). Thanks to Larry Kreitzer for bringing my attention to this book.

43 See Communication, 12 May 1813. BL Add. MSS. 47, 800. F. 162. However, I have not been able to look at this manuscript as I wrote this chapter when the British Library was moving all its manuscript materials to the new site. I have relied upon J. F. C. Harrison for this information and his interpretation of Southcott's comments on Moore in 1813. See *The Second Coming*, 44.

6 JOHN THELWALL AND THE REVOLUTION OF 1649

1 'History of Europe', *Annual Register*, 36 (1794), 267.
2 The name seems to have not had the intended effect on one son at least, as Algernon Sidney Thelwall (1795–1863) became an Anglican clergyman; see *Dictionary of National Biography* 19.593.
3 Caroline Robbins, ed., *Two English Republican Tracts: Plato Redivivus. Or, A Dialogue Concerning Government (c. 1681) by Henry Neville. An Essay Upon the Constitution of the Roman Government (c. 1698) by Walter Moyle* (Cambridge: Cambridge University Press, 1969), 42. Robbins limits the usefulness of her text by modernising the spelling, omitting most of Thelwall's notes, and making other alterations of Thelwall's edition. When possible I will quote from the more accessible Robbins text.
4 Gregory Claeys, *The Politics of English Jacobinism: Writings of John Thelwall* (University Park: Pennsylvania State University Press, 1995), 107.
5 According to Blair Worden, Thelwall's enthusiasm for Sidney led to some outright misreadings, as when Thelwall makes Sidney a proponent of democratic resistance to social oppression in *The Tribune* (1796), III.333. 'The Commonwealth Kidney of Algernon Sidney', *Journal of British Studies*, 24 (1985), 33.
6 In a rare display of something like a religious statement, in *The Rights of Nature*, Thelwall affirms that 'of all religionists' he most reveres and loves the Quakers. Claeys, *English Jacobinism*, 403. Even this statement makes clear he is not a 'religionist'.
7 F. K. Donnelly, 'Levellerism in Eighteenth and Early Nineteenth Century Britain', *Albion*, 20 (1988), 261–9. Thelwall's reference to Lilburne and the Levellers is in *The Tribune* (1796), III.226.
8 Through Gilbert Burnet Thelwall would have gotten much, very sympathetic information on Algernon Sidney and Lord Russell. *Bishop Burnet's History of His Own Time*, 4 vols. (London: A. Millar, 1753): see II:212–24 for Russell, and II:235–9 for Sidney. Burnet's summary of the pre-1660 period contains no information on the Levellers. However, David Hume's *The History of England. From the Invasion of Julius Caesar to the Revolution in 1688*, 6 vols. (New York: Worthington, 1889), while not nearly as sympathetic to the principals in the Rye House Plot (VI:204–18), has much information on the Levellers (V:241, 280–1, 289–90), Quakers (V:428–31), Lilburne (V:290–318, 348, 366), and the Independents (V:168–9).
9 Three of Thelwall's sonnets were Shakespearian and the other nine were 'irregular'. On the sonnet, see Thelwall's essay, 'An Essay on the English

Sonnet; illustrated by a Comparison between the Sonnets of Milton and
those of Charlotte Smith', *Universal Magazine* (December, 1792), 408–14.
See also Daniel Robinson, 'Reviving the Sonnet', *European Romantic Review*
6, (1995), 98–127.

10 Claeys, *English Jacobinism*, 334.

11 In the first edition, Godwin used mother, sister and chambermaid; in the
later editions, he used father, brother, valet. *Enquiry Concerning Political Justice
and Its Influence on Morals and Happiness*, ed. F. E. L. Priestley, 3 vols. (Toronto:
University of Toronto Press, 1946), I:126–8, for 1798 version, and III:146 for
1793 and 1796 versions.

12 John Thelwall, *Poems Written in Close Confinement in the Tower and Newgate, Under
a Charge of High Treason* (London, 1795), 14.

13 Christopher Hill, *The Century of Revolution, 1603–1714* (New York: W. W.
Norton, 1961), 178–9. The invoking by English radicals of the Norman
yoke during the 1790s confirms the persuasive argument in David
Simpson's *Romanticism, Nationalism and the Revolt Against Theory* (Chicago:
University of Chicago Press, 1993) that English culture, anxious about
(possibly French) 'theory', seeks explicitly nationalist models of intellectual
discourse.

14 Hill, *Century of Revolution*, 93.

15 *Ibid.*, 67. See also Christopher Hill, 'The Norman Yoke', in John Saville, ed.,
Democracy and the Labour Movement (London: Lawrence and Wishart, 1954),
11–66.

16 R. B. Seaberg, 'The Norman Conquest and the Common Law', *Historical
Journal*, 24 (1981), 791–806.

17 James Epstein, *Radical Expression: Political Language, Ritual, and Symbol in
England, 1790–1850* (New York and Oxford: Oxford University Press, 1994),
3–28.

18 J. G. A. Pocock's 'Burke and the Ancient Constitution', describes Burke's
use of the constitutionalist idiom. *Politics, Language and Time: Essays on Political
Thought and History* (New York: Athenaeum, 1971), 202–32.

19 For the radical antiquarianism of Joseph Ritson, with whose work Thelwall
was familiar, see Timothy Morton, *Shelley and the Revolution in Taste: The Body
and the Natural World* (Cambridge and New York: Cambridge University
Press, 1994; reprinted 1998), 152–7.

20 The two works are in *Poems Chiefly Written in Retirement* (Hereford: W. H.
Parker, 1801) rpt. by Garland (1978) and Woodstock Books (1989). Only
the first two books of *The Hope of Albion* were published; Thelwall published
further sections of the poem later in periodicals. See Don M. Wolf, ed.,
Complete Prose Works of John Milton, vol. V, 1648?–1671, Part 1 (New Haven
and London: Yale University Press, 1971), 141 n. 59.

21 Claeys, *English Jacobinism*, 21.

22 *Ibid.*, 214–15.

23 *Ibid.*, 298–314.

24 *Ibid.*, 305.

25 *Ibid.*, 303. Thelwall's view of Cromwell is much more positive in an essay in *The Champion* (9 May 1819). Thelwall also runs in several issues a brief, not entirely unsympathetic history of Cromwell (14 November 1819, 21 November 1819, 5 February 1820).

26 Thelwall's attitude towards Napoleon was mixed but surprisingly favourable for someone who viewed Cromwell so harshly. In a December 1805 letter to Thomas Hardy, he dates his disillusionment with the French Revolution from Napoleon's consulate (E. Rickword, 'Thelwall to Hardy', *TLS* (19 June 1953), 402). According to Henry Crabbe Robinson, however, Thelwall was one of the few people Robinson knew who were disappointed in Napoleon's fall from power after Waterloo (T. Sadler, ed., *Diary, Reminiscences, and Correspondence of Henry Crabbe Robinson*, 3rd edn, 2 vols. (New York and London: Macmillan, 1872), 1:257. In the *Monthly Magazine* of 31 July 1825 Thelwall wrote of Napoleon that he was 'with all his faults, the most munificent patron of arts, intellect and science, of the modern world' (623). For Thelwall's most nuanced response to Napoleon, see the lead article in *The Champion* (7 July 1821).

27 Claeys, *English Jacobinism*, 307–08.

28 *Ibid.*, 309.

29 *Ibid.*

30 Mrs Thelwall (Cecil Boyle), *Life of Thelwall* (London: Macrone, 1837), 47–8.

31 *Ibid.*, 51.

32 John Thelwall, *Political Lectures. No. 1*. (London, 1794), 40.

33 Claeys, *English Jacobinism*, 400.

34 *Monthly Magazine*, 49 (May 1825), 330.

35 See *The Champion* for the following dates: 6 December 1818, 13 December 1818, 27 December 1818, 17 January 1819.

36 For the Spenceans, see Iain McCalman, *Radical Underworld: Prophets, Revolutionaries and Pornographers in London, 1795–1840* (Cambridge: Cambridge University Press, 1988), and David Worrall, *Radical Culture: Discourse, Resistance and Surveillance, 1790–1820* (Detroit: Wayne State University Press, 1992).

37 See *The Champion* for 26 September 1819, 31 October 1819, 7 November 1819, 21 November 1819.

38 To Thelwall's credit, when the Spenceans were in peril after the Cato Street Conspiracy in 1820, Thelwall muted his criticism of the Spenceans and provided very favourable coverage of the trial and execution in *The Champion*.

39 *Considerations on Lord Grenville's and Mr Pitt's Bills*, in Mark Philp, ed., *Political and Philosophical Writings of William Godwin*, 7 vols. (London: William Pickering, 1993), II:130.

40 See the three *Tribune* lectures on the food riots, Claeys, *English Jacobinism*, 138–209.

41 *Enquiry*, 1:270–1.

42 *Ibid.*, III:286.

43 *Ibid.*, IIII:282.

44 John Thelwall, ed., *Democracy Vindicated. An Essay on the Constitution and Government of the Roman State; From the Posthumous Works of Walter Moyle* (Norwich: J. March, 1796), iv. For Thelwall and the tradition of civic humanism, see Claeys, 'Introduction', *English Jacobinism*, xxxv–lvi; Gregory Claeys, 'Republicanism and Commerce in Britain, 1796–1805', *Journal of Modern History*, 66 (1994), 249–90; Iain Hampsher-Monk, 'John Thelwall and the Eighteenth-Century Radical Response to Political Economy', *The Historical Journal*, 34 (1991), 1–20; Iain Hampsher-Monk, 'Civic Humanism and Parliamentary Reform', *Journal of British Studies*, 18 (1979), 70–89; Geoffrey Gallop, 'Ideology and the English Jacobins', *Enlightenment and Dissent*, 5 (1986), 3–20.

45 In a 1965 essay Pocock characterises Thelwall's and Cartwright's appropriation of ancient constitutionalism as 'eccentric' and naively simplistic in part because an anti-historical, Lockean, rights-based radicalism had assumed centre stage. 'Machiavelli, Harrington and English Political Ideologies in the Eighteenth Century', in *Politics, Language and Time*, 145–6. However, recently J. A. Epstein has argued persuasively that the constitutionalist idiom was in the mainstream of radical discourse even through the Chartist period; *Radical Expression*.

46 See H. T. Dickinson, ed., *The Political Works of Thomas Spence* (Newcastle-upon-Tyne: Avero, 1982), vii–xviii, and Malcolm Chase, *'The People's Farm:' English Radical Agrarianism 1775–1840* (Oxford: Clarendon Press, 1988), chs. 1–3.

47 Claeys, *English Jacobinism*, 299.

48 John Thelwall, *An Appeal to Popular Opinion* (Norwich: J. March, 1796), 25. The other texts Thelwall used were Tacitus, Polybius, Plutarch and especially E. Spelman's edition of Dionysius of Halicarnassus, *Roman Antiquities*.

49 British Library catalogue number 12270, 5 (3).

50 Displacing revolutionary precursors is a well-established pattern discussed brilliantly by Karl Marx: 'Cromwell and the English people had borrowed speech, passions and illusions from the Old Testament for their bourgeois revolution. When the real aim had been achieved...Locke supplanted Habakkuk' *(The Eighteenth Brumaire of Louis Bonapart*, trans. C. P. Dutt (New York: International, 1963), 17).

51 Thelwall, *Political Lectures. No.* 2 (London, 1794), 18–19.

52 Thelwall, *Democracy Vindicated*, iii–iv.

53 Robbins, *Republican Tracts*, 247.

54 Thelwall, *Democracy Vindicated*, 14–15 n. 14; also 24 n. 23.

55 Robbins, *Republican Tracts*, 232.

56 Thelwall, *Democracy Vindicated*, 21 n.22.

57 *Ibid.*, 18 n.19, 20 n.20.

58 Robbins, *Republican Tracts*, 230.

59 Thelwall, *Democracy Vindicated*, 18, n.19.

60 *Ibid.*, 20 n.20.

61 *Ibid.*, 36 n.28.

62 Robbins, *Republican Tracts*, 212.

63 In a 1794 essay, he notes that there were far fewer prosecutions for opinion under Cromwell than under Charles II. According to Thelwall, Cromwell the usurper was still far better than the Stuarts largely because of the more lively public sphere under Cromwell. Thelwall repeats the famous 'paper bullets' anecdote concerning Cromwell's lack of concern for Harrington's social criticism. Thelwall, *Political Lectures. No. 2.*, 4–6.

64 Claeys, *English Jacobinism*, 319.

65 *Ibid.*, 361–2.

66 *Ibid.*, 367.

67 *Ibid.*, 116–37.

68 *Ibid.*, 310–11.

7 WOMEN'S PRIVATE READING AND POLITICAL ACTION, 1649–1838

I am grateful to the following people for their generous help in the researching and writing of this chapter: Frances Dolan, Margaret Ferguson, Sarah Peterson Pittock, the editors of this collection and especially Teresa Feroli.

1 Anna Trapnel, *A Legacy for Saints* (London, 1654), first page.

2 Trapnel, *The Cry of the Stone* (London, 1654), 67.

3 As Trapnel says in her *Report and Plea* (London, 1654): 'In all that was said by me, I was nothing, the Lord put all in my mouth, and told me what I should say, and that from the written word, he put in my memory and mouth: so that I will have nothing ascribed to me.'

4 For more on the politics of the Fifth Monarchists, see B. S. Capp, *The Fifth Monarchy Men: A Study in Seventeenth-Century Millenarianism* (London: Faber and Faber, 1972).

5 On the need for more detailed studies of individual reading practices, see Robert Darnton, 'Readers Respond to Rousseau: The Fabrication of Romantic Sensitivity', in Robert Darnton, *The Great Cat Massacre and other Episodes in French Cultural History* (London: Basic Books, 1984), 215–56; and John Brewer, 'Reconstructing the Reader: Prescriptions, Texts and Strategies in Anna Larpent's Reading', in James Raven, Helen Small and Naomi Tadmor, eds., *The Practice and Representation of Reading in England* (Cambridge and New York: Cambridge University Press, 1996), 162–75, 226–46.

6 On definitions of the public sphere, see Jürgen Habermas, *The Structural Transformation of the Public Sphere: An Inquiry into a Category of Bourgeois Society* (Cambridge, MA: MIT Press, 1989). Habermas places its emergence in the early eighteenth century. For claims that a version of the public sphere existed in the later part of the seventeenth century, see David Zaret, 'Religion, Science and Printing in the Public Sphere in Seventeenth-Century England,' in Craig Calhoun, ed., *Habermas and the Public Sphere* (Cambridge, MA: MIT Press, 1992), 212–36; Nigel Smith, *Literature and Revolution in England 1640–1660* (New Haven and London: Yale University Press, 1994), 25–6; Gerald Maclean, 'Literacy, Class and Gender in Restoration England', *Text*, 7

(1995), 307–35; for an argument against this see Lloyd Kramer, 'Habermas, History and Critical Theory', in Calhoun, ed., *Habermas and the Public Sphere*, 236–59. On the relation of print to the public sphere see Habermas, and Michael Warner, *The Letters of the Republic: Publication and the Public Sphere in Eighteenth-Century America* (Cambridge, MA: Harvard University Press, 1990). For women's experience of the transition from an oral to print culture, see Paula McDowell, *The Women of Grub Street.: Press, Politics and Gender in the London Literary Market Place 1678–1730* (Oxford: Clarendon Press, 1998). On women's limited access to the public sphere, see Joan Landes, 'The Public and the Private Sphere: A Feminist Reconsideration', in Johanna Meehan, ed., *Feminists Read Habermas: Gendering the Subject of Discourse* (London: Routledge, 1995), 91–117; and Nancy Fraser, 'Rethinking the Public Sphere: A Contribution to the Critique of Actually Existing Democracy', in Calhoun, ed., *Habermas and the Public Sphere*, 109–143.

For descriptions of the emergence of the private or domestic sphere, see Alice Clark, *The Working Life of Women in the Seventeenth Century* (London: G. Routledge and Sons, 1919); Nancy Armstrong, *Desire and Domestic Fiction: A Political History of the Novel* (New York and Oxford: Oxford University Press, 1987); Lenore Davidoff and Catherine Hall, *Family Fortunes: Men and Women of the English Middle Class, 1780–1850* (Chicago: University of Chicago Press, 1987). The rigidity of this division in practice has been questioned by Amanda Vickery, in 'Golden Age to Separate Spheres?', *Historical Journal*, 36 (1993), 383–414; and Lawrence Klein, in 'Gender, Conversation and the Public Sphere in Early Eighteenth-Century England', in Judith Still and Michael Worton, eds., *Textuality and Sexuality: Reading Theories and Practices* (New York: St Martin's Press, 1993), 100–16, and 'Gender and the Public/ Private Distinction in the Eighteenth Century', *Eighteenth-Century Studies*, 29.1 (Fall 1995), 97–111. Habermas defines the 'private' sphere as the sphere of the market, and calls the family the 'intimate sphere'. He reminds us, however, of the 'ambivalence' of the family, both 'an agent of society [and] . . . simultaneously . . . the anticipated emancipation from society' (55).

On the reading practices associated with private life see J. Paul Hunter, *Before Novels: The Cultural Contexts of Eighteenth–Century English Fiction* (New York: Norton, 1990).

7 Ivan Illich, *In the Vineyard of the Text: A Commentary to Hugh's Didacsalion* (Chicago: University of Chicago Press, 1993), 54.

8 John Dryden, *Religio Laici* (1682), lines 400–1. See also Christopher Hill, *The English Bible and the Seventeenth-Century Revolution* (London: Allen Lane, 1993); and Nigel Smith, *Perfection Proclaimed: Language and Literature in English Radical Religion 1640–1660* (Oxford: Clarendon Press, 1989).

9 Peter Stallybrass and Allon White, *The Politics and Poetics of Transgression* (Ithaca: Cornell University Press, 1986), 97. On the practice of reading in coffee houses see John Brewer, *The Pleasures of the Imagination: English Culture*

in the Eighteenth Century (New York: Farrar Strauss Giroux, 1997), especially 183–4.

10 Illich, *Vineyard*, 54.

11 Dorinda Outram, *The Body and the French Revolution: Sex, Class, and Political Culture* (New Haven and London: Yale University Press, 1989), 158. Quoted in Landes, 'The Public and the Private Sphere', 103.

12 Ian Watt, *The Rise of the Novel: Studies in Defoe, Richardson and Fielding* (Berkeley: University of California Press, 1957), 206. Along very similar lines, Habermas argues that:

> On the one hand, the empathetic reader repeated within himself the private relationships displayed before him in literature; from his experience of real familiarity... he gave life to the fictional one, and in the latter, he prepared himself for the former. On the other hand, from the outset the familiarity whose vehicle was the written word, the subjectivity that had become fit to print, had in fact become the literature appealing to a wide public of readers. (*The Structural Transformation of the Public Sphere*, 50–1)

13 Benedict Anderson, *Imagined Communities: Reflections on the Origins and Spread of Nationalism* (London: Verso, 1991), 35. Anderson himself, of course, sees novels as having quite a similar role in nation-building.

14 Diane Willen, 'Women and Religion in Early Modern England', in Sherrin Marshall, ed., *Women in Reformation and Counter-Reformation Europe: Public and Private Worlds* (Bloomington: Indiana University Press, 1989), 140–66 (146, 144). See also McDowell, *The Women of Grub Street*, 123. See, for example, discussions of Katherine Chidley by Sylvia Brown, 'Godly Household Management from Perkins to Milton: The Rhetoric and Politics of Oeconomia, 1600–1645', PhD thesis, Princeton University, 1994; and Katharine Gillespie, "A Hammer in Her Hand: the Separation of Church from State and the Early Feminist Writing of Katherine Chidley," *Tulsa Studies in Women's Literature*, 17.2 (1998), 213–33.

15 See Miranda Chaytor, 'Household and Kinship', *History Workshop*, 10 (1980), 25–61.

16 Samuel Torshell, *The Womans Glorie* (London: Printed by G. N. for John Bellamie, 1645), 124–5.

17 See Kate Flint, *The Woman Reader 1837–1914* (Oxford: Clarendon Press, 1993). Also Naomi Tadmor, '"In the even my wife read to me"', in *The Practice and Representation of Reading in England* (Cambridge and New York: Cambridge University Press, 1996), 162–75.

18 *Ladies' Magazine*, 43 (1812), 22; quoted in Ina Ferris, *The Achievement of Literary Authority: Gender, History, and the Waverly Novels* (Ithaca: Cornell University Press, 1991), 39. The idea was not strictly applied to women: in 1726 the theologian William Law declared: 'Reading and Meditation is that to our souls, which food and nourishment is to our bodies, and become part of us in the same manner, so that we cannot do ourselves either a little good or a little harm by the books we read' (*A Serious Call to a Devout and Holy Life*,

ed. Paul G. Stanwood (New York, Ramsey, Toronto: The Paulist Press, 1978), 262).

19 John Brewer, 'This, That and the Other', in Dario Castiglione and Lesley Sharpe, eds., *Shifting the Boundaries* (Exeter: Exeter University Press, 1995), 1–21 (7).

20 See Smith, *Perfection Proclaimed*, 33–6.

21 See Tadmor, ' "In the even my wife read to me" '.

22 Willen, 'Women and Religion in Early Modern England', 144.

23 Mary Pope, 'A Treatise of Magistery' (1647). Quoted in Phyllis Mack, *Visionary Women: Ecstatic Prophecy in Seventeenth-Century England* (Berkeley and Los Angeles, University of California Press, 1992), 90.

24 Sarah Wight, 'A Wonderful Pleasant . . . Letter', (London: 1656), 5. Quoted in Elaine Hobby, *Virtue of Necessity: English Women's Writings 1649–88* (London: Virago, 1988), 67.

25 Trapnel, *The Cry of the Stone*, 40.

26 This may be because Trapnel's actions both participated in an established tradition of feminine religious fasting, and to some extent brought those traditions into a more rationalised relation to the state. See Teresa Feroli, 'Toward a Feminine Theory of the State', unpublished manuscript. On Trapnel's fasting, see also Diane Purkiss, 'Producing the Voice, Consuming the Body: Women Prophets of the Seventeenth Century', in Isobel Grundy and Susan Wiseman, eds., *Women, Writing, History 1640–1740* (Athens, GA: University of Georgia Press, 1992), 139–59. Later in 1654, however, Trapnel was arrested for criticising the government in Cornwall, and imprisoned briefly in London's Bridewell.

27 Barry Reay, *The Quakers and the English Revolution* (New York: St Martins Press, 1985), 26.

28 Rosemary Kegl, 'Women's Preaching, Absolute Property, and the *Cruel Sufferings (for the Truths sake) of Katherine Evans & Sarah Cheevers*', *Women's Studies*, 24 (1994), 51–83, 58.

29 Mack, *Visionary Women*, 167. See also Leo Damrosch, *The Sorrows of the Quaker Jesus: James Nayler and the Puritan Crackdown on the Free Spirit* (Cambridge, MA: Harvard University Press, 1996), 163–5.

30 Nigel Smith, 'Hidden Things Brought to Light', *Prose Studies*, 17.3 (December 1994), 57–69: 57.

31 Mack, *Visionary Women*, 184.

32 Phyllis Mack speculates that this was due to the fact that his works seemed particularly in keeping with feminised understandings of the Word (*ibid.*, 200).

33 Damrosch, *Sorrows*, 168.

34 Patricia Crawford, *Women and Religion in England 1500–1700* (London: Routledge, 1993). For a summary of these views see Christine Trevett, 'The Women Around James Nayler: A Matter of Emphasis', *Religion*, 20.3 (July 1990), 258. Indeed, at the time, some Friends thought Nayler had been bewitched by Martha Simmonds.

35 Mack, *Visionary Women*, 205.
36 See Trevett, 'The Women Around James Nayler', 264.
37 See, for example, Hobby, *Virtue of Necessity*, 48, 53.
38 William C. Braithwaite, *The Second Period of Quakerism* (Cambridge: Cambridge University Press, 1961), 227. He discusses some post-1660 signs, 25.
39 McDowell, *The Women of Grub Street*, 287.
40 N. H. Keeble, *The Literary Culture of Nonconformity in Later Seventeenth–Century England* (Leicester: Leicester University Press and Athens, GA: University of Georgia Press, 1987), 83. McDowell reminds us, however, that the transition between oral and print culture during the late seventeenth and early eighteenth centuries was uneven and inconclusive and that 'the religio-political culture of ordinary women was still primarily an oral culture' (*The Women of Grub Street*, 130).
41 Rebecca Travers, *This is for all or any of those . . . that resist the spirit and despise the Grace that brings salvation . . .* (London, 1664), 1.
42 McDowell, *The Women of Grub Street*, 151. See also 145–56.
43 *The Poetry of Elizabeth Singer Rowe (1674–1737)*, ed. Madeleine Forell Marshall (Lewiston, NY: Edwin Mellen Press, 1987), 157.
44 Elizabeth Carter, 'On the Death of Mrs [Elizabeth] Rowe'. Carter here seems to echo William Law's ideas about female piety in *A Serious Call* (1726); women, he argued, possess 'a *finer sense*, a readier apprehension, *and* gentler dispositions' which 'if they were truly improved by proper studies, and sober methods of educations, would in all probability carry them to greater heights of piety that are to be found amongst the generality of men' (262).
45 Brewer, 'This, That and the Other', 9.
46 Hester Chapone, *Letters on the Improvement of the Mind* (1773), in Janet Todd, ed., *Female Education in the Age of Enlightenment*, 2 vols. (London: Pickering and Chatto, 1996), II:192.
47 'Objections against the New Testament, with Mrs Carter's Answers to Them', in *Memoirs of the Life of Mrs Elizabeth Carter*, ed. the Rev. Montagu Pennington, 2 vols. (London: J. C. and J. Rivington, 1808), II.392.
48 Quoted in Christine L. Krueger, *The Reader's Repentance: Women Preachers, Women Writers and Nineteenth-Century Social Discourse* (Chicago: University of Chicago Press, 1992), 27.
49 Chapone, *Letters*, 205.
50 Quoted in T. C. Duncan Eaves and Ben D. Kimpel, *Samuel Richardson, A Biography* (Oxford: Clarendon Press, 1971), 224.
51 Chapone, *Letters*, 47.
52 Quoted in Krueger, *Repentance*, 64.
53 *Ibid.*, 59. The connection to earlier religious women is my own.
54 Klein, 'Gender and the Public/Private Distinction', 102.
55 Kenneth Corfield, 'Elizabeth Heyrick', in Gail Malmgreen, ed., *Religion in the Lives of English Women, 1760–1930* (Bloomington: Indiana University Press, 1986), 41–68, 41.

56 Louis Billington and Rosamund Billington, ' "A Burning Zeal for Righteousness" Women and the British Anti-Slavery Movement, 1820–1860', in Jane Rendall, ed., *Equal or Different: Women's Politics 1800–1914* (Oxford: Basil Blackwell, 1987), 82–112, 82. See also F. K. Prochaska, *Women and Philanthropy in Nineteenth-Century England* (Oxford: Oxford University Press, 1980), 427; and Clare Midgley, *Women Against Slavery : the British Campaigns, 1780–1870* (London and New York: Routledge, 1992), 202.

57 Billington and Billington, ' "A Burning Zeal for Righteousness" ', 83.

58 Quoted in Corfield, 'Elizabeth Heyrick', 49.

59 Vickery, 'Golden Age to Separate Spheres?', 400.

60 *Ibid.*, 401.

61 'A Dialogue between a Well-Wisher and a Friend to the Slaves in the British Colonies, by a Lady' (London: Bagster and Thomas, c.1828), 7.

62 Dublin Ladies' Anti-Slavery Society, *Rules and Resolutions* (Dublin: R. Napper, 1828).

63 *Appeal to the Christian Women of Sheffield* (Sheffield: R. Leader, 1837), 13.

64 Phyllis Mack notes a parallel change in women's relation to the public sphere, though she ascribes it to an increasing interest in sexual difference, rather than changing definitions of privacy (*Visionary Women*, 412).

8 THE STRANGE CAREER OF RICHARD 'CITIZEN' LEE: POETRY, POPULAR RADICALISM AND ENTHUSIASM IN THE 1790S

1 See TS (Treasury Solicitor's Papers, Public Record Office, London) 11/854/2910. Another transcription of the same dialogue can be found at TS11/837/2832.

2 See, for instance, Thompson's *Witness Against the Beast: William Blake and the Moral Law* (Cambridge and New York: Cambridge University Press, 1993), 193. Thompson is contrasting the 'conjunction between the old antinomian tradition and Jacobinism' in Blake's poetry with the 'average supporter of the London Corresponding Society'. While I am not suggesting that the peculiarities of the conjunctions to be found in Blake's poetry are in any way typical of the radical movement, I do want to suggest that the 'old antinomian' traditions were to be found in other guises, among those more closely involved with the LCS than Blake ever seems to have been.

3 E. P. Thompson, *The Making of the English Working Class* (Harmondsworth: Penguin, revised edn, 1968), 155. See also the comments on Lee in Gwyn A. Williams, *Artisans and Sans Culottes: Popular Movements in France and Britain During the French Revolution* (New York: Norton, 1969), 73, 96, 98, and 103. More detail is provided on Lee in a note on bibliography by Edmund and Ruth Frow, 'Charles Pigott and Richard Lee', *Bulletin of the Society for Studies in Labour History*, 42 (1981), 32–5, and Jane Douglas's brief biographical sketch 'Citizen Lee and the Tree of Liberty', *Factotum*, 7 (1979), 8–12, although I disagree with some of the factual details of their accounts and they have

little or nothing to say about his religious beliefs. For Hatfield's comments, see his *The Poets of the Church* (New York: Randolph, 1884), 385. The two sides of Lee's career were succinctly noted in J. Watkins and F. Shoberl, *A Biographical Dictionary of Living Authors* (London: Henry Colburn, 1816), 200, which refers to him as 'a political and religious fanatic'.

4 John Walsh, ' "Methodism" and the Origins of English Speaking Evangelicalism', in Mark A. Noll, David W. Bebbington and George Rawlyk, eds., *Evangelicalism: Comparative Studies of Popular Protestantism in North America, the British Isles, and Beyond* (New York and Oxford: Oxford University Press, 1994), 31.

5 'Preface', *Evangelical Magazine*, 1 (1793), 2.

6 Under the influence of ideas of original genius, the image of the peasant poet was a pervasive part of literary culture and the standard means of representing acceptable working-class literature. Poets such as Robert Burns and John Clare were encouraged by patrons keen to unearth authentic native genius, a process which may have had its origins in a nostalgia for a vanishing rural culture exploited by such educated poets as Wordsworth. The role of patrons in this process was less often by direct financial assistance than by gathering subscriptions or puffing the book in the right circles. In 1831 Robert Southey was instrumental in the publication of *Attempts in Verse, by John Jones, an Old Servant* (London: John Murray, 1831), prefacing the volume with an essay on the 'Lives and Works of our Uneducated Poets', accompanied by selections from their verse. Southey wondered if Jones might not be 'the last versifyer of his class' due to the 'quick step in the March of Intellect', 12. The self-taught writers who sent their products to literary men such as Southey and inundated the periodicals and newspapers often took the idea of the republic of letters at face value. Indeed, some of them followed Burns, who somewhat disingenuously contrasted prostituted learning with his own honest rusticity, but many more modestly disclaimed their own poetic sophistication. For a more detailed discussion of the phenomenon of the peasant poet, see Annette Wheeler Cafarelli, 'The Romantic "Peasant" Poets and their Patrons', *The Wordsworth Circle*, 26 (1995), 77–87.

7 Richard Lee, *Flowers from Sharon; or Original Poems on Divine Subjects* (London, 1794), Advertisement [iii], and James Wheeler, *The Rose of Sharon: A Poem* (London, 1790), n. p.

8 *Evangelical Magazine*, 2 (February 1794), 82–3. The following poems from *Flowers from Sharon* had appeared in the magazine under the pseudonym 'Ebenezer': 'On the Heavenly Jerusalem', *Evangelical Magazine*, 1 (August 1793), 88; 'On the Ascension of Christ', 1 (September, 1793), 132; 'The Afflicted Soul's Refuge', 1 (November 1793), 220; and 'The Christian's Attachment to the House of God', 2 (January 1794), 44. No poems appear under the names 'Ebenezer' or Lee after January 1794.

9 For a discussion of this concern, see Cafarelli, 'The Romantic "Peasant" Poets,' especially 79–80.

10 R. Lee, 'Eternal Love', *Flowers from Sharon*, 1 and 14, David Bogue and James Bennett, *History of Dissenters, from the Revolution in 1688, to the year 1808*, 4 vols. (London: printed for the authors, 1808–12), IV: 392.

11 W. H. Reid, *The Rise and Dissolution of the Infidel Societies in this Metropolis: Including, the Origin of Modern Deism and Atheism; the Genius and Conduct of those Associations; their Lecture-Rooms, Field-Meetings, and Deputations; from the Publication of Paine's Age of Reason till the Present Period* (London: n.p., 1800), 6. For an account of the vicissitudes of Reid's career and opinions on religion and politics, see Iain McCalman, 'The Infidel as Prophet', in Steve Clark and David Worrall, eds. *Historicizing Blake* (Basingstoke: Macmillan, 1994), 24–42. Leigh Hunt, *An Attempt to Shew the Folly and Danger of Methodism. In a Series of Essays First Published in the ... Examiner, and now Enlarged with a Preface and ... Notes. By the Editor of The Examiner* (London: John Hunt, 1809), xiii. Hunt explicitly condemns the *Evangelical Magazine*, 46. I am grateful to Nicholas Roe for confirming that Hunt was the author of these essays.

12 See 'On the *Commencement of a* FRIDAY EVENING LECTURE, *at the* ADELPHI CHAPEL, *by the Rev.* Mr Groves', *Flowers from Sharon*, 85–7. John Feltham, *The Picture of London for 1802* (London: Richard Phillips, 1802), 233. I am grateful to Mr John Creasey, Librarian of Dr Williams's Library, for the biographical information on Thomas Groves. Groves's *The Substance of a Sermon Preached August 26th, 1787, at the Chapel in Tottenham-court-Road and the Tabernacle near Moorfields, on the Death of the Rev. Henry Peckwell, D. D.*, second edn (London, 1787), 11, stresses the importance of preaching 'a *free* and *full* salvation'. Grove's engraved portrait accompanies *Evangelical Magazine*, 3 (August 1795). Obviously his zeal for a full and free salvation did not put him beyond the pale of the Calvinism espoused there and it is possible that he was the sponsor and even reviewer of Lee's poetry in the magazine.

13 For a full discussion of Jordan and Terry, the republication of How and Saltmarsh, and the dissent in Huntington's congregation, see Jon Mee, 'Is there an Antinomian in the House?' in Clark and Worrall, eds., *Historicizing Blake*, 43–58.

14 For Powell's letters, see PC (Privy Council Papers) 1 23/38A. Perchard and Brock are listed as merchants with premises in Chatham Place, Blackfriars, in *The General London Guide* (London, 1794), 3. The *Evangelical Magazine*'s description of Lee as a 'laborious mechanic' suggests something of the haziness of class relations in the period. To a gentleman preacher perhaps a clerk and a mechanic were much the same thing.

15 A letter introducing the 2nd volume of *Pig's Meat*, 3rd edn, 2 vols, n. d. (1795), 3, claims that the previous volume was completed 17th May 1794. Lee's poems all appear in the 2nd volume, as follows: 'The Triumph of Liberty' (II:176–7); 'The Rights of God' (II:204); and 'Sonnet to Freedom' (II:284). See also *On the Death of Mrs Hardy, Wife of Thomas Hardy, of Piccadilly; Imprisoned in the Tower for High Treason* (London, n.d. (1794)), 4, and Thomas Hardy, *Memoir of Thomas Hardy* (1832), in *Testaments of Radicalism: Memoirs of*

Working Class Politicians 1790–1885, ed. with an introduction by David Vincent (London: Europa Publications, 1977), 61.

16 He set up shop first at 2 St Ann's Court, Dean-street, Soho, then 47 Haymarket, then from 1 July at 98 Berwick St., Soho before finally arriving at 444 the Strand. The description of the harassment Lee suffered from his political opponents comes from a handbill, issued from 47 Haymarket and dated 21 March 1795, extant in the archives Library Company of Philadelphia (8362.F). I am extremely grateful to the Company's Chief of Reference, Phil Lapsansky, for supplying me with a photocopy. On the handbill, Lee threatens his opponents with 'the fraternal Salute of a Republican Blunderbuss'. In Parliament, over a year later, Charles Sturt, the Whig MP, claimed that even Lee's mother had been harassed by John Reeves and the Association for the Protection of Liberty and Property against Republicans and Levellers. See *The Senator*, 13 (1796), 368.

17 Richard Lee, *Songs from the Rock*, (London, n. d. (1795?)), note. See note 15 above for the poems which appeared in *Pig's Meat*. Examples of Lee's poetry appearing in pamphlets published (but perhaps not written) by him include 'Let us Hope to see Better Days' from *Songs from the Rock*, 9–10, which appears in the pamphlet *The Wrongs of Man*, 4–5 and the ironically titled *The Blessings of War* (London: n. d. (1795?)), 8, which ends with the final stanza of 'The Horrors of War' from *Songs from the Rock*, 36–40. *The Death of Despotism* is a cheap, four-page pamphlet which gives no publication details. It contains three poems, all from *Songs from the Rock*: 'The Triumph of Liberty' retitled 'The Death of Despotism and the Doom of Tyrants', 'The Rights of God', and 'The Baubles of Courts' retitled 'The Crown a Bauble'.

18 See *Songs from the Rock*, 11–12, 32–5, 13–15, and 69–75.

19 'A Republican', *The Happy Reign of George the Last* (London: n. d. (1795?)), 3. For details of the ways in which Spence exploited a variety of media to get his message across, see Marcus Wood, *Radical Satire and Print Culture 1790–1822* (Oxford and New York: Oxford University Press, 1994), 57–95.

20 See 'On Tyrannicide' in *The Cabinet* (1795), 1:67–80. The paragraphs culled by Lee are from 69–71. The information about the title was passed on to Parliament by Charles Sturt; see Anon., *The History of Two Acts Entitled An Act for the Safety and Preservation of his Majesty's Person and Government against Treasonable and Seditious Practices and Attempts, and An Act for the More Effectively Preventing Seditious Meetings and Assemblies* (London, 1796), 369.

21 See *The History of Two Acts*, 275.

22 See *ibid.*, 369.

23 Reid, *The Rise and Dissolution of the Infidel Societies*, 6. The title page of the British Library's copy of *The Rights of Princes* (London: n. d. (1795?)) at 1389 d. 27 says 'Sturt told the house that Lee had been twice turned out of the London Corresponding Society: Ballard (another bookseller involved in the radical movement) alledges [sic] that it was for disagree[ing] with some of the members in religious sentiments. Lee is a Methodist.' For the LCS's disclaimer of any association with Lee, see *The History of Two Acts*, 330. As

Jane Douglas, 'Citizen Lee', 10, has pointed out, and Lord Mornington gleefully noted, this disclaimer was rather undermined by the fact that Lee's name appears on a list of people's names put out by the LCS on 19 November receiving signatures for a petition to Parliament.

24 See *The History of the Two Acts*, 330.

25 *The True Briton*, 1 December 1795, *The Times*, 19 December 1795, and for Powell's story, see PC 1 23/38A. For the indictment against Lee, naming the three pamphlets, see TS11/854/2910.

26 See Michael Durey, *Transatlantic Radicals and the Early American Republic* (Lawrence: University Press of Kansas: 1997), 187.

27 Quoted in *ibid.*, 682.

28 Details of Lee's contacts in the radical movement in exile can be found in R. J. Twomey, *Jacobins and Jeffersonians: Anglo-American Radicalism in the United States 1790–1820* (New York and London: Garland, 1989), 27, 67, 69, 96–7, 102–3. For Cobbett's abuse of Lee, see *Remarks on the Explanation Lately Published by Dr Priestley*, in *Porcupine's Works*, 12 vols. (London: Cobbett and Morgan, 1801), IX:258. I am extremely grateful to John Stevenson for lending me this volume. Cobbett also provides some corroboration for the story of Lee's escape from Newgate when he later mentions 'citizen Lee, who, like a true sans-culote, slipped out of Newgate in petticoats', *ibid.*, 270. A spy report to the Home Office suggests that Lee may have even survived until 1814. Someone by that name was among a group of former LCS members contacted by the Spencean ambassadors Arthur Thistlewood and Thomas Evans Jr in that year. Given Lee's contact with Spence in 1794–5, the idea of his collaborating with the Speanceans of the early nineteenth century seems plausible enough. See Iain McCalman, *Radical Underworld. Prophets, Revolutionaries and Pornographers in London, 1795–1840* (Cambridge: Cambridge University Press, 1988), 23.

29 Jane Austen, *Persuasion*, ed. John Davie, with an Introduction by Claude Rawson, (Oxford and New York: Oxford University Press, 1990), 24.

30 The term 'author function' is taken from Michel Foucault's influential essay 'What is an Author?', in *The Foucault Reader: An Introduction to Foucault's Thought*, ed. Paul Rabinow (Harmondsworth: Penguin Books, 1991). Foucault is interested in the way that the identity of the author came to be used to regulate discourse in the seventeenth and eighteenth centuries. In the 1790s it was, of course, invaluable as a means by which the government might identify and prosecute sedition.

31 Mark Philp, 'The Fragmentary Ideology of Reform', in Philp, Mark, ed., *The French Revolution and British Popular Politics* (Cambridge and New York: Cambridge University Press, 1991), 50–77 (73).

32 See the handbill, still extant in the British Library, advertising the volume *Proposals for Publishing by Subscription, Sacred to Truth, Liberty, and Peace, Songs from the Rock, to Hail the Approaching Day . . . by Richard Lee* (London, nd (1795?)). All the editions of the collection in the British Library at Rb.23.a.10133 contain the following preamble: 'The Author is induced to forego his Design of printing the Subscriber's Names; so considerable a Number of them,

having (for obvious Reasons) declined thus publishing their Sentiments', end page, recto. On the verso, he lists a number of clergymen who recommend *Flowers from Sharon*. I am grateful to Kevin Knox for taking time to check this for me.

33 Lee's role in the movement in this period is recognised in the hostile burlesque Anon., *The Decline and Fall, Death, Dissection, and Funeral Procession of His Most Contemptible Lowness the London Corresponding Society* (London, 1796), where he appears 'with the Tree of Liberty tied to his back, wheeling a barrow full of seditious pamphlets', 20–1.

34 I take the term 'self-fashioning' from Stephen Greenblatt's *Renaissance Self-Fashioning: From More to Shakespeare* (Chicago: University of Chicago Press, 1980). Although unlike Greenblatt in the Renaissance context, I am not implying that the term continues to involve the idea of a submission to absolute authority or some threatening alterity, I do believe it catches something of the way radicals strove to create identities for themselves in terms of the opportunities available in contemporary print culture and in the face of political repression and cultural assumptions rather than simply expressing some pre-existing popular identity.

35 Durey, *Transatlantic Radicals*, 176.

36 For a discussion and critique of J. G. A. Pocock's work in the context of the 1790s, see Mark Philp's 'English Republicanism in the 1790s', *Journal of Political Philosophy*, 6 (1998), 235–62. For Thompson, see notes 2 and 3 above.

37 See Philp's 'The Fragmentary Ideology of Reform'.

38 Edmund Burke, *Reflections on the Revolution in France*, in *The Writing and Speeches of Edmund Burke*, general ed. Paul Langford, 9 vols, vol. VIII, *The French Revolution, 1790–94*, ed. L. G. Mitchell, (Oxford: Clarendon Press, 1989), VIII:146.

39 See the additional title page in copy RB 23.a.10133 in the British Library on the verso of which this dedication appears. On this additional page the volume is called *Songs for the Year 1795, Sacred to Truth, Liberty, and Peace, Inscribed to the Sovereign People*, the title by which it is often advertised in Lee's political pamphlets.

40 For a discussion of this process, see Jerome J. McGann, *The Poetics of Sensibility: A Revolution in Literary Style* (Oxford: Clarendon Press, 1996), especially chapter 9, 'The Literal World of the English Della Cruscans'.

41 See *The Gospel of Reason* (London, 1795), 1–2. Lee reissued *The Gospel of Reason* as one of the *Political Curiosities* in Philadelphia (1796). The extract also appeared as an 'IMPORTANT AND CURIOUS EXTRACT FROM ROUSSEAU' in the *American Universal Magazine*, 2 (13 June 1797), 348–50. On the reception of Rousseau, see *Critical Review*, 15 (1763), 31 and Edward Duffy, *Rousseau in England: The Context for Shelley's Critique of the Enlightenment* (Berkeley: University of California Press, 1979).

42 See 'The Rights of God' in *Songs from the Rock*, 17–18. The *Monthly Review's* phrase is taken from a review (16 (1795), 208) of Daniel Isaac Eaton's 1794 reissue of John Cook[e]'s Civil War pamphlet *Monarchy No Creature of God's*

Making (London, 1651). The *Monthly* comments: 'we see no end likely to be answered by this re-publication; except it be to show that fanaticism is a useful instrument, which may be employed, at pleasure, in the service of either monarchy or democracy'. The *Monthly*, by no means a conservative organ in the 1790s, nicely illustrates the fear of popular enthusiasm across the political spectrum.

43 See Reid, *The Rise and Dissolution*, 89, William Godwin, *An Enquiry Concerning Political Justice* (1793), in *Political and Philosophical Writing of William Godwin*, general ed. Mark Philp, 7 vols. (London: Pickering and Chatto, 1993), III:118, and for Thelwall, see the discussion in my 'Anxieties of Enthusiasm', *Huntington Library Quarterly*, 60 (1998), 6–7 and 19–21.

44 See McCalman, *Radical Underworld*, 66, and Malcolm Chase, '*The People's Farm': English Radical Agrarianism 1775–1840* (Oxford: Clarendon Press, 1988), 48.

45 See Anthony J. La Vopa, 'Conceiving a Public: Ideas and Society in Eighteenth-Century Europe,' *Journal of Modern History*, 64 (March 1992), 95. See also my discussion of this issue in relation to Lee and William Blake in '"The Doom of Tyrants"', in Jackie DiSalvo, G. A. Rosso and Christopher Z. Hobson, eds., *Blake, Politics, and History* (New York and London: Garland Publishing, 1998), 97–114.

46 It was a connection which Chief Justice Eyre did not scruple to make in his summing up at the trial of Thomas Hardy for High Treason:

> His conduct in all these transactions marks strongly, that he is tinctured deeply with enthusiasm: and I recollect the Counsel in reply mentioned the famous case in which enthusiasm was worked up to its utmost height, in the fifth-monarchy-men, who might be perfectly good moral and religious characters, and it would be upon their religion that the act of high treason would be fixed, to give countenance to the charge. So if a man is an enthusiast, his being a moral and religious man is at least a neutral circumstance, because a moral, religious man, if he chooses to let his enthusiasm carry him beyond his judgement, is exposed to be drawn into the circumstances in which the prisoner now stands.

See Anon., *The Genuine Trial of Thomas Hardy for High Treason*, 2 vols. (London, 1795), II.589. Lee himself was in no doubt that Hardy was a specifically 'CHRISTIAN HERO', as he explained in his note to the 'Tribute of Civic Gratitude,' Songs from the Rock, 107–12:

> Let the Infidel candidly investigate (if Infidelity can possibly be candid) let him candidly investigate this illustrious Character, and then lift his audacious Front to the Heavens and tell the ALMIGHTY, that pure Christianity is inimical to the Cause of Freedom – Rather let him yield to the Power of Conviction, and own with Admiration the *Rationality* of that sublime System which, while it gives GLORY TO GOD, inculcates PEACE ON EARTH, and GOOD-WILL TOWARDS MEN (111).

No doubt the Lord Chief Justice would have felt these words vindicated his summing up. They also indicate that Lee's poem was directed as much at infidels within the radical movement as the established order that the LCS was trying to overthrow.

9 WILLIAM COBBETT, JOHN CLARE AND THE AGRARIAN POLITICS OF THE ENGLISH REVOLUTION

1 John Clare, *John Clare's Autobiographical Writings*, ed. E. Robinson (Oxford and New York: Oxford University Press, 1986), 48. Clare also records the discovery of 'a coin of [Oliver] Cromwells... pickd up in the neighbouring field as large as a crown piece which I gave to my friend Artis' (57). Clare's friend, Edmund Tyrell Artis, was an eminent archaeologist; for further information on Artis see John Clare, *The Natural History Prose Writings of John Clare*, ed. M. Grainger (Oxford: Clarendon Press, 1983), xxxviii.

2 Cobbett used the pseudonym Peter Porcupine for some forty anti-French and anti-Democratic pamphlets published in Philadelphia between 1794 and 1800. Most of these pamphlets were reprinted as *Porcupine's Works*. For further discussion of Cobbett's American sojourn, see David A. Wilson, *Paine and Cobbett: The Transatlantic Connection* (Kingston and Montreal: McGill-Queen's University Press, 1988), 112–45.

3 *Cobbett's Political Register* (London: Cox and Baylis, 1802–35) (15 March 1806), 361–2.

4 William Cobbett, *Rural Rides*, ed. A. Briggs, 2 vols. (London: J. M. Dent and Sons, 1957), I:178.

5 *Ibid.*, I:269.

6 Mikhail Bakhtin develops the concept of 'theoretism' in his essay 'Toward a Philosophy of the Act', composed circa 1924 and first published (in Russian) by the Soviet Academy of Sciences in 1986. For further discussion of 'theoretism' see G. Morson and C. Emerson, *Rethinking Bakhtin: Extensions and Challenges* (Evanston, IL: Northwestern University Press, 1989), 7–10 and 262n.

7 Raymond Williams, *Cobbett* (Oxford and New York: Oxford University Press, 1983), 79.

8 William Cobbett, *A History of the Protestant 'Reformation', in England and Ireland; Showing How That Event Has Impoverished and Degraded the Main Body of the People in Those Countries*, 2 vols. (London: Clement, 1824–6), I: Introduction, para. 6.

9 *Ibid.*, II: para. 363.

10 *Ibid.*, I:243.

11 *Ibid.*, I:243.

12 John Clare, *The Letters of John Clare*, ed. M. Storey (Oxford: Clarendon Press, 1985), 560. For further analysis of Clare's response to Cobbett, see L. Nattrass, 'John Clare and William Cobbett: the Personal and the Political', in J. Goodridge, ed., *The Independent Spirit: John Clare and the Self-Taught Tradition* (Helpston: John Clare Society, 1994), 44–54.

13 Clare's response to enclosure is more fully discussed by John Barrell, *The Idea of Landscape and the Sense of Place 1730–1840: An Approach to the Poetry of John Clare* (Cambridge: Cambridge University Press, 1972), 98–120, and Johanne Clare, *John Clare and the Bounds of Circumstance* (Kingston and Montreal: McGill-Queen's University Press, 1987), 36–55. See also R. Waller, 'Enclosures', *Mother Earth, Journal of the Soil Association*, 13 (1964), 231–7.

14 John Clare, 'The Village Minstrel', *The Early Poems of John Clare 1804–1822*, ed. E. Robinson and D. Powell, 2 vols. (Oxford: Clarendon Press, 1989), II: 162, stanza 99. This poem is hereafter cited in the text of this essay by stanza number.

15 Michael Hudson's royalist uprising is briefly recounted by C. Carlton, *Going to the Wars: The Experience of the British Civil Wars 1638–1651* (London and New York: Routledge, 1992), 320–1. Hudson, a doctor of divinity serving as royal chaplain, had previously accompanied King Charles during his flight from Oxford into Scotland in May 1646. An engraving by William Stukeley, illustrating Hudson's gruesome death at Woodcroft House, was published in a volume of plates to accompany J. Bridges, *The History and Antiquities of Northamptonshire, Compiled from the Manuscript Collections of the Late Learned Antiquary John Bridges, Esq.*, ed. P. Whalley, 2 vols. (London, 1791). See Figure 3.

16 J. Lucas, 'Clare's Politics', in Hugh Haughton, Adam Phillips and Geoffrey Summerfield, eds., *John Clare in Context* (Cambridge and New York: Cambridge University Press, 1994), 154. See also J. Lucas, *John Clare* (Plymouth: Northcote House, 1994).

17 Lucas, 'Clare's Politics', 155.

18 Anon., *Eikon Basiliké: The Portraiture of His Sacred Majestie in His Solitudes and Sufferings* (London: n.p., 1648), 68.

19 John Clare, Peterborough MS., A46, 78–9.

20 *Ibid.*, A46, 79–80.

10 'NOT A REFORMING PATRIOT BUT AN AMBITIOUS TYRANT': REPRESENTATIONS OF CROMWELL AND THE ENGLISH REPUBLIC IN THE LATE EIGHTEENTH AND EARLY NINETEENTH CENTURIES

1 Zera S. Fink, 'Wordsworth and the English Republican Tradition', *Journal of English and Germanic Philology*, 4 (1948), 107–26; Peter Karsten, *Patriot-Heroes in England and America: Political Symbolism and Changing Values over Three Centuries* (Madison: University of Wisconsin Press, 1978); Peter J. Kitson, 'Coleridge, Milton and the Millennium', *The Wordsworth Circle*, 17 (1987), 107–17; Kitson, '"The Electric fluid of truth"', in Peter J. Kitson and Thomas N. Corns, eds., *Coleridge and the Armoury of the Human Mind* (London: Frank Cass, 1991), 36–2; Kitson, '"Sages and Patriots that being Dead do yet Speak to Us"', in James Holstun, ed., *Pamphlet Wars: Prose in the English Revolution* (London: Frank Cass, 1992), 205–30;

Kitson, 'Our Prophetic Harrington', *The Wordsworth Circle*, 24 (1993), 97–102; Olivier Lutaud, *Des Révolutions d'Angleterre à la Révolution Française: Le Tyrannicide & Killing No Murder* (La Haye: Martinus Nijoff, 1973); Nigel Leask, *The Politics of Imagination in Coleridge's Critical Thought* (London: Macmillan, 1988); John Morrow, 'Coleridge and the English Revolution', *Political Science*, 40 (1988), 128–41; Joseph Nicholes, 'Revolutions Compared', in Keith Hanley and Raman Selden, eds., *Revolution and English Romanticism: Politics and Rhetoric* (London: Harvester Wheatsheaf, 1990), 261–76; Kenneth Johnston and Joseph Nicholes, 'Transitory Actions, Men Betrayed', *The Wordsworth Circle*, 23 (1992), 76–96; E. P. Thompson, *Witness Against the Beast: William Blake and the Moral Law* (Cambridge and New York: Cambridge University Press, 1993).

2 John Morrow, 'Republicanism and Public Virtue', *The Historical Journal*, 34 (1991), 645–4 (648).

3 Timothy Lang, *The Victorians and the Stuart Heritage: Interpretations of a Discordant Past* (Cambridge: Cambridge University Press, 1995), 3.

4 Jeremy Bentham, *Legislator of the World: Writings on Codification, Law and Education*, ed. Philip Schofield and Jonathan Harris (Oxford: Clarendon Press, 1989), 158–61.

5 Kitson, 'Sages'.

6 Lang, *Victorians and the Stuart Heritage*, 14; Karsten, *Patriot-Heroes*, 140.

7 David Hume, *History of Great Britain* (1754–61) II:23–4, quoted in Roger Howell, Jr, 'Cromwell, the English Revolution and Political Symbolism in Eighteenth-Century England', in R. C. Richardson, ed., *Images of Oliver Cromwell: Essays for and by Roger Howell, Jr* (Manchester: Manchester University Press, 1993), 63–73 (64–5); Lang, *Victorians and the Stuart Heritage*, 4–13.

8 Catharine Macaulay, *The History of England. From the Invasion of Julius Caesar to the Revolution in 1688*, 6 vols. (New York: Worthington, 1889), II:23–4; Bridget Hill, *Republican Virago: The Life and Times of Catharine Macaulay, Historian* (Oxford: Clarendon Press, 1992), 35–9; Howell, 'Cromwell', 65; Lang, *Victorians and the Stuart Heritage*, 17–19.

9 Catharine Macaulay, *Observations on the Reflections of the Right Hon. Edmund Burke On the Revolution in France*, in Gregory Claeys, ed., *Political Writings of the 1790s: The French Revolution Debate in Britain*, 8 vols. (London: Pickering and Chatto, 1995), I:133.

10 John Millar, *An Historical View of the English Government, from the Settlement of the Saxons in Britain to the Revolution in 1688* (London: J. Mawman, 1803), III:126, 130–3. 140–1, 290–300; James Burgh, *The Political Disquisitions: Or an Enquiry into Public Errors, Defects, and Abuses*, 3 vols. (London, 1775), I:9, II:375–82; Lang, *Victorians and the Stuart Heritage*, 16–17; Kitson, 'Sages', 214–17.

11 Daniel Neal, *The History of the Puritans; or, Protestant Nonconformists from the Reformation in 1517 to the Revolution in 1688 . . . Reprinted from Dr Toulmin's Edition*, 5 vols. (London: William Baynes, 1822), IV:71.

12 *Ibid.*, IV:157–8; II:61–3; IV:182–8.
13 See James E. Bradley, *Religion, Revolution, and English Radicalism: Nonconformity in Eighteenth-Century Politics and Society* (Cambridge: Cambridge University Press, 1990).
14 *Ibid.*, 128–31, 146.
15 George Crabbe, *The Complete Works*, ed. Norma Dalrymple-Champneys and Arthur Pollard, 3 vols. (Oxford: Clarendon Press, 1988), II:85–8.
16 Howell, 'Cromwell', 69.
17 *Ibid.*, 70–3; W. A. Speck, 'Cromwell and the Glorious Revolution' in *Images of Cromwell*, 48–62 (59–60).
18 A. Smith, 'The Image of Cromwell in Folk Lore and Tradition', *Folklore*, 79 (1968), 17–39.
19 John Clare, 'Untitled Sonnet', in *Northborough Sonnets*, ed. Eric Robinson, David Powell and P. M. S. Dawson (Manchester and Ashington: Carcanet and Mid-Northumberland Arts Group, 1995), 59.
20 Edmund Burke, *Reflections on the Revolution in France* (1790), in *The Writings and Speeches of Edmund Burke*, ed. L. G. Mitchell (general ed. Paul Langford) (Oxford: Clarendon Press, 1989), VIII:61–2; see Kitson, 'Sages', 209–11.
21 Burke, *Reflections*, *Writings*, VIII:99.
22 Edmund Burke, *A Letter to a Member of the National Assembly* (1791), in *Writings*, VIII:302, 303, 321, 333, 497.
23 Joseph Priestley, *Lectures on History, and General Policy* (Birmingham, 1788), 262–3, 446.
24 Joseph Priestley, *Familiar Letters Addressed to the Inhabitants of Birmingham* (1790), in *Theological and Miscellaneous Works*, ed. J. T. Rutt, 25 vols. (London, 1817–32), XV:144–8. See Kitson, 'Sages', 211–13.
25 Charles James Fox, *History of the Early Part of the Reign of James the Second* (London: W. Miller, 1808), quoted in Karsten, *Patriot-Heroes*, 140.
26 Karsten, *Patriot-Heroes*, 140–1; M. D. George, *English Political Caricature: A Study of Opinion and Propaganda*, 2 vols. (Oxford: Clarendon Press, 1959), I:144.
27 [John Scott], *A Letter to the Right Hon. Edmund Burke* (Dublin, 1791), in Claeys, ed., *Political Writings*, II:162; Henry Redhead Yorke, *Thoughts on Civil Government* (London, 1794), in Claeys, ed., *Political Writings*, IV:243; *Remarks on Mr Paine's Pamphlet, Called The Rights of Man* (Dublin, 1791), in Claeys, ed., *Political Writings*, V:43; William Sewell, *A Rejoinder to Mr Paine's Pamphlet*, in Claeys, ed., *Political Writings*, V:135; Charles Harrington Elliot, *The Republican Refuted* (London, 1791), in Claeys, ed., *Political Writings*, V:355; Thomas Hearn, *A Short View of the Rise and Progress of Freedom in Modern Europe* (London, 1793), in Claeys, ed., *Political Writings*, VI:358–9.
28 John Thelwall, *The Tribune, A Periodical Publication consisting chiefly of the Lectures of J. Thelwall*, 3 vols. (London, 1795–6), III:226.
29 *Ibid.*, III:219.
30 *Ibid.*, III:190.

31 *Ibid.*, III:192.
32 See E. P. Thompson, 'Hunting the Jacobin Fox', *Past and Present*, 142 (1993), 94–139.
33 Cited in Karsten, *Patriot-Heroes*, 140.
34 Samuel Taylor Coleridge and Robert Southey, *The Fall of Robespierre: An Historic Drama* (Cambridge, 1794), 28.
35 Samuel Taylor Coleridge, *Lectures 1795 on Politics and Religion*, ed. Lewis Patton and Peter Mann (Princeton: Princeton University Press, 1971), 255–6.
36 I have already discussed this in my 'Sages', 220–4; 'Electric fluid', and 'Harrington'.
37 Samuel Taylor Coleridge, *Essays on His Own Times*, ed. David V. Erdman, 3 vols. (Princeton: Princeton University Press, 1978), II:66.
38 Samuel Taylor Coleridge, *The Friend*, ed. Barabara E. Rooke, 2 vols. (Princeton: Princeton University Press, 1969), I: 180–1.
39 For Shelley's *Charles the First* see Johnston and Nicoles, 'Transitory Actions', 84–8.
40 Robert Southey, *Poems* (Bristol, 1796), 59–60.
41 Robert Southey, 'History of Dissenters', *Quarterly Review*, 10 (October 1813), 126, 97, 98–101, 104, 107, 110–11, 130, 135, 138–9.
42 The question of the authenticity of the work had been recently discussed in Christopher Wordsworth's *Who Wrote Eikon Basilike? Considered and Answered* (London: John Murray, 1824).
43 Robert Southey, 'Life of Cromwell', *Quarterly Review*, 25 (July 1821), 287, 288, 286, 298, 294, 324.
44 *Ibid.*, 347.
45 For Hallam, see Lang, *Victorians and the Stuart Heritage*, 23–52.
46 Thomas Babington Macaulay, 'Milton', *Edinburgh Review*, 42 (1825), 304–46 (335–6).
47 It is clear that there was an interest in the Commonwealth period in the Shelley–Godwin circle at this time. As well as Percy Shelley's unfinished drama *Charles the First*, Mary Shelley's futuristic novel of the twenty-first century, *The Last Man* (1826), uses a Cromwellian framework within which to discuss the cult of Byronism. When England becomes a Protectorate the Byronic figure, Lord Raymond, has to choose between the attractions of romance and the world of politics. Shelley's novel is couched in an imagined political context that recalls the constitutional experiments of the 1640s and 1650s and surely is related to Godwin's desire to write a *History of the Commonwealth* from 1818 onwards. For Byron and Napoleon, see Simon Bainbridge, *Napoleon and English Romanticism* (Cambridge: Cambridge University Press, 1995), 134–52.
48 For Godwin's intellectual background see Don Locke, *A Fantasy of Reason: The Life and Thought of William Godwin* (London: Routledge and Kegan Paul, 1980), 12–24; Peter H. Marshall, *William Godwin* (New Haven and London: Yale University Press, 1984), 7–45.

49 Marshall, *William Godwin*, 357.
50 William Godwin, *A History of the Commonwealth of England from its Commencement to the Restoration of Charles the Second*, 4 vols. (London: Henry Colburn, 1824–8), I:335–7, 344; IV:354–7; III:vi.
51 Morrow, 'Republicanism and Public Virtue', 645–4. See also Marshall, *William Godwin*, 357–60, and Lang, *Victorians and the Stuart Heritage*, 94–103.
52 Godwin, *History*, IV:vi–vii, 11, 16, 17, 18–19, 123, 125, 36, 108.
53 *Ibid.*, IV:159, 339, 266.

11 AFTERWORD: THE REPUBLICAN PROMPT: CONNECTIONS
IN ENGLISH RADICAL CULTURE

1 Blair Worden, *The Rump Parliament 1648–1653* (Cambridge: Cambridge University Press, 1974), 40.
2 The entire discussion in this chapter owes more than it knows to J .G. A. Pocock's *The Machiavellian Moment: Florentine Political Thought and the Atlantic Republican Tradition* (Princeton: Princeton University Press, 1975). For one of his adroit expositions of the self-historicising of republican procedures see 207–8.
3 David Norbrook, *Writing the English Republic: Poetry, Rhetoric and Politics 1627–1660* (Cambridge and New York: Cambridge University Press, 1999), 15.
4 Compare Richard Tuck on Bacon's opposition both to Aristotle and to Stoicism ('we should perform only those acts which would definitely bring us an increase in welfare'), *Philosophy and Government 1572–1651* (Cambridge and New York: Cambridge University Press, 1993), 112–13.
5 Johann Gottlieb Fichte, *Machiavell, Nebst einem Briefe Carls von Clausewitz an Fichte*, Kritische Ausgabe von Hans Schulz (Leipzig: Verlag Felix Meiner, 1918). Schulz continues the historicising by himself editing Fichte's essay in a time of *Kriegsnot*, and, with considerable textual justification, he claims that Fichte reads a Machiavelli who '*wurde ihm zum Spiegel schmerzlicher Gegenwart*', vii. I am grateful to Richard Bourke for encouraging this Fichtean comparison.
6 Friedrich Meinecke, *Cosmopolitanism and the National State*, trans. R. Kimber, introduced by Felix Gilbert (Princeton: Princeton University Press, 1963), 77.
7 Alain Renaut, 'Fichte et la politique de l'entendement', in Ives Radrizzani, ed., 'Approches de Fichte', *Revue de Théologie et Philosophie*, 123 (1991), 310 (my translation).
8 Meinecke, *Cosmopolitanism*, 94.
9 David Hume, *Political Essays*, ed. Knut Haakonssen (Cambridge and New York: Cambridge University Press, 1994), 14.
10 *Ibid.*, 222, 31.
11 *Ibid.*, 223. See *De Augmentis Scientarum*, in *The Works of Francis Bacon*, ed. R. Ellis and J. Spedding, 14 vols. (London: Longmans, 1857–74), IV:338–9: ' "Things are preserved from destruction by bringing them back to their

first principles", is a rule in Physics; the same holds good in Politics (as Machiavelli rightly observed), for there is scarcely anything which preserves states from destruction more than the reformation and reduction of them to their ancient manners.'

12 Hume, *Political Essays*, 16.
13 Edward Gibbon, *The History of the Decline and Fall of the Roman Empire*, ed. David Womersley, 3 vols. (Harmondsworth: Penguin, 1994), 1:563.
14 *Ibid.*, 447.
15 *Ibid.*, 482–3.
16 *Ibid.*, 486, 483.
17 Saint Augustine, *The City Of God Against The Pagans*, trans. and ed. George E. McCracken, 7 vols. (London and Cambridge, MA: William Heinemann and Harvard University Press, 1957): 'I shall strive to show that, according to the definitions of Cicero himself, making Scipio his spokesman, when he succinctly laid down what a state is [*quid sit res publica*] . . . that state never existed, because true justice never resided in it . . . True justice, however, exists only in that republic [*in ea re publica*] whose Founder and Ruler is Christ', 1:225 (Book II:xxi). See also VI:207–11 (Book XIX:xxi).
18 Francis Bacon, 'On Atheism', *Essays*, in *Francis Bacon: A Critical Edition of The Major Works*, ed. Brian Vickers (Oxford: Oxford University Press, 1996), 371–3. See Niccolò Machiavelli, *The Discourses*, ed. Bernard Crick, trans. L. J. Walker, revised by Brian Richardson (Harmondsworth: Penguin, 1998), I:xi–xv.
19 Gibbon, *Decline and Fall*, 1:lxx.
20 Andrew Marvell, 'A Horatian Ode Upon Cromwell's Return From Ireland', in *Poems and Letters*, ed. H. M. Margoliouth, rev. edn Pierre Legouis and E. E. Duncan-Jones (Oxford: Clarendon Press, 1971), 91.
21 Burke, *Reflections on the Revolution in France*, ed. J. G. A. Pocock (Indianapolis: Hachett, 1987), 4, 6.
22 William Hazlitt, 'The Character of Cobbett', *Table Talk*, in *Complete Works*, ed. P.P. Howe, 21 vols. (London: J. M. Dent, 1930–3) VIII:50, reprinted 1825 in the second edition of *The Spirit of the Age*.
23 'The Old Song', *The Collected Poems of G. K. Chesterton* (London: Cecil Palmer, 1927), 60.
24 Michael Scrivener, 'John Thelwall and the Revolution of 1649', in this volume.
25 Victoria Kahn, *Machiavellian Rhetoric: From The Counter-Reformation To Milton* (Princeton: Princeton University Press, 1994). Kahn has a brief but interesting methodological discussion of Ricoeur, Habermas and Gadamer in her 'Coda', 237–41.
26 Norbrook, *Writing the English Republic*, especially 18–19 and n.
27 George Puttenham, *The Arte of English Poesie*, A Facsimile Reproduction (Kent, OH: Kent State University Press, 1970), 167, quoted and discussed by Kahn in *Machiavellian Rhetoric*, 90.
28 See especially Blair Worden, 'Classical Republicanism and the Puritan Revolution', in Hugh Lloyd-Jones, Valerie Pearl and Blair Worden, *History and*

Imagination: Essays in Honour of H. R. Trevor-Roper (New York: Holmes and Meieer, 1981), 182–200. On Bacon and Machiavelli, see Lisa Jardine, *Francis Bacon: Discovery and the Art of Discourse* (Cambridge: Cambridge University Press, 1974), 167–8: 'Like Machiavelli, Bacon is more concerned to establish a policy in the present instance, using the past as a guide, than to set up the general precept as a universal principle . . .' Or see Pocock's summary of the problem facing the 'new' prince: 'No *virtù* can so completely dominate *fortuna* as to ensure that the same strategy remains always appropriate', *The Machiavellian Moment*, 180. The classic study of casuistry in Romantic period writing is rapidly becoming James Chandler's *England in 1819* (Chicago: University of Chicago Press, 1998).

29 'Annotations To Essays Moral, Economical and Political by Francis Bacon London MDCCXCVIII' (*c.*1798), in *Blake: Complete Writings*, ed. Geoffrey Keynes (London: Oxford University Press, 1969), 396.

Index

Abel 71; *see also* Bible
abolitionism *see* anti-slavery
abstinence *see* food, fasting
absolutism 33–4, 38
Act of Uniformity (1662) 46
Adam 54, 67, 69, 81, 89–90, 92, 99, 235–6
n. 5; *see also* Bible
Adams, Elizabeth 139
adepts 60
Adorno, Theodor 26
aesthetics 5, 7, 10, 25–6, 49, 61–2, 82, 94,
201, 204, 205, 213; *see also* rhetoric, sublime
Africa 74
African-American culture 18
agency 101, 109, 133–4, 138, 146–7,
149–50, 212–13
Agreements of the People 59
agriculture 167–9, 171, 173–4, 179, 182;
farmers, farms 173–4; agrarian radicalism
76; agrarian socialism 127; *see also* Clare,
enclosure, McKusick, Spence
alchemy 58, 60, 67
alcohol 13, 66, 68, 75, 78, 231 n. 9; *see also*
drink, food, sobriety, temperance
Aldridge, A. Owen 234 n. 99
Alien Act (America) 161
allegory 6, 54–6, 120, 131; *see also* rhetoric,
signs, writing
Allen, D. C. 36, 224 n. 41
Allen, John 110
America, Americans 18–19, 54, 70–9, 83,
111, 126–7, 157, 161, 163, 167–8, 188, 211,
259 n. 2; American Constitution 127;
American War of Independence 65, 196,
211
anarchism, anarchy 51, 62, 120, 185, 190,
196
ancien régime 29–30, 33–4, 36, 38, 43, 96
Anderson, A. 224 n. 42
Anderson, Benedict 136, 249 n. 13
Anderson, M. S. 221 n. 3

androgyny 59, 90, 100, 236–7 n. 15; *see also*
female, gender
Andrew, Donna T. 61, 89–90, 100, 230 n. 81
Anglicanism, Anglicans 11, 31–2, 41–2, 46,
48, 57–8, 101, 109, 111–12, 141, 153, 184,
195, 197, 243 n. 2
Anglo-Saxons *see* Saxons
animals 68, 70–3, 75–8, 84, 89
Anne, Queen 53
anthropology 102
anti-clericalism 29, 32, 35, 38–43, 48, 77
anti-Jacobinism *see* Jacobinism
antinomianism 24, 57, 83, 152, 154–5, 252
n. 2; *see also* Blake, radicalism, religion
antique, antiquarianism 16–17, 20, 123, 128,
184, 244 n. 19
anti-Semitism 172
anti-slavery 24, 70–7, 82, 146, 148, 150, 157,
212; Ladies' Anti-Slavery Societies 24,
146, 148, 150; Sheffield Association for the
Universal Abolition of Slavery 148
Apicius, Marcus Gavius 78
Apollonius 41
Aquinas, Thomas 205
Arendt, Hannah 205
Arianism 95, 238 n. 42
aristocracy *see* class
Aristotle 204–5, 264 n. 4
Arminianism 94, 238 n. 40
Armstrong, Nancy 248 n. 6
army, military 6, 9, 23, 49–51, 54, 78, 162,
157, 168, 172, 175–6, 178, 187, 194, 208;
New Model Army 54, 56; standing army
9, 50, 53, 128, 168
Arner, Robert D. 234 n. 94
artisans *see* class
asceticism 102
Ascham, Roger 214
Askew, Anne 138
Ashcraft, Richard 61, 230 n. 83
Astell, Mary 59

274

Index

Hemans, Felicia 14, 219 n. 41
Henderson, Alexander 111
Herbert of Cherbury 39
Herder, Johann Gottfried 206, 210
heresy 7, 13; *see also* Arianism, Christianity,
  heterodoxy, orthodoxy
hermeneutics 67
hermetic, hermeticism 54, 58, 97
hermits 65
Hervey, James 239 n. 50
Herzog, Don 228 n. 35
heterodoxy 11, 13, 23, 41, 43, 101
Heydon, C. 221 n. 12
Hill, Bridget 261 n. 8
Hill, Christopher 122–3, 183–4, 223 n. 35,
  225 n. 47, 218 n. 28, 244 n. 13–15, 248 n. 8
historicism 202, 206, 209–10, 214–5; New
  Historicism 20
historiography 1, 29–32, 35–6, 43, 152, 169,
  183–4, 186, 209, 212; *see also* philosophy,
  political theory, theory
Hite, Lewis F. 240 n. 64
Hoagwood, Terence 15, 216 n. 1, 219 n. 44
Hobbes, Thomas 14, 35, 37–9, 68
Hobby, Elaine 250 n. 24, 251 n. 37
Holbach, Paul Henri Thiry, Baron d' 29,
  34–5, 37, 40–2, 220 n. 1, 223 n. 31–2
Holcroft, Robert 16
Holcroft, Thomas 2
Hole, R. 32, 222 n. 14
holiness 105, 109, 133; *see also* Christianity,
  Eucharist, God
Holland, Dutch 35, 37, 41, 57
Holmes, Richard 77, 233 n. 62
Holy Roman Empire 209
Holy Spirit 2, 95, 115, 140; *see also*
  Christianity, God
home, house 22, 29, 33, 37, 47–8, 106, 113,
  135, 137–9, 144, 147, 149, 161, 189; *see also*
  domestic
Hone, William 20
Hooker, Richard 209
Hopkins, James K. 242 n. 42
Horne Tooke, John 156
Horns, J. 222 n. 22, 224 n. 38
House of Commons 7, 123; *see also*
  government, Parliament
How, Samuel 'Cobbler' 48, 155, 164, 254
  n. 13
Howard, Robert 39
Howell, Jr, Roger 189, 261 n. 7–8, 262
  n. 16–17
Hubberthorne, Richard 140
Hudson, Michael 175–7, 260 n. 15
Hughes, Derek 227 n. 22, 229 n. 76

Hulme, P. 221 n. 4
Hume, David 26, 121, 128, 169, 186, 197,
  207–8, 235 n. 4, 243 n. 8, 261 n. 7, 264
  n. 9–11, 265 n. 12
Hunt, James Henry Leigh 84–5, 154, 158,
  235 n. 102, 254 n. 11
Hunter, A. C. 223 n. 29
Hunter, J. Paul 248 n. 6
Huntington, William 155–6, 254 n. 13

idealism 18, 29–30, 96, 195, 207
identity 7, 11, 86, 91, 97, 134, 151, 163;
  see also self-fashioning
ideology 7, 20–1, 120–1, 123, 161, 163, 172,
  177, 185–6, 190, 192, 194, 201, 215
Illich, Ivan 248 n. 7, 249 n. 10
imagery 5, 7, 58–9, 65, 68, 94–5, 98–9;
  see also rhetoric
imagination 16, 59, 67, 73, 90–3, 96–9, 142,
  155, 158, 214; *see also* dreams, prophecy,
  visions
imperialism 19, 24, 130–1
Independents 10, 103, 106, 128, 187, 190,
  193, 198–9, 209, 243 n. 8
individual, individualism 83, 87–8, 135, 136,
  138, 145, 149, 205
Industrial Revolution, industry 2, 125, 168;
  see also bourgeoisie, capitalism, labour,
  working class
interiority, inwardness 14, 22–3, 58, 67,
  69–72, 78, 122, 124–5, 142, 138–40, 219
  n. 40
Interregnum 8, 11, 24, 57, 60, 65, 104–5,
  136, 138–9, 149, 171, 184, 190, 202; *see also*
  Commonwealth, Cromwell, English
  Revolution
Ireland, Irish 50, 52, 56, 107, 148, 210–11,
  216 n. 4
Ireton, Henry 216 n. 4
irony 16, 209, 214; *see also* rhetoric
Isaiah *see* Bible
Islam 37, 39, 41; *see also* Mohammed
Israel 94, 140; *see also* Jews
Italy, Italians 54, 84

Jacob, James C. 217 n. 19
Jacob, Margaret C. C. 32, 221 n. 4, 222 n.
  15, 223 n. 28
Jacob, W. M. 222 n. 12
Jacobean age 206
Jacobinism, Jacobins 17, 65, 120–1, 128,
  152, 164, 185, 192–5, 252 n. 2;
  anti-Jacobins 130, 173
Jacobitism, Jacobites 52–3, 65
James II 53, 110, 190